Perl for the Web

Contents At a Glance

Perl for the Web

Chris Radcliff

New Riders

www.newriders.com

201 West 103rd Street, Indianapolis, Indiana 46290
An Imprint of Pearson Education
Boston • Indianapolis • London • Munich • New York • San Francisco

Perl for the Web

Trademarks

Warning and Disclaimer

Publisher
David Dwyer

Associate Publisher
Al Valvano

Executive Editor
Stephanie Wall

Managing Editor
Kristy Knoop

Development Editor
Laura Loveall

Product Marketing Manager
Stephanie Layton

Publicity Manager
Susan Nixon

Project Editor
Caroline Wise

Copy Editor
Jill Batistick

Indexer
Christine Karpeles

Manufacturing Coordinator
Jim Conway

Book Designer
Louisa Klucznik

Cover Designer
Brainstorm Design, Inc.

Cover Production
Aren Howell

Proofreader
Katherine Shull

Composition
Amy Parker
Rebecca Harmon

For Karen, my true love.

Table of Contents

x   Contents

About the Author

Chris Radcliff is a Perl programmer and chief evangelist at VelociGen Inc. He has been programming in Perl and designing Web sites since 1995, and he is convinced that neither technology is a passing fad. He is an advocate of open source software, practical Web applications, and user-centered design. Outside the world of software, Chris is fond of permaculture, architecture, physics, gardening, philosophy, travel, and science fiction. He has considered both cloning and temporal engineering as possible solutions to the problem of too many ideas and not enough time. He currently lives in San Diego, California, with his wife, Karen, and two friendly cats.

About the Technical Reviewers

These reviewers contributed their considerable hands-on expertise to the entire development process for *Perl for the Web*. As the book was being written, these dedicated professionals reviewed all the material for technical content, organization, and flow. Their feedback was critical for ensuring that *Perl for the Web* fit our readers' needs for the highest-quality technical information.

Klent Harkness has been a programmer and network administrator since 1984, and he has been developing Perl programs and Internet-based applications since 1995. He is an advocate of the open-source software movement, Linux, and the utilization of the Internet in daily life. Klent's interests are long-distance bicycle touring, cooking, traveling, literature, history, and philosophy. He currently lives in Wichita, Kansas.

Doug Welzel is currently a software engineer at Amazon.com. Prior to joining Amazon, he attended Carnegie Mellon University (CMU), where he double majored in information systems and computer science. Following this, he stayed at CMU for a master's in information systems. Outside the office, he enjoys reading, snowboarding, hiking, and other outdoor activities. Doug currently resides in Kirkland, Washington. Doug can be contacted at welzel@linuxmail.org.

Acknowledgments

This book would not have been possible without the efforts of the folks at VelociGen. Their support for my wild crusades and flights of fancy is greatly appreciated. Alex Shah wrote my favorite development environment and taught me everything I know about persistent Web application architectures. Parand Darugar gave me the chance to write a killer app based on his killer app. Shahin Askari rewrote VeloMeter from scratch specifically for this book and made it all look easy. I wish every programmer had the chance to work with people this brilliant, or at least the amazing technology they produce.

Many thanks go to the staff at New Riders, as well. Karen Wachs had the insight to see this book's promise even while it was disguised as a dull tutorial. Laura Loveall had the diligence to edit the book despite missed deadlines and wild changes in content. Stephanie Wall had the grace to shepherd the book to its finish amidst a flurry of activity and the eccentric requests of the author.

Much of my Perl and Web knowledge came from excellent books and articles by Larry Wall, Randal Schwartz, Philip Greenspun, and Jakob Nielsen. They all set outstanding examples for me to follow, and I thank them for that. I'd also like to thank Eric Hedström for introducing me to Perl in the first place. Terry Pratchett deserves both my thanks and my admiration for writing books that are so bloody enjoyable. Most of all, I thank my wife, Karen, for making this all worthwhile.

Tell Us What You Think

As the reader of this book, you are the most important critic and commentator. We value your opinion and want to know what we're doing right, what we could do better, what areas you'd like to see us publish in, and any other words of wisdom you're willing to pass our way.

As Executive Editor for the Web Development team at New Riders Publishing, I welcome your comments. You can fax, email, or write me directly to let me know what you did or didn't like about this book—as well as what we can do to make our books stronger.

Please note that I cannot help you with technical problems related to the topic of this book, and that due to the high volume of mail I receive, I might not be able to reply to every message.

When you write, please be sure to include this book's title and author as well as your name and phone or fax number. I will carefully review your comments and share them with the author and editors who worked on the book.

Fax:	317-581-4663
Email:	stephanie.wall@newriders.com
Mail:	Stephanie Wall
	Executive Editor
	New Riders Publishing
	201 West 103rd Street
	Indianapolis, IN 46290 USA

Introduction

Designing a Web application isn't brain surgery. Really, it isn't that complex, and the uses to which it will be put are usually lightweight compared to the kinds of things a single-user or enterprise-level application is expected to do. Using Perl to write the application makes the job even easier. As simple as Web application design is, however, there are fundamental ideas involved that are missed entirely by most application designers. These aren't complex ideas; the truly important parts of this book could be summed up in a page or two. These aren't stupid people, either; most of the programmers and designers producing Web applications are the most advanced members of their team. The real reason that these principles are missed so often by so many people is that they're new enough that no one has written them down before.

I should modify that; no one's ever written them down in the same place. They're all there for those who look for them, but the ideas are all over the place—not to mention the technologies to implement them. I first learned some of these principles by accident while reading through documentation. I learned others by trial and error by trying to put together a Web application that wasn't hideously slow and then improving it by bits and pieces. Some of these ideas are my own invention entirely; I've had them as working principles long enough that they are integral to the rest of this book.

So, if the fundamentals can be summarized in a page, why the 400-page tome to back it up? One answer is that you never would have picked up a one-page leaflet and used its principles to develop a million-dollar Web application. Another answer is that you could never convince your boss that the one-page leaflet was sufficient reason to build your application the way that you did. This problem is especially acute when the technology being discussed is Perl, which has neither a billion-dollar company advertising it nor sufficient new hype to compensate for years of misconceptions. Proposing a Perl solution can be an uphill battle. Thus, it helps to have a complete and relevant reference based on real-world experience.

Mostly, though, the reason for the book is that one page isn't sufficient to cover all the important ideas in detail. It might cover the fundamentals, but it misses many of the important reasons for those ideas. It wouldn't cover the architectural model that makes CGI slow or the business process that makes template-based HTML design necessary. It wouldn't talk about the 15 little things that add up to make Web-based database access slow, and it couldn't cover the reasons why it's not always best to be efficient. Most of all, it couldn't reiterate its points in a dozen different examples, any of which could be the one example that makes the idea click.

Target Audience

If you're a Webmaster, a Web site project lead, a CTO, a database administrator, or Just Another Perl Hacker looking for better ways to develop for the Web, this is the book for you. The target audience for this book includes programmers looking to improve the performance of their Web applications, managers trying to evaluate Web technologies in terms of suitability to a project, and HTML designers hoping to add application processing to their Web pages without sinking into the mire of CGI programming. This book also is designed to be useful to anyone trying to convince one of these groups to adopt a better strategy than they have now.

I fully expect that many people will read this book because they're fed up. Some might be fed up with the abysmal performance of CGI programs. Others might be fed up with the poor scalability of Cold Fusion, ASP, or Java servlets. Still more readers are likely to be fed up with the need to write object-oriented mod_perl programs. Managers might be fed up with programmers constantly harping on the need for performance testing, better hardware, and more Perl.

Nontechnical readers and technical readers who are new to Perl will find the most valuable insights for decision-making in Chapters 1–7. I've tried to make the rest of the book clear enough for a nonprogrammer to understand, and the introduction and summary sections of each chapter should definitely be within everyone's grasp.

Prerequisites

To be truly comfortable with this book, you should have a pretty firm grasp of both Perl programming and Web design. Any programmer with some experience writing CGI applications in Perl should have all the background necessary to take advantage of the principles in this book. Perl programmers with no Web experience might want to get familiar with HTML before proceeding. Similarly, HTML designers with no programming experience might want to pick up an introduction to Perl before tackling the examples.

Alternately, if you're a whiz at PHP and ebXML (insert your favorite language and XML variant here) and you're making the switch to Perl, you'll find everything familiar enough to get by. If you want to do the next great thing with Perl and XML, you don't need to know anything about HTML per se; the examples work just as well from an XML perspective, and Part III of the book, "Solutions for the Future," is right up your alley.

With that said, this book does not attempt to teach the fundamentals of Perl, the history of HTML on the World Wide Web, the basics of database query design, or the intricacies of XML languages. There are enough wonderful references on each of those subjects (and many others touched on in this book) to teach you everything you need to know; I've included a group of them in Appendix A, "Alphabet Soup—Glossary and References," to give you a starting point.

Organization of This Book

This book is divided into three parts that cover the problems, solutions, and future directions of Web application development. Part I, "The Problems," defines some of the problems that come up in Web application design, and it is designed for a technical audience that might not know Perl. For programmers, Part I (consisting of Chapters 1–6) is best used to get confirmation of the problems you've faced and descriptions of the ones you can look forward to. For decision makers, it gives an overview of the problems that Web application designers face from initial deployment to years down the road.

Part II, "The Solutions" (consisting of Chapters 7–15), is geared primarily for the Perl programmer solving problems in a Web application setting. These are the solutions you're probably looking for right this moment: improving performance, creating faster prototypes, adding more modularity, pleasing site designers, and testing site performance. If you think you have all those bases covered, read that first section again and rediscover fear. If you still think you have it all covered, write a book; the world of Web applications needs you.

Part III, "Solutions for the Future" (consisting of Chapters 16–21), is a sampling of the things that are possible after you've solved all the problems from the first two sections. It's fully buzzword compliant, so be sure to get your boss to pay for the book: XML, SOAP, WAP, WML, DOM, XHTML, UDDI, and WSDL are all present. There also are some impressive tricks to play with clustering, decompiling, and multiplexed record sets, so don't think it's all work.

Conventions Used in This Book

Perl is based partially on English. Thus, a monotype font is used where there might be confusion between English and Perl terms. For instance, the Perl directive `use strict` shouldn't be confused with the way nuns use strict discipline when teaching Catholic school students. Monotype text also is used to specify command line utilities, XML and HTML tags, and sections of code. New terms are introduced in *italics* just before they are defined.

Code listings are provided with both listing numbers (for example, Listing 1.1) and line-by-line numbering. Of course, the line-by-line numbering is not part of the code itself. It is there simply for cross-referencing purposes. The same code without the line-by-line numbering is available on the companion Web site. Numbered listings are usually complete Perl programs that run as listed, but some listings require the appropriate Perl application environment to be installed. In all cases, I've assumed Perl 5.6 syntax, which should be compatible with later versions of Perl 5 as well. Additionally, some listings might depend on other files or systems not included in the text. These additional files are included with the listings on the book's companion Web site (`http://www.newriders.com` or `http://globalspin.com/thebook/`), when applicable. See the inside back cover for details about the Web site.

Additional code, file format, configuration, and output examples are set in a monospace font with no line numbers. These sections should be considered explanatory rather than exhaustive, as they might be incomplete or simplified to emphasize a point. Specific installation and configuration instructions for servers, application environments, and Perl modules won't be included in the text due to the changeable nature of these programs. However, the book's Web site or others listed in the glossary are likely to have all the information necessary to get these systems up and running. I did it; how hard can it be?

I

The Problems

1

Sources of Unexpected Traffic

O N THE WEB, ONE WORD CAN SIGNIFY BOTH A BOON and a danger to an application: traffic. There's no surer death to a Web application than a lack of traffic, which indicates a lack of interest and usually ends up with a lack of sales. On the flip side, though, increased traffic can mean greater demands on limited hardware and software resources, and many a site has been buried under its own success.

Sites That Suffer Outages

Every site is hoped to be a site for the ages...one that never gets old, goes out of style, or fails for any reason. Yahoo! is one of these sites; the core content on Yahoo! has been the same since its inception, the design of the site has changed very little in the years it has been available, and it's reliable enough that many people use it to determine if their Internet connection has failed. In other words, if you can't reach Yahoo!, you can't reach anything.

Of course, not every site is Yahoo!, and not every site is accessible, fast, and reliable. When site response is slow, when pages are intermittently returned, or when the site is inaccessible, it can cause a lot of problems for both the people accessing the site and the people running the site.

I've collected some examples of Web site outages from my travels. Most of these sites became inaccessible not due to extraordinary circumstances, but due to more traffic than the designers expected. It's an easy thing to run into; I've designed sites that operated for years longer than their expected lifetimes. When they fail, it's seen as less a disaster than the end of a miraculous run that was never expected.

The Macadamia Story

The holidays are a time of love, joy, and consumerism. As much as I try, I'm still not out of the woods where that is concerned. Of course, being the twenty-first-century man that I am, I like to do the shopping I have to do online. It means that if I can't keep from getting the people I love tacky, overpriced gifts that they'll never keep, I can at least buy those gifts from a Web site while wearing boxers, listening to the Muppets sing carols, and drinking egg nog while playing Minesweeper in another window.

Unfortunately, the 1999 holiday season made this less convenient than I originally had hoped. It was my first season shopping entirely online, and I was feeling very merry about the prospect of doing all my shopping over the course of an afternoon while the rest of my neighborhood engaged in a blood match for the last Furby down at the local mall. In fact, I was so optimistic about my ability to buy everything online that I waited until the last minute to order; I had heard that most sites wouldn't guarantee on-time delivery unless the order was placed that day. Of course, most sites didn't mention this outright, but I figured I'd better be safe.

The last gift I had to buy was one of the most important: my mother's. She's a sweet woman who likes macadamia nuts. So, I figured the choice was clear. I'd find a site that offered a nice assortment of macadamias in a bright shiny package, and my shopping would be complete. Being the savvy comparison shopper I am, I also planned to visit a few locations to make sure I found the perfect package at the right price. You know, multiple browser windows offer the kind of shopping experience that a mall just can't duplicate. My first destination was Harry and David, a company I was used to dealing with through mail order and brick and mortar. I had just noticed that they had a Web site. So, it seemed the perfect place to search for those macadamia nuts.

The Harry and David site was well laid out, but I noticed a performance problem as soon as I opened the first page. I'm used to waiting for Web pages, though, and I tend to give sites the benefit of the doubt when surfing because I know how it is to be under the gun when designing a Web site. I was willing to wait for those macadamia nuts because there are always other browser windows and other sites to visit while a page loads. Unfortunately, I had to wait for longer periods of time for each page; the site must really be getting hit hard, I thought. Finally, pages started taking too long for the otherwise infinite patience of my Web browser; I still persevered, though, reloading each page repeatedly until something came back. At the very last step, just before I got the chance to look at the macadamia assortment I thought would be best, the site returned an ASP application error and refused to show me any further pages. I was shut out; there would be no macadamias from Harry and David.

I was determined to go on, though. Certainly there had to be another site that would provide the macadamias I wanted to buy and the stability I needed to actually process the order. I went to site after site, big names and small, but they were all slow, damaged, or both. Some sites timed out when I tried to order, others gave application errors when I searched for that devil term "macadamia," and many more just quit without letting me know whether nuts were available at all. It was getting to the point where I had to decide whether to continue this hellish endeavor or give up and join the fray at the mall. I couldn't, though. It had reached the point where it was a matter of principle. Somewhere, someone was going to sell me some macadamia nuts.

My final destination was a true desperation move. I went to the corporate Web site for Mauna Loa, makers of macadamia nuts. Their headquarters are in Hawaii. The site wasn't geared for e-commerce; in fact, it practically shunned me from actually purchasing actual food. Not to be deterred, I navigated to the samples section where nuts could be shipped to those without the benefit of other macadamia outlets. I gave my credit card number and my mother's address. No gift wrap was available, no message could be included, and the tin would contain just nuts. In short, it would look like it came from a supermarket. No promises were made about shipping dates, and it would probably be sent through the U.S. mail. Still, it worked; I was able to order it online, and that was all that was important at that point. I let Mom know that the macadamia nuts were on their way, and she was happy enough with the thought involved.

Incidentally, I called my mother back a few weeks after the holidays to ask if the macadamia nuts had arrived safely; they never did. It could have been the vagaries of the postal service or a shipping error at the Mauna Loa plant. The order itself could have been ignored due to the sheer idiocy of a man in California ordering nuts from Hawaii to be shipped to Wisconsin when they're already available there. Whatever the reason, the nuts never arrived. I sometimes imagine that they're making their way around the country, looking for my mother the way that the fugitive looked for the one-armed man, destined to search for eternity.

Case Study: WFMY

Chris Ellenburg knows how important it can be to prepare for unexpected traffic increases. Ellenburg is director of new media at WFMY, a television station in Greensboro, North Carolina, and webmaster for the Web site the station launched in August 1999. WFMY was the first station in its market to offer a Web site, which saw its success overwhelm it when traffic became too much for the site to handle.

Ellenburg initially developed the WFMY Web site using Perl CGI to connect to a MySQL database that provided dynamic content for use throughout the site. News stories, weather forecasts, program listings, and archival content were all processed by Web applications because most pages on the site needed to provide

continues

continued

up-to-the-minute information. This information made the site an instant success with viewers throughout the region and around the country, but that popularity quickly led to a collapse.

Shortly after the WFMY site was made public, Hurricane Floyd—possibly the worst storm in North Carolina's history—caught national attention and the site received a flood of requests for information about the hurricane. WFMY was the definitive Internet news source for the region. Therefore, the site was pummeled with requests—site logs recorded over 3 million hits that month. The traffic onslaught proved to be too much for the CGI applications on the site, as Ellenburg quickly found out; the site became slow to respond, taking up to 20 seconds to return each page. Eventually, the site stopped returning pages at all, and the Web server itself went down every 10 minutes due to the load. There was little time to take steps to improve performance or stem the flow of traffic before the wave of interest—and the hurricane—passed. Site usage dropped below 1 million hits per month afterward, which the server was able to handle.

Ellenburg realized that something had to be done to prevent the same thing from happening again. So, he evaluated potential solutions to the performance problems plaguing the site. A Web server upgrade was initially considered, which would involve either increasing the server's memory beyond its original half-gigabyte of RAM, or clustering a group of servers using load-balancing hardware. Both of these options were prohibitively expensive for the station, however, and either option would give at best an incremental improvement in speed. Ellenburg also considered using static HTML files for the entire site to remove the overhead due to CGI processing, but the timely information that was the site's core would have suffered as a result. Despite the performance hit they entailed, dynamic pages and Web applications were indispensable.

Clearly, the solution to the problem had to come from performance improvements to the site's Perl processing. Ellenburg came across mod_perl and VelociGen, both of which claimed to provide performance improvements over CGI by caching and precompiling Perl-based Web applications. (mod_perl, VelociGen, and other tools for improving Perl performance are detailed in Chapter 10, "Tools for Perl Persistence.")

Both packages performed as advertised and then some. Tests that compared the original CGI with a persistent application using embedded Perl showed the persistent application performing up to ten times faster than the CGI version (see Chapter 12, "Environments For Reducing Development Time"). In the process of testing, Ellenburg also found that he enjoyed the ease afforded by embedding Perl directly into his dynamic HTML pages.

A new WFMY site was developed using embedded Perl applications, and it launched in October 2000 to unanimous approval. Site visitors immediately noticed a marked improvement in site responsiveness, and, more importantly, so did Ellenburg's boss. The site recorded 3 million hits for the month once again, this time without so much as a hiccup. Remember, this was after a year stagnating at only a million. No longer constrained by site responsiveness, traffic continued to increase up to 7.6 million hits for December 2000 with 2 million hits from page views alone. Ellenburg estimates that the site could easily handle 20 million hits per month in its present configuration. When the next hurricane hits, whether it be digital or meteorological, Chris Ellenburg will be ready.

Evaluating the Cost of Down Time

WFMY didn't lose any business due to the slow responsiveness of their site, but businesses with e-commerce sites would certainly feel the impact of a sluggish or unavailable site. In the case of an e-commerce site, the cost of being slow or unavailable is easy to estimate based on the revenue lost for that time period. For instance, if Amazon.com had revenues of $1.8 billion for 2000, that translates to a cost of $280,000 per hour of down time. That means a performance solution that improves Amazon's uptime from 99.9 percent to 99.99 percent—a reduction from 90 seconds to 9 seconds a day of unavailability—would be worth over $6,300 a day in revenue alone, or about $190,000 a month. This doesn't even count the cost of lost productivity among site staff, delays to site improvements, or other internal costs.

The numbers are no less compelling for the cost of performance degradation. Even if a server is up 99.9 percent of the time, it could still be slow enough to discourage potential customers from exploring the site. A slow site can deter visitors drastically, as WFMY can attest; their site usage fell off when the site was slow, but grew rapidly when performance was improved. Estimating the cost in this situation is less reliable, but more compelling. If Amazon had discouraged just 25 percent of its customers overall, it would have lost $450 million in those 9 months. If it improved performance like WFMY and saw a 600 percent increase in customers, it could stand to gain $11 billion in revenues. (Money is never a bad thing for a company struggling to be profitable.) The idea of expansion isn't revolutionary or untested; any brick-and-mortar establishment would find it an obvious choice to increase the capacity of a popular store before turning customers away at the door.

Obviously these numbers are estimates and would vary widely from business to business, but the principle holds true: Basic Web site performance improvements can translate to large gains in visitor interest and revenue. When evaluating the cost of performance improvements and site architecture upgrades, you should weigh the opportunity costs of not upgrading against the costs of the change.

The Cost of Readiness

Preparing a Web site to handle traffic increases can be costly, but cost overruns can be avoided if the true costs of readiness are known and budgeted before the upgrade begins. Knowing the hidden costs of an upgrade has an additional benefit: Better architectural decisions that improve efficiency and decrease hidden costs will become more attractive to managers looking to get the most bang for their buck.

The costs of a performance overhaul fall into four categories:

- Time spent researching performance problems and deciding on solutions
- Hardware upgrade costs
- Software upgrade costs
- The cost of training (or hiring) staff to develop and administer the new systems

Usually, only the cost of new hardware and software is considered; the assumptions are that research and development time are already paid for and staffing costs are equivalent for all solutions. However, choices made in each of the four areas can have enormous effects on the costs of the others.

Evaluating all areas as a whole provides a better indication of the true cost of a solution. For instance, Windows is sometimes chosen as a server operating system with the idea that Windows administrators are easier to train and less expensive to hire than Linux administrators. Unfortunately, this choice would lead to an increased hardware cost due to the need for more Windows servers to handle the same load as equivalent Linux servers, which—in combination with increased down time and reconfiguration needs—would necessitate hiring more administrators. This additional hiring usually cancels out individual salary savings.

Sudden Traffic Increases

Sudden increases in site traffic can come from many sources and become more likely as the Web increases in size and consolidates around a few very popular points. A Web site can cause its own traffic surge due to new marketing or popular interest in the site's product, service, or information. The site also could become popular by being linked to another popular site or service, which causes a sudden increase in traffic with little or no warning.

Fame and the Slashdot Effect

Slashdot (http://www.slashdot.org) is a site that aggregates news and product reviews that might be of interest to the geek community on the Web. The site's motto is "News for nerds. Stuff that matters," and it has gotten a devoted following since its inception in 1998. The stories on Slashdot are designed to showcase a new idea or declare the availability of a new technology rather than comment on the state of something ongoing, as the nightly news is likely to do. However, Slashdot doesn't limit itself to technology articles; any new discovery, theory, product, service, or idea that might have some interest to geeks is fair game, and hundreds of thousands of submissions a day are posted from Slashdot devotees looking to have their name listed under the latest headline.

In early 2001, Slashdot had a readership of millions. Many visit the site every day; some (like me) read the site many times over the course of the day as a running summary of the geekosphere at any given time. Because of this, millions of Slashdot readers are likely to respond to a story at any given time, as opposed to weekly or even daily news sites that are visited over the course of an entire day.

Because of its format, Slashdot concentrates the majority of reader focus on one article at any given time. The site lists about a day's worth of headlines directly on the home page, usually with a link to the site or news story being discussed. As headlines are supplanted by new stories, they move down the page—eventually getting listed in a separate archive area. Because of the quick availability of these few links, many Slashdot readers are likely to click on the same link within the same short period of time. The result of this extreme interest by so many people in such a short time is known as the *Slashdot Effect*.

The Slashdot Effect causes enough of a spike in traffic to crash many of the Web servers that are lavished with the site's attention; afterward, comments attached to the Slashdot story mention that the site had been *Slashdotted*. This usually happens to relatively unknown sites because the Slashdot Effect is larger in comparison to their usual site traffic.

The Slashdot Effect can be made even larger when the Slashdot readership is less likely to have seen the linked site already. In fact, small sites can misdiagnose the Effect as a distributed denial of service attack. If a site's connection to the Internet is being saturated by incoming requests, it's difficult to distinguish a difference between legitimate interest and malicious intent. In most cases of legitimate interest, however, the Web server is overloaded long before the network connection, which makes the difference easier to discern.

No site or subject is safe from the Slashdot Effect, even if the site's content or function is outside the stated focus of Slashdot. Because the editors of Slashdot have independent editorial control, it's possible that any one editor might deem a story fit for posting.

Other Sources of Fame

There are many sites on the Web that create effects similar to the Slashdot Effect, but traffic from these sites builds over a longer period of time. Sites like Yahoo! News or C|Net can focus a lot of attention on a previously unknown site by simply mentioning it in an article; the effect is magnified if Associated Press or Reuters syndicates the article. With such syndication, the article appears on many news sites simultaneously. News writers on the Web also are known to use each other as sources; even a story with very little information can be quoted again and again as parts of other news items.

A Web site also can see sudden increases in traffic when it provides a Web application that becomes an integral part of another application or toolkit. For instance, the XML Today Web site (`http://www.xmltoday.com/`) saw a ten-fold increase in traffic when its XML stock quote service was included as a test in an XML development kit released by IBM. Each new test of the IBM software caused an automatic burst of traffic to XML Today, and users of the development kit found the service interesting enough to continue using.

Cumulative Increase

Luckily, not all increases in Web site traffic are as sudden or as short-lived as the Slashdot Effect. Gentle increases are just as likely as a site becomes more widely known. Additional increases in site traffic come with the general expansion of the World Wide Web (WWW) as more Web sites are created and more people connect to the Internet. With these types of increases, it's much easier to estimate the need for additional site resources well before performance problems occur. Still, it's necessary to keep an eye on traffic increases because they can add up quickly and keep a site from handling larger spikes.

The Network Effect

Traffic increase due to the increase in connections to a site from other sites is known as the *Network Effect*. This occurs when new Web sites are brought online with links to your site, with a fraction of that site's traffic added to yours. For instance, every new Amazon.com partner bookstore that is created provides new links back to Amazon.com. These new links increase the total traffic to that site. A traffic increase also occurs when existing sites add new links to the site, as in the case of SourceForge, an open source development site that links to software projects in progress. A new link on SourceForge attracts visitors interested in that kind of project.

The Network Effect can cause the traffic to a site to increase even if the total number of links doesn't increase. This increase occurs because the sites that are already linked get more traffic as time goes on, and they transfer a portion of that increase accordingly. Thus, a link from the Yahoo! directory to a site provides more and more traffic over time, simply because Yahoo! itself gets more traffic due to promotions and consolidation. It is possible for this principle to work in reverse—sites providing less traffic to linked sites as viewer numbers decline—but that case is much less likely due to the overall increase in people and sites connected to the Web. (See the "Web Expansion and New Devices" section later in this chapter.)

Site Log Indicators

It's possible to determine the average traffic a site receives by studying Web site activity logs. These logs are created by nearly every Web server available, so they should be available for use in determining the traffic to any Web site, regardless of which or Web server it uses. In addition, most activity logs are stored in variations on a standard format. This allows standard analysis software to be used across different sites. Usually, activity logs are analyzed in terms of pages that are most popular or the overall amount of traffic a site gets. This is a holdover to the early days of the Web when any traffic at all was a sign of prestige and webmasters were mainly interested in determining the popular pages. Site traffic was viewed in the same light as Nielsen ratings for a television show; a site was seen as a success if it increased its number of *hits*, or requests for files. This style of log analysis is still used to determine viewer intent by ranking popular areas of a site; the resulting data is sometimes used to determine which parts of a site are worth the devotion of resources.

When analyzing the effect of increased traffic on Web applications, however, it's important to separate the idea of hits from the real usage a Web application gets. For instance, a processing-intensive Web application, which uses four dynamic pages and twenty images (icons, advertisements and such), registers as 24 hits in a traditional log analysis. However, another application with 1 dynamic page and 23 images also registers as 24 hits. If a server log shows only the total hit count for a period of time, it becomes difficult to determine how many of the hits are due to static files and how many are due to Web applications. If requests for the first Web application increase while requests to the second decrease, the overall increase in server load would go unreported by a hit count.

To get a clearer picture of the current load on a Web application server, more emphasis needs to be placed on the dynamic pages served overall. If a site sees an increase from 3,000 hits one month to 6,000 the next, for instance, it might seem that load on the server has doubled. If the dynamic pages served by the site have increased from 1,000 to 4,000 in the same time period, however, it's more likely that server load has quadrupled.

Estimating Time to Full Load

Estimates of future site activity should take a few different factors into account. Existing traffic, past trends, seasonal patterns, and traffic changes due to site redesigns all can be used to get an estimate of the activity a site can expect. By taking server load under current conditions into account, it's possible to get a good estimate of when a server upgrade is necessary to keep up with traffic increases.

Determining Traffic Patterns

If a site has been available long enough to show a trend of increasing site traffic, a base estimate of future site traffic can be determined by assuming that traffic increases will follow the same general curve as previous increases. Again, dynamic page usage should be weighted higher in determining overall load, and the trends in dynamic page usage should be estimated independently to get a sense of their effect.

If the content and usage of a site follows a seasonal pattern, take the seasonal pattern into account when estimating future traffic. E-commerce sites, for instance, are likely to see an increase of traffic before the holidays, and financial sites are likely to see the greatest spike before tax season. News sites are likely to see seasonal increases as well; WMFY counts on an increase in traffic during hurricane season, and sites in tourist-oriented markets can count on more visitors during peak season. Site sections also can show seasonal patterns; during ski season, a news site in Colorado might see a disproportionate increase in traffic to the Web application that displays weather. Logs that go back over a year would be the best way to gauge seasonal changes, but the current revisions of many sites are less than a year old.

Dramatic changes to a site, usually caused by redesigning the site or adding new sections or services, should also be taken into account. A site redesign is likely to affect the number of files present overall, the number of images requested per Web page, and the relative number of Web applications in use on the site. For instance, if a news article that uses one static page and five images is replaced by one that is broken into four dynamic pages with ten images overall, the number of hits and dynamic page accesses both increase, regardless of overall traffic increases. If the site this article is part of records a 300 percent increase in hits and a ten-fold increase in dynamic pages generated, only a fraction of that increase is due to the increase in visitors. So, when determining trends on such a site, the traffic levels before the site redesign should be scaled (up in this case, down in some others) to match the traffic levels directly afterward. For instance, if site traffic increases 70 percent from the week before a redesign to the week after while the number of visitors stays constant, traffic before the redesign can be scaled up by 70 percent when figuring traffic trends.

Determining Maximum Load

Once estimates of future traffic are available, it's possible to estimate how soon a Web server will need upgrading to handle the increased traffic. You can't necessarily determine this from current server statistics alone. A server can experience performance problems due to a variety of factors, and each possible bottleneck would have to be considered. For instance, static file performance is rarely going to peak before database connections have hit their maximum. Fortunately, the maximum load a server can handle can be determined directly through testing.

First, get an idea of the maximum load the server supports. Test the server using a load simulator to get the maximum number of requests the server can support in a given amount of time. For instance, if the server can process 100 dynamic page requests per second at peak capacity, that translates to 260 million dynamic page requests per month. Likewise, if the server can handle 1000 mixed requests—applications, static files and images—per second, that translates to 2.6 billion hits per month. A discussion of load testing and performance analysis tools is available in Chapter 15, "Testing Site Performance."

Then, check this number against the estimates of traffic. If a server can handle four times the current load and that number will be reached in six months according to traffic estimates, for instance, it's time to start planning. These numbers also can be used when evaluating performance improvements to a site. If a server upgrade will double the server's capacity but traffic increases will outstrip that value in nine months, more work might be necessary to extend the life of the server.

Of course, this doesn't take sudden spikes of traffic into account. If a server can handle four times the current traffic, it still gets Slashdotted when sudden interest increases traffic by ten times or more. As a result, it's a good rule of thumb to keep server capacity at least ten times the current traffic levels at all times, and plan server upgrades to maintain that level. This isn't likely to cost a great deal more than maintaining a lesser readiness, and it provides a much-needed buffer when making decisions about how to serve visitors' needs in the future.

Web Expansion and New Devices

Of course, not all Web traffic will come from the same sources as today. The Web itself is a very young medium, and as such, it reinvents itself at an alarming pace. Sites that are popular one moment can be gone the next, and entirely new genres of sites can be invented within months. The growth of the Web adds to the growing pains; the growth is from traditional computers being connected to the Web and from new devices, such as cell phones and palmtop computers, gaining Web access.

The Web Doubles Every Eight Months

The number of Web sites available to browsers doubles every eight months, according to numbers published by Alexa Internet in 1998. More recently, that rate was verified by server totals published by the Netcraft Web Server Survey in December 2000. Although this number seems phenomenal, the number of people and businesses not connected to the Web is still large enough to support this kind of growth for years to come.

This growth doesn't automatically mean that site traffic to every site also doubles every eight months. Although the potential for a traffic increase is doubling at that rate, the actual increase (or decrease) of traffic to any given Web site is governed more by the interest in that site than by the sheer number of people and possible connections that are available on the Web. However, the likelihood that a site with consistent performance will see this kind of growth is good.

WML and Slow Connections

With new Web-enabled devices come new possibilities, as well as new headaches. A cell phone connected to the Web sounds like a good thing at first; it provides mobile Web access to millions of people who wouldn't carry wireless laptops. Unfortunately, the interface on a cell phone is not nearly as rich or detailed as the one most Web browsers use today; thus, a special set of technologies had to be developed to give cell phone and wireless PDA users a way to get Web content, without dealing with the high-bandwidth, visually-oriented sites that are currently available. The answers were the Wireless Access Protocol (WAP) and Wireless Markup Language (WML).

WAP provides a low-bandwidth way for wireless devices to access the Internet without incurring the overhead of the usual TCP/IP connection. A detailed description of WAP is outside the scope of this book, but the important thing to remember about WAP is that it appears to a Web server as a very slow—but otherwise standard—client connection.

WML is a markup language based on XML (Extensible Markup Language) that uses a completely different way of organizing Web content than does the more-familiar HTML. WML organizes content into decks of cards—similar to the way a slide presentation or a stack of flash cards would be organized. A deck is a single document with a collection of demarcated sections, called cards. A card is a snippet of HTML-like content with no graphics that can have links both within the deck and out to other WML decks. This represents a radical departure from the full-screen HTML pages to which Web users and designers have become accustomed. This departure means that existing HTML content would have to be translated into WML before it could be repurposed for wireless devices. In practice, this has generally meant the complete redesign of a Web site for WML presentation, with all the decisions and hassles that entails. The end result is two versions of the Web site, both of which have to be updated whenever site information changes.

Once a site is made available through WML and WAP, the slow connection speed of the current set of Web-enabled wireless devices can cause additional headaches for Web site administrators. Slow connections can have a marked effect on site performance; because the Web server has to keep a slow connection open longer than a speedy one, it's possible to degrade the performance of a site by tying up all its available connections with wireless devices. Unfortunately, this can't be easily rectified; it simply has to be accounted for when planning. See Chapter 17, "Publishing XML for the Future," for more information on WML support in Web applications.

XML and Automated Requests

Eventually, the majority of Web application traffic might not come from viewers at all. The rise of business-to-business (B2B) and peer-to-peer (P2P) communications provides new avenues for computers and applications to interact with each other directly, as well as new reasons for them to do so. The CDDB (Compact Disc

Database) protocol, for instance, enables a compact disc jukebox in someone's home to contact a Web site and request information on an album or song. This connection enables the jukebox to display the song's title and artist while it's being played, without requiring the owner to type in any information at all. As a result, though, sites that provide information in CDDB format are likely to get requests every time a song is played or a disc is loaded, regardless of whether an actual person is viewing the resultant information.

These sorts of requests are likely to become more common as Web applications are developed to enable other Web applications to query them in ways in which users would not. Employment sites, for instance, might receive many more requests for job listings and resumes if they made those listings available to other job sites in a standard format. The same sites would also generate requests by querying the same information from other sites. Maintaining these interfaces will be just as important as maintaining the HTML interface to customers because the site becomes less usable if its sources of information become unavailable.

The favored language for these kinds of requests is XML. XML is a flexible way for all types of information to be marked up in ways that both humans and computers can understand. In practice, it's become the watershed for a new generation of languages that can be used to represent data specific to a business or other population on the Internet. For instance, the human resources (HR) and job search community has proposed HR-XML, a set of XML languages that can be used to describe job postings, resumes, and other documents used in the field.

A standard way of sending requests automatically for such HR documents comes in the form of interprocess communication protocols. These protocols include the Simple Object Access Protocol (SOAP) and XML Remote Process Communication (XML-RPC). These give a standard set of protocols that can be used by one program to access documents from another program remotely, without having to develop a specific protocol for each pair of programs. These standard protocols, combined with service directories using the Universal Discovery and Description Interface (UDDI) and the Web Services Description Language (WSDL), give programs a generic interface to a whole range of remote applications by implementing support for just these languages and protocols. This is similar to the same way in which a Web browser has a generic interface to a whole range of remote documents using HTML, HTTP, and Internet search engines. The catch is that the protocols and languages themselves are as difficult to implement as HTML and HTTP—if not more so. This fact once again gives Web application programmers more to support with the same architecture. For some solutions to this problem, see Chapter 17, Chapter 18, "XML as a B2B Interface," and Chapter 19, "Web Services."

Summary

Traffic comes from many sources, and it can be both a blessing and a curse. Sites like WFMY have found that too much traffic all at once can cripple a site and deny service to additional site visitors. When this happens to an e-commerce site, it can mean lost revenue and lost opportunities. However, it's sometimes difficult to tell just when traffic will spike. Traffic can increase quickly due to exposure on a site such as Slashdot. It can increase slowly due to exposure on other sites. By evaluating overall traffic patterns, it's possible to determine the margin a site has before the Web server becomes overloaded. Also, by considering the possible effects of new technologies such as WAP and XML, it's still possible to stay ahead of the curve and keep site visitors happy while avoiding performance problems.

2

Budget and Schedules Aren't Ideal

I F THE ONLY PROBLEMS A WEB APPLICATION DESIGNER had to surmount were technical, solutions would be simple. Men have walked on the moon, a computer has beaten a Grand Master at chess, and entire Thanksgiving dinners can be made with soy products. There's never been a technical problem that couldn't be overcome by extraordinary amounts of technical effort, but the real difficulty lies in applying technical solutions to real-world problems without expending the same effort over and over.

The problem, of course, is that the resources we have available to expend on technology are limited. In fact, they're limited even further by the primary goal of technology, which is to make our lives easier and more productive as well as to make new things possible. This mantra means that expending a decade's worth of effort to put a man on the moon was a wonderful thing, but expending an additional decade's effort for each person that wants to go to the moon would be out of the question.

On the Web, the problems are similar. If all users had broadband connections, and if all servers were supercomputer clusters with OC-12 lines, and if all webmasters had infinite amounts of time and money to throw at a problem, there would be no difficulty in providing everyone with a rich, rewarding, and productive Web experience.

Unfortunately, the reality is that computers are obsolete as soon as they're out of the box, customers are demanding more features that are easier to use and that consume less bandwidth, and your network is starting to get old and creaky. To top it off, the boss is asking for a whole slew of new buzzword-compliant technologies for every Web application within the company. Oh, and it all has to be done by yesterday, thanks. It's enough to send a sane Webmaster around the bend.

The Web environment also creates problems that are even less responsive to technical solutions. Web applications are likely to involve custom programming that brings together disparate technologies, departments, and people to address an issue that they all have in common. Of course, this is the same problem that hundreds of years of business planning and organizational theory have been unable to solve. So, it seems logical to add an organizational solution to all the technological requirements. As a result, the Webmaster is also taskmaster, reporter, presenter, and arbitrator. In addition, all this must be done in less time, for less money, and with fewer requirements on the rest of the staff because they're busy doing important things.

Slow Decisions Versus Fast-Approaching Deadlines

Corporations are slow about nearly everything. It's a fact of life in the business world, and there's very little that can be done to change the decision-making process of a 7,000-employee business that stands to lose billions of dollars if it makes the wrong choice. On the other hand, every individual in a corporation demands that everything under his or her control be available as soon as possible to try and combat the overall slowness of the organization. If the other departments are slow and unresponsive, the reasoning goes, at least one group's results can be made available yesterday.

A bureaucracy is an anathema to the Web application design process, which requires quick thinking, flexibility, and time to produce a Web experience that is on par with the user interfaces that site visitors have come to expect. The price of failure is high on the Web; people go elsewhere if their needs aren't being met. If it takes six months before a new service is made available to customers, that might be the six months necessary for a fast-moving competitor to start, get funded, develop a revolutionary technology, and provide a service that outstrips the one offered by the slower company. The result is obsolescence and downsizing. Welcome to the Web.

The Weight of Progress

On the Web, new technologies are made, used, and overridden within the span of a few months. As a result, a four-to-six month span of time is called a *Web year*, with the implied notion that new products, services, and companies come out every "year."

With all this churn, it's difficult to stick to the basic goals of a Web application project. If the project was originally supposed to provide a service for home buyers looking for a loan over the Web, for instance, a whole host of new technologies and services might become available by the time the project is underway. New partnerships with realtors, new links to lender networks and their technologies, and new vendor contracts can all be made while the initial goals of the project are being implemented.

Management could also demand new features from a Web application based on interest from customers or directors, regardless of whether the new features are easy to implement.

Technology is usually outdistanced by the hype surrounding it in the press. As this book is written, there are many technologies, standards, and industry movements that are popular in the press but completely unimplemented. The Universal Description, Discovery, and Integration (UDDI) specification, for instance, is a standard being touted by IBM, Microsoft, Hewlett-Packard, and others as the answer to directory listing of automated Web services. But, as of January 2001, there were few companies listed in the UDDI databases and only one Web service. Meanwhile, companies around the world are scrambling to build UDDI compliance into their products because they're being told that it's the next big thing. If it fails instead, which it has 50-50 chances of doing, those companies must write off all UDDI-related development and start fresh with the next standard touted by the big players.

The result of all this progress is a Web environment that uses a lot of "pre-release" software. The Web server implementation community has become a nation of early adopters and technology implementers who have to take whatever technology is available as long as it performs even part of its intended job. Gone are the days when software was expected to work right out of the box; the need for an army of consultants and custom programmers now is assumed when implementing a Web application project. In fact, expecting instant usability from these programs has become so unusual that programmers and implementers are surprised when a program works as advertised without any unpleasant side effects.

Evaluating New Technology

The evaluation process is rarely a smooth one; it tends to unearth more issues than it solves. Evaluating new technology or technology upgrades would be simple, if only one person were doing all the evaluating, deciding, and implementing. Unfortunately, the managers with the purchasing power usually make the decision, and the engineering staff must implement it. The task of evaluating a solution tends to be assigned to a mix of the two groups with varying degrees of authority given to each group. In reality, the decision-making process is influenced as much by vendors, consultants, media perceptions, and politics as it is by feasibility.

Decision-making isn't made easier by vendors and consultants. No vendor wants to explain the aspects of its technology that don't work, and very few even acknowledge that there are situations for which their products aren't suited. No vendor mentions the platforms they don't support, the aspects of the program that are still in beta, or the reasons why other products are faster or more reliable. Consultants, at least those sponsored by a particular vendor, aren't much different. Their solutions always are biased toward their sponsors' products, no matter how bad the fit might be; their solution is a hammer—so every problem must be a nail.

Independent consultants can provide an opinion free of corporate bias, but their pronouncements might be geared more toward the perceptions of the client than toward technical reality. They might recommend a single suite of products that offers partial solutions to each client need, rather than explaining the individual roles of disparate technologies that would solve the problem more effectively.

Even reviews and articles in the mainstream media can be misleading when evaluating a new technology. Trade journals and computer magazines show a bias toward products and technologies that are new and exciting. These new technologies provide an endless supply of new specifications and marketing descriptions to use as source material. The source material eventually becomes articles that describe the new technology to readers who have never encountered it.

On the other hand, old technology—especially stable, ubiquitous technology—isn't news because it provides limited draw to introductory or speculatory articles about it. Thus, "push" technology was all the rage in the press while the Apache Web server made quiet inroads into thousands of sites, and every magazine gushed about VRML (the ill-fated Virtual Reality Modeling Language) while database-backed Web applications generated real income. The continued disparity between the popular conception of hot new technologies and the technical reality causes real conflict when decision-makers are doing the reading and engineers are doing the implementing.

Even after finding a suitable technology, it's possible that political decisions will make it unavailable for a particular project. This technological standoff often occurs within project groups that are formed by merging the talents of several existing groups, for instance when companies merge or are taken over. Each group might have its own solution set implemented using a different technology, but consolidation efforts invariably require one group to abandon their existing solutions in favor of "standardized" technology, even when the solutions would not be technically incompatible. This forces entire groups of developers to use technology that is, at best, unfamiliar to them, and, at worst, unsatisfactory to the their desired ends.

Sometimes, engineers have to use a technology unofficially because of the politics surrounding it. For years, UNIX servers had to "go underground" because the prevailing view was that Windows NT would overwhelm the server market and provide everything the UNIX servers did and more. Magazines and trade journals declared the death of UNIX weekly, and managers spoke of the inevitability of their switch to Microsoft products. Developers who saw UNIX as the best solution for their particular needs were forced to implement servers quietly while giving lip service to their "transition" to Windows. Fortunately, the exponential growth of Linux as a server environment gave a boost to the visibility of UNIX in the media, and stories about the death of UNIX tailed off considerably. Interestingly enough, after this happened, corporations started noticing that many of the systems they thought had been implemented using Windows were actually Linux systems masquerading as such.

Dealing with Unexpected Decisions

All the plans and decisions made when designing Web applications can be crushed with a few simple phrases like these: "We're standardizing on Oracle," "We're going to use Windows from now on," and "Everything has to be made available to WAP phones." Snap decisions about technology are always a possibility in an environment in which new insights from partners, consultants, and investors can change the technology direction of a project overnight.

Changes in vendors can be the most damaging to a project. The decision to switch database vendors, for instance, might require all database-backed Web applications be rewritten to support differences in query syntax between the old and new databases, even though the vendor might insist that the database is "fully standards compliant." What this really means is that the old and new databases support the same core standard, but that they provide their own "enhancements" to it. Although some sudden decisions can be averted by knowing the true nature of the changes involved, many times these decisions are made without developers' knowledge. The decision to switch vendors can also be affected by company mergers and purchases; when this happens, the company usually decides to use the newly-acquired product, regardless of whether it's compatible with what's currently being used.

Decisions that change the platform requirements of a project are easier to deal with when developing Web applications. Web technologies were designed from the start to be as standards-compliant as possible, and that history has fostered the need for cross-platform tools as the basis of Web technologies. This need also has been helped by the UNIX-centric nature of Web application environments; UNIX was designed to be portable, with little dependence on hardware or specific implementations. As a result, core Web technologies like the Web server, Perl, Java, and the Web browser itself are available on almost every server platform, and derivative standards like TCP/IP, HTTP, XML, and HTML have implementations across many platforms and environments. Even some proprietary systems, such as Oracle, have few differences between versions for different platforms. Thus, it's possible to change server platforms without impacting the design of a dependent Web application. The few exceptions include Microsoft server technologies, such as ASP and COM, which tend to tie themselves to Microsoft platforms as much as possible. Other exceptions include MacOS platforms before MacOS X. These platforms had limited support for common Web application tools. The limited support problem is addressed by MacOS X and future MacOS systems, all of which are based on BSD UNIX and all of which integrate standard services such as the Apache Web server.

Adding an additional technology to a specification can be easy or difficult to implement, depending on the scope of the technology involved and the difference between the technology's requirements and the requirements of the rest of a project. For instance, adding support for WAP phones, as discussed in Chapter 17, "Publishing XML for Wireless Devices," can be very simple from the standpoint of the Web server; however, it requires a duplication of effort from the standpoint of Web content production. This difference might not be factored into the decision-making process, however, and consultants or articles might gloss over the potential difficulties when describing the benefits. In the case of WAP phones, articles might emphasize the idea of "the Web on a phone" and the number of additional clients this provides. However, the articles might not emphasize the fact that most Web content has to be specially repurposed for the WML browsers on these phones.

The best protection against change is selecting technology that is flexible and that interacts with a multitude of potential systems—not just the ones originally present in a specification. Even the most flexible framework is not compatible with every new technology and delivery mechanism, but many trends in Web application design can be anticipated well in advance of their inclusion in project specifications. So, it's reasonable to design the current generation of Web applications with the next generation of Web technologies in mind. This idea is explored in Section III of this book, "Solutions for the Future."

Small Budgets Versus Grand Ambitions

Decisions are usually made more difficult by the lack of money for technology purchases and implementation. Sometimes, the best solution to a technical problem is prohibitively expensive, and partial solutions have to be implemented instead. For Web applications, this often happens when evaluating server hardware and network infrastructure. Vendors would love to sell every Web application designer a colocated, load-balanced server cluster with hardware fail-over and near-infinite bandwidth; however, in reality, many Web applications have to provide the same performance on a single low-budget server that operates through a less-robust connection to the Internet.

Of course, the lack of money doesn't stop decision-makers from dreaming up the largest possible set of features for a Web application to support. A system with more features is always more impressive than a system with fewer features. In fact, new features are more likely to be added than old ones are to be taken away. When this happens, you must keep track of the features that are most essential to a project. It's also helpful to set proper expectations within the time and money allocated to a project. You also should budget for the inevitable flood of new features that get proposed when initial versions of a Web application come available. This flood happens because users always find uses for a Web application that require new features to be implemented.

Making Room for Essentials

Even the most poorly defined project has a core set of goals that have to be met at a basic level to satisfy everyone involved. No matter how many wish lists and feature requests are added to a project's scope, these main goals are the things without which the project can't be considered a success.

Hardware and software requirements are usually the first set of essentials to be defined, but there's more flexibility in implementing these solutions than would usually be acknowledged. For instance, a decision to use the Solaris operating system on Sun server hardware might seem to imply a fixed cost, as determined by Sun's current pricing model for performance that a Web application demands. It's often possible, however, to gain additional performance by the efficient use of server software. This software can range from clustering software on multiple systems to optimized software for older systems. In addition, it can enable less-expensive choices to be made while still meeting the core requirement. As another example, the seemingly-fixed cost of doubling the amount of RAM in a server can be reduced by reducing the memory requirements of the Web application software that the server runs. The former incurs a monetary cost, but the latter uses development time to achieve the same result. If a project has more development time than money to spare, the decision becomes clear. (Perl modules, open source software, and the techniques in this book are examples of using the development time of others as well. By implementing solutions other people have developed to reduce hardware requirements, it's possible to save money without a penalty.)

When determining the features of a Web application that should be implemented first, it's wise to consider how these features could share common technology components. This consideration enables a solution to be implemented and tested with one feature and then adapted to related features as they are implemented. Generally, a large group of features can be found that implement a common technology, which can then be included in the list of essentials with highest priority. Even though the common technology might take up a large chunk of the budget, after that core technology is implemented, new features of that type can be implemented more quickly and cheaply. As an example, consider that implementing a publishing-centric site around XML technologies might cause additional work and require more technology purchases to assure high performance in XML parsing and translations. The decision would be warranted if new features such as syndication or wireless device support could be added for a fraction of the cost in a fraction of the time. Of course, not all features are easily grouped into classes, and it's sometimes better to implement a quick solution rather than attempt to fit radically different features into a common framework. It's perfectly acceptable to implement a feature multiple times in different ways instead of spending the same amount of time finding a common solution to all possible implementations.

Setting Expectations

When developing a project, it's important to make sure that decision-makers and end users have an accurate view of the work that will actually be done and the problems that will actually be solved. Setting the proper expectations can make the difference between a project that is considered successful and one that is sent back to the drawing board.

The idea of setting expectations is one that independent contractors learn very early in their careers. If a client asks for the moon on a platter originally but is convinced by the contractor to accept a more reasonable solution within the scope of the project, it's often the case that the client reaffirms his or her need for the moon when the product is delivered. It's as if the client doesn't remember the "reasonable solution" discussion. Without a written record of the expectations that were set originally, many contractors would not get paid until the client exhausted every possible feature desired in a product.

For developers working within an organization, it's possible to get the same effect by making the accepted scope of a project explicit at every opportunity. When developing an application that will be accessible by Web browsers and Palm devices but not WAP-enabled cell phones, for example, you might need to state that up front and repeat it frequently to remind decision-makers and managers that the project has a limited scope. If the proper expectation is set originally, later changes to the scope of the project can be seen as additions to the project. These addition can be decided upon and budgeted for separately. In the WAP example, if managers see an increased need for WAP devices as well, the decision to add support for WAP devices can be evaluated and the appropriate budget can be allocated. More often than not, separating out features in this way can keep superfluous and expensive features from sneaking into a specification after the project is already underway.

Living Up to the Demo

Sometimes, success can inflict its own punishment, even under the best development circumstances. Interest in a project can seem impossible to generate initially, and feedback from early users and testers is great for usability testing. After the project is successful, though, it's possible to get inundated with requests for product fixes and new features.

A demonstration of product capabilities can offer a concrete example of how a Web application can be used. Until users get a chance to see the program in action, it might be difficult for them to visualize the way in which it really works. Seeing the demo gels the application in their minds and gives them a basis by which to evaluate their plans for using it. The demo also gives users a chance to express preferences that they wouldn't have been able to articulate without specific examples in front of them.

Unfortunately, a successful demo also can give rise to usage ideas that weren't anticipated when choosing the initial scope of the project. Viewing a demo can give users more insight into the workings of the application, but it also gives the impression that the application is complete and looking for new ideas. Instead of giving feedback on the technologies demonstrated, users are likely to comment on a dozen other tangential solutions they'd like to see from that Web application. If each tangential solution is added to the project's list of required deliverables, the project can quickly drown.

Initial demonstrations of a developing Web application should be seen as a part of the decision-making process as well as a time to do informal usability testing. User feedback is important, but only when it fits in with the established goals for the project. Does solving the user's issue require changing the focus of the Web application, and would the change require delaying the application's release? If so, it might be better to include the requested feature on a list of revisions to carry out after the initial release. To avoid growing a long list of these, which might detract from the success of the application as users wait for the next release, it usually helps to keep the scope of the application flexible enough to allow at least some features to be implemented quickly, if requested.

Some Help is No Help at All

It starts innocuously, but it ends up being the downfall of your project. You ask for a graphic designer, and the boss brings in his 11-year-old daughter who's "a whiz at these things, really." You ask for a new Web server, and the boss brings out a 10-year-old minicomputer from the depths of the server closet. You ask for usability studies, and the boss shows the Web application demo to his buddies at competing companies and gives them your phone number. You ask for timely content, and the boss gives you old data in an archaic format stored on a backup tape that might or might not be readable. Every time you ask for help, in fact, you're given another technological challenge instead of solutions for the current ones.

Some help is truly no help at all. A Web application designer looking to provide a cutting-edge interface using the latest technologies—on time and under budget—can be hampered as much as helped by old data, old systems, staff with indeterminate Web experience, and unwanted feedback from an audience that isn't likely to use the site regularly. In many cases, though, this is the only help that's available. The old systems are the only hardware budgeted for the project, there's no money to hire staff with actual Web knowledge, and a usability testing firm would be entirely too expensive. So, the best has to be made from the materials at hand.

Working with Legacy Systems

Legacy data is a term that's tossed around a lot in the industry, but it basically means "data from any software that isn't directly supported by this software." By lumping all external software into a category with data tapes and punch cards, software vendors can escape the responsibility of interacting with many of the systems to which their customers would ordinarily like to connect.

A Web application designer doesn't have the luxury of dismissing legacy data, even when the tools used to develop Web applications do. Never mind that there isn't an Enterprise Java Bean built to read records from old FoxPro databases; if that's where the data is, it needs to get to the Web somehow. If a company's business logic is contained in an IBM mainframe accessed through CICS, the Web application had better speak the language and operate on the resulting data in a meaningful way.

These data connection needs are where the choice of a Web application environment is most important. Does the environment support adding additional sources of data? How easy is it to do so? Better yet, is the existing base of support for data sources broad enough that adding support for legacy sources is both rare and trivial? These concerns are important when you are evaluating Web environments (servers, programming languages, and middleware suites). No matter how easy an environment makes the core 90 percent of Web application design, it's not a good choice if the other 10 percent is difficult enough to erase any productivity gains.

Delegating Web Development

Web application technology aside, it's a good idea to let your Web application benefit from the work of others. Graphic artists, system administrators, database administrators, user interface designers, copy editors, and other potential contributors should all be given the easiest route possible to offering input and making improvements to a Web application.

Delegating aspects of Web application development requires planning and forethought. If it's difficult to make graphic and layout changes to the pages of an application, for instance, those changes are unlikely to be made in a timely manner. Designers and usability testers will be discouraged from making modifications freely, and the application interface suffers as a result. See Chapter 3, "Site Design Versus Application Design," for further discussion of this subject.

Involving the Audience

Any Web application, be it a public Web site or a private intranet application, has a built-in source of data that's rarely acknowledged when building the application—users. Since the scope of the site assures that the primary audience has at least one thing in common, it's important to allow users to modify application structure and contents to the full extent possible. The more work users do in shaping a Web application, the closer it's likely to be to the application they'd prefer. Besides, any modification or addition that users make to a Web application without developer support is an additional feature added to the application for free.

On the other hand, giving users that level of control over a Web application can require as much or more development work as creating the application in the first place. User administration forms and other site meta-interaction pages are designed the same as any other user input; however, there are additional concerns because of the more fundamental changes users are making to the site. Allowing visitors to a news site to add headlines to the front page, for instance, also brings the risk that any user input might modify the page in a way that is aesthetically unpleasant at best and disastrous at worst. You can mitigate these concerns by defining explicitly what a user is allowed to add or change. You want the controls as tight as the content allows, but you should remember that accounting for every unwanted circumstance can be time-consuming.

Some users can be a boon to a Web application. In the news site example just discussed, no mention was made about the way headlines get on the home page if site viewers aren't submitting them. In many cases, site personnel or other privileged Web application users need to use the same interfaces that unprivileged site visitors would use. So, the choice is not between offering and not offering user interfaces, but between offering interfaces only to a few users or putting the time in to make them available to all.

Summary

Not all problems are technological, and not all technology solutions are affordable or feasible in the time allotted for a project. New technologies are vital to a robust Web project, but any new technology must be evaluated before it can be trusted on a live site. This doesn't stop managers and decision-makers from asking for everything and demanding it yesterday, but it does set limits on what can be promised and what suggestions should be considered. Also, the cost of a Web project can't outstrip the value it produces, so not all goals can be met within the allotted time and budget. However, you can bring in the work of others whenever possible, which can provide additional features without additional cost. It's also helpful to use pre-existing tools to develop a Web application and delegate aspects of development to those who are most capable, including the application's intended audience.

3

Site Design Versus Application Design

A FULL-PAGE MAGAZINE ADVERTISEMENT CAN BE THE PERFECT venue of expression for corporate graphic artists. The only inherent restrictions are the size of the page (which is huge) and the resolution of the color imagery (which is so tiny as to be infinite.) The challenge is to reach a reader who spends less than a second looking at the ad, draw the reader in, and deliver the advertising message. The tools are varied, and the creative process is individual to each artist.

A Web site can have just as wide an impact as a magazine advertisement. HTML and modern Web browsers enable pages to be laid out with the same creativity, detail, and control as print—albeit in a smaller space. A Web site also offers interactivity and multimedia, both of which open up the artistic possibilities of the medium and enable more compelling expressions of information to be portrayed.

On the other hand, a commercial application can be the best form of expression for a computer programmer. An application has one main metric of success: if it doesn't do the job, it's worthless. Programs usually have other restrictions and optimizations, as well; performance, memory footprint, and efficient use of resources all have to be taken into consideration. Human factors are important, but they usually come second to a clean, efficient program that operates without errors. Creative impulses are less of an ally than a solid set of solutions upon which the programmer can draw to solve problems quickly and reliably.

Web sites have become applications in their own right. Some of the most popular Web sites are applications at their core. For instance, an e-commerce site is really a shipping and ordering database front-end that incorporates business logic and data mining capabilities with a graphic user interface, and a news site is really a real-time publishing and syndication engine with data collection and distribution interfaces. In addition, a business-to-business (B2B) portal is really an integration infrastructure with quality assurance, security, and administrative interfaces. These sites require the same scalability, performance, and reliability as any other enterprise-level application.

The line between Web sites as venues of artistic expression and Web sites as applications is a thin one that is blurring more with each new technology. Convergence— a buzzword usually thrown around in reference to Web sites and multimedia outlets such as television or radio—is a reality for these artistic applications, and the opportunities it opens up are only surpassed by the problems it creates. A Web application is judged not only by the way it works, but also by the way it looks and feels. A site that provides accurate information or useful services 100 percent of the time is valuable, but one that does so while presenting the information or service in a pleasing, easy-to-access fashion gains much more support.

Because Web applications are being created jointly by graphic artists, programmers, and other types of developers, it's important to meet the needs of all groups. Graphic artists need the flexibility to create aesthetically pleasing interfaces, programmers need a stable environment in which to develop clean code, and other groups need clear interfaces to the work that is available.

What Graphic Designers Want

Web site design is a lengthy process, even when programming is not involved. Content production, editing, layout, and graphic design all have their respective processes and problems. Content takes time to gather, and it is sometimes not available until the site is live. Editing Web copy takes time, and the process it uses is sometimes a duplicate of content production. Layout has to walk the fine line between consistency and suitability to specific content. HTML itself is not an easy language in which to provide content; it's less complicated than page layout programs, but it's less sophisticated as well.

Graphic artists would prefer to have a definite goal to which they can work; the more uncertainty there is in the design environment, the more likely it is that an assumption made during the design process will not be accepted. Consistency across the site is an additional hedge against potential changes to the design; consistency enables the graphic artist to make design decisions once and carry them through the rest of the site.

Consistent Look and Feel

Site design is made considerably easier for a graphic artist when page elements are repeated consistently from page to page. For a commercial site, this makes it easier to create a brand identifying the content. Branding is more important on the Web because a site can be accessed in an indefinite order by viewers referred from an unknown source. Consistency also provides improved navigability to sites by allowing viewers to discover a site without having to relearn basic navigation elements.

In the early days of the World Wide Web, HTML pages had very little resemblance to each other, even when they were performing similar functions on the same site. The nature of Web servers was to provide a different page for each request without any knowledge of pages that were accessed previously; thus, each page was treated as a complete document with its own formatting and structure. Unfortunately, this presented a navigational nightmare as users were forced to choose between wading through monolithic pages with the site's content laid out linearly or following links from one page to the next without an overall picture of each page's ownership or relation to other pages. Site designers quickly learned to use consistent design elements on related pages to provide continuity and navigability within larger sites.

Originally, consistency was addressed by designing one page with the desired look, and then copying the page and modifying it for each subsequent page of the site. This worked fine for the initial development of small sites, but modifications to any design elements had to be copied manually to every page each time they were made. Developers of larger sites with hundreds of similar pages learned this lesson the hard way, as changes to the look became cumbersome and time-consuming to implement one page at a time. Sometimes, new changes became necessary while earlier changes were still being implemented, thus creating a site with as many navigational variations as before.

Frames, introduced by Netscape for the 2.0 version of Navigator, seemed to be a good solution to the problem of consistency. The common elements of a page would be broken out into separate frames, and only the information that changed from page to page would be reloaded. Unfortunately, the implementation of frames was a disaster; site design had to become much more complex because a frame set was made up of a group of HTML pages, each of which could be accessed directly by the browser. Rather than providing a consistent look across an entire site, frames created disparate pages that contained navigation structures without content, content pages without navigation, or branding elements with neither content nor navigation.

Template-based design is a more recent way to provide a consistent look to many pages without the need to break the design elements into pieces or make hundreds of unchangeable copies of them in each page or application. Tools such as Macromedia Dreamweaver and Adobe GoLive enable templates to be created during the design process. The templates are then applied across a site. However, they don't make the job of transferring the updated site to the Web server any less complex or time-consuming. They also aren't likely to support the Web applications that are present on the site; this is the reason why many sites have a less interesting look for dynamic pages than they do for static ones. A better solution would enable graphic artists to use the templates for both static and dynamic content.

Round-Trip HTML Design

Of course, the tools used by a programmer to write and test code are not the same tools a graphic artist uses to compose HTML pages or other Web-ready content. For instance, a Web Perl programmer is likely to use a basic text editor to write Web application code, and then he or she would test the code by running it in a Web environment. Simulating the final runtime environment is usually very difficult. Thus, intermediate steps between creation and implementation are few. As a result, the code produced by programmers is likely to be inaccessible to the designer's tools and processes.

For instance, a CGI application such as the one in Listing 3.1 has HTML elements along with the Perl code, but it would be very difficult to extract the HTML in a form usable to an HTML editing application. Within the Perl application, the HTML could be in blocks of text, quoted strings, or even composed on the fly. The only way to extract it in the final form is to execute the program.

Listing 3.1   **CGI Program with HTML Output**

```
01 #!/usr/bin/perl
02
03 print "Content-type: text/html\n\n";
04
05 print <<EOF;
06 <html>
07 <head>
08 <title>Problems with CGI</title>
09 </head>
10 <body>
11 EOF
12
13 foreach my $number (1..3)
14 {
15 print "<p>$number. Embedded HTML.</p>\n";
16 }
17
18 print <<EOF;
19 </body>
20 </html>
21 EOF
```

A one-directional solution involves the site designer providing application developers with a template page to use when writing the HTML output sections of the Web application. Unfortunately, this approach assumes that the applications are updated to match new templates as they are made available, which can cause delays to implementation. It also assumes that programmers are comfortable with taking the time to replace possibly hundreds of lines of HTML embedded in their code with nearly-identical HTML supplied by the site designer, and that graphic artists are comfortable entrusting the timely update of their HTML designs to programmers.

This situation also makes it difficult for graphic artists to incorporate changes to the template made by programmers when adapting it to Web applications. If Web addresses in an image map are changed to point to different parts of an application, for example, the changes won't be reflected in the original template. This gets more complicated with the inclusion of JavaScript or other client-side scripting; the lines between HTML text to print and programmatic code to develop become blurred.

The best solution would be to base the look and feel of both static pages and Web applications on a single template file (or set of files) in a single location that is accessible to both graphic artists and programmers. The applications and pages would derive their look from the template, and modifications made to the template by either application changes or site redesigns would be available to all groups.

What Programmers Want

Images of start-up companies with Nerf armories and all-night coding sessions might make the programming world seem as chaotic as any creative endeavor, but that chaos masks the underlying rules and structure programmers rely on when producing code for Web applications. A programmer works best when given a clear goal to meet (for example, to display a given query in a given format or to deliver a provided piece of information to a given database) and a clear set of guidelines to use in reaching it.

Programmers are looking for any shortcut that gets them to the goal faster; conversely, they resist any process that might pose a threat to their progress. Readable code helps a programmer understand code faster, modularity keeps the programmer from reinventing the wheel, and future-resistant code keeps programmers from having to modify it as often.

Clean Code

If there's one axiom that is constant throughout all program development, it's that all code needs to be changed sooner or later. Whether it's due to new bugs, incompatibilities with new software or hardware, or the addition of new features, any application is likely to be modified at least once—and more likely, many times—over its lifetime.

Code rewrites aren't automatic, though. They are performed by programmers, no matter how much automation is put into the process. Programmers are also human, which means they have priorities, style preferences, and idiomatic ways of creating code. For instance, it's possible to write code that is impossible to decipher. The practice is called *obfuscation*, and it can be the result of deliberate effort—usually for a competition or for artistic value. It also can happen inadvertently when programmers write unreadable code due to inexperience or the conditions under which the code was written.

Obfuscated code also can be written by code generators, such as applications that create code based on templates or other high-level languages, as discussed in Chapter 12, "Environments for Reducing Development Time." Although this code can be perfectly usable after it is created, it can wreak havoc on a development cycle by requiring programmers to completely decipher the obfuscated code before they modify it, rather than simply finding the part that needs changing and making the modification. The answer in a development environment seems simple: Write clean, understandable code.

Producing clean code isn't such a simple matter, though; there isn't one "good style" that is learned by programmers everywhere. Clean code is also the product of good business practices. The readability of code that is written by a team of programmers can be greatly improved by having a clear road map of functions, naming conventions, and a high-level structure. For instance, the code in Listing 3.3—a segment of the forum code written for VeloMeter.com, as detailed in Chapter 14, "Database-Backed Web Sites"—is written to conform to a style guide agreed upon by VeloMeter.com developers. Listing 3.2 is a work-alike segment, which follows a different style.

Listing 3.2 **Code in a Default Style**

```
01 squeal($q,'Please try again.');
02
03 sub squeal {
04 $_[0] or return; $_[1] =~ tr/ /+/;
05 print $_[0]->redirect("/forum/confirm.psp?error=$_[1]&".
   ⮑$_[0]->query_string);
06 exit;
07 }
```

Listing 3.3 **Cleaner Code in the Author's Style**

```
01 show_error($q,'Please try again.');
02
03 # redirect the user to the input page with an error if needed
04 sub show_error ($$)
05 {
06   my $q = shift || return;
07   my $error = shift;
08   $error =~ tr/ /+/;
09
10   my $query = $q->query_string;
```

```
11
12    print $q->redirect("/forum/confirm.psp?error=$error&$query");
13
14    exit;
15 }
```

The subroutines in Listings 3.2 and 3.3 perform the same function, are called with the same arguments, and work nearly identically. The difference is striking, though, and Perl's indifference to variations such as these is usually seen as a drawback to programming in the language. However, the idea that a language should force programmers to create clean code makes little sense; it's much easier to develop and enforce a style at the project or team level than at the language-design level.

Some improvements in the readability of Listing 3.3 come from basic Perl style rules; it's much easier to tell that the error message is being printed when it's named $error, instead of the more Perlish $_[0], in line 12. In addition, the $q object is easier to recognize when it's named the same in line 6 as it is in line 1. Also, basic whitespace and indenting rules help group functions in a logical way throughout the program.

Further enhancements come from style rules developed by the project's authors. Program blocks begin with a curly brace on its own line, as in line 5. The ending brace in line 15 is at the same indent level to enable easier matching. Cute function and variable names such as squeal are eschewed in favor of functional descriptions such as show_error, which use whole words separated by underscores for easier reading. The $q object is an exception to this rule because the object it references is common in Web programming and likely to be used frequently; a shorter identifier, as in line 10, is less obtrusive when calling methods. The $dbh database handle object—used frequently in the examples throughout this book—is another example of this idea.

For Web applications, clean code can make the difference between a quick site modification and a major rework. If a five-minute modification to the content on a Web page requires a six-day trek through the inner workings of a complex application that consists of code in a style such as Listing 3.2, more important modifications might never have the chance to be made.

Modularity

Components, beans, modules, objects, layers, and plug-ins—they're all ways of providing program modularity. Program modularity enables each part of a program to be developed and modified separately, without impacting the overall usability of the program. The plug-in interface to Netscape Navigator, for instance, enables third-party programmers such as Macromedia to produce extensions, such as the Shockwave, to the Navigator program player without having to change them every time a new version of Navigator is developed. Similarly, a new version of the plug-in can be developed without requiring modifications to Netscape itself.

Modularity goes hand in hand with abstraction, which is the capability to address part of a program in a standardized way, regardless of the underlying implementation. For instance, the Shockwave plug-in makes calls to the Netscape plug-in API, which is a defined set of methods that Navigator responds to in a consistent way even when the underlying functions being executed change. Abstraction can be codified in a standard such as HTML, which provides a common language that is used regardless of what the Web browser or Web server actually does to create or interpret it.

Subroutines, modules, and object interfaces are the main structures used to provide modularity and abstraction in Perl. Objects are found also in Java, C++, C#, and Python, and modules are similar to headers or includes in procedural languages such as C. Subroutines are common in most languages and are generally used as the first examples taught to computer science and other programming students. Each layer enables a program to be developed in parts that interconnect in formalized ways.

Modularity doesn't just work at the language level, though. Programs are rarely self-sufficient, and they frequently combine features with other programs to make more complex applications. In fact, this idea of small programs that "do one thing and do it well" is a founding principle of UNIX-like operating systems. For instance, an email retrieved through the `mail` program could be searched with `grep` and the resultant lines could be counted with `wc` to produce a tally of the occurrences of a particular word. Because each program both takes in and emits text, neither program needs to know how the other is implemented.

Web sites enforce their own modularity by implementing the Hypertext Transfer Protocol (HTTP) and the standard uniform resource locator (URL) notation. These two standards break a site into a hierarchy of directories with discrete files, any of which can be accessed at any time from any network-accessible locale without the need for previous exposure to any other file. Because of this simple structure, a Web server can provide thousands of files per second by applying a simple translation between the URL requested and the location of the file on the disk. The server also can cache files or compose them on the fly as long as the basic needs of HTTP are met.

Web applications have to merge the document-based statelessness of Web sites with the reusable persistence of application objects. Unfortunately, this usually means that parts of a Web application that should be shared—such as the look of a navigation bar or previously-selected user preferences—are likely to be expressed in a multitude of file locations, as seen by the Web browser. This can cause problems when neither the browser nor the server is saving program information; recreating state information with each request can create additional load for the server and discontinuity for the browser.

Modularity is a must also when extending a Web application to provide new features and functionality. It's easier to develop and test a small, independent piece of a large Web application than it is to test a piece on which the entire application is dependent. Abstraction also restricts the possible ways that the larger Web application interacts with the piece being modified.

Future Resistance

Of course, the best way to avoid rewriting a piece of code is to write it with the future in mind. The future comes all too quickly for Web applications, and the pace of change requires that old programs do work they were never designed to do because there's no time to write a new program for each new function. Unfortunately, it's usually difficult to predict all the possible uses of a Web application when it's first designed, and it's practically impossible to design an application that is compatible with every future technology.

Code that is written to a standard is more likely to be flexible when the demands on it change. The Web server is a perfect example of this principle; even though Web browsers have changed significantly since the Web was first implemented and Web sites have grown to incorporate countless new applications, Web servers themselves have been able to focus on their primary goal of serving more files in less time with more flexibility. This is possible because the Web server is written to standards such as HTTP, Multipurpose Internet Mail Extensions (MIME), and the Common Gateway Interface (CGI). To a Web server, a Java applet is just another MIME document, a data mining application is just a set of CGI scripts, and a load testing application is just another HTTP client.

The standards themselves are usually repurposed for use with new technologies. MIME was originally proposed as a standard way to identify file attachments embedded within an Internet email, but Web servers started using MIME descriptors to identify files as they were returned through HTTP. CGI was originally designed as a way to pass arguments and environment variables to external programs called by a Web server, but the conventions of CGI are used also by technologies such as FastCGI and mod_perl to make them more understandable to the programmers using them.

What Everyone Wants

Of course, the Web application landscape isn't a battleground. Programmers, designers, and other staff members do agree on some aspects of the process. Everyone involved would like to see shorter development cycles, consistent results, and help from other teams. After all, everyone wants the end result to be a site of which they can be proud.

Shorter Development Cycles

Nothing can possibly happen quickly enough on the Web. If any information relevant to a Web site changes, the Web site needs to reflect that change as soon as it happens, no matter when it happens. If there is any delay, the possibility exists that someone will access the site, get the incorrect information, and lose confidence in the accuracy of the site's information.

As a result, content producers need the ability to change site information at any time with little or no notice. This applies to all types of content, whether it's advertising copy prepared by the marketing department or a home listing entered by a user of a real estate site. Self-determination allows content producers to work to their own schedules, applying changes and updates whenever needed without adding more work for programmers and site administrators.

This idea has worked well for news and comment sites that integrate content production into the basic framework of the site. By allowing any site visitor to post news stories or add comments, these sites provide a richer experience to future visitors without additional effort. If this type of content required intervention by programming staff or site administrators, it would cause much more work than it was worth.

Application programming and graphic design have their own tight schedules. In both cases, changes and new development have to be acted on as soon as possible to allow time to implement them, and the finished product has to allow for changes that come to light after it is available for review. If either graphic designers or programmers have to wait for the other group to implement a change before it can be reviewed, the result is a site that doesn't fit the requirements or a deadline that is missed.

With a Web year lasting only six calendar months, schedules are tighter than usual and advance notice of design changes is in short supply. If a site requires a quick change and it relies on someone who is out of the office for a week, any process that relies on that person loses that week as well, and site visitors spend an entire week either looking for a change that hasn't been posted or using out-of-date information.

Clear Division of Labor

Nothing brings site design to a grinding halt sooner than making everyone wait for a manager to decide who needs to implement each new change. When there is no acknowledged ownership of a file, project or process, it becomes difficult to determine where even the smallest change should be made, and by whom.

Programmers want to program; they don't necessarily want to learn the intricacies of graphic design every time an application needs to provide a new visual interface. If programmers are left to their own devices without a clear route to the work of graphic artists and other site designers, they either ignore needed changes entirely or implement them in a way that seems reasonable to them. This can result in a Web application that is unappealing at best and unusable at worst. With clear guidelines to follow when drawing the line between site look and feel and application function, programmers are more likely to fit application structure into the site design seamlessly.

Graphic designers want to design; they don't necessarily want to learn the intricacies of a program listing every time the look of an application changes. They might become frustrated if the changes they make to the look of a site create errors in the site's Web applications. If forced to choose leaving applications in an outdated state, asking for programmer assistance in updating the look and feel, or breaking functionality, graphic designers are likely to update the accessible parts of the site at the expense of Web applications. If graphic artists have a clear path to updating the site's look and feel and they can do so safely, easily, and with instant results, they are more likely to make each change across the board to keep the site consistent.

Usability testers want to churn; they don't necessarily want to learn the intricacies of graphic design or programming when an interface change is dictated by usage patterns. They certainly don't want to wait a week to test a slight variation to a widget when there are a dozen other variations to test before the application goes live. If given the choice between hacking together code and graphics that fit the usability criteria or waiting for graphic artists to match the site look and feel and programmers to optimize the code, usability testers will make the change first and attempt to sort out the conflicts later. If usability testers are given an intermediate level of code generation that is clearly separated from site look and feel and underlying implementation programming, they can make broad changes to the operation of a Web application and test the results immediately with confidence that the changes will carry intact through to the final site.

Content providers want to write and edit; they don't necessarily want to dive into the sea of usability, design, and code whenever there's a new piece of information to present or an old bit of copy to change. Unfortunately, administrative interfaces to application data are as difficult to write as the Web applications themselves. If a site is designed with modularity and abstraction in mind, however, administrative interfaces can be added to a site just as easily as other application components can be added.

Every team wants to know what its domain is, what its limitations are, and where to go for help in other areas. With the right approach, this idea can be extended to the design of Web sites and Web applications as well. Each group can have its own area of expertise, and each area can be abstracted for use by other groups.

The Cool Factor

Everyone involved in producing a Web application wants a site that looks great and that provides the latest and greatest features. Programmers want to show off their skills in producing the fastest, most capable applications, graphic artists want to win design awards for their avant-garde work, user interface designers would love to see repeat traffic from satisfied users, and they all want to impress the boss, the viewer, and the folks back home. The chance to elicit the "Wow!" response is difficult to pass up.

Unfortunately, the coolest programming tricks aren't necessarily the most stable or extensible. When Java was developed, for example, the urge was to add Java functions to all parts of the site without regard to their real utility. The result was a lot of sites with "nervous text" or mouse-over animation that either slowed site responsiveness or crashed Web browser software. These useless features were quickly dropped from sites after the problem of updating potentially unstable Java applet code for simple site changes was revealed. Of course, after Java technology matured, it became possible to find areas where applets were truly needed.

Likewise, the coolest graphic designs aren't always the most usable or conducive to performance. A site with the fastest Web applications imaginable can still be brought to its knees serving 15-megabyte Macromedia Shockwave files or QuickTime background music. If system resources are nearly all being devoted to supporting style, it's difficult to provide Web application substance with the remaining resources. At the other extreme, sites can be made unusable by relying on all the latest features from Cascading Style Sheets, JavaScript, and the Document Object Model (DOM), even if they would enable simple underlying code and a rich graphic interface. Browsers that support only a subset of the features used might cause navigation to behave strangely, increasing the need for server-side assistance in checking user input and determining browser compatibility.

Web applications might eventually benefit from cool new features and exciting graphic design, but a more sustainable approach might require waiting for some technologies to achieve wider adoption and greater stability.

Summary

Programmers, graphic artists and other site personnel have different needs and priorities when designing Web applications. Graphic designers want artistic freedom with the look and feel of a site, but programmers are looking for stable, extensible architectures that can be modularized and optimized as the site grows. Everyone involved would like a clear division of labor and a result of which they can be proud.

4

Prototypes Versus Live Sites

Web applications are commonly seen as the programs we interface with while using a site that's already in production, but they can just as easily be prototypes of those same sites. Because of the fluid nature of Web development, even sites that don't have a formal prototype stage have prototypes. The Web enables sites to change from day to day. Thus, initial releases of a site can be updated to include new or updated Web applications as the need presents itself. Each revision of the application can be seen as the prototype for the next. Therefore, each iteration is a chance for more development to be done with the application.

With large-scale Web applications, the prototype process is likely to be lengthy. A prototype on the Web with many people evaluating it goes through lots of changes and many revision cycles. During most of the process, features won't be implemented in their final form. Rather, they are implemented in a vague approximation that behaves similarly to the final form. This makes it difficult to determine a detailed structure for the prototype because the underlying functionality might change dramatically, rendering the details obsolete.

Perl is used to prototype many sites because of the speed and ease with which Perl Common Gateway Interface (CGI) can be used to mock up a site in a near-complete form. As they are being designed, smaller sites might use Perl CGI exclusively because it's readily available to site programmers. Larger, more established sites still use Perl

CGI to create prototypes of new features for the same reason and with the intention of reimplementing the design using another language and environment when the details are finalized.

The switch from prototypes to live sites usually leaves Perl CGI behind, though. CGI doesn't provide the performance that a Web application needs in production, and using CGI for live sites can sometimes cause the sites to be slow or inaccessible because the CGI processes consume every available clock cycle and megabyte of the Web server.

Perl Means Fast Prototyping

One of the most attractive reasons to use Perl for Web site design is the ability to prototype a Web application in great detail with little effort. Perl is designed to be a problem-solving language that glues disparate systems together to form a coherent whole—a description that fits most Web applications precisely.

Perl also benefits from its "interpreted" nature, which eliminates the need for a compile step when developing applications in Perl. (Perl isn't really interpreted at all; programs are actually compiled when run, as is discussed later in this chapter in the section entitled "The Cost of Compilation.") This makes Perl CGI development follow the process used in Web site development, where modifications to source files can be viewed immediately by reloading the resultant page in a client browser. This enables instant feedback to the programmer by presenting intermediate results for modification and exposing errors as soon as they occur.

Perl's history as a glue language also enables prototypes to be created without having to write much underlying implementation code. Publicly available Perl modules contain interfaces that provide database connections, error-handling routines, network interaction, and other common tasks that Web applications perform; thus, it is easy to find a group of modules that can be combined easily to fit the needs of the prototype application. Programmers also can find examples of Perl CGI on the Web that implement common Web applications such as user forums, news publishing, and data browsers.

The object-oriented features of Perl also provide a way to prototype a Web application one feature at a time, by designing simple interfaces to the parts of the application without needing to know details of the implementation behind the interface. This is how most public Perl modules work, and converting an existing piece of Perl code to an object module is trivial. Few restrictions on variable types or scoping are enforced by default, so disparate program sections can be included and patched together with a minimum of effort.

Case Study: Amazon.com

Amazon.com uses Perl to create prototypes for its main site and in production for many of its internal and auxiliary sites. The company has found Perl to be an excellent choice for creating quick prototypes of new systems in a matter of weeks. The production team has used Perl for application automation and workflow tasks for years, but more recently, the team has started to rely on Perl more for Web application design and development.

When the production development team at Amazon creates applications for the live site, they develop the entire application as a C-based monolithic program. This environment was developed early in the company's history to overcome CGI application overhead and to ensure that the site's e-commerce back end could scale along with hardware improvements to meet the demands of increased traffic and transactions. Originally, application prototypes were developed using the same system, but the rigid style of C programming and the time spent waiting for compilation were obstacles to quick prototyping of new features. Also, the need to address implementation concerns, such as memory leaks, even in the earliest prototypes added to the overhead of designing in C.

In 1999, when faced with the need to prototype a new auction site (`http://www.amazon.com/auctions`), the production software group at Amazon.com turned to Perl. The group was able to develop a complete auction site in three weeks, including full bidding functionality, customer feedback, and other advanced features. This was made possible mostly because the team was able to reuse existing code and object modules from other projects in the prototype. The team also was able to test different data models as the prototype was constructed to determine the most efficient way to store and handle data. However, after the Perl prototype was complete, development of the site had to switch back to the compiled C environment for performance reasons. Because of this, not every feature developed for the prototype was implemented in time for the initial launch of the production site.[1]

1. Houston, Lori [online]. *Amazon's Production Software Group Builds Auction Site Prototype.* [cited Feb. 1, 2001]. Available from Internet: `http://perl.oreilly.com/news/ amazon_0100.html`.

continues

continued

> More recently, the team has experimented with implementing the live site in mod_perl or other persistent, Perl runtime environments. Using mod_perl would help the development team bridge the gap between prototypes and production code, freeing up more time and effort for additional development and application performance tuning. (See Chapter 10, "Tools for Perl Persistence," for more details on mod_perl and other persistent environments.) A persistent Perl environment also would enable round-trip development between prototypes and live applications, which makes performance data from live site usage patterns directly applicable when designing the next revision of the prototype.

Perl Modules for Common Tasks

Part of the attraction of writing a Web application prototype in Perl is the number of modules Perl provides to perform common Web-related tasks. Most languages have application program interfaces (APIs) and libraries for integrating disparate systems into an application, but Perl excels in this by bringing the majority of those interfaces together in a single module architecture that can be navigated easily.

The Comprehensive Perl Archive Network (CPAN) lists hundreds of modules for use with Perl. The functions are as varied as database connection (DBI), graphics production (GIMP::), Web browsing (LWP), XML processing (XML::*), and even Telnet access (IO::Telnet). All modules on CPAN are arranged by author or name and are available for immediate download—many with complete documentation for both installation and use. CPAN itself is truly a network with mirrors on dozens of sites around the world. Many interfaces to CPAN exist. The interfaces even include a Web-based portal site with search engines and documentation at `http://www.cpan.org`.

Each module on CPAN provides a lightweight and general interface to the module's functions, usually with module documentation that emphasizes usage examples first and detailed instructions later. Many of the code samples included in module documentation are designed to run as-is in user programs, which makes incorporating the features of a module into a prototype that much easier. The DBI module, for instance, has extensive documentation for its API and features. It also includes sample code for common functions, and hints on optimizing database access using the module.

If a module that meets the specific needs for a Web application prototype isn't available on CPAN, it's still likely that some section of code can still be applied to the prototype as a module. Perl modules are just Perl routines in a generically accessible location, so it's very easy to convert any algorithm or code snippet into a Perl module for use in a prototype.

The greatest strength of most Perl modules is the fact that they are released under the Artistic License, the open-source license under which Perl itself is made available. The Artistic License was created specifically to provide the greatest flexibility to Perl programmers when writing and using Perl modules. Modules released under the Artistic License might be used in any fashion, individual or corporate, public or private. This enables modules to be used in proprietary or open-source projects without fear that a license will be violated in future use, which can be a real concern when developing a Web application which is then sold as an original work. Not all Perl modules are made available under the Artistic License, but nearly all modules on CPAN are. Check the documentation for each module if there is a concern; language such as "This module is released under the same terms as Perl" indicates that the Artistic License is in effect.

A Profusion of Available Perl CGI

Perl also suits Web application prototyping well because of the Perl CGI scripts that are already available. These scripts address many of the common forms a Web application might take, so it's often easy to find a CGI script that is close to the desired final result and modify it to suit a specific Web application prototype. Scripts have already been written that implement Web forums, user administration, database access, site searching, and a host of other standard Web application tasks.

CGI's ubiquity as a Web programming protocol can't be overestimated. CGI is not only available for every platform and Web server, but also is almost always included as a default application environment. Perl, as well, is present by default in practically every UNIX Web server installation, and it is made freely available to less common Web server platforms, such as Windows or Macintosh. In fact, the combined ubiquity of Perl and CGI causes neither technology to register on lists of popular server add-ons while PHP, Java servlets, and similar technologies rise to the top of such lists with only 50 percent acceptance or less. This gives the impression that Perl and CGI aren't being used in Web server environments at all, even when a quick tour around the Web shows that they're just as common as ever.

As a result, common aspects of Web applications are likely to have been implemented by CGI programmers already. Even if most of these solutions are never offered as examples for download, that still leaves a wealth of available Perl applications that can be used as fodder for new prototypes. Perl's lax style enables code from similar applications to be incorporated into a prototype with little fuss. This makes it possible to take a number of existing Perl CGI programs and combine functions from them into a new prototype using Perl glue to smooth out incompatibilities in the code. After this hybrid is created, it's then much easier to insert the few new functions that might be necessary to make a prototype workable.

There's More Than One Way to Do It

The philosophy behind Perl development is to get the job done first and worry about the implementation later. Because of this, the language has been designed to enable a simplistic programming style—called *baby talk* by Larry Wall, Perl's creator— to be used alongside more mature and optimized code with no detectable difference at runtime. This makes it easier to develop a Perl application that performs functions that are unfamiliar. Because the application itself can be expressed in its simplest form first, the general structure of the application can be defined in terms of real working code before more complex features—such as advanced error checking or higher-performance algorithms—are added. In fact, in cases where quick, temporary solutions are needed, the complex code might never need to be added at all.

Perl also is designed to reduce the impact of style variations in the operation of code. This is a programmatic version of "Do what I mean, not what I say," which enables programmers conversant with one style of programming (in C, for example) to program in that style instead of a more "Perlish" style. The Perl compiler then uses the most efficient method to implement either style, usually with quite a bit of overlap between the implementations of similar functions implemented in different ways. The value of this style neutrality is discussed in greater detail in Chapter 7, "Perl For the Web." This philosophy makes prototyping a Web application in Perl simple because style isn't an issue when developing the prototype. Languages such as Java, on the other hand, enforce restrictions on programming style and interface design, making the initial architecture of an implementation much more important than it would be in Perl.

Perl then allows code to be revised and optimized at a later time by abstracting away features of the code. The object-oriented features of Perl can be used to provide a generic interface to common application functions. The code underlying these functions can then be optimized independently of the main program code and potentially reused in other applications. To assist optimization, Perl has adjustable levels of strictness that give the programmer the ability to define regions of code with strict or loose styles pertaining to variables, subroutines, or references. A Perl application also can be made to emit more stringent warnings in situations in which the program is likely to do something different from what is expected. Because enabling or disabling these warnings is as easy as specifying `use warnings` or `no warnings` at any point in the code, it's possible to achieve a very fine grain of control over which ranges of code need strictness and which don't.

Perl CGI Means Poor Performance

Perl CGI can be a common way to develop a site initially, but performance problems become apparent when a Perl CGI application is put under load. This situation is encountered frequently when a prototype application is placed in a production environment with the potential for slow response times, unusual behavior, and system failures. After a site encounters performance problems due to one Perl CGI script, it's likely that no others will be allowed in a production environment again.

Perl CGI works fine when testing a Web application initially, but as the site gets more usage and the application is under more load, the CGI process inflicts more and more overhead and eventually outstrips the capabilities of the Web server. The processor gets overloaded, memory fills up, the database runs out of available connections, and the system grinds to a halt much sooner than would be expected.

It's here that Perl's on-the-fly compiler has the biggest drawback; much of the CPU load of executing a Perl CGI process comes from compiling and initializing the application. The obvious conclusion is that Perl is too slow for the task at hand; there certainly aren't any companies lauding the impressive speed of Perl CGI, and there are fewer examples of speed-optimized Perl programs in everyday use. (Problems with this conclusion are covered in greater detail in Chapter 5, "Architecture-Based Performance Loss.")

One-Time Tasks Under Load

Perl CGI processes work very well in a prototype-testing environment. Only one user is generally accessing the Web application at a time, with all interface lag perceived by that user caused solely by the processing of the user's requests. This is analogous to the way a Perl program is used outside of Web processing, so all the assumptions inherent in that architecture are true; only one request occurs at a time, and after the request is fulfilled, the program and its data are no longer needed.

These assumptions also are correct when a prototype is being demonstrated. The demonstrator is the only user accessing the system, and any delays caused by normal processing are minimal and can be covered by explaining the process while waiting. As a result, any slowness caused by CGI processing is unlikely to be caught during the demonstration or usability testing phases. Even if sluggishness is noticed by individual users, it's likely to be so mild as to be ignored in favor of more pressing concerns.

Moving a prototype into production is a different story. The assumptions of one user, few requests, and no competition for resources are no longer valid. As more visitors use the Web application simultaneously, the load on the application increases exponentially. This is due to the nature of Web requests; they don't come in one at a time the way they would in a single-user application, and they aren't fixed in scope in the way most multiuser applications (such as databases or groupware) are fixed in scope. Web requests can come in simultaneously in ever-increasing quantities, with no simple way of queuing up requests for orderly processing. Instead, a Web server starts up as many processes as there are requests. The load of the additional processes makes the existing processes even slower, so more requests come in while earlier requests still are being processed. Under load, this situation can easily spiral out of control, causing all the Perl CGI processes to grind to a halt. All requests then are lost in the process.

Memory Footprint of Perl Processes

A Perl CGI process can use anywhere from 1MB to 15MB of RAM. Taken individually, processes taking this amount of system memory are easily manageable and unlikely to overwhelm even the least sophisticated Web server. However, the Perl compiler executable used in CGI processing is likely to be linked statically rather than dynamically, resulting in a Perl interpreter that isn't shared between processes. If many CGI processes are running at the same time, the Perl interpreter might be duplicated dozens of times, taking up even more memory in overhead.

If a new process is started before an old process finishes, the new process takes up even more system memory. This is likely to happen repeatedly as a site gets more frequent visitors, which causes more overlap and a greater drain on system resources. For example, if a site gets even 20 requests per second for a CGI application that requires as little as two seconds to process, 40 CGI processes might be starting and stopping continuously, taking up to half a gigabyte of RAM overall. As the rate of requests increases—100 per second is still a very conservative number for a production Web application—the memory requirements increase not just additively, but geometrically. Each process adds CPU load that slows down other requests, increasing the number of processes necessary and feeding the cycle again. The limits of available RAM can quickly be exceeded in even the most expensive Web servers.

When available RAM is exceeded by the needs of CGI processes, most servers start using swap space on disk to create virtual memory for the processes. At this point, the processes become phenomenally slow; processing time per request increases by tenfold, increasing the number of active processes by the same factor. The overall load of the processes quickly becomes too much for the system and all processing grinds to a halt. Once again, requests are lost and connected systems might be left in an indeterminate state, causing unusual behavior and administrative nightmares.

The Cost of Compilation

The main reason for most of the overhead of Perl CGI is compilation into bytecode and instantiation of program data. Every Perl program is compiled before execution, and any program—no matter what language it's written in—needs to initialize the memory structures and system libraries it uses during runtime. Compiling is necessary for any program that is run directly in a system environment without an interpreter.

Compilation is rarely a step that's seen when running a single-user program. C programs, for instance, are compiled over the course of minutes or hours. The compilation step also is where much of the system-related error checking takes place, so compilation might take even longer if the first compile step isn't successful and numerous tries are necessary. As a result, the compilation step is usually performed before the program is ever shipped to the user. Even open-source programs, which are shipped as source code, generally are compiled only once before being installed on the destination system.

Perl programs, however, are designed to be compiled just before they are executed. This makes Perl more immediately responsive to system environment changes and enables Perl programs to be more portable across platforms than a compiled executable would be. The Perl runtime compiles each program in a matter of seconds (or milliseconds), including all libraries and core utilities. The compile and execute steps are both started when a Perl program is started, which adds to the impression that Perl programs are interpreted rather than a compiled. This impression is strengthened by the fact that the Perl runtime—sometimes called the Perl interpreter—needs to be invoked to compile and execute each Perl program.

For some Perl programs, compilation can take longer than a few seconds. This becomes more likely the larger a program becomes, with modules adding significant bulk to the program. Instantiating variables, system connections, and large data structures also can add considerably to the overall time a program takes to start. Parsing large XML documents into Perl data structures, for instance, is likely to take a noticeable amount of time. This additional compilation and instantiation time creates an upper limit to the range of Perl CGI solutions because more complex processes would involve prohibitive performance losses.

Compiling a Perl program is a larger CPU drain than simply executing the compiled program. This holds true for all but the most processor-intensive Perl programs because compiling the program requires the same text manipulation, system integration, and disk I/O that a Perl program itself would perform, but on a more complex scale. In fact, in most cases, a Perl CGI process uses up to twenty times more processor time starting up that the same process would use if precompiled. The reasoning used to determine this overhead is discussed in more detail in Chapter 9, "The Power of Persistence."

Summary

Prototypes for Web applications are a great use for Perl, and many Perl programs start out as Perl prototypes. Perl's flexibility and powerful system integration modules make prototype design and implementation particularly easy. Perl CGI performance hits the wall in a short time, though, and Perl CGI processes take more memory, use more CPU time, and can eventually overload the system and stop Web server processing entirely. This is mostly due to the overhead of compiling a Perl process on the fly, which only takes a second or two, but which requires even more processing power than the application alone.

5

Architecture-Based Performance Loss

WHEN CONSIDERING THE OVERALL PERFORMANCE OF a Web application, the system architecture is the most important factor on which to focus. Both hardware and software architecture create the environment under which a Web application operates, and both play a role in determining the maximum efficiency possible for a Web application. Inefficient architecture can create bottlenecks that are the limiting factor in Web application performance, regardless of the individual cause.

Performance loss due to an inefficient architecture affects every aspect of a Web application. A sluggish application causes dependent applications and other system processes also to perform slowly, which can cascade into every part of a server environment. If each application is affected by the same architectural performance limits, the effects can accumulate to the point at which the entire system is unusable even when individual applications are supposed to perform with much greater efficiency.

With Perl CGI applications, the major contributor to an inefficient architecture is the Common Gateway Interface (CGI) itself. The CGI protocol was designed to fit an environment that didn't have persistent applications in mind. Thus, it inherited an execution model that was well-suited to early Web programming, but that is inefficient when placed under load. Whether written in Perl or other languages, CGI programs start and stop with each Web request, regardless of whether the requests are coming in once every few days or hundreds of times a second. Performance is reasonable in the former case, but as soon as requests start coming in at a pace that is faster than the CGI applications can process, the overhead of starting and stopping the applications overwhelms the system.

The performance characteristics of a CGI architecture can affect the performance of related Web application systems as well. Database servers, for instance, assume that an application connects once to the system and that it continues to process transactions interactively—disconnecting only when all transactions are complete. Systems like these respond poorly to the stop-and-go pattern of a CGI applications, which causes the database server to process the client connection repeatedly over the course of its interaction with the Web application. The performance of both the Web application and the database suffers as a result, creating a theoretical limit to the number of database transactions any Web application can process in a given time period.

The only way to really find architecture bottlenecks is by stressing the system and checking the outcome. With a complex system, this process can be difficult even with the best diagnostic tools. Unfortunately, the nature of most Web applications makes load testing a low priority for the development team. The low priority results in shaky testing methods with ineffective tools that shed no light on potential trouble spots. Developing the right testing practices isn't impossible, but it requires a clear understanding of how to really test Web applications in a form that's representative of the actual load they'll have to deal with in production.

The Nature of CGI

It might seem that for a book about efficient Web applications, we are spending a lot of time discussing a technology—CGI—that isn't efficient at all. The reason is that most Web application developers equate Perl with CGI and vice versa, and they assume that the performance problems caused by CGI require switching to an application language such as Java or C. However, this "solution" isn't a solution at all; it merely replaces the application development language with a new one without changing the architecture used to access the application. A Java application accessed through CGI (as many servlets are) has all the performance bottlenecks of an equivalent Perl CGI program, as does a CGI program written in C, COBOL, or shell scripting.

In short, CGI has performance problems. In general, the performance problems are solely due to the architecture of CGI processes in relation to the Web server. More specifically, CGI is slow because of the assumptions made when using it. These assumptions all are based on the Web server performance model rather than on the application performance model. CGI processes are managed poorly, accessed inefficiently, and restarted without need.

In comparison, most interactive applications would fail miserably under such a model. If a common application, such as Microsoft Word or the GNU Image Manipulation Program (GIMP), were implemented using a stateless request-and-response model, it would be nearly impossible to use because the application would be constantly exiting and restarting to handle even the most basic interactions with the user. Instead, these applications apply a more reasonable model to handle interactions as events while keeping the program in memory and running.

One Process Per Request

CGI is based on the same model that Web servers use for every other file: a file is requested, the file is accessed, and the file is delivered. For static HTML and image files, which are the mainstay of the Web, this model works well because it simplifies the relationship between the browser and the Web server. The only information a browser needs to pass along to a Web server is the location of the file to be accessed, which is encoded in a uniform resource locator (URL). The URL gives basic information about the server from which the file should be accessed, the path to the file on that server, and the name of the file. For instance, a URL to the file that contains an HTML representation of this chapter might look like this:

    http://www.globalspin.com/thebook/chapter05.html

This URL indicates that the file chapter05.html can be retrieved through the HTTP protocol from the computer called www in the domain globalspin.com, in a directory called thebook. This idea of a single generic way to locate any file on the Web is the Web's greatest strength, even though URLs won't necessarily correspond to an actual file of that name in a file system directory with the specified name. Because each interaction between the browser and the server can be given a distinct URL, it's possible to start the interaction at any point. You then can continue through hyperlinks to any other point of interaction in any order. This behavior is called *stateless*, and it's the backbone of the World Wide Web.

When you need to provide dynamic responses to Web requests, the CGI protocol can access server-side applications in a fashion similar to static files. Each application would still have a URL of the same form as static files. However, the Web server understands that files in certain directories should be accessed as executable programs instead of as files to be transferred. The CGI application would then be responsible for returning a result to the Web server, which would be passed back to the client browser. (See Figure 5.1.)

As Figure 5.1 shows, the interaction between the client browser and the Web server is essentially identical even though the Web server is handling the two requests differently. Thus, a URL for the second interaction would look like this:

    http://www.globalspin.com/cgi-bin/chapter08.cgi

Like the URL for a static file, this URL would indicate that the file could be accessed from the computer www.globalspin.com by executing the program chapter05.cgi from the cgi-bin directory. Again, the interaction specified by this URL should provide a consistent result, regardless of which URLs the browser has accessed previously.

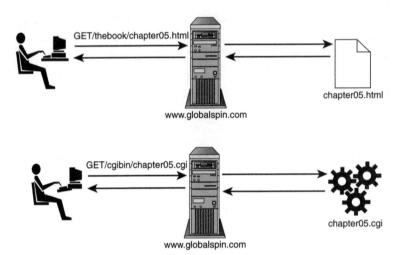

Figure 5.1   Accessing a CGI application (bottom)
is analogous to accessing an HTML file (top).

Because the HTTP protocol and the requested URL define the transaction between client and server, the CGI protocol specifies the interaction that takes place between the Web server and the executed application. For each request, CGI requires the Web server to start the application and provide a predefined set of information about the environment and the request itself. In return, the application is expected to emit a Multipart Internet Mail Encoding indicator—such as `text/html` for an HTML document—followed by the document to be returned to the client. (CGI also defines ways for the Web server and CGI application to communicate more robust information, such as form variables and headers, but the core interaction remains the same.)

Comparison with Word or GIMP

Although the CGI model of request processing might look reasonable, it falls apart when used to create the kind of interactive applications most Web visitors are used to. Web users don't just use the Web; they also use a host of applications on their local machines to perform a wide variety of tasks. The Web browser itself is running on the client machine to provide responsive behavior when using interface elements, such as the Back button or drop-down menus. Because this is the environment with which most users are familiar, it's not surprising that so many people expect the same kind of response when using Web applications. With CGI, however, the Web application itself isn't designed to produce this kind of behavior, so performance suffers and users are left unsatisfied.

As an analogy, consider the way a desktop application works. A word processing program, such as Microsoft Word, or a graphics manipulation program, such as GIMP, works different from a CGI application. When a user runs Word or GIMP, an application is started that then takes requests in the form of keyboard and mouse input. The application doesn't stop and restart every time a new menu choice is made; if it did, the continuous stopping and starting would make the program unusable—and this book would take even longer to write. Instead, each new request is handled as a part of the overarching program, whether it's a minor aspect of the program (display a particular screen) or a core function (check the spelling in the document). These applications spend a relatively long time initializing a monolithic application because the understanding is that the initialization happens only once each session.

This underscores the reason why neither application is likely to be replaced by a Web application in the near future. If Word was reimplemented in HTML with a CGI back end, for instance, every request to make a word bold or add a line of text would require another call to the Web server. The CGI architecture would require that the Word executable be restarted for each request, and the result would be an application that took minutes to perform even the simplest action. If this situation sounds familiar, it's because most Web applications—such as online stores, Web news services, and Web mail—operate under the same conditions and end up being as painfully slow as Word would be.

The Nature of Databases

Databases are optimized differently than are CGI applications. Standard database access software is likely to support a fixed (if large) number of users who access the database simultaneously with continuous connections that need to be optimized for faster transaction processing. The server is optimized to provide the best performance possible in this environment with an emphasis on providing a smooth performance curve for client applications and their users.

CGI applications access databases differently than do custom clients, however. A CGI Web application is capable only of connecting to the database for as long as it's active, which means that the application connects to the database anew with each request. This runs contrary to the continuous way a database is normally used, so many of the aspects that haven't been optimized on the database server are receiving a disproportionate amount of load. As a result, database performance from a Web application becomes much slower than the performance that the database would otherwise provide.

It is possible to get a fixed number that represents the theoretical limit of CGI-to-database processing speed. Because databases are limited in the number of simultaneous connections they support and the time spent connecting to the database is known, it's possible to calculate the maximum number of requests the database supports each second. This upper limit is a telling reminder that the performance limits due to CGI are restrictive despite the capabilities of the hardware or database server.

Many Users, Many Connections, and Continuous Access

Database servers are optimized to support connections from many clients at the same time, but there are basic differences in the way traditional clients and CGI processes access a database. These differences aren't a function of Perl style or the database server, but the architecture of the CGI interaction itself.

A database server is likely to be optimized for access by individual named users who connect to the database, prepare and execute a reasonable number of transactions, and finally disconnect from the database after all transactions have been completed. Because performing the sum total of these steps as quickly as possible is the usual goal when optimizing a database, database server vendors are likely to optimize the steps that are performed most often—transactions. As a result, the time taken by a standard transaction, such as a SELECT on a million-record table, is likely to be optimized while the time required to connect to a database is not. After all, time saved in performing transactions is likely to be multiplied dozens or hundreds of times in a single database session, while a connection happens only once. Half a second shaved off the overhead of performing each transaction is worth minutes of time per session, for example, while the same half a second is barely missed from a three-second connect time. Database benchmarks reinforce this focus by testing the maximum throughput of transactions in a single long session while ignoring connect time entirely.

The database also is likely to be optimized to human interface speeds. This means that any specific part of the database interaction can take as long as a few seconds if the user is expecting an immediate response, and interactions that are expected by the user to be complex can take as long as necessary. This is because the client software indicates to the user—by displaying an hourglass icon, for instance—that more complex processes are expected to take time, so the only interactions that have to be quick are those that aren't acknowledged by the client interface as being complex. Still, "quick" is defined as taking less time than the user notices, so the amount of time available can be counted in seconds.

Another assumption made when optimizing the database server is that client connections are created infrequently and held open continuously while the user interacts with the database. For user interactions handled through a custom database client, this assumption is perfectly reasonable—users connect once at the beginning of a session and stay connected throughout the session. In most cases, a connection is used continuously for minutes or hours before being closed by the user. However, CGI applications accessing the database open and close database connections as quickly as the applications run their course, which means that dozens of applications might be opening connections every second. This increases the relative importance of connection time disproportionately and exposes delays that would otherwise be unnoticed.

The Theoretical Limit of CGI-to-Database Connections

One easy (if disturbing) way to calculate the theoretical limit of CGI access to a database is by taking the total number of simultaneous connections that the database enables (100, for instance) and dividing it by the average connect time for the database (say, 3 seconds.) Because a database does not enable a new connection to be made until the old connection is released, the result is the theoretical maximum number of CGI requests per second that the database will support (33, in this case.)

The reason this number is so discouraging from an architectural standpoint is the fact that it's a *theoretical maximum*. Even if the individual query from a CGI request takes a fraction of a millisecond, overall those requests can't be processed faster than the database makes connections. The numbers get worse fairly quickly for difficult database transactions, which can take ten seconds or more to process. Because even the easiest transactions are weighing down the real response time of the database, it's difficult to compensate for such slow transactions, and overall performance suffers even more.

This limit also can be a cause for great concern if the maximum number of database connections is reached and exceeded. Depending on the database server, results might vary from a fatal error in the CGI process to unusual behavior among all database connections. Data integrity is a prime concern when designing a Web application. Thus, behavior like this can be very distressing if it happens unexpectedly—yet another reason to invest time in determining the performance characteristics of Web applications.

The limit can't be raised much by upgrading the database to accept more simultaneous connections. It would seem that upgrading the database to enable ten times the number of connections would increase the limit by the same factor, but the effect isn't so direct. The total number of database connections enabled by a database might be just an issue of licensing, but the number of connections the database server can start each second is a function of the processor power available to the server. Thus, even if a license is purchased to increase simultaneous connections ten times over, the individual connection time might increase by the same factor if the server can't support those connections.

Because the theoretical limit is caused by the way a CGI application accesses the database, the solution to the problem is to change the architecture of the system. Again, a small change to the processing model releases much of the overhead of CGI processing and raises the theoretical limit to rely on factors for which the database is optimized. These factors include transaction speed and total data retrieved. A detailed discussion of how to implement a better database connection architecture can be found in Chapter 14, "Database-Backed Web Sites."

The Nature of Performance Testing

Probably the least mature part of the Web programming process is the poor attempt at performance testing most developers employ before unleashing their applications on the Web. Compared to commercial applications, the amount of testing performed on most Web applications is minimal.

In many cases, performance testing is practically nonexistent. In good cases, performance might be tested by simulating a flood of Web requests. In the worst cases, the simple fact that the site is accessible by one user—usually the developer—is considered proof enough that the application is capable of production-level performance. Either way, the results of such tests are rarely indicative of the true load an application will see in production.

Even in cases in which performance testing is performed with some rigor, the testing utilities themselves are incapable of providing an accurate replication of the production environment.

Ten Employees Click Submit

An embarrassing but recognizable way in which many companies handle "performance testing" is by manually stressing a site with continuous single-user access. The most pitiful case of this is ten employees trying to access a Web application at the same time, supposedly simulating "ten simultaneous users."

As robust as this test might seem at first glance, it really doesn't simulate the kind of load that would truly stress test an architecture. In fact, it's not likely to stress even the least efficient Web applications because it underestimates the expected load on a standard Web application by hundreds of times. "Simultaneous users" are a fiction when applied to Web applications because the term implies user sessions that are continuous from start to finish. The real measure of Web performance is the number of requests that can be answered in a particular time period, usually standardized at one second. Ten developers clicking the Submit button at the same time won't create more than a temporary spike of a few requests per second, which isn't much of a test when the production server might sustain a load of hundreds of requests per second.

Besides, testing the performance of a Web application should not focus on determining if the application supports the load expected in normal use. Rather, performance tests should determine the amount of load that overloads an application, which then can be compared to estimated traffic levels to determine how much of a margin there is between the two. (If an application is capable of supporting 300 requests per second and traffic is expected to average 30 requests per second, for instance, there is a better margin for growth than there would be with a maximum of 35 requests per second.) Determining the point of overload also gives a benchmark against which later performance improvements can be tested.

Built-In Performance Tools

Many times, the tools included with an application development environment are inadequate for determining the maximum load a server can handle. In some cases, the performance tools are designed solely to monitor the usage statistics of an application already in production, so there's no way to determine the circumstances under which the application would be overwhelmed with requests. Even if tools are included to produce requests in a test environment, they might be incapable of generating the load that would normally be seen in production. For instance, if it takes a tool longer to generate, process and record a request than it takes the Web server to respond to it, the tool might reach saturation before the Web application does. Also, in some cases, the tools are designed to run in the same environment on the same machine, which means that the performance tools compete with Web applications for system resources.

Another downfall of most performance tools is that they rarely pinpoint the cause of a bottleneck, even when one is indicated. A program that stresses an application to the point where it starts to drop requests, for instance, still is unlikely to indicate the conditions under which the requests were lost. Was the network overloaded with requests, which caused request packets to be lost en route to the server? Was the Web server daemon overloaded with file access and request processing, which caused it to queue incoming requests until some were lost? If requests were handled correctly by the Web server, were no responses returned from an overburdened Web application? If a performance tool isn't capable of determining the cause of a failure, the wrong assumptions might be made about the source of the problem. This might lead to an inappropriate solution, which doesn't actually address the real problem.

Good performance tools have a few things in common. They take the structure of the Web application into account, or at least enable that structure to be considered when developing tests of the application. They also simulate real-world requests garnered from log or proxy information to prevent artifacts of the testing process from clouding the results or breaking the application's flow. Good performance tools would simulate a number of requests that would far exceed the current capabilities of the Web application. They would do this even if that would mean simulating millions of users with high-speed access, all throttling the server at the same time. Of course, all these features would be meaningless if the results of the tests weren't made available in a complete, understandable format that could be used to track down bottlenecks. (Further discussion of performance testing can be found in Chapter 15, "Testing Site Performance.")

Summary

Perl CGI applications are notable for poor performance in production environments, but a major source of overhead and instability is the architecture inherent in any CGI application. Just as inefficient hardware architecture can hamper application performance no matter how well the application is written, inefficient system architectures such as CGI can limit the performance that an otherwise-efficient Perl Web application can achieve. The stop-and-start nature of CGI doesn't just affect the application itself, but also any connections to other systems on which it might rely. This causes inefficient interactions that slow overall performance even more. The real solution to these problems is a combination of testing to determine the circumstances causing performance loss and architectural changes to smooth over the differences between the way in which high-performance applications are designed to work and the way in which Web requests are likely to be received.

6

Often-Overlooked Problems

WHILE PERFORMANCE CONCERNS ARE PARAMOUNT in this book, you also want
to do real work with a Web application. This often means that the Web application has
to cover areas that other applications can ignore; after all, a Web site devoted to workflow or other high-level concepts requires all pieces of the puzzle, not just a few.

One difficult aspect of complex computer environments is legacy applications that
need to be brought into the Web site framework. Mainframe and custom applications
are designed to be accessed from specific hardware systems with narrow requirements;
thus, applying a more robust interface on these systems for use by Web applications
can range from difficult to expensive to impossible.

Licensing issues also come up when developing Web applications because offering a
service that relies on other servers can create additional usage and incur costs that
weren't anticipated when designing the Web application. If Web developers aren't
aware of licensing concerns, they can incur unanticipated costs for an organization
simply by making a connection between applications or by making an application
available to a new class of users. Some licenses protect against such concerns, but it's
usually not the Web developer's role to determine whether this is the case.

The general idea behind enterprise integration and automation overarches these
concerns. Every technical advance tends to promise integration of all business
processes into one efficient structure, but implementing such a system often results in
almost as much work created as is automated away.

Legacy Applications

Existing applications can be a real pain to integrate into a Web environment. It's not so bad when the applications can be accessed over the network through an established protocol, but applications that assume a human interface can be nearly impossible to access in any other way. Nevertheless, many organizations still use legacy applications for critical systems, so you often need to add these systems into the mix when designing a robust Web application. Although it takes some custom programming and a little creativity to solve these kinds of tricky integration problems, it is possible to solve them.

Mainframe applications are some of the hardest to integrate. Many were developed at a time when all users accessed the system with the same proprietary interface, so there was no need to provide alternate interfaces, let alone automation. Most mainframe development environments assumed a pre-Internet network that had no reason to integrate with other network services because those services were all running as part of the mainframe environment itself. The interface to such systems was simple—a screen-by-screen display that was dictated verbatim by the mainframe application, with input provided by a user at a terminal. To add a Web perspective to this environment, you had to build an additional interface over the human-centric text interface, with a simulated terminal for input and data skimmed from the screen-by-screen results.

Other custom applications can be just as difficult to integrate because they're completely opaque and have only one thin interface. In some cases, the application is compiled, and it provides few clues about how it could be modified for use in a new environment.

Terminal-Based Mainframe Applications

Mainframe applications, the hard-working dinosaurs of enterprise server environments, still can be found operating critical systems at large organizations around the globe. Financial applications, power regulation systems, and a whole host of other mission-critical applications have been written for environments such as CICS, which was developed for use with IBM mainframes. These environments have been updated over the years to interact with more modern hardware and software, but they're still not easy to integrate into Web applications.

Although some mainframe applications are designed to be accessible by common network protocols such as Telnet or remote procedure call protocols, others use proprietary interfaces that require emulation to provide any automated interface at all. Some IBM mainframe applications use the 3270 terminal protocol, for instance, which has many emulators available for use as direct-access clients, but few ways to integrate such applications into a more robust automated interface. The assumption made when developing these systems was that all access would come interactively by way of terminals, not automatically by way of client programs.

To integrate with mainframe applications from nonstandard client systems, developers commonly use text-filtering systems that process the screen-by-screen results of terminal interaction. These systems are generally called *screen scrapers* because they have to extract meaningful data from a screen's worth of undifferentiated information—an inefficient method at best. Screen scraper interfaces are some of the least robust interfaces possible because of the many assumptions that have to be made when determining what data from each screen is important. Very little can be done to catch errors or provide for unusual situations with a screen scraper because the interface definition is so arbitrary. If the third through fifth characters of the second line of the fourth screen are used to indicate the three-digit product code of a widget, for instance, the entire interface could be thrown off by having four-digit product codes come into use after the interface is developed.

With this kind of environment, it would be too much to ask for any sort of data markup, let alone adherence to standards such as Extensible Markup Language (XML). This is unfortunate because the data contained in these legacy systems is sometimes the richest source of integration potential an organization has available. In addition, making that information available by encoding it in XML would be a boon to many future applications in a wide variety of uses.

Custom Applications

Custom applications are usually written to fit one purpose within an organization, often because no other software performs that task. A custom application to capture technical support information from phone technicians, for instance, could be written in C++ or Visual Basic with networked access to a central support database that is custom-written for the purpose. Such an application could be a poor fit for off-the-shelf server environments such as Oracle or Lotus Notes if it needs to interact with phone systems or employee time clocks. It might be more cost-effective to build the application from scratch than it would be to assemble it from expensive server products.

Like mainframe applications, custom applications generally have no interface other than the user-centric controls provided for the environment in which the application was developed. A point-of-sale (POS) application, for instance, is usually developed to run on specific cash register hardware that has only basic network connections to a POS server on the same network. It might be difficult to abstract the interface to system functions away from code that operates the hardware, and it can be virtually impossible to simulate the terminal environment because the interface is written specifically for touchscreen terminals.

Even worse, there is often no vendor to contact for support for adapting a custom application for Web use because the application is usually developed in-house. Because the pace of information technology changes causes frequent shifts in the workforce, programmers who no longer work there might have written the application. In some cases, little documentation is available for extending the application because emphasis was placed on covering user-interface issues instead. Whatever the cause, it can be difficult or unreasonable to adapt an application for use on the Web because the application itself would be too difficult to modify.

Database Connections and Licensing

Licensing issues can be tricky even when a server application is being used in a traditional framework. However, Web applications provide additional twists that make licensing even more difficult to keep track of. With traditional application use, it's possible to keep track of users who access an application and restrict access to only those who are authorized in terms of the end-user license purchased from the vendor. Functionally, this is usually rolled into the same server restrictions that provide security and access control by tracking named users that have limited access to a central system. Server licensing is usually provided in terms of either the total number of named users or the number of users allowed to access the server simultaneously, with some servers enforcing license restrictions on both.

When using Web applications to access these same servers, however, the distinction between users becomes blurred and the need for simultaneous access can become more of a performance issue than overall server usage. In many Web application cases, large numbers of anonymous users access the application sporadically and with varying frequency, so it's difficult to separate these users into named groups, let alone named users. Even if that were possible, it would probably lead to an explosion in the number of named users registered for system access. This explosion would occur even though most of the users would have accessed the system only once for a short period of time. As a result, most Web applications provide their own layers of system access and conglomerate all Web access into a single named user with multiple simultaneous connections to each server system. This goes against the vendor's licensing model, though, so many vendors have changed their policies to reflect Web usage more realistically, with varying results.

Microsoft and MySQL have two different ways of looking at the solution, but both approaches are opportunistically trying to get the most out of Web environments. Microsoft changed its SQL Server database product from a user-centric licensing model to an enterprise model to capture more licensing dollars from Web use. They did this after realizing that most Web application developers were getting by with the least expensive licensing option, regardless of the amount of Web traffic they were processing using the product. MySQL AB, on the other hand, went in a different direction with their MySQL database server. MySQL was originally licensed based on platform and use, but concerns by Web developers convinced the company to make the server available under an open source license.

Microsoft's View of the Web

When Web applications started using databases as backend storage, Microsoft didn't realize that this kind of usage presented a special concern for their SQL Server product. Like Oracle, Microsoft was licensing SQL in terms of a per-processor cost, plus an additional cost for each named user accessing the system at any time. Each named user would have a Client Access License (CAL), so a Web application developer had to purchase additional licenses as the server was used by increasing numbers of people within the organization.

This licensing model assumed that client applications accessing the server would each require a CAL from the user operating the application, but Web applications were designed to use the same named connection for all requests. Thus, the Microsoft pricing model enabled Web sites to operate using the cheapest licenses for SQL Server because only one named user was ever invoked at any one time. The server enabled a single named user to open multiple simultaneous connections from an application. In addition, the Web application could submit all its requests from the same user, so there was no reason to purchase a license for more than one user. Because the price for these licenses ran into the thousands of dollars, it was possible to save a considerable amount of money by routing more information through the Web application. Also, new e-commerce businesses were getting more mileage out of cheaper licenses by purchasing only a single processor license and a single CAL, and then spending the money left over on improving the performance of the server hardware itself.

Microsoft was concerned that a new class of applications in a growing market was capable of bypassing its standard pricing model. To close the pricing loophole and make up for the additional usage being seen by SQL Server in Web environments, Microsoft introduced a pricing addition called the Internet Connector. The Internet Connector provided no additional functionality for SQL Server, but it let Microsoft differentiate between servers that were allowed to process Web requests and those that were not. Simply put, it was an Internet tax levied by Microsoft against any application accessing SQL on behalf of an Internet user. Servers required an Internet Connector license for each processor in addition to the base license and CAL user licenses. Thus, Web use was clearly defined as something that required additional payment to Microsoft, regardless of whether other licenses had been purchased.

Later, Microsoft changed the pricing model to mask the tax-like nature of Internet licensing of SQL Server by offering an additional tier of per-processor pricing. Now it's possible to purchase either a traditional license with per-server and CAL costs or a per-processor license for SQL Server that does not limit the number of clients. The latter license covers both traditional users and Internet use. The per-processor license is considerably more expensive, however, so the tax has turned into a multiplier that makes SQL considerably more expensive for Internet use than it is for traditional use.

For Web application designers, a difficult aspect of these licensing issues is the fact that the software always operates the same, regardless of whether it's violating its license. In addition, because the licenses have little effect on the software that's actually installed, Web applications can access SQL Server, regardless of whether the Internet Connector or later licenses have been purchased. This puts Web application designers in a precarious position; it's possible that adding an integration layer to a Web application using systems that are already fully licensed might violate the license of those systems or incur additional costs above those of Web application development. Because most Web developers are not part of the license procurement process, it's possible for a developer to inadvertently incur thousands of dollars worth of additional licensing simply by making a server more widely available or using it as part of a Web application.

MySQL's View of the Web

MySQL is a database server designed to provide a lightweight, high-performance alternative to Oracle or SQL Server. Using MySQL for basic Web applications is a natural choice because many of the environments used for Web development—including Linux distributions and Perl modules—either included noncommercial copies of MySQL or assumed it was available.

Unfortunately, licensing concerns came to light when applications based on MySQL were put into production. The first concern involved the fact that MySQL was freely licensed only on a noncommercial basis; this meant that development use of the MySQL server was free, but that the software had to be purchased as soon as Web applications based on it went into production on commercial Web sites. Making matters worse, the line between commercial and noncommercial had been fuzzy on the Web because some noncommercial sites were offered by commercial entities and some noncommercial sites ended up raising money for one purpose or another.

The second concern involved the fact that MySQL was licensed differently for Windows and UNIX platforms, so adapting Web applications for use on a new platform had the potential to incur new licensing fees. This made Web application developers wary because the possibility existed that the free license under which they developed would go away at some point in the future; the free license would be replaced by a paid license if they crossed some boundary between platforms or between commercial and noncommercial use.

MySQL AB, makers of the MySQL database, answered the licensing concerns of Web application designers in a different way than did Microsoft; however, the motives behind each were rooted in profiting from increased Web use. While Microsoft offered unlimited Internet usage at a premium, MySQL AB offered their database product as open source under the GNU General Public License (GPL). This unified the licenses for Windows and UNIX platforms and enabled both commercial and noncommercial use of the software on any platform, without additional fees or licenses.

This change opened up MySQL to even broader groups of application designers because it now could be included with all sorts of application environments and used by any Web application, with no fear of later restrictions or unnatural distinctions between platforms. MySQL AB hopes that the increased use of MySQL fuels the need for support licenses and consulting contracts, which eventually should offset the costs of developing and marketing the software.

Although this particular situation turned out for the best for Web developers, it underscores the broad range of licensing possibilities each integrated application presents over its lifetime. As Web services and application syndication become more prominent, the line between an application user and a product reseller will blur even more; thus, it will be more difficult for Web application developers to consider all the licensing problems that might crop up if an application gets used in a previously unanticipated fashion.

Business-To-Business Automation

Enterprise Application Integration (EAI) is a hot topic, especially with companies trying to Web-enable their applications and capitalize on the success of Web interfaces. With each new Web interface comes the need to integrate it with other applications' Web interfaces; thus, more and more applications are coming under the domain of the Web developer. This unprecedented access to enterprise applications from a central interface makes it possible to integrate business processes that were previously inaccessible within an enterprise application framework. This makes the overall process more efficient.

Vertical markets, however, pose a big challenge when creating an integrated Web application to bring partners and suppliers together. Because control can't reasonably be exerted over the software and hardware choices made by each company, the need for standards and common implementations becomes more crucial. At the same time, the special needs of some vertical markets pose particular challenges to Web developers trying to fit a robust infrastructure into a Web interface.

On-Site Integration

EAI creates an interesting opportunity for Web applications. Its goal is to integrate and automate all applications used by a business, including business logic, data storage, communications, and groupware applications. Because Web applications provide a good network interface to traditionally server-bound applications, the whole is greater than the sum of its component applications.

Web applications can perform tasks that were previously possible only with lots of custom programming. In addition to integrating applications that are already being accessed individually, Web applications can also integrate network processes (such as email) and physical processes (such as fax or print). With these processes, it's possible to use a Web application to bring people into the process that aren't otherwise using the enterprise applications.

As an example of integration, consider an ordering system. It can take orders from a Web interface, use business logic to determine a pricing model, record the order in an order database, make inventory requests to a stock management system, create a customer record in a Customer Relationship Management (CRM) application, email an invoice to the customer, and fax a packing slip to the fulfillment company. Because each step happens within a system provided by a different vendor or internal department—and some of them happen outside the system entirely—Web-based EAI can provide a new level of continuity and reduce the need for human intervention in each step of the processes.

Unfortunately, many Web application development environments are not built with EAI in mind. They're designed to build dynamic consumer Web sites and are sometimes capable of little else. Some support is generally provided for network activities such as email or socket access, but rarely is there support for Web-client simulation or off-network systems such as voice or fax. Most Web development environments have started to support databases for backend data storage, but integration with other enterprise systems usually requires more custom programming, if the development environment allows it. This widens the gap between what can be done within the framework of mainline Web application development and what will require more in-depth programming, which adds additional time and effort to a process that usually has little to spare.

As a result, developers who want to add enterprise applications to a Web environment usually wait for the Web environment or the application vendor to provide an interface between the two. Enterprise application vendors are starting to provide Web interfaces to their products, but in many cases, the vendor confuses Web integration with the mere integration of a Web server and the provision of an HTML interface to the application. For Web applications looking to integrate enterprise systems, interfaces such as these are nearly impossible to automate, and thus are as useless as having no interface to the application at all.

Vertical Integration

Integration with business partners and suppliers is another focus of many businesses on the Web. After internal business processes are integrated into a coherent Web application, it's useful to automate the relationships that the application has with other companies. Much attention has been given to supply-chain integration for companies producing and selling products. The integration provides automated interfaces for each supplier, shipper, reseller, and support organization to streamline the order fulfillment process.

Other types of companies and organizations also benefit from automated interaction with their suppliers and consumers. For instance, news agencies and other content syndicators on the Web were early adopters of this idea, offering content to aggregators and portals through automated network interfaces. Companies that haven't used the Web for internal applications to date are starting to take notice of the potential this idea creates for their partners' applications and associated data.

Reams of data are being passed from company to company and from company to consumer, so there's a pressing need for systems to process and deliver it all. Just a few years ago, it was unusual for a company to provide a Web interface to its order system, even if the company had a Web site; now, companies and consumers are used to the availability of Web applications for business-to-consumer use, so they want the same ease of use when dealing with partners and suppliers.

Some vertical markets have unusual needs that require more than just interaction with suppliers and partners. Medical invoice and insurance tracking, fault-tolerant messaging for infrastructure monitoring servers, and similar high-importance systems are being developed to enable any market to benefit from the same kind of integration and ease of use that existing Web applications enjoy. With these advances come difficulties for Web application designers, however, because traditionally lax standards for Internet data security and robustness are clashing with the accountability and security needed by these new markets.

XML is a promising technology that seems to provide a standard way to encode and distribute application data, but few vendors seem to have a handle on what to do with XML and how to deal with it from an integration standpoint. Many companies pay lip service to the XML idea, but few are actually implementing solutions by marking up data and dealing with other marked-up data in a standard fashion. The flux surrounding XML implementations is creating additional uncertainty for Web application developers because vague standards and changing implementations create an environment that is both difficult to avoid and tough to work with. Further discussion of the future of XML for application integration is available in Chapter 18, "XML as a B2B Interface."

Summary

Although integration issues are usually overlooked in favor of user-interface concerns and feature sets, developers have their work cut out for them when attempting to integrate enterprise systems into Web applications. Some enterprise systems, such as mainframe applications or custom programs, pose technical problems because the interfaces are archaic and difficult to adapt. Other systems are easy to integrate technically, but provide licensing difficulties because of the special circumstances Web applications create. Solutions to these issues are pressing, though, because the need for application integration is growing. Users are getting acquainted with the possibility of a single Web interface to all enterprise systems, and the promise of even more integration with business partners and application syndicators is just around the corner.

II

The Solutions

7

Perl for the Web

PERL IS SOMETIMES SEEN AS YESTERDAY'S WEB APPLICATION language. It is not as well-advertised as Java or C#, and many new application servers and content management systems are making their names with technologies such as Python, PHP, or Java Server Pages (JSP). Perl, in contrast, is advanced mostly by noncommercial organizations with little interest in buzz and a real focus on solutions that work quickly and quietly.

Of course, within the Perl community, there's a different story. Perl programmers communicate with each other at a frantic pace. Their communication consists primarily of new and updated modules, solutions to new challenges, and changes to Perl itself. To those who listen more to technical explanations and design specifications, Perl is a vibrant language with a strong following and an excellent future. Perhaps this is why Perl programming manuals consistently top the technical book bestseller lists at online stores and brick-and-mortar booksellers alike.

All buzz aside, Perl is an excellent Web development choice for many reasons, including the following:

- Perl programmers are easy to find and easier to train.
- Modules ease Web interaction and database and legacy system access.

- Integration between Perl and the system environment allows Perl programs to access disparate systems with a uniform interface.
- Perl's flexibility with text handling makes data collection from external Web sites possible.
- The "Swiss Army chainsaw" has more tools available than ever.

This chapter provides some basic insights into the advantages that Perl brings to Web development. The insights are from the standpoint of the technical evaluator and the programmer who might be new to Perl, Web applications, or both. The chapter also contains concrete examples of the work that Perl does for Web sites at development time and beyond. Perl is useful not only for delivering information over the Web, but also for serving as an excellent systems management and discovery tool.

Any Programmer is a Perl Programmer

One of the most overlooked benefits of building applications in Perl is the abundance of Perl programmers. This reality stands in stark contrast to the myth that most programmers use Java or C, which comes about from the use of those languages to teach computer science courses. Perl programmers generally don't come from a class-room. They usually learn the language when performing system administration, integration, or Web development tasks. As a result, Perl has become both an easy-to-learn programming language as well as a popular one.

Many programmers learn Perl as a scripting language for common system tasks. The programmers use Perl to write test harnesses and to install scripts and command-line utilities for compiled applications. Programmers don't write these programs in a compiled language such as C because these types of programs are usually too changeable. They also don't write these programs in an abstracted language such as Java because they require integration with too many other system utilities. As a result, many one-time or evolving programs are written and revised in Perl.

Other programmers learn Perl by developing extensions for preexisting compiled programs. In addition, they use Perl to provide application program interfaces (APIs) for applications that allow custom access through plug-in extensions. One such API is the plug-in API for the GIMP, an image editor that provides automation and filter plug-ins through a Perl interface to the internal graphics API. All the GIMP's functions, from graphics file translation to pixel-level editing, are available through the Perl API.

The GIMP API was originally written in a proprietary language called Script-Fu, but the GIMP's creators later decided that Perl provided a more robust interface and would be easier to develop with. Incidentally, the same GIMP API can be accessed within stand-alone or Web-based Perl applications, which provide a powerful way to create graphics programmatically. Many other program interfaces are added to Perl's tool set this way.

Alternately, some people become programmers by learning Perl first. In Web development, this occurs most often when a graphic artist or content producer learns Perl Common Gateway Interface (CGI) scripting to add functionality to a site. Many of these programmers learn Perl in bits and pieces in response to a particular need, and Perl's shallow learning curve encourages them to develop their skills as new needs arise. As a result, the line between Web designer and Perl programmer is blurring to form a new group of programmer/designers—Web application developers.

Perl's glue language background and flexible syntax means that experience with C/C++, PHP, Python, JavaScript, and even HTML can be applied immediately to Perl programming. Thus, there are many types of programmers who would be comfortable using Perl to start developing a Perl-based Web application.

Programmers with a C Background

C programmers find the structure of Perl programs familiar because C was a design inspiration during Perl development. Many of Perl's most basic constructs—such as looping, conditionals, and function calls—are duplicated faithfully from C with only minor variations. In fact, C style is one of the dialects of Perl, as shown in Listing 7.1.

Listing 7.1   **C Style in a Perl Program**

```
01 $num = scalar (DBI->data_sources);
02 for ($i = 0; $i < $num; $i++) {
03    push @datasources, {DBI->data_sources}[$i];
04 }
```

Listing 7.1 is a modified fragment of Listing 7.7, a SQL query processor, brought forward to illustrate the similarities in C and Perl coding styles. See Listing 7.7 for the complete program.

In Listing 7.1, an HTML list is generated using the values contained in a Perl array returned by a function. A `for` loop is used to step through the array, just as it would in a similar C program. The arguments to `for` are the same as in C:

- The initial value of the loop variable `$i`
- The conditional that is checked for truth after each iteration
- The change to the loop variable `$i` after each iteration
- The block to execute each time

Within the block, the loop variable `$i` determines which element of the array returned by the `DBI->datasources` function is added to the `@datasources` array.

The `for` keyword is a synonym for the more Perlish `foreach` keyword; both accept the C-style arguments, as listed in Listing 7.1, and the customary `foreach` syntax, as listed in Listing 7.2. The example could have been written either way without so much as a hiccup on the part of the Perl compiler.

Listing 7.2   **Perlish Dialect Version of a C-Style Loop**

```
01 foreach (DBI->data_sources($_))
02 {
03   push @datasources, $_;
04 }
```

The main difference between Listings 7.1 and 7.2 is the focus of the loop. The C style uses an explicit loop variable and requires the programmer to extract the appropriate member of the array returned by DBI->data_sources, as needed. The returned array could have been assigned to its own variable, for example, @raw_datasources, but confusion between that and the more important @datasources array would result. Instead, the Perlish version uses the $_ variable, which is set automatically by the foreach (or for) loop to point to the current member of the array specified. Perl provides many of these convenience variables to reduce the amount of explicit variable definition. Nonetheless, it is always acceptable to define variables explicitly.

Because this book's focus is on performance, it is helpful to note that the for and foreach synonyms are identical in terms of speed, and the C or Perlish dialects post similar benchmarks. The variation in Listing 7.1 would require the Perl interpreter to assign more variables and would request the array of data sources from DBI more often. However, the resulting speed difference most likely would be unnoticeable. See Chapter 8, "Performance Myths," for a discussion of Perl benchmarks of loop processing and similar constructs.

Another benefit of Perl's C heritage is the tight integration between many C libraries with their Perl interfaces. An example of this integration is the set of object classes and methods based on the Document Object Model (DOM). This model most commonly is used with HTML or XML document description and navigation. These libraries use the same method calls, object classes, and exception types as their C or Java brethren. So, programmers familiar with the libraries in other languages are right at home using them in Perl. See Chapter 18, "XML as a B2B Interface," for more information on the Perl interface to DOM.

Overall, C programmers have an easy time transitioning to Perl programming. Solution sets from C are generally applicable to C and the idiomatic differences between C and Perl can be discovered while programming, resulting in a shallow learning curve that can be overcome almost immediately.

Programmers with a PHP Background

PHP was developed specifically to address many of the needs presented by this book. These needs include easy database access, embedded programming, and faster prototyping. To a great degree, it has succeeded. The language is based in large part on C syntax, with modifications made to accommodate Web-style programming, to reduce unnecessary restrictions on variable types, and to allow object-oriented programming.

PHP is an interesting case of the influence Perl has on recently developed
programming languages. PHP programmers find Perl very familiar, largely because
PHP (like C) has very Perl-like syntax. In addition, PHP object dereferencing, variable
notation, looping, and subroutines are almost identical to Perl. Also, the rest of Perl's
constructs are similar enough to PHP that programmers spend little time adjusting.
Last, the project life cycle afforded by an interpreted language, which involves more
frequent changes and less structured debugging than is required by compiled
applications, is already familiar to PHP programmers.

The PHP and Perl examples in Listing 7.3 and 7.4 access a database and deliver
SQL queries through methods on an object class. The similarities are striking.

Listing 7.3   **Object Method Access in PHP**

```
01 //connect to the database
02 $db = new DB;
03 $db->connect("test","localhost","root","")
04    or $error = "Connection failed";
05
06 //if the database connection worked, send the query
07 if (!$error) {
08   $db->query($query)
09        or $error = "Query failed";
10 }
```

Listing 7.4   **Object Method Access in Perl**

```
01 # connect to the database
02 $dbh = DBI->connect($datasource, $user, $password)
03        or $error = "Connection failed: $DBI::errstr";
04
05 # if the database connection worked, send the query
06 unless ($error)
07 {
08   $sth = $dbh->do($query)
09        or $error = "Query failed: $DBI::errstr";
10 }
```

Aside from the C-like syntax—using curly braces to denote a program block, grouping attributes with quotes, and ending statements with a semicolon—the PHP example and Perl example both use the same variable notation (e.g. $error), the arrow
operator (->) to call object methods off an object stored in a variable, and short-circuit
operators such as or. In fact, the PHP example is syntactically valid Perl; the only
reason to use the latter style is for convenience—unless $error is more English-
inspired than if !$error—or because of underlying data structures like the DBI
object, which is described in more detail later in this chapter.

As a result, migrating to Perl can be simple for a programmer with PHP experience. Idiomatic differences would be overlooked by the Perl interpreter, and programmers can learn underlying modules quickly as applications are designed and developed. The addition of Perl's many available interface modules (such as DBI) would help PHP programmers by providing object interfaces that offer a useful layer of abstraction.

Nonprogrammers

Perl was designed with first-time programmers in mind. The forgiving nature and do-what-I-mean philosophy of Perl were big factors in making it the de facto standard for CGI programming.

The object-oriented language constructs that were added in Perl 5 are an example of Perl's flexibility. A Perl program could be written in a completely object-oriented fashion to facilitate reuse and extensibility. On the other hand, a Perl program could be written using only procedural code with no object notation at all, or with a mix of objects and procedural style. Compared to strict object-oriented languages such as Java, Perl is unusually flexible in allowing the programmer to choose the programming style, instead of the language imposing it.

This friendliness and flexibility in the Perl language was no accident. From the beginning, Larry Wall, Perl's creator, intended Perl to be as much like English in structure and syntax as it is similar to C or awk. Like English, Perl has many ways to state the same functional messages. The comparisons between Perl, C, and PHP syntax in the previous sections of this chapter are examples of the flexibility of programming style built into Perl. This flexibility at the core of the language reflects not only the diversity of Perl's language ancestors, but also the diversity of programming styles that Perl programmers are expected to need. In fact, some programmers take this flexibility to the extreme by choosing to make their Perl seem as much like English as possible. Listing 7.5 is an example.

Listing 7.5 **Perl Poetry by Ryan Koppenhaver**

```
01 #!/usr/bin/perl
02 if ($^I =~ m/cool/) {
03     go("clubbing")
04 } else {
05     go('hack', 'Perl')
06 }
07
08 sub go {
09     print "Guess I'm just another @{[reverse @_]}er.\n";
10 }
```

This poem is actually a functional Perl program that produces the answer to the poem's question as output. Note the use of keywords such as if, else, and print to fill both the roles of poetic substance and programmatic function. The poem also uses Perl simplicity shortcuts (such as omitting the semicolons that would normally come at the end of the third and fifth lines) to improve readability and to keep the focus on the central message. This poem was listed on the PerlMonks Web site (http://www.perlmonks.org), which is discussed in more detail later in this chapter.

Perl poetry is a common form of creative expression among Perl programmers. Programs in any language can be poetic in their own right to those who understand the function of the program, but Perl is unique among programming languages in that it enables complete English sentences to be used in functional programs. In fact, Perl poetry contests are held yearly to find new ways of expressing the same concepts both poetically and functionally. The poems can get very elaborate; many poems print themselves as output, and others produce additional poems when run. One Perl poem even uses poetic functions to turn a sad poetic input into a happy poetic output.

These poems are perhaps best appreciated with a knowledge of Perl; however, the ability to get a sense of a program's inner workings simply by reading the program as an English text is invaluable to anyone who wants to evaluate a program quickly. By using the English syntax that Perl provides, it's possible to create code that is both aesthetically pleasing and functional.

HTML markup is another skill that's generally seen as more art than programming, but in-depth knowledge of it is essential when creating Web applications. Even when creating a Perl-based Web application, HTML might make up the majority of the code because it is also the majority of the program's output. In fact, a common practice is to embed small sections of Perl code within a standard HTML page to keep the HTML and other content sections readable.

Listing 7.6 is an example of Perl embedded in HTML. The Perl code in this example is used only to enumerate a list in an otherwise HTML-centric page; so, the emphasis is placed on the HTML formatting, not Perl.

Listing 7.6   **Perl Embedded in HTML with PSP**

```
01 <template file="page.psp">
02 <p>Font sizes on this browser are in the following range:</p>
03 <ul>
04 <perl>
05    foreach $size (1..7) {
06        print qq{<li><font size="$size">Size $size</font></li>\n};
07    }
08 </perl>
09 </ul>
10 </template>
```

In this case, readability of the page is improved by embedding the Perl function in an HTML-like `<perl>` tag similar to the `<script>` tag used to denote client-side scripting languages, such as JavaScript. The Perl functions are evaluated just as though they were contained in their own program. The output is blended with the rest of the HTML page before the page is delivered. The `<template>` tag works in a similar fashion, but it references Perl code that is included from another page. By separating Perl functions out and including them separately, you can emphasize the HTML aspects of the page, which are more likely to resemble the final output than stand-alone Perl code. Further discussion of Perl templates and embedding can be found in Chapter 13, "Using Templates with Perl Applications."

HTML experts won't have a difficult time making the transition to Perl when programming for the Web. Perl's procedural nature makes it easier to learn than JavaScript's object-oriented functions. In addition, the capability to embed Perl into an HTML page or to use HTML-like tags to express program functions enables Perl to be learned one function at a time while Web applications are being developed.

The Perl Programmer Next Door

Although "Perl Developer" is a title rarely seen in corporate America, many computer professionals have enough Perl programming knowledge to develop a Web application. Systems administrators, analysts, database administrators, and many other programmers use Perl to perform their jobs. These programmers might not consider themselves Perl experts, but they are likely to have the skills necessary to develop for the Web using Perl.

Systems Administrators

Systems administrators, especially UNIX administrators, almost certainly have a working knowledge of Perl. The complexity involved in administering a complex UNIX system encourages administrators to develop customized tools that help them perform repetitive tasks more quickly and easily. In addition, the core UNIX philosophy of having many simple programs that do one thing and do it well creates the need for a glue language such as Perl. A glue language can use groups of system programs to perform a task that is more complex than could otherwise be done with any of the programs individually. Perl's ease of use and interpreted nature also enables it to be used in developing single-use applications that would otherwise be prohibitive to develop in a compiled language. As a result, administrators develop applications in Perl even when the applications are used only once. However, each application might take on a life that is longer than the developer initially envisioned.

In addition, UNIX system administrators with no direct Perl knowledge know more about Perl than they realize. Many of Perl's built-in functions are identical in both name and function to the system utilities found on UNIX or Windows systems. Functions such as `crypt`, `grep`, `localtime`, and others are either UNIX function work-alikes or direct links to system functions. Other common Perl keywords, such as open, close, fork, and exec, refer to system functions that are familiar enough to enable any system programmer to grasp their meaning in Perl and to use them effectively with little additional training.

Perl regular expressions also should be familiar to the UNIX system administrator. The regular expression syntax in Perl is based on awk, a common UNIX regular expression utility. Because regular expression syntax is both the most powerful and the most difficult part of Perl to learn, awk knowledge can give you a good head start on Perl programming. Awk also is likely to be used in conjunction with shell script programming. Thus, a system administrator familiar with awk is likely to have used it in a context very similar to the way in which regular expressions are used in Perl.

In Web programming, a thorough knowledge of system administration can be a valuable asset. Web applications frequently interact with all levels of the systems on which they reside. These levels include database drivers, system files, or compiled programs. An understanding of the issues that can arise concerning Web server access to these systems—including file permissions, which are a common source of confusing error messages—can make the transition to Web application programming in Perl smoother.

Analysts

Generally not regarded as systems programmers, Quality Assurance (QA) analysts, systems analysts, and data analysts are nonetheless likely to have developed Perl-related skills on the job for many of the same reasons as have systems administrators. Data compilation, batch processing, and system discovery processes are all made more accessible by using Perl programs at the system level.

QA analysts are likely to use Perl to design test harnesses, especially when performing long sets of custom tests against a specific program or system utility. Perl also enables sections of a program to be accessed directly through module interfaces. With such access, QA analysts can test database access, network interaction, or other secondary program functions that might not be accessible by the program itself.

Systems analysts use Perl to discover information about a system and to compile and analyze data produced by the respective system. Perl's capability to interact with the server environment at all levels enables systems analysts to write programs that determine if aspects of the environment are available. This testing is done prior to testing them individually to determine their capabilities. Perl also offers the rest of its facilities to system analysts who need to compile the information into text or database repositories, which then can be aggregated by additional Perl programs and presented in a usable form.

Data analysts, including those who perform numeric analysis or data mining on large sets of preexisting data, use Perl to facilitate the analysis of potentially unique data sets without requiring the extended programming that compiled applications would entail. These analysts also use Perl's glue language capabilities to connect directly to the databases and other data set formats that they need to analyze without having to translate into an intermediate format.

Any analyst is likely to have the necessary skills to develop Web applications in Perl, especially when the application involves the analysis and presentation of data derived from a large source. Analysts are likely to be familiar with programming style (if not specifically Perl style) and familiarity with the systems and interfaces used by Perl make the transition even easier.

Database Administrators

Database administrators, although they might never have interacted with Perl or Perl-like languages, are well-suited to Web application development in Perl. Databases are an essential part of Web application infrastructure; the data provided in most medium- or large-scale applications comes from a database through the Structured Query Language (SQL). To use SQL effectively requires a solid understanding of the underlying structure of the database, and database administrators are likely to have created the databases themselves.

Good database design lends itself to good Web application design because many of the principles are the same. Certainly, a well-designed database is essential to a high-performance Web application that frequently accesses the database to insert or retrieve data. SQL queries themselves can be either written poorly or optimized greatly, and a database administrator usually knows the most efficient way to retrieve data from the database. In addition, database administrators can alter the database itself to enhance the performance of Web applications, as is discussed in Chapter 14, "Database-Backed Web Sites."

Database administrators are likely to have programmed in a Perl-like fashion because of the need for shell scripting when designing a complex database schema. Because SQL is a programming language that makes immediate changes to a database, it's usually a good idea to create complex schema-creation queries in a more structured and repeatable fashion than most SQL interfaces allow. Database administrators create shell scripts or Perl programs to automate the process of testing complex queries in a way that enables them to be undone as a whole rather than in parts. They also might create Perl scripts to perform database maintenance on a regular basis.

Database administrators are likely to use Perl-type programming within the database itself through languages such as PL/SQL. PL/SQL is a procedural language that executes functions in the Oracle database and that creates stored procedures that can be called from other SQL queries. Although the languages provided by database manufacturers are not likely to be as robust as Perl, they bridge the gap between the data-centric nature of SQL and procedural programming enough to give database a taste of what is possible.

The transition from database design to Web application development might be a leap for some database administrators, but in general, they are likely to take to the programming tasks of a database-backed Web site very quickly. The benefits of having a solid grounding in database concepts—and potentially an intimate knowledge of the database schema being accessed—make database administrators a valuable asset to any Web-application design team.

Thousands of Lines of Existing Web Code

The Web contains a large base of developed and tested Perl code. Perl programmers tend to be a gregarious bunch. So, the first thing a new Perl hacker is likely to do with his five-line "Hello, world!" program is to share it with the nearest archive site for comments and corrections. This urge gets stronger as programmers become more prolific, so the end-result is an ocean of well-designed Perl examples for any possible situation.

A central repository for the best of this code, called the Comprehensive Perl Archive Network (CPAN), was formed to give more structure to the process of sharing Perl modules and documentation. Modules are considered fit for public consumption after they're published on CPAN. Other types of code are too specialized or too unfinished to qualify for a CPAN listing. They reside on other sites that offer their own archives of Perl code to meet particular needs.

Catalog sites, such as CGI Resources, are devoted to organizing and presenting Perl-based CGI or mod_perl software for use by others. There also are Perl-related news and discussion sites such as PerlMonks, which include archives of Perl code that has been submitted for discussion. In addition, mainstream sites, such as Slashdot (`http://www.slashdot.org`), use Perl as a Web application environment and sometimes post the code that operates the site.

CGI Resource Index

The CGI Resource Index (`http://www.cgi.resourceindex.com/`) is a Web site that collects links to CGI scripts and programs written in a number of languages, including Perl, Tcl, and C. As could be expected, though, over ninety percent of the CGI programs the site has collected are written in Perl.

The site has dozens of application categories, from auctions to image indexing. Site visitors rate each CGI program listed on the site, and the highest-rated programs in each category appear at the top of the list. Not all of the archived programs are well-written, but they serve as a good starting point when deciding how to approach a Perl-based Web application, regardless of whether it is represented in the archive.

It's interesting to note that not all the programs listed in the CGI Resource Index are free, as contrasted with program archives such as CPAN that assume all archived software is available for free download. Both approaches can be helpful when evaluating Perl programs to use as the basis for a Web application; commercial applications might fill in where public modules aren't available.

PerlMonks

PerlMonks (`http://www.perlmonks.org/`) is a discussion and archive site devoted to the Perl programming community, with a specific emphasis on improving their Perl skills by interacting with more advanced programmers.

The PerlMonks site has a code library on par with CGI Resources Index, but its main attraction is the smaller snippets of code that abound in the development forums. Code might be offered for comments and criticism, or it might also be offered as the answer to a query or the result of a challenge. Together, the combination of working code and expert commentary makes a search through the PerlMonks libraries a worthwhile experience.

PerlMonks also shines as an example of the cooperative spirit that pervades the Perl community. The most prominent names in Perl development are the same people that teach and inspire other Perl developers by offering help for beginners, tips for advanced users, and interesting challenges for Perl experts.

The Seekers of Perl Wisdom section, for instance, is a clearinghouse for questions regarding Perl style, technique, and experience. The site also contains sections for Perl poetry, meditations on life as a Perl hacker, and cool uses of Perl in the real world. The latter is a good place to look for inspiration when starting a new project. PerlMonks also has a special place for the most infamous of Perl styles—obfuscation. The fascination with indecipherable Perl code has given Perl a reputation as a language only for the initiated. In truth, however, it's merely an expression of love for the language. It has little effect on mainstream use.

SlashCode

The programmers at Slashdot.org (`http://www.slashdot.org`), perhaps the most visible of high-traffic sites driven by Perl, have taken a unique view regarding the Perl programs they created over the years to handle the unique needs of their popular site. Instead of hiding their code or packaging it to sell to other sites in the same situation, they've taken the time to create an open-source distribution of the code, appropriately named Slash.

SlashCode (`http://www.slashcode.org`), the site devoted to distributing and discussing the Slash code base, also serves as a working example of how to customize Slash for another site. Discussions of Slash applications, development, and distribution are carried out using the Slash modules and templates.

The SlashCode site also lists dozens of examples of other sites that have applied Slash to their own ends, from the Berkeley High School student newspaper to earthDot, an environmental advocacy news site. Each site gives visual clues to its Slash origins as well as new techniques to explore when adapting the Slash code base to a particular end.

Standard CGI Example

To get an idea of the simplicity that Perl CGI offers a new programmer, an example of Perl connecting to a database is included in the following section. This example is in the simple CGI style, but it is reiterated in Chapter 12, "Environments For Reducing Development Time," within a higher-performance, more sustainable design model.

Universal SQL Query Processor

Accessing a database might seem to be a straightforward process, and the advent of standards such as SQL might reinforce that notion. However, good tools to access databases are still few and far between, so most database users still browse databases through custom programs. Worse yet, many database users are forced to plod through a schema, one query at a time, by using a command-line interface and the formatting nightmare it presents.

The Web, however, provides an excellent venue for exploring and manipulating data. The flexibility of HTML formatting enables data to be presented attractively, regardless of whether the style is specific to the current schema or general to all SQL-accessible data.

Before designing a specific format for Web presentation of database content, you should browse the data in a universal format to get a sense of what is available. The most flexible way to do this is by offering a generic SQL portal to any database accessible by the Perl CGI engine.

Form Access with CGI.pm

Most Perl CGI programs begin with CGI.pm, the Perl module that handles Web server interaction through CGI. CGI.pm provides a simple interface to headers, form variables, and other architectural elements that comprise the communications layer between a Web server and a CGI application. See Chapter 5, "Architecture–Based Performance Loss," for an architectural overview of CGI.

With Web programming in mind, CGI.pm offers methods for creating forms and other HTML structures, as well as methods for accessing form variables and modifying page attributes. As Listing 7.7 shows, HTML forms can be written entirely using method calls to the CGI object.

Listing 7.7 **Database Access Through SQL** (*sql_query.pl*)

```
001 #!/usr/bin/perl
002
003 #----------------------------------------
004 #
005 # sql_get.pl - CGI application example
006 #
007 #----------------------------------------
008
009 # include libraries
010 require 5.6.0;
011 use strict;
012 use warnings;
013 use CGI;
014 use DBI;
015
016 # declare some variables
```

continues

Listing 7.7 **Continued**

```perl
017 my ($q, $dbh, $sth, $query, $datasource, $user, $password, $error,
018 $field, $result, $results);
019 my (@datasources);
020
021 # initiate CGI parser object
022 $q = CGI->new;
023
024 # begin the page
025 print $q->header,
026        $q->start_html('SQL Database Viewer'),
027        $q->h2('SQL Database Viewer');
028
029 # build a (safe) list of data sources
030 foreach (DBI->available_drivers)
031 {
032   eval {
033     foreach (DBI->data_sources($_))
034     {
035       push @datasources, $_;
036     }
037   };
038 }
039
040
041 # display the entry form
042 print $q->start_form;
043
044 print qq{<p>Choose a datasource:</p>\n};
045 print $q->popup_menu(-name => 'datasource',
046                      -values => \@datasources);
047
048 print qq{<p>Specify username/password:</p>\n};
049 print $q->textfield(-name => 'user',
050                     -size => 10);
051 print $q->password_field(-name => 'password',
052                          -size => 10);
053
054 print qq{<p>Enter a SELECT query:</p>\n};
055 print $q->textarea(-name => 'query',
056                    -rows => '5',
057                    -cols => '40',
058                    -wrap => 'virtual');
059
060 print $q->p, $q->submit;
061 print $q->end_form;
062
063 # get form variables
064 $datasource = $q->param('datasource');
065 $user = $q->param('user');
066 $password = $q->param('password');
067 $query = $q->param('query');
```

```
068
069 # check form variables
070 if ($query)
071 {
072   $error = "Improper datasource specified" unless
      ⮡($datasource =~/^dbi/i);
073   $error = "Query should start with SELECT" unless
      ⮡($query =~/^select/i);
074 }
075
076 # if a query is specified and form variables are OK,
077 if ($query and !$error)
078 {
079   # connect to the database
080   $dbh = DBI->connect($datasource, $user, $password)
081         or $error = "Connection failed: $DBI::errstr";
082
083   # if the database connection worked, send the query
084   unless ($error)
085   {
086     $sth = $dbh->prepare($query)
087           or $error = "Query failed: $DBI::errstr";
088     $sth->execute or $error = "Query failed: $DBI::errstr";
089   }
090 }
091
092 # if any errors are present, display the error and exit
093 if ($error) {print $q->p("Error: $error"), $q->end_html and exit;}
094
095 # if the query produced an output,
096 if ($query and $sth->{NAME})
097 {
098   # start a data table
099   print qq{<table border="1">\n};
100   print qq{<tr>\n};
101
102   # display the fields as table headers
103   foreach $field (@{$sth->{NAME}})
104   {
105     print qq{<th>$field</th>\n};
106   }
107   print qq{</tr>\n};
108
109   # display the results in a table
110   while ($results = $sth->fetchrow_arrayref)
111   {
112     print qq{<tr>\n};
113     foreach $result (@$results)
114     {
115       print qq{<td>$result</td>\n};
116     }
```

continues

Listing 7.7   **Continued**

```
117     print qq{</tr>\n};
118   }
119
120   # finish the data table
121   print qq{</table>\n};
122 }
123
124 # finish the page
125 print $q->end_html;
126
127 # disconnect from the database
128 $dbh->disconnect if $dbh;
```

After including the necessary libraries and setting up some variables for use in the program, line 021 of the sql_query.pl program creates a new CGI query object, $q. The $q object provides a unified interface to all CGI methods, including form creation and query variable access.

After setting up the environment, lines 029 and 032 call methods off the DBI object to build a list of available data sources. Then, lines 041 through 060 create a basic HTML form with a drop-down box for choosing the DBI data source, text boxes for username and password entry, a textarea box for the SQL query, and a Submit button. (DBI access methods are covered in more detail in the following section, "Accessing a Database with DBI.pm.")

The program is designed to be accessed multiple times with different information. Forms generated by the program submit information back to it with more information added each time the user submits. This style of programming is common with CGI, but it is much less common in more modern Web programming styles because it leads to monolithic code bases as programs get larger. Large, single programs become difficult to develop in a Web environment, especially on the time scales that Web programming requires. For this example, however, the multiple-access style is useful in keeping the program portable and compact.

Checking Variables with Regular Expressions

Form variables returned by the browser should almost always be checked for validity. The only time they shouldn't be checked is when any possible input is acceptable, as in the case of the $user and $password variables. These variables can blank or contain any characters. No matter what controls are added to the HTML form itself, the HTTP response enables any data to be passed as form variables. Most of the time, it is enough to check that form variables are not empty or that they do not contain data that will crash the application after they are used.

In the case of a database browser, you should restrict the possible SQL queries to those that won't alter the content of the database. To do this, line 073 uses Perl's regular expression engine to check the $query form variable provided by the $p object. The simple regular expression /^select/ returns a true value only if the query starts with the keyword SELECT, and the i modifier relaxes the restriction to enable both uppercase and lowercase versions of the SELECT keyword.

Similar checking is performed on the data source itself in line 072 to gracefully catch obviously malformed data sources, which might result in an uglier error if passed to the database connect method. This type of error checking becomes more important if the page does not display correctly—or at all—due to a fatal error in the program.

Accessing a Database with DBI.pm

In this example, any database that is visible to Perl is available to the query processor. The module that provides this functionality is DBI.pm. This module unites a number of secondary database drivers (called DBD modules) under a common object structure and method syntax. DBI is a boon to Web application programmers because it enables database-generic code to be used with any database without modification. This comes in handy when developing a prototype using an inexpensive database system, such as PostgreSQL, and transferring the resultant programs to a production database such as Oracle.

Because DBI offers connections to many databases, the query processor needs a way to indicate which database and data source the query is intended to access. DBI provides convenience methods for enumerating available database drivers and data sources. So, lines 029 and 032 use the available_drivers and data_sources methods to get lists of possible data sources available. (An eval block catches errors from the available_drivers method; DBI installs many drivers by default. Not all drivers apply to every system running this program.) DBI takes these data sources as connection strings in the same form in which they are given by the data_sources method. Therefore, it's possible to list the sources without any translation or parsing.

Once a data source is chosen and a query is submitted, lines 079 to 089 pass the query to the specified data source, and lines 098 to 121 format the output in as generic a way as possible. This is assisted by the NAME attribute of the statement handle $sth used in line 96, which references a list of the field names returned by the query. By listing these names as headings in an HTML table in lines 103 to 106, you can provide an understandable view of the results without knowing in advance either their size or contents.

Error Handling

Because something can always go wrong, it is important to check for potential errors and declare them in a format that the Web server and browser understand.

One way to catch error messages is by redirecting them to the Web browser as they appear, perhaps even setting them apart in red text. This method is commonly seen in ASP-style applications when a particular snippet of code fails to run or returns an error. Unfortunately, the error messages produced by Perl are of more interest to the programmer of the application than the user. Thus, you should treat common or foreseeable errors with a little more charm.

Perl errors are produced in plain text and don't necessarily require the program to halt, so common errors can be found and restated in a way that is more understandable to the program's user. For example, a query that is rejected by the specified data source might give a cryptic error message and a useless line number if allowed to halt the program on its own. Catching the error and presenting it in plain English can greatly improve the usability of a program.

It's also important to give the user a chance to correct any typos or other errors without having to type the entire query again. This is a situation in which the form creation qualities of CGI.pm come in handy. If the user has filled in the form fields and the values are present as variables—as the data source and query variables are likely to be—the CGI query object inserts those values into the form's input fields as it creates them, as illustrated in Figure 7.1. The form creation methods don't have to be modified for this case, which reduces both duplication of effort and the complexity of the program.

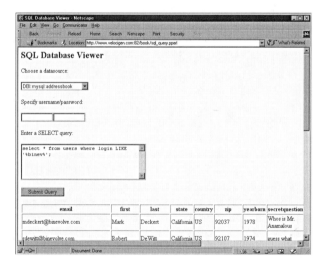

Figure 7.1   Script output and prefilled fields.

System Administration Example

Perl's unrivaled systems administration facilities make it a natural for back-end Web tasks that would otherwise be performed by hand (or not at all). Tasks that are usually performed at the command line—such as regular searches on a database or continuous monitoring of a network-accessible resource—lend themselves to Perl-based automation and the eventual provision of a Web application interface to the same functions.

Downtime Logging and Notification

Immediate notification of a server failure can be valuable, especially when the failure occurs after hours when it would ordinarily go unnoticed. For public Web services and e-commerce sites, quick notification can mean the difference between a temporary blip and a major outage; Web users do retry a site a few minutes after an initial setback, but few keep trying to reach an inaccessible site for much longer than that. An outage of even half an hour can lose significant business, but a Web failure might go unnoticed by site staff for hours—or in the case of a late-night Saturday fault, for days. Checking the availability of a Web site continuously would be an impossible chore if done manually; a Web developer's time can always be better spent.

Fortunately, Web servers can check on other Web servers and notify staff of inaccessible pages and server faults no matter what time of day the outage occurs. A simple Perl application running as a time-triggered independent process can perform this job admirably, and additional notification—to email, cell phone, or pager—can be added without much fuss, as shown in Listing 7.8.

A log of downtime can come in handy during later analysis, as well. For example, uptime as a percent of total can be used to evaluate a server for replacement or upgrades. Customers of a Web-based service might ask for certification of uptime performance as well.

Listing 7.8   **Server Monitor Through LWP** (*server_monitor.pl*)

```
01 #!/usr/bin/perl
02
03 #-----------------------------------------
04 #
05 # server_monitor.pl - LWP monitor example
06 #
07 #-----------------------------------------
08
09 use 5.6.0;
10 use warnings;
11 use strict;
12 use LWP::UserAgent;
13 use HTTP::Request::Common;
14 use Net::SMTP;
```

continues

Listing 7.8 **Continued**

```
15
16 # set up variables
17 my ($server_url);
18 my ($ua, $result);
19
20 # set environment
21 $server_url = $ARGV[0];
22
23 # check the URL
24 $ua = LWP::UserAgent->new;
25 $result = $ua->request(GET $server_url);
26
27 # was the check successful?
28 # if so, write the current time to the uptime log
29 if ($result->is_success)
30 {
31   # not so fast! check for the string "success"
32   if ($result->as_string =~ /success/)
33   {
34     my $time = localtime;
35
36     open (LOG, '>>/tmp/server-monitor.log');
37     print LOG "$time - 200 - $server_url\n";
38     close LOG;
39   }
40   else
41   {
42     # call the page fail subroutine with an error code
43     page_failed(500, $server_url);
44   }
45 }
46 # if not, email a notification and log the failure
47 else
48 {
49   # call the page fail subroutine with the result code
50   page_failed($result->code, $server_url);
51 }
52
53 # email a notification and log the failure
54 sub page_failed
55 {
56   my $error = shift;
57   my $url = shift;
58
59   my $time = localtime;
60
61   # send an email notification
62   my $smtp = Net::SMTP->new('mail.server.com');
63
64   $smtp->mail('sender@server.com');
65   $smtp->to('recipient@server.com');
```

```
66
67   $smtp->data();
68   $smtp->datasend("To: recipient\@server.com\n");
69   $smtp->datasend("Subject: $server_url not responding\n");
70   $smtp->datasend("\n");
71   $smtp->datasend("The page at $server_url is not responding.\n");
72   $smtp->datasend("Please check it.\n");
73   $smtp->dataend();
74
75   $smtp->quit;
76
77   # send a text message
78   $result = $ua->request(POST
     ↪'http://www.messaging.sprintpcs.com/sms/check_message_syntax.html',
79                          [mobilenum   => '8885551212',
80                           callbacknum => '8885551234',
81                           message     => 'Server down.']);
82
83   # write a line to the downtime log
84   open (LOG, '>>/tmp/server-monitor.log') or die "Log file: $!";
85   print LOG "$time - $error - $url\n";
86   close LOG;
87 }
```

Accessing a URL with LWP

At its core, the downtime logging application simply checks a server URL the way any browser would, by accessing it over the Web and evaluating the result. This is made possible by LWP, a module that provides HTTP, HTTPS, and FTP interfaces to Perl programs. LWP is actually a collection of individual modules that access servers, wait for a response, and parse the result—all are offered through a high-level interface that masks many of the individual parts.

There are many ways to use LWP, but the simplest is to invoke the HTTP::Request::Common module in conjunction with the LWP::UserAgent module. HTTP::Request::Common makes assumptions about HTTP session variables so that they don't have to be defined explicitly. The module also provides streamlined method calls for use in basic request and response queries.

The server monitor uses LWP to access the page as a browser would to determine whether the page is accessible. If not, the error reported by LWP (usually an HTTP error code such as 404 for "Not Found" or 500 for "Internal Server Error") is passed to a subroutine, which logs the error and notifies site personnel that the site is inaccessible.

Finding Success with Regular Expressions

A nonerror result code doesn't necessarily mean that the Web site is accessible, however. Databases and other secondary systems sometimes produce human-readable errors that don't catch the attention of LWP. These errors are translated into HTML, much like the SQL query program we just discussed. Thus, they do not affect the overall status code of the document returned to LWP. To test that secondary systems are available and responding to requests, it's good to write an application on the server side that returns a trivial string (such as "success") if and only if the system is accessible and functioning normally.

Finding the desired output within the HTML page is an ideal use of regular expressions. Perl can very quickly search through a large string, such as the HTML results of a test page, to find a string that matches the pattern specified. In this case, the pattern is the simple string /success/, which returns a true value if any occurrence of that string is found in the returned HTML document. Note that this also includes substrings of words or tags, so be sure to use a string that is unique to a successful document. The pattern /ok/ would be a bad choice, for instance because it is a substring of 'broken' or 'token', while a pattern such as /database success/ is much less likely to appear erroneously.

Regular expressions also can be used to check arbitrary data with a finer grain than success or failure. For example, the update time on a page could be checked against the current time to make sure the page was updated recently. In addition, an aggregate query from a database could be checked to make sure the total always increases with time. Regular expressions can be used to find almost anything in an output page, and the resulting values can be used in a conditional, as shown in the following code:

```
...
my ($total) = $result =~ /<b>Total: (\d+)</b>/;
if ($total <= 0)
...
```

This regular expression returns a section of the result determined by a series of digits, which come after the word Total in a bold string. The total is then checked before continuing with the conditional statement. The perlre section of the Perl documentation contains an in-depth explanation of regular expressions and their syntax.

Notification Through Email or Instant Message

At run time, the most important function of this program is notification. Instant notification of site outages can be crucial, so it's important to notify in multiple ways simultaneously, such as through email and an SMS message to a phone.

Notifying an email address is relatively simple. Net::SMTP is a module included with the standard distribution of Perl. It is implemented entirely in Perl, which means that it relies only on basic network services. It does not require Sendmail or an equivalent mail server to be installed on the same machine. This is important both for portability and performance, as is explained in detail in Chapter 11, "Problems with Persistence."

In this example, Net::SMTP is invoked with the simplest message possible: "Help!" A new $smtp object is created, and then the message is composed and sent with the mail(), to(), and datasend() methods.

Adding the ability to send a text message to a cell phone is made easy by the LWP module and a Web-based SMS gateway (see Figure 7.2). The example uses a gateway supplied by Sprint for its PCS customers, but other cellular carriers provide similar services and the corresponding URL could be inserted in place of the Sprint site. When doing so, it is usually necessary to find a Web-enabled form and determine the necessary form variables and destination, as in Listing 7.9.

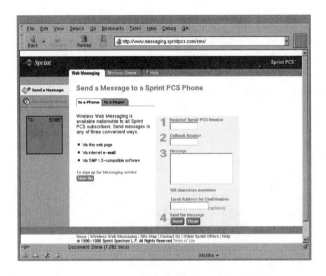

Figure 7.2 Sprint SMS gateway form.

Listing 7.9   **Excerpt of Sprint SMS Gateway Form**

```
01 <form name="frm" method="post" action="check_message_syntax.html">
02 <b>Recipient Sprint PCS Number<br></b>
03 <input name="mobilenum" size="10" maxlength="10" type="TEXT">
04 <b>Callback Number<br></b>
05 <input name="callbacknum" size="10" maxlength="10" type="TEXT">
06 <b>Message<br></b>
07 <textarea wrap="VIRTUAL" name="message" cols="21" rows="5"
   ➥onfocus="count_text(this.value)" onchange="count_text2(this.form)"
   ➥onblur="timer_stop()"></textarea>
08 <b>100 characters maximum<br></b>
09 <b>Email Address for Confirmation<br></b>
```

continues

Listing 7.9 **Continued**

```
10 <input name="ack_add" size="14" type="TEXT">(optional)
11 <input type="image" src="/images/SendButton3.gif" width="40"
12  height="22" border="0">
13 </form>
```

In this case, the important pieces of information to find are the form action, which is used as the destination URL for the LWP query, and the form variables, which are combined with the phone number and message to make up the query string. In Listing 7.9, the form action is check_message_syntax.html, which can be fully-qualified using the base URL of the form page. The form variables are mobilenum, callbacknum, and message, which are fed to the LWP user agent with their appropriate values.

When posting form variables to a Web page, it's necessary to encode the variables so that illegal characters are escaped as standard sequences of allowable characters. Thus, the message string The server is not responding must be reformatted into The+server+is+not+responding before being sent to the Web server. LWP escapes form variables automatically, but there are some cases in which you must escape the values manually, such as when posting a Location: header to redirect a user to another page.

Logging Results

In this application, the results are logged in a detailed format, but a more abbreviated form could be made available if necessary. The choice could be gathered from command-line options and defaulted to the abbreviated log format. This choice, along with log file locations and other parameters, could just as easily come from a preferences file. Preferences could be read and parsed at startup and stored for later use by the program.

A detailed log entails writing the time and status of each attempted connection to a log file, which then can be analyzed at a later date to determine the relative percentage of uptime. This might be necessary to provide accountability when certifying system uptime to a third party. An additional benefit to a continuous log is the possibility of checking the uptime monitor itself by making sure there are no gaps in the recorded log.

The abbreviated log format involves overwriting a file with the most recent successful connection and keeping a separate file with the times and circumstances of failed connections. One reason to use the abbreviated format is to save disk space; the assumption is that downtime is much more rare than uptime. In a situation with 99 percent uptime overall and a connection check every minute, for instance, the detailed log would gain five megabytes per URL per month, while the abbreviated log would gain only fifty kilobytes per URL per month. Another compelling reason to use the abbreviated log is to reduce the load experienced by log analyzers that need details on failed requests, but that need only a summary of successful requests.

Either way, a server monitor produces lots of good data for analysis, as well as the immediate notification that makes it invaluable.

Text-Processing Example

Producing reams of useful data has a downside. Analyzing text-based logs and reports has generally required the work of a dedicated C program or a patient UNIX shell script writer. Perl, however, was written specifically to solve problems like these with a minimum of effort.

Web server logs are the most readily accessible example of this idea. A Web server generates one line in an access log for every page, image, or script accessed by any user at any time. It takes only a short time for a Web server log to present a challenge that is both daunting and tempting. Many other logs and data sources create similar challenges, which usually go unmet due to time and money constraints.

Downtime Log Analysis

A basic analysis of the logs produced by the server monitor might involve a simple calculation of uptime as a percentage of total time logged. This is the calculation that's usually referred to when servers and applications boast of a 99.99 percent uptime.

Additional levels of analysis can be performed on the same data, including plots of errors as a function of time or a listing of sites with the most errors in a given time period. The opportunities are as rich as the underlying data; this emphasizes the importance of a rapid development environment in which to try many different data models as soon as they are imagined.

```
Mon Dec 11 19:21:57 2000 - 200 - http://www.perl.com/
Mon Dec 11 19:24:40 2000 - 200 - http://www.globalspin.com
Mon Dec 11 19:25:12 2000 - 500 - http://www.globalspin.com/lost.html
Mon Dec 11 19:28:34 2000 - 404 - http://www.globalspin.com/lost.html
Mon Dec 11 19:28:46 2000 - 200 - http://www.globalspin.com/
Mon Dec 11 19:29:17 2000 - 500 - http://www.perl.com/
Mon Dec 11 19:40:49 2000 - 500 - http://www.perl.com/
```

The log that this program reads is formatted with a date, an error code, and a site URL, as in the preceding example. The format is simple, but it's easy to see how thousands of lines of the same type of data could obscure any meaning the data could potentially provide. The log analyzer in Listing 7.10 provides a simple example of how to read the file a line at a time while building a statistical compilation of the data contained therein.

Listing 7.10 **Log Analyzer with HTML Output**

```
01 #!/usr/bin/perl
02
03 #----------------------------------------
04 #
05 # log_analysis.pl - text analysis example
06 #
07 #----------------------------------------
```

continues

Listing 7.10   **Continued**

```
08
09 # include libraries
10 use 5.6.0;
11 use warnings;
12 use strict;
13
14 # initialize a few variables
15 my %site;
16 my $latest;
17 my $log_file = $ARGV[0];
18
19 # open the specified log file
20 open (LOG, $log_file) or die " Log file: $!";
21
22 # check each line
23 while (my $line = <LOG>)
24 {
25   # extract the month, result code and url
26   my ($month, $code, $url) =
27     $line =~ /^... (...) .+?- (\d\d\d) - (.+?)$/;
28   ($latest) = $line =~ /^([^-]+)-/;
29
30   # add one to the appropriate site, result, and date hashes
31   $site{$url}->{total}++;
32   $site{$url}->{result}->{$code}->{total}++;
33   $site{$url}->{result}->{$code}->{date}->{$month}->{total}++;
34 }
35
36 close LOG;
37
38 # display the collected results by site
39 print "<html>\n";
40 print "<h2>Log Analysis</h2>\n";
41 print "<h3>Site totals:</h3>\n";
42 foreach my $url (sort keys %site)
43 {
44   my $total = $site{$url}->{total} or 1;
45   print "<p><b>$url</b>: $total monitor request(s)\n";
46   print "<ul>\n";
47
48   # display the site results by code
49   foreach my $code (sort keys %{$site{$url}->{result}})
50   {
51     my $total = $site{$url}->{result}->{$code}->{total};
52     print "<li><b>$code</b>: $total monitor request(s)</li>\n";
53     print "<ul>\n";
54
55     # display the results by date
56     foreach my $month
57       (sort keys %{$site{$url}->{result}->{$code}->{date}})
58     {
```

```
59        my $total =
60            $site{$url}->{result}->{$code}->{date}->{$month}->{total};
61        print "<li><b>$month</b>: $total monitor request(s)</li>\n";
62        }
63      print "</ul>\n";
64    }
65    print "</ul>\n";
66
67    # determine percent uptime
68    my $successes = $site{$url}->{result}->{200}->{total} || 0;
69    my $uptime = sprintf("%2.2f", $successes / $total * 100);
70    print "Percent uptime: <b>$uptime</b></p>\n\n";
71 }
72
73 # write the summary results to a summary file
74 my $summary_file = "/tmp/log_analysis_summary.txt";
75 open (SUMMARY, ">$summary_file") or die " Summary: $!";
76 # write the summary data
77 foreach my $url (sort keys %site)
78 {
79   foreach my $code (sort keys %{$site{$url}->{result}})
80   {
81     foreach my $month
82       (sort keys %{$site{$url}->{result}->{$code}->{date}})
83     {
84       my $total =
85           $site{$url}->{result}->{$code}->{date}->{$month}->{total};
86       print SUMMARY "$url - $code - $month - $total\n";
87     }
88   }
89 }
90
91 # write the latest time summarized
92 print SUMMARY "Latest: $latest\n";
93
94 close SUMMARY;
95
96
97 print "</html>\n";
```

Line-By-Line Parsing

Perl provides a basic interface to line-by-line parsing of text files, which works well
in a case like this. As the log file is read in, only one line is kept in memory at a time.
This allows files to be analyzed even when they are much larger than available
memory. It also prevents the resulting data structures from being cumbersome.

Building a Results Hash

As lines are processed, a regular expression is used to extract the relevant data into more understandable chunks, namely $month, $code, and $url. These are then used to determine which data structures to increment; in this case, the data structures are created automatically when data is present to fill them. After it is aggregated, this single data structure holds a summary of the entire log file, no matter what individual dates, codes, or URLs are present. By enabling the data itself to determine the structure of its summary, the program can be applied to more varied situations without the need for a rewrite.

Writing Results as HTML

Printing the results of the aggregated data in a readable format is as easy as producing an HTML list (see Figure 7.3). The lists are nested in the same fashion as the data structure, so a simple set of foreach loops can be used to produce the HTML lists of lists. If a graphic interpretation of the data is desired, you can create images with data points specified by the Perl data structure's values.

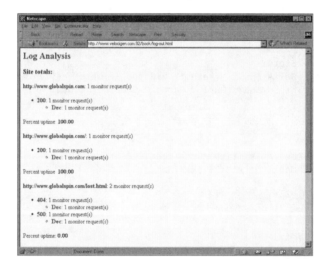

Figure 7.3   Log analysis summary in HTML form.

Logging Results Summaries

In addition to the human-readable results produced by the log analyzer, you should produce aggregate results that can be reused by the program. By summarizing the results of a long log file and using the results as a base for further summaries, time is saved when analyzing subsequent logs. This time saving is especially important when processing Web access or error logs, which can be too large to process in a single run and might be processed repeatedly over the course of months or years.

When recording summaries for use by the log analyzer, you should write the summary logs in a format that matches the internal data structures as closely as possible. The log analyzer separates results by error, URL, and month and keeps a simple count of the errors recorded for each class. Thus, you should record a separate line in the summary log for each combination of the categories.

Note, however, that aggregate data does not need to be recorded if it can be easily arrived at by manipulating the other recorded data. Functions such as the uptime percentage can be generated on the fly, regardless of whether the data comes from a summary log file or the original logs.

The summary log format used by the server log analyzer would produce output as follows:

```
http://www.globalspin.com - 200 - Dec - 1
http://www.globalspin.com/ - 200 - Dec - 1
http://www.globalspin.com/lost.html - 404 - Dec - 1
http://www.globalspin.com/lost.html - 500 - Dec - 1
http://www.perl.com/ - 200 - Dec - 14
http://www.perl.com/ - 500 - Dec - 5
http://www.perl.com/lost.html - 500 - Dec - 3
Latest: Mon Dec 11 20:05:01 2000
```

Processing summary log data would be done before any other log data is processed by reading the summary log as though it were the original log, but adding the total value listed instead of a single line.

Summary

Perl presents a world of opportunities to Web developers, both in terms of the wealth of programming experience in the Perl community and the sheer number of tools available for the Perl programmer. By digging a little deeper than the buzzwords and headlines, it's possible to find a rich Perl culture that encourages growth and new solutions. Perl is an excellent choice for Web development, and it will remain so for a long time to come.

8

Performance Myths

BEFORE ANY PERFORMANCE PROBLEMS CAN BE SOLVED, it's important to understand the pitfalls a Web developer can encounter while attempting to optimize a Web application. It's difficult enough to come to the conclusion that an application should be tested for performance before it's offered to the public. But after the decision is made, it's sometimes even more difficult to get beyond technology preconceptions to discover the aspects of an application that might cause performance bottlenecks when put into production. For applications that are already being used by site visitors, it can be difficult to realize that problem areas aren't always obvious and that the solutions to performance problems aren't necessarily straightforward.

It isn't always easy to pinpoint the real reason why an application is perceptibly slow. There are many links in the chain between the Web server and the site visitor, and any one of them can suffer from performance degradation that is noticeable by the user. A perceived lag in image load time, for instance, can be the result of a slow connection between the user and the Internet, or it could be caused by the Web server's connection. In addition, load from other users accessing the same images could cause the same effect, as could load from users accessing unrelated applications and tying up server resources.

Performance problems also can affect each other, causing greater- or lesser-per-ceived slowdowns. In the case of slow graphics, a slow connection from the user to the Internet could mask a slow connection from the Web server to the Internet, but it also could exacerbate any delays in the transmission caused by server lag. When a site is deemed slow overall by disgruntled visitors, it's difficult to tell which of these factors had the most effect on the slowdown and which of the factors are solvable within the scope of the Web server.

Perception itself can be misleading. A slow site can appear slower when site elements rely on unusual browser tricks or high-bandwidth technologies for basic navigation or form input. A Flash interface that takes two seconds to download might take ten seconds to initialize on a computer with a slow processor, for instance, and the user might not be able to tell the real reason for the slowdown. Even a site that relies on mouseovers to activate meaningful elements of a visual navigation interface might run into trouble when the "on" graphics take more time to load than it takes the user to overshoot the graphic and move on to the next menu choice. In cases like these, simple confusion over interface elements might make a site seem less responsive than it should, which makes duplicating the source of the slowdown even more difficult for site personnel who have no such difficulties.

With Web applications, the same uncertainties apply. Perceived lag can be caused by server-side slowness or network delays. Server-side performance loss can come from many sources, including system architecture, network connection, and simple server overload from too many interested visitors. Because each visitor feels like the unique user of the Web application, it's all too likely that performance loss from any source is intolerable and will cause users to go elsewhere.

Luckily, Common Gateway Interface (CGI) applications all share a few common performance bottlenecks that can be easily identified and removed. On the flip side, Perl CGI programs won't be helped by many performance enhancements that would seem obvious in other environments. Optimizing the application at the source code level, benchmarking the application at runtime to gauge the performance differences between one style and another, and switching to a different database based on external benchmark scores are all unlikely to solve performance problems that plague Perl CGI programs. Even worse, switching the development language from Perl to a compiled language such as C or Java is likely to do more harm than good. Each "solution" is more likely to drain development than fix performance issues because it doesn't address the real reasons for performance loss.

Program Runtime

As odd as it might seem, the time it takes a Perl CGI application to run is rarely ever a factor in the application's performance. To understand this, it's important to know the difference between program runtime and the total time and system resources taken when using a program to complete a specific task.

With a normal instance of a program written in Perl, the program is run interactively at the command line. After this happens, the program is loaded off disk, and the Perl compiler:

- Also is loaded off disk

- Is executed
- Configures itself based on files it loads from the disk
- Accepts the Perl program as an argument
- Parses the program and checks for syntax errors
- Compiles the program and optimizes it
- Executes the resultant bytecode

Because the first seven steps usually take less than a second, a simple Perl program run in this fashion seems to run instantaneously (that is, in less than a second). Similarly, the total execution time of more complex programs seems to depend solely on the length and complexity of the program being run. A log analysis program that takes twelve seconds from start to finish spends most of that twelve seconds analyzing logs, so the fraction of a second spent on the first seven steps are seen as trivial in ordinary use.

Perl CGI programs are run using all the same steps, but the relative importance of each step becomes skewed greatly because of the demands placed on a Web server in normal use. Although an administrative Perl program is likely to be run once by a single user willing to wait for a response, a Web application written in Perl is more likely to be accessed hundreds of times per second by users expecting subsecond response times—most of whom are likely to run the same or similar Web applications again within a few seconds. With this environment, the time spent in the first seven steps is no longer trivial; that is, "less than a second" becomes much too long when compared to a runtime of a few milliseconds. The processor power used in performing the main task of the Web application has to be divided up between the running instance of an application and dozens of other copies, which are in the process of being loaded off disk, compiled, and instantiated.

Compile Time is Much Longer

When any Perl program is run, the Perl runtime first compiles it from source code. This process isn't trivial even for the tiniest of Perl programs; in those cases, Perl spends much more time and processing power compiling the program than it does running the program itself.

This should make perfect sense to anyone familiar with the process necessary to compile programs in a language such as C. For C programs, the compile step is one that takes minutes or hours, even for a program designed to run for only a few seconds. Perl is similar in this regard, even though the time scales are seconds and milliseconds, respectively, for most Perl Web applications.

The effects of the compile step aren't usually noticed when executing a Perl program. This is because the compile step of most Perl programs is only a second or two when executed by a single user, far less than most users would notice when executing an average system program. This happens no matter how long the program itself takes to run. The program either executes very quickly, in which case the added compile time is seen as a reasonable total runtime, or it executes over a longer time period than the compile time, in which case the time spent compiling is inconsequential compared to runtime.

If the same circumstances were to apply to a C program, the effect would be much more noticeable. If a standard program took half an hour to initialize before performing a simple two-second task, the overall perceived runtime would be interminable. Even if the program took an hour to run after the initial half hour of compiling, it would still seem like an incredible waste to compile the program before every use.

On the time scale used by most Web applications, this is exactly the case. A Web application usually needs to respond in milliseconds to keep up with the rate of incoming requests, so a half second spent compiling the program is an eternity. Compared to that eternity, a millisecond faster or slower isn't likely to make much of a difference.

Disk I/O is Much Slower

The first optimization any Web server makes to its operation is caching files in memory instead of accessing them from the disk. The reason for this is raw speed; a file in memory can be accessed much more quickly than a file on disk. Because a Web site is likely to be made up of hundreds of small text files that change very infrequently, it's possible to keep a large number of them in memory for quicker access. If files are accessed a thousand times a minute, the Web server gets an orders-of-magnitude speed increase by loading the files off disk once a minute instead of each time they're accessed. On top of this, it's usually possible to check each file to see if it's been changed since it was last read from disk. This saves the need to reload files unless they've been altered.

The Web server isn't able to cache files used by a CGI Web application, however. The main program file has to be read from disk each time, as do Perl module files, data files, and any other supporting files for the application. Some of these files might be cached within the Perl CGI program if they're being called from within the program itself; however, none of the files associated with compiling the application is going to be cached by Perl because the files are used only once throughout the compilation process.

Even if files used during runtime are cached for use later in the same program, within the CGI model, there's no way to cache these files for use by later instances of the program, let alone for other Perl programs that use the same files. A text file being searched for the words "dog" and "cat," for instance, could be loaded into memory once and used both by the "dog" search routine and the "cat" search routine; however, the next time the program is called to perform the same search on the same file, it has to load the file from disk all over again. This repeated disk access is likely to be much more time-consuming than the algorithms that actually perform the search.

Data Structure Setup Takes Time

A program that provides access to an external data set has to have access to that data internally before it can deal with the data in a meaningful way. An Extensible Markup Language (XML) document, for instance, has to be translated from the text representation of the document into a Perl data structure, which can be directly acted upon by Perl functions. (This process is generally called "parsing the document," but it can involve many more steps than simply breaking the document into chunks. More detail on handling XML can be found in Chapter 16, "XML and Content Management.") Similar processes have to occur when accessing a database, reading a text file off disk, or retrieving data from the network. In all cases, the data has to be translated into a form that's usable within the Perl program.

The process of setting up data structures as a program runs, also known as *instantiation*, can be very time-consuming. In fact, the time taken by instantiating data might be hundreds of times greater than the time spent actually processing it. Connecting to a busy database can take as long as five or six seconds, for instance, while retrieving data from the same database might take only a fraction of a second under the same circumstances. Another example would be parsing a log file into a hash structure for easier access and aggregation, which could take seconds while the actual aggregation functions take only milliseconds.

Again, note that the time scales on which a Web application operates are likely to seem miniscule, but the important relationship to consider is the relative time and processing power taken by instantiating a Web application as compared to running it. The combined total of these two steps might still be much less than a second, but when evaluating the source of performance bottlenecks, it would be counterproductive to concentrate on a process that takes up only a small percentage of the total runtime while ignoring parts of the process that take up the majority.

The Effect of Minor Optimization

Understandably, the first thing a Perl CGI programmer looks at when trying to make an application run faster is the program code, even when the time it takes to run that code is a fraction of the time spent loading and compiling it. The urge comes from Perl's reputation as a beginner language. If it's so easy to write a program in Perl, the idea goes, most early Perl programs must be written badly with many inefficiencies. This idea is particularly popular among programmers with a background in C. Much of the design work that goes into a C program addresses the need to optimize the program's memory footprint, processor load, and runtime.

From a Perl programmer's perspective, though, optimization is a secondary concern. The primary concern for many Perl programmers is to complete the tasks required of the program using as many existing Perl techniques and modules as possible. In this respect, Perl can be seen more accurately as a solution set rather than a simple programming language. The final result is to make creating a particular application possible with the tools Perl makes available. For Web applications, this becomes even more crucial; in many cases, it's more important for a Web programmer to meet a deadline and deliver a complete and functioning Web application than it is to achieve the greatest possible performance within that application. Performance is seen more as a pleasant side effect than a primary goal, especially when the goal is getting the job done, not merely getting it done faster.

Luckily, Perl does most of the optimizing for the programmer. Because Perl programs tend to use similar styles and techniques, many of those techniques have been quietly optimized over the years to give common programs a performance boost without the need to explicitly optimize the program. In addition, many Perl optimizations are expressed in programmatic hints that have made their way into desired Perl programming style.

Because of these subtle optimizations that Perl recognizes and encourages, it's actually possible to waste time modifying a particular piece of Perl code that already is being quietly optimized behind the scenes. In fact, it's more likely than not that optimizing code written in a Perl style by rewriting it using the rules of another language (such as C) might actually cause more harm than good.

There is an exception to this rule, but it involves major optimization outside the bounds of Perl rather than minor optimization within them. Modules can be written in C or other compiled languages for use with Perl, and within these modules, it's possible to optimize data structures and algorithms that give real performance improvements in cases in which Perl isn't capable of providing them on a general scale. Many common Perl modules use compiled code to provide performance improvements to often-used algorithms and data structures, so it's possible to benefit from these optimizations without having to develop them from scratch.

Optimization Can Increase Development Time

Web programming is a special discipline that spans a variety of skills, but it usually ends up falling between the cracks when it comes time to plan the budget. Web applications are likely to be misunderstood because the possibilities of Web sites are still being explored, and the timelines and decisions surrounding Web applications are likely to vary from nebulous to terrifying.

In a situation like this, the cost of optimizing a Web application can be prohibitive when compared to the potential benefits of spending that time improving the application by adding new features or fixing interface errors. Better yet, it would be a boon to Web programmers to find ways to improve performance across the board without incurring so much of a penalty to development time. In this way, simple optimizations that cause large improvements in performance are far more valuable than minor optimizations that cause only incremental performance increases. Minor optimization always can be carried out at a later time, but in most Web development environments, it's much more likely that new features and updated interfaces will create new work and tighter schedules before that point is ever reached.

An Exception: XS-Optimized Modules

One optimization that can make a real difference when dealing with Web applications is XS, which is the interface language provided by Perl for extending the language using compiled modules written in C. The idea is analogous to the programmer's ability in C to optimize algorithms by writing them in assembly language for a specific processor—a technique that is widely used in programs that need to perform specific calculations with high performance. XS bridges the gap between compiled C—with all the restrictions and processor-specific performance optimizations—and Perl.

Modules written using XS can provide noticeable improvements to both runtime and processor load by compiling optimized handlers for large data structures and complex algorithms that Perl would be less than efficient in handling by itself. It does this by enabling a module developer to specify the interface to a Perl module in the XS language, which is then compiled into a shared library. The XS language can contain complete C functions or it can reference existing C header files to provide a direct or indirect interface to those functions. After it is compiled, the shared library and its associated Perl wrapper module can be used as any other Perl module would be. This enables XS-optimized modules to replace existing all-Perl modules if there's a need to improve performance or to provide a link to existing C code.

Two areas in which XS noticeably improves performance is in database access and XML processing. In the case of database access, the Perl DBI module provides a Perl interface to database driver modules written in C. This enables the individual drivers for each database to be written using C-based interfaces, which are more commonly found in vendor-provided development toolkits than pure Perl interfaces would be. It also encourages driver modules to optimize the raw transfer of data to and from the Perl interface routines in the main DBI module, while providing a seamless interaction between the driver layer and those routines. For XML processing, similar XS modules enable Perl XML processors to use existing parsers and algorithms written for C applications, which optimize the handling of data structures that would otherwise be unwieldy if represented as native Perl references and variables.

Luckily, most of the common cases in which XS is needed already have been addressed by the modules that are most commonly used. DBI, as mentioned before, uses XS to optimize data transfer speeds whenever possible. XML parsing performance is improved using the expat parser (through the XML::Parser module), and interactions with the parsed documents can be optimized by using Xerces for Document Object Model (DOM) processing, Sablotron for XSLT transformations, and Orchard for XML stream handling. (More details on XML processing using Perl is available in Chapter 16.) In each case, the interface to the module is left up to Perl, and C is used simply to accelerate those parts of the modules that are likely to get the most frequent use.

Of course, additional XS modules can be created as the need arises to incorporate C libraries or compile code for performance enhancements. Graphics libraries, windowing toolkits, and proprietary communications protocols are some of the many uses that XS modules can be written to address. This frees the core of Perl to handle the interfaces between these libraries. The development of compiled modules using XS is a topic that is outside the scope of this book, but it can be noted here that most of these performance enhancements are similarly outside the realm of minor optimization and are generally exceptions to the rule.

Perl and C Differences

It would seem logical that the performance problems Perl sees are due to it being an interpreted language. There's no distinct compilation step seen when running a Perl program, so it's easy to come to the conclusion that the Perl compiler is actually an interpreter; it's also common to hear Perl referred to as a scripting language, which lumps it into the same category as shell scripting languages or high-level languages, such as Lisp. Both of these are interpreted and neither is known for high performance. These ideas are reinforced by Perl programmers' recent forays into graphic user interface programming, which usually results in an application that is less responsive overall than a comparable C program.

Most programs in the Web environment that can be compared to Perl CGI applications are both compiled and optimized for performance. The Web server, for instance, is almost always a compiled C program optimized to serve files to remote clients as fast as possible. Server modules, as well, are compiled in with the Web server and optimized to provide their services—such as authentication or encryption—with as little overhead as possible. Because these applications are optimized for performance and all are compiled, the connection between compiled applications and performance optimization is a strong and obvious one.

Writing a compiled application in C to avoid the overhead of interpreting Perl programs might seem to be the answer. This also would seem to enable more thorough optimizations to be made using the standard techniques developed for other compiled C programs. As common as it is, however, this answer is wrong. Compiled CGI applications are just as slow as their Perl brethren because the differences seen between Perl and C programs in other arenas aren't nearly as pronounced when encountered in Web applications.

Even if it did improve the performance of a Web application in use, compiling a Web application presents its own problems during development. Traditional single-user applications have slow development cycles that end when the application is shipped to a user. This comes from the complexity and robustness of end-user applications, such as Microsoft Word, that are required to perform many tasks in a coordinated fashion with few errors and very little chance to fix errors.

On the other hand, Web applications are likely to change rapidly, and they are likely to be created and modified by the same developers who use them. This comes from the Web tradition of editing text files—usually HTML or plain text—for immediate distribution by way of the Web site. Changes are made interactively as errors show up on the pages displayed. In many cases, a page is changed and changed again many times over the course of a few minutes as variations of page layout or word choice are made and tested in context.

Because Web applications are edited and tested in an environment that encourages near-instant feedback, the time spent compiling a C application after every change might become cumbersome when developing for the Web. Developers might be discouraged from trying different variations of an implementation because the time spent compiling each possibility would be prohibitive.

C CGI is Still Slow

Compiled CGI programs are still CGI programs. Chapter 5, "Architecture-Based Performance Loss," describes a bottleneck that can afflict any CGI process. A compiled C program is no exception; C programs still have to be loaded from disk and executed, program variables and data structures still have to be instantiated, and any files related to the program still have to be loaded fresh from disk each time the program runs.

Any optimizations a C process would normally benefit from in single-user use are still tiny in comparison to the overhead caused by CGI invocation of the program. In fact, the major difference in overhead between a CGI program written in C and a work-alike written in Perl is the compilation step necessary before the Perl program is executed. Because the Perl program has to pass through this compile step every time it is executed, and because the C program is compiled once before it is executed the first time and then run as a system binary from then on, it would seem that Perl could never catch up to the performance achievable by the equivalent C program. Fortunately, both compilation overhead and instantiation overhead are artifacts of the way CGI programs handle requests, so even this difference between Perl and C can easily be overcome by switching away from the CGI protocol.

C Optimizations Aren't Automatic

It's been said that it's easier to write a bad C program than it is to write a bad Perl program. Conversely, it's easier to write an optimized Perl program than it is to write an optimized C program. C enables great flexibility when developing a program, but this flexibility can be detrimental when writing Web applications.

Issues such as memory allocation and garbage collection are an anathema to Web programmers because they add complexity and difficulty to the application design process. A Web programmer doesn't want to have to deal with transitory memory leaks, data type mismatches, and system corruption due to incorrect memory allocation when there are more important issues with which to be concerned, including consistent user interfaces and easy access to data sources. Perl's assumptions might not produce the pinnacle of optimized code, but that is more than made up for by the sheer number of optimizations and corrections Perl makes that the Web programmer never has to know about.

Perl offers optimizations that are automatic, like the optimized regular expression engine and the XS-optimized DBI module, which interfaces with a database (see Chapter 14, "Database-Backed Web Sites"). In Perl 5.6, for instance, many optimizations were made to the Perl compiler itself, which affected common Perl keywords, such as `sort`, by increasing the optimization of nonstandard ways of calling the function. These improvements are present in each version of every module or core release made available.

Because of the high-level abstraction inherent in developing a Perl program, future optimizations to Perl will be utilized by Perl-based applications automatically. This can't be said for a compiled C program for two reasons. First, the optimizations present in a particular version of a C compiler or in a particular version of a system library aren't likely to be so common as to improve the performance of all—or even a majority of—the Web applications written in C. Even if that was the case, though, the applications would have to be recompiled against the new version of the compiler or libraries, which requires a separate step to be performed each time the improvements were made available.

C Programs Still Connect to a Database

One similarity between Perl programs and C programs when creating Web applications is the supporting applications and services to which either application would need to connect. Because a Web application is likely to interact with system resources such as database servers, network support applications, groupware, and other server applications, a Web application written in Perl is likely to rely on transactions between these system applications as much as it relies on internal processing within the Perl application. Similarly, a Web application written in C or Java would have to integrate the same system-level applications, so any bottlenecks caused by system applications would cause the same performance problems for Web applications written in either Perl or C.

A database server, for example, is going to be accessed in similar ways by both a Perl application and a C application. Either one is likely to use the same underlying network interface because Perl module developers generally use the C libraries made available by database server developers. Even if the modules so created behave differently from the standpoint of the programmer who is developing Web applications in Perl, transactions between the database and the Perl application are still likely to be identical to those between the database server and a C application. This is especially true for database servers such as Oracle that rely heavily on network protocols to facilitate database interaction because the network protocols bridge the gap between any specific implementations of the protocols in C or Perl.

One important difference between database access in C and Perl is the ease with which Perl applications can be written to access a database. Database access from Perl has become both efficient and easy to develop in the past few years due to the DBI interface module, which creates a generalized database for use within Perl programs. Optimized interfaces to each supported database can then be written to conform to the DBI specification, which enables database driver developers to concentrate on the details of interfacing with a particular database without having to develop an understandable application program interface (API) for use by application developers. It also enables application developers to learn one database interaction API and apply it to any database made available to DBI. The DBI module is covered in more detail in Chapter 14.

Java, a language commonly used for Web development, illustrates this myth perfectly. Although Java is a precompiled language, database performance from a Java application is likely to be slower overall than database performance from a Perl application. This is due in large part to the available Java Database Connection (JDBC) drivers being used to access database servers from Java servlets and Java applications. These drivers aren't nearly as optimized for performance as are their C or Perl counterparts, so any application that sees heavy database use is likely to be slowed considerably by the inefficiency of JDBC drivers.

Misleading Benchmarks

Another myth when testing a Perl CGI program for Web performance is that reasonable information can be garnered from the benchmark facilities provided within Perl. The mere presence of these tools would seem to indicate that they would be useful in diagnosing the cause of performance loss, but the tools themselves aren't suited to diagnosing the problems a Web application would face. In fact, most of the results given when using these tools on a Web application are confusing at best and ludicrous at worst.

Perl benchmarks are designed only to test the relative performance of algorithms within the scope of a Perl program. These benchmarks, even when run against an entire Perl program, would measure only runtime and would completely ignore compile time and the other steps necessary to run a program. Because those other steps are much more likely to affect the overall performance of a Web application, the results themselves are useless even when they seem to make sense.

Benchmarking also doesn't take the special nature of Web requests into account. Differing connection speeds cause variable effects on a Web server, which in turn can change the performance characteristics of the Web application being accessed. Because these effects can be duplicated only within the Web server environment itself, the aspects of the applications that need to be tested are outside the scope of the benchmarking tools. Better tools are available, but they would have to operate outside of Perl entirely.

Benchmarks Measure Only Runtime

One common mistake when benchmarking a Perl CGI Web application is using the Benchmark module to time the program from start to finish. It would seem reasonable that capturing the time when the program starts and the time when the program ends, and then subtracting the former from the latter, would give a reasonably accurate measure of the total time the program takes to run. Benchmark.pm provides a group of convenience methods that gives a precise system time that is partitioned into user and system CPU time as well as "wallclock" or perceived time. It also can perform calculations on pairs of these times to determine the difference between them. Listing 8.1 gives an example of how Benchmark is used in such a fashion.

Listing 8.1   **Benchmarking a Program**

```
01 #!/usr/bin/perl
02
03 require 5.6.0;
04 use warnings;
05 use strict;
06
07 use Benchmark;
08
09 my $t1 = Benchmark->new();
10
11 print "Content-type: text/plain\n\n";
12
13 print "This is a CGI script...\n";
14
15 for my $x (1..99)
16 {
17    my $square = $x * $x;
18    print "The square of $x is $square.\n";
19 }
20
21 print "...which does something silly.\n";
22
23 my $t2 = Benchmark->new();
24
25 my $total_time = timediff($t2,$t1);
26
27 print "\nThis script took ". timestr($total_time)   . " to run.\n\n";
```

The program in Listing 8.1 illustrates a basic way in which the Benchmark module might be used to determine the total runtime of a program. Lines 03 through 05 include the basic reference checks and modules that are essential to any well-written Perl program. Line 07 includes the Benchmark module itself, and line 09 instantiates a new Benchmark time object, which is assigned to the variable $t1. (Note that this object is more complex than the time stamp given by the built-in localtime function, but for the purposes of this program, it can be thought of in the same way.) The time stored in $t1 is the start time of the program proper. It should be noticed at this point that this isn't really the start time of the benchmarking program, but the start time of the first accessible part of the program; it isn't feasible to get a time before this point.

Lines 11 through 21 of the program make up the core of the program being benchmarked. In theory, if we weren't benchmarking the program, these lines would comprise the program in its entirety. In this case, the program does very little and does it pretty inefficiently; it prints a line of text, uses a simple but inelegant algorithm to determine the square of each number from 1 to 99, and then prints each result. Line 21 declares the folly of such an enterprise and ends the program proper. This section of the program could be replaced with any Perl program, CGI or otherwise.

After the central program has finished, line 23 instantiates a second Benchmark time object to capture the moment. Because we now have the start time and end time of the program, line 25 uses the `timediff` function provided by the Benchmark module to determine the difference between time `$t2` and time `$t1`, which is returned as a third time object and stored in `$total_time`. Line 27 then converts that into a string and displays it.

The first problem with timing a program in this fashion becomes apparent as soon as the program is run. Running this program from the command line produces the following output:

```
Content-type: text/plain

This is a CGI script...
The square of 1 is 1.
The square of 2 is 4.
The square of 3 is 9.
...
The square of 97 is 9409.
The square of 98 is 9604.
The square of 99 is 9801.
...which does something silly.

This script took 0 wallclock secs ( 0.01 usr + 0.00 sys = 0.01 CPU) to
run.
```

Something doesn't look right in this output; the last line states that the program took no time to run. As it turns out, the Benchmark module records "wallclock" time only in increments of seconds, so a program like this—which takes only a few milliseconds to run—won't even register as having taken any time. Also, it would appear that this process required only 10 milliseconds of CPU time, which gives some indication of the load on the processor caused by executing the program; however, that still doesn't translate to any meaningful demarcation of time that could be used to test the overall performance of a Web application.

It might be argued that the program itself does nothing useful, causing the output to be skewed toward the zero direction. Unfortunately, most common Web applications return a similar value because the time taken by Perl to execute this type of application is usually less than a second. For instance, substituting Listing 7.7 from Chapter 7, "Perl for the Web," gives very similar output:

```
Content-type: text/plain

Content-Type: text/html

<!DOCTYPE HTML PUBLIC "-//IETF//DTD HTML//EN">
<HTML><HEAD><TITLE>SQL Database Viewer</TITLE>
</HEAD><BODY>
...
</BODY></HTML>
This script took 0 wallclock secs ( 0.32 usr + 0.00 sys = 0.32 CPU) to
run.
```

Again, very little information was actually given about the total runtime of the program, even though the CPU time taken by this program appears to be about 30 times greater than the previous program. It would seem that even a program that does real work should take so little time as to be practically instantaneous, so the idea that Perl CGI is slow would seem to have no merit.

No Internal Benchmarks for Compile Time

Benchmarks like this only tell half the story when dealing with a Perl program. The idea of benchmarking a compiled program from within the program itself would make some sense; there isn't much that happens before the program is run, and the runtime of the program (or parts of the program) is important only if it's noticeable to the single user interacting with it.

In Perl, however, steps that occur before the benchmarking section of the program is ever reached cause much of the effective runtime and processor load. Notably, the time taken by loading the Perl compiler and compiling the program are ignored completely by benchmarks of this type. Because the Perl compiler also compiles the benchmark code, there's no way to start the timer earlier and catch the time spent before the core program is reached. The beginning of the program in terms of source code is executed only after it is compiled at runtime. Before that point, no Perl can be executed because it hasn't yet been compiled.

It's not possible to get around this problem by embedding the entire program inside a separate timing program, as was the case with Listing 8.1. Any code embedded in this way is considered a part of the main Perl program, and it is compiled at the same time. As a result, the Perl compiler has already been loaded and the program has already been compiled before any embedded code is reached and executed, so the timing results still would exclude compile time. In fact, there is no way to get a benchmark of the total runtime of a Perl program from within itself or an encompassing Perl program. In all cases, the time spent loading the Perl compiler and compiling the program falls outside the scope of the Perl-based timing code.

There are ways to trick the Perl compiler into compiling the timed code after the rest of the program is running, but they result in benchmarks that are so unique as to be useless. You can compile and evaluate the code at runtime using eval, for instance, by loading the program off disk, assigning it to a string variable, and processing it with `eval`. Tricks like these are made possible because Perl enables the program to take a finer grain of control over sections of code, if necessary. (Applications like this are explored in Chapter 9, "The Power of Persistence.") However, there's no guarantee that the process used to compile and execute the code in this modified way will have any relationship to the process used by Perl to compile and execute the program independently; thus, any benchmarks given by this process would not be indicative of real performance. This problem is compounded further by the fact that time taken by loading the Perl compiler is still being ignored.

The Effect of Connect Time

An additional factor in application performance that shouldn't be ignored is the speed of visitors' Internet connections and the time it takes to connect to the site and retrieve the results of a page. Connection speed can affect site performance in more ways than one, and it's even possible for visitors with slow connections to disrupt the performance of an otherwise-fast site for visitors with more bandwidth. It's very difficult to test a site based on connection types, but considering the effects in a general sense might avoid some surprises.

When benchmarking a Web application written in Perl, it's easy to forget that the application will be accessed through a network connection that doesn't provide instantaneous access to the information being provided. A Web application might respond in a matter of milliseconds, but high latency between the visitor's computer and the Web server might add seconds to the time it takes to establish a connection. Independent of latency, available bandwidth might be limited to the point in which page contents returned by the Web application take even more precious seconds to be transferred downstream to the visitor. Although there isn't much that can be done within Perl to improve the performance of an application over a slow network connection, it's still important to keep this kind of overhead in mind when determining whether an application is providing reasonable performance at a particular rate. (This idea is discussed in more detail in Chapter 15, "Testing Site Performance.")

A slow connection can affect other visitors' experience as well. Depending on the Web server and the Web application, it's possible that an application will have to stay connected and running as long as it's processing the request, which would include the time necessary to transmit the results back to the visitor's computer. This means that an application that technically takes only a few milliseconds to process a request can remain open hundreds of times longer while transferring the results. This prevents that server process from answering any other requests in the interim. If enough of these slow requests come in simultaneously to clog the pipes, it's possible that visitors with fast connections could be kept waiting for a connection to open up before their requests can even start to be processed. Situations like these are more common than they should be, unfortunately, because network congestion can create an environment in which otherwise fast connections can become slow enough to create the same effect.

Slow upstream connections can become as big a performance drain as slow downstream connections. A Web application that requires large files or other data streams to be sent from the client to the Web server for processing can suffer doubly from a slow connection speed. A forum application that accepts long text submissions, for instance, will have to wait until the entire request is transmitted to the server before it's possible to start processing the request. Because the Web server process is occupied while this is happening, and then occupied while the information is being processed and the result is being returned through the same slow connection, it's possible to have a Web application that posts decent benchmarks in local testing take long enough to time out the visitor's Web browser connection.

This kind of upstream lag is very common due to the asymmetric nature of most DSL and cable modem connections; a connection that has a decent downstream transfer rate might have only a tenth of that bandwidth open for an upstream response. Because upstream and downstream connections can interfere with each other on both the client and the server, it's doubly important to check the performance of a Web application under slow network circumstances.

Unfortunately, it's very difficult to test a site based on connection speeds. Most benchmarking applications assume that the site should be tested by overloading it with as many requests as possible as quickly as possible. With these, the goal is to saturate all available bandwidth with simultaneous requests and see how many requests the Web application can process before losing performance or shutting down entirely. In many cases, it's not even possible to set preferences on the benchmarking application to test connections that are slower than the one used for testing. Generally, the test connection is a LAN with hundreds of times more bandwidth than a site visitor would have. On top of that, it's very difficult to tell the average speed of visitor connections—even after the fact. Chapter 15 discusses a few ways to simulate slower connections while maintaining a reasonable server load.

Database Benchmarks Expect Different Circumstances

Despite the lip service paid to testing the performance of Web applications, in practice they aren't likely to be tested or benchmarked frequently. Database servers, on the other hand, are some of the most aggressively benchmarked applications available. As a result, it would seem that the task of performance testing the database-enabled aspects of a Web application has already been done to satisfaction. Most database benchmarks take for granted circumstances that are very different from the kind of usage patterns a Web application would impose on a database server; thus, benchmarks produced in regular server testing—even those from third-party groups—are likely to be inadequate when testing the performance of a database in terms of the Web applications it's supporting.

Databases are likely to be benchmarked in terms of transactions per minute. Few databases are likely to be compared in terms of the number of seconds it takes to connect, however, so the connection time from a CGI application still has to be factored in when testing the performance of a database-backed Web application.

The usage patterns of a Web application are unlike most database transactions. Most database front-end applications are likely to access the database in a straightforward fashion; they connect to the server, log in, and start processing a stream of transactions in response to interactive commands. When testing a database in this context, the most important aspects would be the number of concurrent connections, the maximum rate at which transactions can be processed, and the total bandwidth available to returning results. These would correspond respectively to the number of users who could access the system at the same time, the complexity of the programs they could use to access the database, and the amount of time they would have to wait for a complete response. This makes it more reasonable to test the database by having a group of identical applications access the database simultaneously, process as many transactions as possible to determine the maximum transaction rate, and retrieve as much data as quickly as possible to determine the maximum transfer rate.

With a Web application, however, the usage pattern would be very different. A CGI Web application is likely to connect to a server, log in, process a single transaction, retrieve a subset of the results, and disconnect, only to reconnect again a moment later. As a result, testing in a Web context would need to concentrate more on the total time taken by connecting to and disconnecting from the database, the overhead due to logging in and processing a transaction, and the elapsed time necessary to retrieve the necessary subset of data needed by the application. (Chapter 14 has more detail about how to make Web applications access a database in a more continuous manner.) As it turns out, the best way to simulate such odd request patterns is by running the Web application itself in production testing.

The Real Cost of Optimization

When I first went to a meeting of the San Diego Perl Mongers, a local Perl user group, another attendee explained a problem he was having with the performance of a Web application. Bill was working for a university in San Diego as a Web programmer, and one of his duties was the care and feeding of an application used to process class registrations through the school's Web site. At the start of every quarter, the site would get pounded by traffic as the students all logged in at the same time to search through and register for classes. Unfortunately, the application wasn't able to handle the traffic, and it responded to the flood of requests slowly—if at all. This made the students furious with the site, and it caught the attention of Bill's superiors.

He had inherited this application from a previous Webmaster. It was written in Perl for use with CGI, and the application itself was full of twists, convoluted functions, and hard-to-follow pathways. Bill was having a devil of a time just understanding the program enough to fix errors or add features. So, he had no idea how to optimize it to make it react more efficiently to the temporary surges of traffic it was likely to see. Previous attempts had been made to improve the speed of the program by optimizing the code in sections of it, but none had improved the application's performance to the point where it was usable under load. (Unfortunately, they didn't realize this until the next registration period started and more students got angry at the system.)

continues

continued

At some point, the decision was made to rewrite the entire application in a compiled language such as Java. As a result, Bill's job wasn't to fix the application completely, but to patch parts of it wherever possible to improve performance while the new application was being written. With this in mind, he latched on to an idea that the database accessed by his Web application was itself slow, so if it was possible to increase the performance of the database, it might be possible to improve the performance of the application to the point where it was usable. Bill came to the Perl Mongers meeting with this goal in mind, but he ended up getting a tutorial on the mechanics of CGI instead.

Bill's problem was not that the application itself was slow, but that it was being overwhelmed by overhead whenever a large group of users accessed it simultaneously. Having read this book up to this point, you should recognize that Bill's problem wasn't going to be solved by tuning the database or optimizing sections of code, and it wasn't going to be solved by translating the whole mess into Java, either. The crux of the problem was that Bill's program was running as a CGI process, which by now should send shivers of apprehension down your spine. The overhead of starting, compiling, and instantiating his complex program and connecting to an already-overloaded database was completely overshadowing the main task of the program—processing the students' requests. At that meeting, Bill was told what you've read here: tuning the application itself wouldn't help more than incrementally, but running the application in a persistent environment would give exponential performance improvements, especially in the circumstances he was seeing.

I don't know if Bill was ever able to act on that knowledge, or whether the university eventually did rewrite the entire application in Java. Hopefully clear heads and reasonable performance testing prevailed. I do know that I've seen the same situation many times since then, which is the main reason why I've written this book.

Summary

When it comes to Perl CGI, performance myths abound. Most people place the blame for poor performance on Perl because it's not precompiled or hand-optimized, but in truth, neither of these factors has much effect on CGI performance. Optimizing the runtime of Perl programs doesn't help (aside from a few exceptions), and rewriting Web applications in C doesn't make a difference if the application is still being called through CGI. When determining the cause of a performance problem, internal Perl benchmarks are likely to give misleading data because there's no way to add in the compilation and instantiation time required to get a complete picture of how long a CGI Web application really takes from start to finish.

9

The Power of Persistence

CHAPTER 8, "PERFORMANCE MYTHS," COVERED THE ASPECTS of Web applications that won't help the performance of a CGI application, but it begs this question: "Where *can* Perl performance be improved on a Web server?" The answer is simple: Don't exit. Another word for this idea is "persistence;" a persistent program is one that hangs around as long as it's needed without having to restart. Each new request to a persistent program is handled as part of a continuous stream instead of in fits and starts.

Implementing the solution is trickier than it looks. The core assumption of the Common Gateway Interface (CGI) and CGI programs is that the program is called, it responds to the call, and it is tossed away. Thus, the first thing to do when setting up persistence for a Web application is to replace the CGI interface entirely. CGI isn't set up to work in a persistent form. CGI has no way of accessing a program that's already running because it assumes it is starting a program. The replacement for this protocol has to provide the same bridge between the Web server and Web applications that CGI does, with the new assumption that it always is accessing programs that are already running. After that happens, it's still necessary to set up the persistent application itself. Because Web applications written for use with CGI assume that they are started fresh for a specific request, it's likely that an application that works well in a CGI environment needs some work to be made persistent.

There are a few ways to implement a persistent interface between a Web server and applications. The Web server usually provides one of its own, known as the server *application program interface (API)*, which treats applications as extensions of the server process itself to be started at the same time. Another way of implementing a persistent interface is by using a Web server extension to start and manage external programs as they are accessed by incorporating them into the extension at runtime. Perl makes this possible by providing a mechanism by which external programs can be compiled into a Perl program while it's running. A third way to achieve persistence is by using a network-like protocol to communicate between the Web server and an external process, which contains the Web application. Additional forms of persistent Perl applications can be created using a mix of these three techniques as well.

These changes don't just affect one aspect of the CGI performance bottleneck. When applications are persistent, it's possible to tune performance even further by taking real advantage of the hardware and environment. Persistent applications can be clustered to use memory more efficiently, cached to provide instant response, and balanced across physical servers to provide high availability. Additional aspects of the applications, such as database access, can be made persistent after the applications themselves are persistent. We discuss this in Chapter 14, "Database-Backed Web Sites."

Basically, Don't Exit

The principle behind persistent applications is simple, but it's not simple enough to go without some explanation. In fact, for most Perl programmers, the idea of continuing after a request is fulfilled is foreign. Perl programs are generally written with a straight path from beginning to end, aside from a few loops and conditionals. Even system utilities written in Perl are designed to run once, from beginning to end, to provide one result, and to exit. This way of behaving comes from Perl's roots as a command-line scripting language for UNIX systems; many UNIX programs simply accept arguments, process them, and return the result before exiting.

Interactive programs don't operate this way. Familiar programs, such as Microsoft Word or the GNU Image Manipulation Program (GIMP), load all their program code into memory when the program starts, and then execute program sections as they are needed. They do this by way of an event loop, which is basically a program loop that doesn't specify the conditions for its own end. Instead, it continuously checks for the occurrence of system events, including keystrokes, mouse clicks, and network requests. Events usually cause parts of the program to be executed, but in some cases, events are handled by additional code called *plug-ins*. These plug-ins are provided by third-party vendors. These program modules are loaded into memory with the program at runtime and serve as extensions to the core functions of the program.

GIMP and Word Revisited

As stated in Chapter 5, "Architecture-Based Performance Loss," common programs with graphic user interfaces (such as GIMP and Word) would be unusable if they used the CGI model for handling user requests. If either program ended after every keystroke or mouse action and started up again with each new one, the user would spend most of his or her time waiting for the program to perform even simple tasks. The program would have great trouble keeping track of state information, too; any action the program performed would have memory only of the steps performed during the current request. As a result, external data structures would be needed to store information about the current size of the main window, the position of the cursor in a document, or even the current document being worked on. Writing an application that works this way would be ludicrous; thus, most applications that interact with a user are persistent as a matter of course.

How do these programs get consistent performance? Basically, they stay put. Very little of the program's structure is dependent on any one action, so the core of the program can stay constant while specific routines take care of incoming requests. This is very different from a CGI application, which can't be very complex. CGI applications have to start from scratch with each request, so they're usually written to perform a single task with no data structures shared between instances or between different aspects of the interface seen by a user.

Persistence improves these applications in many ways. One thing a persistent application can count on is the capability to set up complex or time-consuming data structures only once—usually when the program starts up—and have them available from that point forward. Word, for instance, needs to load a dictionary for spell checking, which might take up megabytes of storage (either on disk or in memory). It would be prohibitive to create such a massive data structure every time spelling is checked, especially if it's checked after every new word is typed. Instead, the entire dictionary is loaded into a standard memory structure before the program starts executing, so any further action taken has that structure at its disposal without having to create it. Many such data structures can be created when the program starts up, and each one enriches the possibilities of what a program can do as its running.

Another difference between Word or GIMP and a CGI application is that the former can take much longer to compile without incurring performance penalties at runtime. GIMP, for instance, can be compiled once when new versions are released, and then used a thousand times before the next version is compiled. Because of this, compilation can take much longer than a user is willing to wait for the program to start because compilation happens separately from runtime. For a Perl program, this isn't possible—Perl assumes that a program is compiled from source code every time it is run. However, it is possible to use the same principle when running Perl applications in a Web server environment. As long as an application is compiled before the user first interacts with it, that application can have the same benefits of a long compile time that a compiled program enjoys. This idea is explored in greater detail in the "More Power: Clustering, Precaching, and Balancing" section later in this chapter.

Word and GIMP also provide the means for additional code to be run within the same persistent environment. This gives users and third-party vendors the ability to write simpler programs that take advantage of the environment provided by the program to perform more complex tasks. Plug-ins for GIMP, for instance, can use any GIMP tool by invoking its corresponding function call from the plug-in scripting language. The languages GIMP provides for these plug-ins include C, a custom language called Script-Fu, and Perl. Using these languages, plug-ins can be written that perform complex operations on the current document using the GIMP tools to achieve an overall effect. A plug-in written to create drop shadows behind an image, for instance, might invoke GIMP functions to duplicate the image, fill the duplicate with black, and then blur the duplicate. Because the plug-in is running persistently in the same environment as GIMP, it appears to the user as though the plug-in is simply another function provided by GIMP.

The Event Loop

The way most programs handle the simple task of continuing to run is through an event loop. The event loop is a continuous loop that cycles through some trivial task while waiting for a request to come in from the keyboard, mouse, or other input stream. GIMP, for instance, gladly sits and does nothing if no user input is given to it; however, it springs to life the moment a key is pressed or the pointer is moved or clicked. Each keystroke or click is then dealt with as though it were a singular event, with a specific set of input arguments and a specific result. For instance, clicking the About menu choice when using GIMP is a single event that causes a window containing program information to be displayed. Most event loops are designed to process many events at essentially the same time, either by keeping a list of events that need to be processed or by processing them in parallel through simultaneous subprocesses called *threads*.

To deal with events as they occur, each possible event is assigned a subroutine or program section called an *event handler*, which is responsible for performing an action. For instance, the event handler assigned to the About menu choice event might be a subroutine called show_about_box() that displays a window with a graphic and some text. Event handlers can perform more complex tasks as well, including changing the program environment and operating on the current document. In fact, event handlers do most of the work of a program such as GIMP because almost all program functions are the result of events.

As discussed in the previous section, plug-ins for a program such as GIMP are treated as parts of the main program. In fact, each plug-in serves as a special kind of event handler, which is invoked when the corresponding menu choice is made and given the current document as a working environment. Plug-ins might be written in a language other than the main program, though, so it's necessary for common program functions to be translated into the plug-in language and made available to the plug-in environment. This set of program functions is known as an API, which comprises the complete set of functions any plug-in can perform. In the case of GIMP, the API is integrated into the Script-Fu plug-in language and offered as a set of documented Perl modules that can be used when writing a GIMP plug-in in Perl. The API encapsulates all the functionality of the main program that is accessible by each plug-in, plus the requirements of a plug-in program that enable it to be called by the main program as an event handler.

A Web Application as a Single Plug-In

One way to get persistence in a Web application is to write a Web application the way you would write a plug-in module for GIMP, with the Web server taking the role of the central program. Like a plug-in for GIMP, a Web server plug-in serves as an event handler for events received by the main program. The Web server itself serves as an event loop, processing requests as they come in—from the network in this case, rather than from a keyboard or mouse—and then distributing the requests to handlers assigned to each class of events. Web applications written in this fashion are accessed the way in which the Web server itself is accessed. The new code becomes an extension of the Web server and becomes persistent as a result.

Of course, rewriting the Web server as part of the application—instead of the other way around—is possible, but not advised. Web servers such as Apache have been optimized over the course of years to serve Web pages and related files as quickly as possible. This functionality would be difficult to duplicate in a Web application, and it's likely that the new implementation would be significantly slower at serving the Web application. In addition, standard Web files that include static pages and images are likely to be served with much less efficiency than a dedicated Web server would be able to give, so the overall performance of the Web site would suffer appreciably.

The Web Server API

A plug-in Web application is integrated into the Web server through an API that is like the one used by GIMP. Different Web servers have different APIs, including Apache API, Netscape Server API (NSAPI) for Netscape and related servers, and Internet Server API (ISAPI) for Microsoft Internet Information Server (IIS) and related servers. Plug-ins written to address an API can rely on the Web server to listen for network traffic and route that traffic accordingly, invoking the plug-in when necessary to handle incoming request events that warrant it. In turn, the plug-in is responsible for retrieving the request and related environment information and returning the result through the same API.

Because Web server applications use the server process as an event loop, they can rely on some basic assumptions:

- The Web server handles each request as it comes in, whether by threading the request handlers or by keeping a list of requests to be processed. As a result, no requests are lost due to a busy handler.

- The Web server calls plug-in code as needed to process requests, with all information needed to process that request provided by the given environment. As a result, no additional programming is needed to provide network listeners or similar constructs.

- The Web server provides an internally consistent set of methods for accessing information about the request and the system environment. The server also provides standard functions for modifying and delivering the response to the client.

One benefit of writing Web applications as plug-ins to the Web server is the tight integration this affords. Complex applications that take up a large fraction of the requests a Web server processes are good candidates for this kind of implementation because more of the Web server's tasks can be taken over and customized by the plug-in. For instance, an application might be designed to respond to requests for HTML pages by translating XML files on disk into HTML. (Similar applications are discussed in Chapter 16, "XML and Content Management.") For this application, it would be useful to override the Web server's default way of translating page request URLs into filenames. You would do this by processing those URLs indirectly within the Web application plug-in itself. The Web server API is likely to provide functions that make this possible without requiring the plug-in to perform other functions provided by the Web server.

On the other hand, that tight integration is also a major drawback to writing Web applications as Web server plug-ins. Because plug-ins are written to integrate with a specific Web server API, most applications written this way are incompatible with any other Web server API. In fact, some Web server APIs change from one version of the server to the next, so Web applications written to one version of the API do not work under subsequent versions of the same server. This incompatibility is worse for plug-ins written in compiled languages because they are likely to be incompatible even with the same Web server running on a different platform. All these incompatibilities can provide a major obstacle to deploying a Web application in a diverse environment, and they can make the application a barrier to upgrading the Web server architecture at a later time.

Another drawback to writing plug-ins based on an API is the steep learning curve for programmers with a CGI background who make the switch to API programming. The Web server API provides a fine grain of control over all the Web server's functions, but inherent in this control is the expectation that the programmer specifies explicitly every aspect of the Web application's interaction with the Web server and the network. Most CGI-style programmers—especially those who use Perl—are used to environments that assist application development by preprocessing input variables and buffering and post-processing output. These programmers sometimes balk at a whole new layer of interaction that has to be addressed by the Web application. Even if Web programmers are up to the task, the relative merits of better performance or shorter development cycles should be weighed before deciding to develop a Web server plug-in. (Other alternatives are discussed in the "Web Applications in One Modular Program" and "Web Applications as Persistent Separate Programs" sections later in this chapter.)

Apache API, NSAPI, and ISAPI

The Apache Web server, the most popular server at the time of this writing, provides an API in the C language. Apache plug-in modules can be incorporated into the server in one of two ways, at compile time or at runtime as a *Dynamic Shared Object (DSO)*. After Apache is compiled for a specific system, it is possible to provide modules that are compiled directly into the program. Because it's not always feasible to recompile the entire Web server when a plug-in Web application changes, Apache provides the ability to write plug-ins as DSOs, which are compiled as separate object modules and relinked to the Web server at runtime. The DSO interface does not provide any additional portability, however, so DSOs are not exempt from the main drawback of API-dependent plug-ins. An Apache DSO module still has to be compiled against the precise version of Apache with which it is used because the server API is likely to change between versions.

A third way to write plug-in modules for Apache is provided indirectly by the mod_perl module. This module provides the entire Apache API as a set of Perl functions, similar to the way in which GIMP provides its API to Perl. With the Perl version of the API, it's possible to write Perl plug-in modules for Apache, which are compiled into the Web server at runtime. These plug-ins are treated the same as DSO or compiled C plug-ins, so they have most of the same benefits and drawbacks as any other API-dependent application. (mod_perl is discussed in greater depth in Chapter 10, "Tools for Perl Persistence.") One benefit to writing plug-in modules in Perl, however, is the portability across operating systems that Perl offers—plug-ins written in Perl for Apache under Linux, for instance, probably work without modification under FreeBSD. Portability across versions also is more likely because the process of translating the server API into Perl functions adds inertia to the interface and potentially slows the pace of changes. Neither of these benefits is set in stone, however, because the choice of when to make changes still is up to the API designer.

Assigning an Apache plug-in module to a class of events is done by configuring the Apache server to use the module for a defined group of requests. A module might be assigned to handle requests in a particular virtual directory, or it might be assigned to handle any request with a particular file extension in the URL. One familiar module that works in both ways is mod_cgi, the module that processes CGI requests for the

Apache server. The mod_cgi module usually is assigned to handle any requests to the virtual `cgi-bin` directory, and it might also be configured to handle any request for files with the `.cgi` extension. As a result, both of the following requests would be handled by mod_cgi:

```
http://www.example.com/cgi-bin/sql-query.pl
http://www.example.com/forum/build_hash.cgi
```

Like Apache, the Netscape line of Web servers (sometimes called iPlanet servers) provides a server API for plug-in applications. The programming API for this server is appropriately named the Netscape Server API, or NSAPI. NSAPI modules are implemented similarly to Apache API modules, with the Netscape server providing the event loop and the plug-in modules serving as event handlers. At the time of this writing, NSAPI servers do not provide a Perl interface to the API, so the NSAPI interface is tangential to the scope of this book. However, some solutions for persistent Perl on Netscape and iPlanet servers are listed in Chapter 10.

Microsoft IIS also supports a similar plug-in programming interface, called ISAPI. Again, at the time of this writing, no ISAPI servers have a direct interface to the API in Perl, but persistent Perl solutions for ISAPI servers are detailed in Chapter 10. Incidentally, support for ISAPI is slated to be included in version 2.0 of the Apache Web server for Windows.

Threading and Perl 5.6

Threading is a method of event loop processing by which events can be handled by the same process at the same time by executing program sections in parallel. The Netscape and Microsoft IIS Web servers are threaded, and the NSAPI and ISAPI interfaces also enable plug-in code to be threaded. As of version 2.0, the Apache Web server enables threading within the server process.

At first glance, threading a Perl environment would seem to be an excellent idea. Threads would increase the amount of compiled code shared between processes and would reduce the overall memory requirements of Perl processes. It would be simpler to create shared data structures if it could be assumed that all requests would be handled within the same memory space. Also, persistent connections could be pooled between threads to reduce the total number of connections necessary at any given time. Overall, the benefits of a threaded model are very enticing.

However, the threading model requires both the Perl environment and all code running within it to be *thread-safe* code, or code that behaves consistently with or without threads. Support for threaded code is present in the current version of Perl (5.6 as this is written), but Perl threading is still considered experimental and many modules are not written to be thread-safe. This is due in part to the fact that threading models are platform-specific, so duplicating the same threading behavior in all varieties of Perl has been difficult. Some modules have had success in cleaning out any code that isn't thread-safe, but not all modules are thread-safe for all platforms. Because thread safety in Perl programs can be a concern in terms of application stability, its generally advised to avoid threaded Perl environments for Web applications until Perl threading support is more mature.

Web Applications in One Modular Program

Another way to achieve persistence in a Web application is by writing a single Web application in parts and incorporating the parts into the main process at runtime.

This method enables each program section to be written more simply than a combined Web application based on the Web server API would be written. Aspects of persistent API programming that are common to each application can be written once in a core translation module, and additional code for specific functions can be written in separate programs that are combined implicitly at runtime. For instance, Perl programs written to address the standard input and standard output devices can be combined with a translator application. This translator application preprocesses request input through the server API and buffers the standard output device and post-processes it back into API calls. In fact, there are already Perl modules, such as Apache::Registry, that perform this task.

This also enables many different Web applications to be combined into a single persistent application, which enables the development of a persistent Web application to more closely follow the way in which CGI-based applications and Web sites are designed. As discussed in the "The Nature of CGI" section in Chapter 5, CGI applications are developed using the same one-file-per-request paradigm that governs HTML files. Because each page is developed to address one request, it would be unwieldy to redevelop these individual applications into a monolithic application that handles classes of requests based on factors other than the page URL. If this type of application didn't rely on Web conventions for filenames and directory structures, an alternative organization would have to be developed anyway.

Subroutine-Based Execution

The API interface to a Web server can be accessed directly by writing plug-in modules, or it can be used indirectly by incorporating individual CGI-style programs into a larger Perl program, which then can be used directly as a plug-in module. The key to this translation is the capability of Perl programs to rewrite another Perl program as a subroutine and compile the subroutine into the main program. Perl provides the `eval` keyword to accomplish all sorts of program modification and recompilation at runtime. Compiling code with `eval` at runtime makes it possible to process the source code of a Perl program as though it were any string, modify it for use as a Perl subroutine, and then compile it into the main program as though it had been present all along.

In addition, Perl namespaces provide a convenient way to keep track of code that has been compiled into the program environment. After modification, each subroutine generally is placed in a package named for the original program file. This enables code to be reused by accessing the same subroutine in the same namespace again, which provides the full performance benefits of persistence without having to explicitly write code that accesses the API directly. By adding an additional processing step, which translates nonPerl structures into Perl code before compiling, this method also can be used to process template code or Perl code embedded into HTML pages. Applications of this method, such as Apache::Registry, HTML::Mason, and VelociGen, are discussed in more detail in Chapter 10.

Monolithic Application Drawbacks

Even though the source files for this method of persistence might be stored separately on disk, the result at runtime is in fact a single running program, known as a *monolithic application*. This kind of application architecture is closer to the single-program architecture found in Web applications written for a specific server API than it is to the multiple-program architecture described in the "Web Applications as Persistent Separate Programs" section of this chapter. This is true even if the program changes over time and loads sections of itself interactively as new page types are requested from the network. The server process still shares one memory space between all parts of itself and requires no communication protocols other than the server API. The program is a monolithic application even if many copies of the server process are running at any one time because each copy has the potential to be a duplicate of all the others. In addition, the processes can't communicate with each other after they have been started.

Keeping the program together as a monolithic application can be efficient in terms of system resources. However, monolithic applications can have serious drawbacks when used in a Web environment. Because each process has the potential to duplicate the entire Web application, it's possible to have server processes that are all very large due to the size in memory of a few functions.

Also, monolithic applications—especially those made up of many smaller programs compiled in at runtime—have the potential to be unstable if any of the smaller subprograms or plug-ins crashes or behaves erratically. For instance, a Perl program incorporated into a server through Apache::Registry might be modified incorrectly during application development or maintenance, inadvertently introducing an infinite loop or memory leak that causes the program to behave erratically. Because the misbehaving subprogram is compiled into the Web server itself, crashing the subprogram causes the Web server itself to crash, along with any other Web applications that have been compiled into the server process. Worse yet, after the Web server restarts after crashing, it loads the same subprogram again in response to the first Web request that calls for it.

Because all copies of the Web server are being disrupted by the misbehaving code, it's possible that all other requests to the server are being ignored or mishandled while the server crashes and restarts.

Another drawback to monolithic application architectures is the inability to separate out sections of the Web application for independent processing. For large-scale sites with broad areas of focus, a Web application covering all the different functions of the site might become unwieldy to load entirely into one Web server process. A Web application that keeps an in-memory cache of parsed Extensible Markup Language (XML) structures, for instance, might quickly grow to fill available memory, causing the application to use virtual memory on disk and perform poorly. This situation is made worse when the Web server uses multiple processes because dozens of processes might each create a duplicate of the oversized program. It would be helpful in this case to split the Web application into independent sections, each of which processes a portion of incoming requests and loads only a fraction of the subprograms required by the entire Web application. However, this is difficult to set up within a monolithic application because decisions as to which Web server process handles a specific request are usually made before any modules are executed, so modules themselves can't route network requests within the process.

It should be noted that application environments that provide persistence by incorporating smaller applications into the Web server process already are available, so it's generally not necessary to develop an environment like this from scratch. These tools are detailed in Chapter 10.

Web Applications as Persistent Separate Programs

In the UNIX world, a program that runs continuously and that waits for external processes to access it to perform tasks is called a *daemon*. Similar constructs— sometimes called listeners or servers—exist for any networked operating system and provide the same functionality, regardless of what they're called. For example, the Web server process itself is a daemon, usually listening on port 80 for requests from a Web client. Other common network daemons include Telnet for remote terminal access, SMTP and POP for email transfer, and FTP for file transfer. Each listens at a different port for incoming traffic. The ports used by these applications aren't set in stone; Web servers are known to listen to ports from 82 to 8000, and responses to requests usually are sent out to ports in the 10,000 range on the client machine.

This flexibility enables new daemons to be created that provide services that are not so common, but that are likely to be used more by local applications. A database server such as Oracle, for example, serves as a daemon for client processes accessing the database over a network. The Oracle server provides a standard interface to the database assigned to a specific port, such as 1521, and client programs connect to that port when it's necessary to retrieve data. This method provides persistence in contrast to simpler database systems, such as dBASE or Microsoft Access, which invoke the database server off disk whenever the client program is launched. The network connection between client and server need not take place between two machines that are physically separated on the network; in many cases, the client and the daemon are on the same machine, and the network simply provides a standard interface between the two.

A Web server can be considered a client as well because the Web server process can execute code that connects across the network to another daemon. For instance, in our Oracle example, the database server might be accessed by code running within a Web server, which in turn is processing a request sent by another client. This leads to a chain of persistent network daemons and provides another way to separate functional components of an application while maintaining the persistence of the application as a whole. In contrast, if the database server functionality needed to be incorporated into the Web server along with network interaction and data processing code, the application as a whole would quickly become unwieldy, and it would be difficult to add robustness to either the Web server part of the application or the database part of the application without impacting the other part negatively. Similarly, if the client had to access the Web server and the database server independently, the overall utility of the endpoint application would be greatly limited. By combining the utility of a single client endpoint (the Web server) and a chain of more robust services (the Web server and the database, among others), this enables application designers to concentrate on the task at hand without worrying unduly about how to integrate other applications into the endpoint.

The daemon idea can be extended further to provide persistence to Web applications. Just as the database server was kept separate from the Web process to enable each program to become independently robust, the Web application process can be separated out from the Web server to enable a more robust Web application while keeping a persistent link to the Web server process. Again, this provides a consistent interface to the client by providing a single endpoint for server interaction (the Web server) while using a chain of robust services (the Web server and the Web application, among others) to provide the body of the response. Because the Web application is separated from the Web server process, it's also possible to tune the performance characteristics of the Web application without having to modify the performance of the Web server. For instance, this provides a solution to the problem of threading, as mentioned in the "A Web Application as a Single Plug-In" section earlier in this chapter. The Web server process can be threaded for greater performance and uniform caching, even if the Web application runs as separate processes to provide more stability for Perl processing.

Most daemons listening at network ports are likely to require any incoming requests to adhere to a specified protocol. A Web server requires the Hypertext Transfer Protocol (HTTP), a file server requires FTP, and remote procedure call daemons might require the Simple Object Access Protocol (SOAP). In this usage, a protocol is the format of the data stream sent from the client to the server; it governs things like the format of meta-information, the location of the content length if necessary, and the symbols used to indicate the end of the data stream. Similarly, Web applications designed as stand-alone network daemons would need to specify a protocol for the Web server process to use when transferring request information and receiving response information. This protocol might be custom developed for a single Web application, or it could use one of the preexisting protocols, such as FastCGI, that were developed for just this purpose.

Subroutines Revisited

It's possible to set up a Web application daemon that runs Perl programs the same way Apache::Registry does. Because the application daemon is running persistently, it's possible to use the same techniques to process CGI-style Perl programs within a stand-alone daemon. The Web application daemon can accept preprocessed request information from the Web server and load the corresponding Perl application from the compiled cache to process the request. The Web server still handles the majority of Web requests, including static HTML and image files, and implements all the network interface code necessary to provide a robust Web site.

Just as in the case of an Apache::Registry module, a Web application daemon can translate each application into a subroutine in its own namespace, creating a fairly clean environment in which the application can allocate its own variables and create its own data structures. Unlike Apache::Registry, however, a stand-alone process can interact with any Web server that supports its protocol. This gives greater freedom to system administrators when deciding on server architecture because the Web applications no longer dictate a choice of Web server.

Another important difference in this case is that fine-grain control over the Web server process is no longer available. Because all communication between the server process and the Web application daemon is taking place through a network protocol rather than through a server API, it's unlikely that the Web server would provide a protocol that enables daemon processes to modify the environment greatly. However, some control over the Web server process can be gained by configuring the client module, which does interact with the server through the server API.

CGI Compatibility

Greater compatibility with complex CGI programs can be gained by making each individual program a separate daemon. A CGI search engine, for instance, can be separated out from the rest of the Perl applications if it has been written to handle many different types of search requests within a single application. Some CGI programs were designed in this fashion because it more closely resembled traditional interactive programs, even though the nature of the CGI protocol kept these applications from benefiting from traditional applications' persistence. In the case of such a complex program, it's sometimes more sensible to set the program up as its own Web application daemon because the code necessary to handle network protocol requests would be a minor addition.

Separating a CGI-style Perl program out as an individual daemon also provides greater compatibility with the way CGI programs execute. Because some stand-alone Perl programs assume they are running as unique processes, little regard is given to naming conventions, namespaces, and other style issues that make it possible to combine Perl programs the way that Apache::Registry does. If a Perl program is written in a style that would cause it to behave erratically under a shared environment, separating the program out would give the program free reign over its own process. At that point, problems caused by executing the program in a persistent environment can be discovered and solved individually without trying to fit the application into a shared environment at the same time.

This idea also works for CGI programs that aren't written in Perl, although those applications are outside the scope of this book. By implementing the same Web application protocols in these applications that are used in the Perl applications, it's possible to provide a persistent interface to all Web applications, no matter how they are implemented. This additional level of abstraction also provides the opportunity to change the implementation of any Web application daemon at any time without impacting other Web applications.

Variables, Objects, and Memory Issues

Persistence compatibility for average CGI Perl programs can be helped greatly by simulating the conditions of a clean restart every time a program is accessed. This can be implemented within a program by keeping track of variables manually and resetting each variable at the end of the program. Those kinds of modifications tend to be costly to implement—if not practically impossible—because existing code would have to be searched by someone as knowledgeable about the program as the original developer, with the added capability to tell when subroutines and additional modules create variables and data structures implicitly. In most cases, this problem can be overcome by using good Perl coding style because Perl has facilities for automatically cleaning up my-scoped variables. In addition, some of the tools listed in Chapter 10 reinitialize Perl variables by searching the symbol table and keeping track of variables independently of Perl.

Objects can present specific difficulties when relying on Perl to clean up memory allocated, especially if the objects have circular references to themselves. Objects in Perl are stored as references to data structures that might contain references to other data structures as well. Perl decides when to dispose of an object by checking its *reference count*, which is the number of variables that hold a reference to the object at any point in the course of the program. Because objects can also store references, it's possible for an object to reference another object that references it in return. Because both objects maintain a nonzero reference count until either object is disposed, it's possible that neither object will be disposed even after the program is finished using it. In a persistent environment, this can result in objects continuing to stay in memory long after the programs (or subroutines) that started them have exited. Disposing of these objects automatically can be difficult, so it's lucky that this situation does not occur very often.

Again, environments that handle the conversion from CGI applications to persistent Perl programs already are available, so it's generally not necessary to write cleanup routines for these from scratch. These tools are detailed in Chapter 10.

More Power: Clustering, Precaching, and Balancing

Persistence isn't the only performance improvement made possible by these architectural changes. When Web applications are persistent, clustering, precaching, and balancing applications can provide additional performance tuning. Most of these techniques are possible with only one of the architectures mentioned in this chapter—from the "Web Applications as Persistent Separate Programs" section—but other architectures might be able to use variations of these techniques.

Clustering Web applications enables individual programs to become more responsive while reducing the memory requirements of a particular daemon, or *application engine*, as it's sometimes called. Although the usual approach to improving Web server performance in a multiprocess environment is to create identical duplicates of a process in memory, clustering takes the approach that each application engine has a preferred group of programs it hosts. With the first approach, any available application engine is considered to be equivalent when deciding which engine should process a request. Clustered engines, on the other hand, are weighted by their preferred group of programs, so requests are routed to the first open engine that has the appropriate program to handle each request. This makes it more likely that any given request reaches an application engine that has recently handled a similar request, which increases the use of cached code and reduces the amount of duplicate code.

Precaching Perl modules and data structures is important because much of the time spent compiling program code and instantiating data should be spent before the first request gets handled. Perl makes caching modules easy because each module has its own package and namespace that is referenced in the same way, regardless of the namespace of the program or subroutine that accesses it. Precaching data structures and application code is a little more difficult, but only because the data and applications are more likely to change over the course of the application engine's lifetime.

Balancing is the performance improvement most Web server installations are likely to implement in hardware, but the intelligence behind most balancing doesn't take Web application structure into account. The assumption is that all Web site sections are being accessed equally and that they cause the same load on the server, so a simple duplication of all the Web servers would improve performance across the board. With a clustered Web application, though, it's possible to load balance on a smaller scale, shifting the load of higher-use applications to more application engines and even to additional Web application servers.

Clustering Application Engines

Because daemons can be accessed independently of the Web server processes, it's possible to cluster useful programs in each daemon so that the overall size of the daemons in memory stays as small as possible. This is an architectural change that should have no effect on the way applications are accessed; programs are simply grouped behind the scenes into clusters that are more manageable for the server environment. This idea is similar to Web server clustering, which uses network hardware to determine which Web server should respond to a class of Web requests to provide as uniform a stream of requests as possible to any one Web server.

Applications can be clustered within application engines in a number of logical configurations:

- Programs can be clustered based on the directories in which they reside or other URL information. For instance, requests for programs residing in the `/search/` directory might be routed to one application engine, while requests for programs in the `/wml/` directory might be routed to another. This type of routing is the easiest to set up in most Web server environments.

- Programs also can be grouped by function. If a group of programs comprise a search application that takes considerably more time and processing power than other applications, that group can be routed to a specific application engine to improve the response time of other applications.

- Programs can be grouped even by the Perl modules they use. If a group of programs uses the XML::Parser module, for instance, it might be advisable to separate those programs out to reduce overall memory usage. This grouping probably is useful in few cases, though, because many Web applications use the same core set of modules and differentiating between similar combinations would be difficult.

Additionally, it's possible to cluster applications automatically using a balancing algorithm to decide which application engine should respond to each request. The development of such an algorithm is outside the scope of this book, but the general idea is to funnel incoming requests to engines that have previously processed similar requests. Thus, the application needed to process any particular request is less likely to be duplicated across multiple engines because the balancing algorithm assign priority to the engines that already have that application cached. Subsequently, each application engine is likely to cache fewer applications because requests outside its scope are likely to be handled by other engines.

Precaching Modules

One way that persistence techniques using subroutines can help the performance of Perl Web applications is by enabling modules to be shared between applications without any changes to the individual program. This is made possible by the way Perl separates modules into their own namespaces, which are accessed through an absolute path from anywhere in the program. For instance, variables and subroutines from the DBI module can be accessed directly by prefacing them with DBI, so the `connect` subroutine could be accessed as `&DBI::connect()`. Object notation adds an additional layer of abstraction to these calls by enabling subroutines in a specific package to be accessed as methods off an object, which then inherently calls the appropriate package. Thus, `DBI->connect()` calls a subroutine from the DBI package, but so do `$dbh->quote()` and `$dbh->disconnect()`.

Because modules are shared between the subroutines that pass for individual programs, it's easy to load the modules before any requests are accepted at all. A list of common modules can be kept either manually or determined automatically from the scripts to be cached by a particular daemon, and each module can be loaded into memory by calling it from the main daemon program as it is initialized. Similarly, a list of the Perl programs that are likely to be invoked by a particular daemon can be used to load those programs into their own namespaces as soon as the daemon initializes. In both cases, the modules and program subroutines then are available in precompiled form to all requests, and any new modules or programs are added in as they are requested.

The difference is seen during the first request to a particular program after the server or daemon has been started. If modules have been precached, the first request takes just as long as any other request. However, if modules haven't been cached, the first request to a particular engine takes much longer than subsequent requests. In fact, the first request takes almost as long as an equivalent CGI request would take because the same compilation and instantiation overhead is seen in both cases—only the Perl compiler itself is already in memory.

Precaching Data Structures

If each daemon has a specific set of programs it hosts and each program is precompiled within that application engine, it's also possible to preload the data structures for those applications in which the daemon is first started. Perl doesn't assist this process inherently the way it makes module caching possible, but a few changes to the modules used by a Web application can do a similar job. For instance, the DBI module has a corresponding Apache::DBI module, which enables applications in a persistent environment to create database connections when the application engine is first invoked so that they are available when the first request is handled by the engine. Similar techniques can be used to precache parsed XML files, compiled template code, or lengthy data files. Precaching these kinds of data require more specific knowledge of the data structures the Web application uses, but in some cases, the performance benefits are well worth the additional effort and care.

Of course, additional checks must be performed when a request comes in for each program to make sure that the program's data structures haven't changed or become invalid. A database connection, for instance, might be closed by the database after a period of inactivity. If a persistent application tries to use the connection without checking its status, the application might behave erratically. A simple check needs to be added to make sure the connection still is available. Similarly, an XML file used as an on-disk data repository might have been modified by another process since it was last cached, so it would be useful to check the timestamp on the file against the cached version, update the file if it has changed, and purge the file if it is no longer present.

Many Perl modules have persistent versions or Web-centric add-ons that enable this kind of preloading and persistence management to occur transparently. The DBI module is an example that is discussed in detail in Chapter 14. The persistence-enhanced versions of other modules might be found by searching for `Apache::*` versions on the Comprehensive Perl Archive Network (`http://www.cpan.org`).

Load Balancing Across Engines

Another benefit to separating Web application engines from the Web server process is additional control over the number of engines available to process a given type of request. If a Web application requires many more Web server processes than application engines, for instance, it's possible to balance the load from all Web server processes across a smaller set of application engines. Load balancing this way generally requires a more complex algorithm for routing requests than the standard one-process-per-server approach, but the results can be more flexible and configurable.

This type of load balancing also can benefit Web server performance by enabling an administrator to limit the number of engines available to process certain types of requests. For instance, if a database used infrequently by Web applications is licensed for only a small number of simultaneous connections to save money on licensing fees, it is possible to cap the total number of engines capable of accessing the database server. Because this number can be set independently from other Web application and Web server performance tuning variables, it's possible to fix a value without impacting negatively on the performance of the Web site as a whole. This same technique also can be used to limit the impact of a specific user's Web applications in a multiuser environment, as would be found in a shared Web-hosting situation.

Application engines also can be spread across multiple machines to create a Web application cluster. Because each application engine is also a network daemon, it doesn't matter whether the engine is running on the same system as the Web server or on another system connected to it through a network. The protocol is the same, the request is the same, and the response is the same. Because of this, it's possible to run any or all application engines on separate servers, with the additional possibility of clustering application engines based on the servers that have those applications available. Of course, those servers have to be connected through a suitably fast connection, but in most cases, the internal connections between servers on a Local Area Network (LAN) are much faster than the connection between the Web servers and the Internet.

In practice, a combination of automated load balancing and clustering techniques provides the most robust and responsive environment possible. Because it's impossible to determine the relative load on a server caused by requests to one Web application or another, it's good to load balance engines that have been clustered. This enables each engine type to have as much processing power devoted to it as necessary without creating unnecessary duplicates of engines that aren't under as much load.

Two Important Principles to Remember

I really can't emphasize enough the importance of two simple principles in Web application design:

- Don't exit.
- Keep connections open.

The first is discussed here and in subsequent chapters, and the second is discussed in terms of databases in Chapter 14. In truth, though, the two principles would be invaluable even without explanation because they underlie every major performance increase this book has to offer.

It's amazing to me how often these two simple principles are overlooked. I was programming in persistent environments with continuous database connections before eBay was popular, but I still run across executives from Fortune 500 companies who are confused by the concept of a persistent environment. Most are convinced that their performance problems will be solved by rewriting entire Web applications in a different language or for a different operating system. They ignore the fact that both the old and the new systems they're using are made inefficient by throwing compiled and instantiated programs away after every request and creating and destroying database handles every time they're used. Even more amazing was the arrogant explanation that I got from one e-commerce CTO: "I have sixty programmers working night and day to optimize code. I don't need a new architecture."

Although this chapter described a few important types of Web server architectures, there are many more possibilities waiting to be discovered. In fact, as the performance limitations of each architecture are reached, it becomes possible to see the next level of architectural improvement necessary to meet exponential growth yet again. In all cases, though, the same two questions can be used as a filter for architectural performance improvements:

- Does the improvement add any persistence to the application or its data?
- Does the improvement keep connections open that otherwise would have to be closed?

To keep the idea even simpler, the two principles can be combined into one over-arching goal: recycle everything. Don't throw any piece of compiled code away. Hold on to that database connection as long as possible. Keep a cached version of those XML files, and update only the sections of them that have changed. Use idle clock cycles on other machines to augment Web processing. Provide cached copies of results when the data isn't likely to have changed. Above all, recycle those resources that are more precious than all the processing power in the world: reuse the code that cost so many programmer hours to produce.

Summary

Persistence is a Web server concept that has many possible implementations. The general idea behind a persistent Web application is to mimic the way in which an interactive application, such as GIMP, would process incoming requests through an event loop and event handler code. One way to duplicate this in a Web server environment is by writing the Web application as a server plug-in that interacts through the Web server's API. A second approach is to take the existing CGI applications and rewrite them automatically by incorporating them as event handler subroutines into a larger Perl program. Both approaches create monolithic applications that are difficult to modify for greater performance, however. A third approach separates out the Web application code by creating a network daemon that communicates with the server through a protocol layer. By combining these approaches, it's possible to create an environment that is configured for persistent performance but that accepts CGI-style code as well as persistence-specific applications. Furthermore, it's possible to use these techniques to cluster applications into functional engines and balance application processing over multiple servers without needing to modify the Web application code itself.

10

Tools for Perl Persistence

MANY TOOLS EXIST FOR ADDING PERSISTENT PERFORMANCE to Perl-based Web application environments. Products such as mod_perl, FastCGI, VelociGen, and PerlEx provide persistence for Web applications on a wide variety of platforms using widely varying architectures. This list is far from complete, although it is a sampling of the most common tools available at the time this book was written. In fact, most readers are likely to run across one of these tools—mod_perl—much more often than all the rest combined. This is simply because the server for which it is written, Apache, is the single most popular Web server in the world. Each product has its strengths and weaknesses, though. Thus, the decision to use one over another is based as much on the Web application being deployed as on any comparison among the tools.

A combination of approaches is also possible. One product, VelociGen, uses a variety of architectures to provide a range of possible solutions based on environment. You can create similar solutions by using a combination of tools. Any of these solutions provides a marked improvement in performance; they all implement architectures that provide persistence and that do away with most of the overhead due to Common Gateway Interface (CGI) application processing. The main differentiation points between these tools are subtle architectural differences that are likely to make notable differences only when tested using individual Web applications in production-class environments. More information about simulating these environments is available in Chapter 15, "Testing Site Performance."

Other factors to consider when choosing a persistence environment are platform, price, and ease of use. Some tools are available for only a handful of platforms, and some platforms rule out all but one persistence environment. For instance, an iPlanet Web server running under Solaris won't be able to use mod_perl or PerlEx, and FastCGI might also be difficult to find for that platform. Thus, the choice would be narrowed to VelociGen. The Apache Web server running under Linux, on the other hand, has a wide range of Perl persistence choices. In that case, the relative price of each tool could be the deciding factor when it is weighted against the relative difficulty of implementing one persistent solution over another.

mod_perl

One popular environment for providing Perl persistence is mod_perl, which is offered as a product by the Apache group (http://perl.apache.org). mod_perl is implemented as a Perl interface to the Apache application program interface (API). Thus, mod_perl applications are compiled into the server process and run within it. mod_perl provides persistence for Perl programs by embedding the Perl interpreter into the server process and caching the compiled Perl code as it is executed.

mod_perl is offered under the same open source license as the Apache Web server. In this context, an open source license grants users the right to download, execute, modify, and redistribute both the Apache Web server and mod_perl without prior permission from the Apache group. Because of this openness and the wide deployment of the Apache Web server, mod_perl has developed a large user base and is used by many other open source Web applications and site development systems made available for download. In fact, mod_perl is the most popular Perl persistence package in use at the time this book was written.

The tight integration between Apache and mod_perl can be both a strength and a weakness for the environment. Full access to the Apache server API gives mod_perl a unique advantage when creating server extensions, but the distinct API programming style used to create mod_perl extensions is often daunting for CGI programmers who are not used to the object-oriented Perl style. mod_perl comes with an Apache::Registry module to provide a CGI compatibility mode for these developers, but some care must still be taken when using complex CGI programs in a mod_perl environment.

Architecture of mod_perl

Apache offers mod_perl as a direct Perl interface to the Apache API. As a result, the architecture of a Web application written for mod_perl is based around the architecture of the Apache server itself. At runtime, mod_perl programs are considered direct extensions of the Apache server process rather than separate programs, even though mod_perl extensions are written independently of the compiled server.

mod_perl operates by embedding a Perl interpreter into each server process. The Perl interpreter compiles mod_perl programs into the server process at runtime. In addition, these programs can compile Perl subprograms into the server process at compile time or as requests come in. This latter approach is how Apache::Registry is used to compile CGI programs. Embedding the Perl interpreter into the server process saves the overhead of loading and executing it every time a request comes in. It also offers the capability to compile and cache Perl programs as persistent parts of the server process, which saves the overhead of loading and compiling these programs each time a request comes in.

However, the one-to-one relationship between Apache server processes and mod_perl processes can cause a performance problem for servers with exceptionally high volumes of traffic. This problem stems from the default behavior of Apache server processes. This default behavior creates as many server processes as there are simultaneous requests. In some cases, hundreds of Apache processes might be running simultaneously. Because mod_perl embeds the Perl interpreter in every Apache process, these processes are likely to be much larger in terms of memory than Apache server processes would be alone. Note that all Apache processes are considered equal when deciding which process handles a specific request, regardless of whether that request is for a static file or a Perl program; thus, it's possible to have hundreds of Perl interpreters loaded in server processes, even though most requests handled by those processes won't need mod_perl at all. This situation can cause secondary inefficiencies with caching Perl programs; with hundreds of server processes, there could be hundreds of copies of each Perl program, which causes even more memory to be used.

Open Source

Both Apache and mod_perl are open source programs offered under the GNU General Public License (GPL). The GPL gives Apache and mod_perl users and developers permission to use, modify, and redistribute the source code to both programs. The only condition imposed on these permissions is that modified or redistributed versions of the programs must also be licensed under the GPL with the same permissions. (Incidentally, programs written in Perl for mod_perl or Apache are not bound by this license because they are considered dynamically linked libraries and therefore separate from the licensed programs.) In addition, both the Apache server and mod_perl are made freely available for download from the Apache project Web site.

Open source licenses embody a philosophy that has served the Web community well, and the Apache project specifically. In fact, one of the major reasons for the Apache server's overwhelming popularity and exponential growth has been the fact that it's readily available to any Web developer. Similarly, mod_perl has become a popular way to achieve Perl persistence because it is made just as readily available. In addition, both products have become faster, more robust, and more stable because the open source development model encourages programmers to add features and fix errors in the code, regardless of whether they're directly allied with the project. Perl itself has been offered under a similar license called the Artistic License, which gives similar permissions to users, but which imposes no restrictions on the license used for derivative works. Because of their shared open source philosophy, the Perl and Apache communities have a good working relationship, with current technology and future plans shared between the groups. This results in recognition of mod_perl and persistence when developing Perl modules, many of which are optimized to perform well in persistent environments.

The fact that mod_perl is offered under an open source license also hedges against the possibility that the software's original developers will shift their focus away from mod_perl and leave it undeveloped. In the case of closed source commercial software, a project can suffer significantly if a vendor decides to discontinue development of a crucial product. The software still is available, but it soon can become obsolete without regular updates to make it compatible with current technologies. With open source software, however, it is possible to take control of crucial software if the vendor decides to discontinue development. The vendor's product then is moved from the list of purchased products to the list of internally developed applications. Also, in some cases, development of a product is taken over by a new group if an existing group stops development. In fact, many open source projects (including Perl's XML::Parser and DBI modules) were developed initially by programmers from related projects, and then taken over and implemented by different programmers.

Tight Integration with Apache

Apache and mod_perl are integrated very tightly, which can be both a benefit and a drawback. When viewed as a Perl interface to the Apache API, mod_perl can be a very powerful tool for changing the Apache server environment and creating extensions for complex tasks that CGI-style Web applications are not efficient at performing. However, when viewing mod_perl as a CGI replacement for persistent Perl environments, the tight integration of mod_perl into the Apache server can be a deterrent to developing portable Web applications.

One of the unique benefits of developing Perl Web applications in mod_perl is that it gives complete access to the Apache API. However, because mod_perl provides little in the way of an abstraction layer between mod_perl programs and the API, programs written for a specific version of mod_perl are subject to changes in the Apache API. For instance, if a call that generates a specific error message (for example, "500 Server Error" or "301 Moved") changes from one version of the Apache server to the next, modules written using mod_perl with this functionality behave erratically or cease to work.

Of course, the main difficulty with mod_perl's tight integration with Apache is that it requires the Apache server. This would seem to be a minor issue because Apache is currently the most popular Web server software available and the acknowledged performance leader. In addition, Apache is available for most operating systems, including

most UNIX variants and Windows. Unfortunately, this assumes that the only considerations when choosing a Web server are Perl integration and platform availability. If
some other reason to switch Web server platforms arises, converting mod_perl programs to operate in the new environment would be a nontrivial task.

Large User Base

As a popular module for the most popular server in the world, mod_perl benefits from
a very large user base. mod_perl programmers have developed many different types of
applications, ranging from development environments to complete Web site administration systems. Many systems have been written with mod_perl in mind, including the
Slash news site generation system mentioned in the SlashCode section of Chapter 7,
"Perl for the Web."

In addition, many modules have been created to enable existing Perl modules to
take advantage of the persistent environment offered by mod_perl. These applications
are usually listed under the Apache:: branch of the Perl module tree, which includes
important modules such as Apache::DBI. More information on Apache::DBI and its
role in persistence can be found in Chapter 14, "Database-Backed Web Sites."

Object-Oriented Programming

Although there are many Perl programming environments built on top of mod_perl,
the standard form of mod_perl programming takes the form of Apache API calls
through an object-oriented interface. Although this provides a powerful way to interact directly with the Web server, some Perl programmers are less than comfortable
with Perl's object-oriented programming style. In fact, a few Perl programmers might
have a specific aversion to object-oriented style because of occasional programmatic
awkwardness such a style entails.

In addition, the persistent nature of mod_perl programs requires them to have a
stricter style that is more suitable for a persistent environment. Again, this can be a
style that is different from that which is used by many Perl programmers in a stand-
alone or CGI environment. Specifically, adapting existing CGI programs for use as
mod_perl modules might be a daunting task because the differences between the
mod_perl style and the CGI style can be present at such a fundamental level that it
might seem easier to write the entire application from scratch.

Many of these issues are common enough that they have been addressed in modules designed to soften the sharp differences between the mod_perl programming style
and the CGI style. The Apache::Registry module, for instance, provides a way to use
CGI programs in an unmodified form within a mod_perl environment. This process is
not without its caveats, however; Apache::Registry does not account for the needs of
CGI programs that stray from the norm (for example, programs with nonparsed headers),
so additional changes to the environment or the program might be necessary to fit
with the assumptions made by Apache::Registry. The module also doesn't solve the

problem of global variables used in a persistent context, which still can cause some CGI-style programs to behave erratically when run persistently. For new program creation, additional functionality is provided by modules such as Embperl and HTML::Mason, which enable mod_perl programs to be created in sections that make more sense within a Web site framework. Environments such as these are discussed in Chapter 12, "Environments for Reducing Development Time."

FastCGI

FastCGI is a protocol designed to replace the CGI protocol and provide a more platform-neutral approach to API programming for Web servers. As a replacement for CGI, it was written to provide a language-independent framework for persistent connections between a Web server and application engines running in separate processes. As a broader solution for API programming, the FastCGI architecture adds greater control over the performance characteristics of application engines, as well as an abstracted interface that enables the deployment of FastCGI applications in various load-balancing configurations, including over a network of application processing servers.

FastCGI was originally developed by Fast Engines, and then released as open source software and maintained by a group of programmers. Modules implementing the FastCGI protocol are available for Apache Web servers from the FastCGI Web site (http://www.fastcgi.com), and Zeus servers include support for the FastCGI protocol as a native API.

The architecture of FastCGI applications is different from both CGI applications and mod_perl. FastCGI applications are deployed as independent persistent processes that communicate with the Web server through the FastCGI protocol. On the other hand, CGI applications are run once per request by the Web server, and they communicate through standard program output channels. Despite the differences, FastCGI holds true to the CGI programming style. FastCGI applications are written in a style that is similar to the style used with CGI programs, although some modifications have to be made to accommodate the persistent environment and to handle the FastCGI protocol.

Architecture of FastCGI

FastCGI programs are run as independent processes—either as network daemons or application engines, as described in Chapter 9, "The Power of Persistence." The FastCGI processes communicate with a module embedded in the Web server process or processes. FastCGI engines written in Perl embed the Perl interpreter in each application engine process, providing a persistent Perl interface to the Web server that is similar to the one mod_perl provides. However, the FastCGI interface is abstracted away from the Web server API by the FastCGI protocol. Thus, FastCGI programs are more resistant to changes in the Web server environment.

FastCGI processes can be implemented as daemons, which communicate with the Web server over the network, or as application engines, which communicate with the Web server through named pipes or similar structures. FastCGI processes might also be implemented as threaded applications, but Perl processes are unlikely to take advantage of FastCGI threading because its not advisable to run Perl programs in a threaded environment. However, some Perl-related programs, such as VelociGen, use FastCGI threading to reduce the overhead of having multiple FastCGI processes in memory.

Because FastCGI application engines are kept separate from the Web server process, its possible to execute a different number of application engines than there are Web server processes. This can be a benefit to environments in which hundreds of Web server processes are running to deal with large volumes of static page requests while only a few application engines are needed to handle the less-frequent requests for dynamic pages. The opposite case also is possible, such as when there is only a single-threaded Web server process handling static requests with many more application engines supporting it.

In addition, the separation between FastCGI and Web server processes adds a layer of stability by isolating potentially unstable code in the FastCGI processes. Because the FastCGI protocol conveys only a limited amount of information between the Web server and the application engine, an engine can fail without taking down the Web server process. This level of separation is crucial for threaded Web server processes because there is likely only one process running and all current client connections would be lost if that process were to crash.

Like the CGI protocol, FastCGI was designed to be language-neutral. FastCGI applications can be created in any language as long as the application implements the FastCGI protocol. Toolkits with FastCGI libraries and sample code are available for the C, Perl, Tcl, and Java languages. These toolkits are made available under open source licenses. Thus, programs can be developed with them without the need for licensing agreements or fees. For Perl programmers, the FCGI module provides all the functionality necessary to create a FastCGI application engine in Perl.

Familiar CGI-Style Code

True to its name, FastCGI implements an interface that should be familiar to CGI application developers. In fact, the core of a FastCGI application engine can simply be a CGI application written in the same style as any other CGI program. This core is implemented as a subroutine that is similar to the way Apache::Registry compiles CGI programs as subroutines, but FastCGI programs are likely to have just one core subroutine that handles every request.

Of course, CGI programs as written are not FastCGI applications. An additional layer of code has to be added to each application engine to handle the communication between the engine and the Web server and the persistence of the application engine. The FastCGI module makes this code as easy to implement as possible, but modifications still have to be made to each CGI application being translated into a FastCGI process. It is possible to combine the functionality of the Apache::Registry and FCGI modules to produce a FastCGI program that loads other Perl programs and that processes the differences automatically; however, the work involved can be more diffi-cult than rewriting the applications individually.

One notable difference between CGI and FastCGI styles is that global variables have to be declared and initialized at the beginning of a FastCGI program. In contrast, CGI-style global variables are generally declared in place, if at all. The upside of this initialization phase is that complex data structures can be explicitly initialized outside the event handler loop so that they are instantiated only once over the lifetime of an application engine. This process can reduce the overhead of creating these data struc-tures each time a request comes in, which can be considerable for complex data such as XML parse trees or other parsed files. This procedure should *not* be used to create databases in memory to store state information because more than one application might be used to process the same type of request. In addition, the process loses all in-memory data when the application engine is restarted, so it's generally safer to store state information outside the application engine, in a database or session server, for instance.

Other aspects of persistence need to be coded in a FastCGI application as well. CGI programs rarely have to consider the effects of global variables versus local or file-scoped variables. In a persistent context, however, global variables can hold on to their values from one request to the next, providing inconsistent results for each request. In addition, FastCGI programs run CGI-style code as a subroutine the same way Apache::Registry does under mod_perl. Thus, unanticipated behavior might occur due to CGI subroutines being shifted outside the main subroutine. Some of these issues are covered in Chapter 11.

VelociGen

VelociGen is a commercial Web application server offered by a company of the same name (`http://www.velocigen.com`) that provides Perl persistence and a series of Perl development environments. VelociGen is available for Netscape Enterprise Server, Apache, Microsoft Internet Information Server (IIS), and Zeus on most UNIX and Windows platforms.

The VelociGen server architecture combines many of the techniques mentioned in Chapter 9 to take advantage of every performance improvement provided by any technique available. As a result, the specific architecture used by any one installation of VelociGen can vary widely depending on the capabilities of the operating system, the hardware configuration, and the Web server software and deployment style used on any specific instance of the server environment.

Common to all VelociGen servers, however, is an abstracted programming environ-ment that uses the same style, regardless of the underlying architecture. This environ-ment is designed to provide comprehensive CGI compatibility for existing programs with no program modifications necessary. Additional environments are provided for new Web application programming. These environments include a full persistence mode with no overhead, which is for power-hungry applications, and an embedded mode, which addresses simpler programming tasks in more complex HTML or XML environments.

Architecture of VelociGen

The architecture of a VelociGen server varies depending on the environment. For instance, VelociGen for Netscape Server API (NSAPI) servers uses a threaded plug-in module that communicates with application engines, while VelociGen for Apache servers uses Dynamic Shared Objects (DSO) or FastCGI connections between application engines and the Web server. In fact, variations on both the monolithic architecture (the "Web Applications in One Modular Program" section in Chapter 9) and the independent architectures (the "Web Applications as Persistent Separate Programs" in Chapter 9) are possible depending on server choice and the configuration of the VelociGen engines. For instance, VelociGen engines can be deployed as DSOs for the Apache server under Linux, and each in turn can control a Perl processing engine on the same machine. In another configuration, a threaded VelociGen load balancing plug-in for the iPlanet server under Solaris can control a number of clustered Perl engines on multiple machines.

The most common architecture used by VelociGen servers consists of a number of application engines controlled by a load-balancing plug-in module. Each application engine is a persistent Perl program started by the plug-in modules, which is sent requests as the Web server delivers them. The application engines communicate with the VelociGen plug-in through a named pipe or socket, depending on the server and configuration used, so that they can be deployed on local or remote machines.

Each application engine is designed to operate in a fashion similar to Apache::Registry by compiling independent programs as subroutines within an overarching persistent Perl program. The engines can be set up to run for a specific number of requests before restarting, which enables the environment to be purged of cached elements if they are likely to grow over time.

Caching and Clustering

In addition to basic process control over the number of application engines present, the plug-in module provides load balancing and automatic clustering for application engines. Each request is dispatched to an appropriate Perl engine based on a load-balancing algorithm. The algorithm takes into account which engines have processed similar requests in the past as well as which engines are currently in use or unavailable. As a result, program engines are clustered automatically based on execution patterns and relative application popularity. This results in engines that take up less memory because fewer programs are being cached in each engine. The engines also are more responsive to requests overall because the odds of a request being processed by an engine with the necessary program and connections cached increase dramatically.

Because applications in a persistent environment are compiled and cached in memory and those applications might be running in a persistent mode for days or months, it's necessary to check for changes in the application or other cached files every time a request is received. VelociGen tracks the age of each file cached in memory, checks that age against the file on disk, and reloads and recompiles the file (if necessary) before processing the request. Although this capability can be important when developing a Web application, this functionality can be turned off to save overhead and improve the performance of deployed applications.

As mentioned, Perl application engines can be clustered across machines to provide greater scalability to a Web application. To do this, identical copies of the programs and their shared environment—including database connection managers and other driver software—must be present on each machine used as an application environment. After those copies are present, however, each new machine can be pressed into service interactively as additional performance is needed, without modifying any of the applications.

Full CGI Compatibility

VelociGen was developed to provide a complete solution to companies that want to accelerate existing CGI programs without the need to rewrite any code. To this end, the VelociGen architecture and environment is built around providing high-transaction support for persistence in as transparent a fashion as possible. In fact, VelociGen is tested to ensure that any valid CGI Perl program—no matter how complex or sloppy— produces the same output in a persistent context as it would in a CGI environment. To do this, VelociGen provides a CGI compatibility environment that simulates a CGI environment as closely as possible. The environment checks programs before they are compiled to make simple changes automatically, and then it checks the Perl environment after each instance of the program is executed to clean up global variables or other memory structures that might not have been disposed of by the program itself. The CGI compatibility environment also provides environment variables expected by many CGI programs that might not be present in the persistent environment.

VelociGen provides persistent environments with stricter style rules as well. After existing CGI programs are made persistent within the compatibility framework, it's possible to develop new applications in full persistence mode. Persistent applications built without the CGI compatibility layer achieve even better performance because the environment no longer keeps track of global variables or preprocesses input parameters. This saves a bit of overhead and offers an incremental performance improvement, but it requires extra care when writing programs. Often, however, the requirements for this mode can be met simply by using the `strict` and `warnings` pragmas to check code during development and the CGI module to process input parameters when necessary.

For development that more closely resembles HTML than CGI programming, an environment that provides embedded Perl code and abstracted HTML-like tags also is available. This environment, which is known as *Perl Server Pages (PSP)*, enables Perl code to be embedded into HTML pages in a manner similar to Active Server Pages (ASP), Java Server Pages (JSP), and PSP pages. The Perl code then can be treated as though it will be executed to fill in the page at runtime, which enables smaller sections of Perl to be used within more complex HTML pages by site designers without the cumbersome CGI style. The specifics of PSP syntax and usage are explored in Chapter 12, "Environments For Reducing Development Time." An important architectural note is that these pages are translated into full persistent Perl programs at runtime and treated much like other persistent programs handled by VelociGen.

In fact, all the environments offered by VelociGen provide persistence, database connection caching, precompiling, and script caching. Because the VelociGen server is based on a robust persistence architecture, performance benchmarks in any of the available modes are similar, and even the slowest of the modes still posts benchmarks that are orders of magnitude faster than CGI environments.

PerlEx

PerlEx is a similar commercial CGI Perl accelerator offered by the ActiveState software company (http://www.activestate.com). The software is generally less expensive than VelociGen, but it is not offered under an open source license, as are FastCGI and mod_perl. Unlike mod_perl, however, PerlEx provides persistence for Perl programs under Windows. In addition, accelerating Perl Web applications might be simpler and might require less modification using PerlEx than with a FastCGI implementation. PerlEx can be a good solution for noncritical Perl programs that need basic persistence.

PerlEx utilizes a plug-in architecture, embedding Perl interpreters directly into the Web server process. The plug-in is available for IIS, O'Reilly WebSite, and Netscape (or iPlanet) servers. As this book is being written, PerlEx is available only for Web servers running under the Windows operating system; versions of PerlEx for UNIX or other operating systems have not been announced. Similarly, a version of PerlEx for the Apache Web server has not been announced.

Architecture of PerlEx

PerlEx is implemented as a plug-in for Windows Web servers. The PerlEx environment embeds a threaded Perl interpreter in the Web server process, which provides persistence by compiling Perl programs into an encompassing Perl program. The resulting architecture is most similar to the "A Web Application as a Single Plug-In" section of Chapter 9. No separation is maintained between the Web server process and the Perl environment, and there is only one server process. Thus, any unstable Perl code is potentially capable of bringing down the entire Web server process.

Web application performance in PerlEx can be improved by designating scripts for preloading and precompiling in the PerlEx registry entries. In addition, PerlEx can support persistent database connections or custom file caching by specifying one-time code in the program's BEGIN and END blocks. Code in the BEGIN block to create a database connection, for instance, is run once when the program is compiled. The resulting connection then is available to subsequent requests as the program is executed. This method is not as transparent as the method employed by Apache::DBI, however. (Apache::DBI is described in detail in Chapter 14.)

As mentioned in Chapter 9, threading is experimental in Perl implementations through version 5.6. Though many Web servers are threaded, it is generally not wise to introduce threaded Perl into a high-transaction Web application. PerlEx is designed to work in threaded mode, however. Thus, thread safety of Perl programs running under PerlEx is a concern. A list of thread-safe Perl modules is available from the ActiveState Web site (http://www.activestate.com), but the list is far from comprehensive. In general, any Perl module written solely in Perl (that is, without any compiled extensions) is likely to be thread-safe, and a few common compiled modules, such as DBI, are considered thread-safe as well. Because the threading implementation is likely to change, however, many modules considered thread-safe in one version of Perl might not be so in another.

ASP-Style Programming

PerlEx provides persistence for both CGI and ASP-style code. Many CGI programs can be used with PerlEx without modification, but a few caveats should be observed when using PerlEx to add persistence to a complex CGI Web application. PerlEx doesn't always automatically account for global variables, and common modules, such as CGI.pm, should be used only in object-oriented mode. Luckily, PerlEx enables programs to be excluded from the persistent mode by specifying them in a registry entry used by the environment. Unfortunately, though, programs excluded in this fashion do not benefit from any performance increases PerlEx provides other programs.

PerlEx also provides an environment for new development using ASP-style embedded Perl code. Perl code can be embedded in HTML pages using the <% and %> tags, which are familiar to ASP programmers. These pages then are processed to replace the Perl code with its output at runtime—similar to the way a Server Side Include (SSI) works.

Summary

Although there are many tools that provide Perl persistence in a Web server environment, there are four that are most commonly seen:

- mod_perl provides a direct interface to the Apache Web server, and it can be used to provide persistence to derivative Perl environments such as Apache::Registry.

- FastCGI, available for a wider range of servers and Web application languages, provides a more abstracted interface and network-enabled architecture.

- VelociGen uses both approaches as well as others to provide a platform-neutral environment for Perl persistence, but its ease of use and CGI compatibility aren't free.

- PerlEx, another commercial tool, is specifically tailored to Windows environments, but its use of threaded Perl interpreters and tight integration makes Web applications potentially unstable in a PerlEx environment.

Overall, each environment should be evaluated in terms of the Web application being developed, as well as budget, platform, and development time constraints, because each tool provides a marked improvement in performance over a comparable CGI solution.

11

Problems with Persistence

THE PERFORMANCE BENEFITS OF PERSISTENCE ARE WORTH nearly any cost. Persistence tends to provide exponential improvements in performance with additional benefits when Web applications see more traffic and need to become more robust.

When implementing a persistent solution, it's necessary to watch for pitfalls, however. Specifically, some of the programming techniques commonly found in Perl Common Gateway Interface (CGI) programs can lead to unusual behavior or unanticipated performance loss when transplanted into a persistent environment. Some of these problems can be overcome automatically by choosing the right environment, but stylistic solutions to persistence problems can provide further benefits with little effort and few drawbacks.

The most common pitfall when writing Perl for the Web comes from global variables. The behavior of these variables can be very different between a CGI environment and a persistent environment. Luckily, there is an easy solution to global variable problems built directly into Perl. The my keyword provides a way to limit the scope of variables, and the strict and warnings pragmas provide runtime checks to ensure that it is being used correctly.

More difficult than variable issues are subtle problems that cause performance degradation even when the application operates correctly. The use of scoped variables is good Perl programming practice in any situation, but speed killers are specific to persistent Web applications and might not be obvious to programmers coming from a CGI background. The solutions to these performance issues are varied, but it's usually possible to find a solution based on the function being performed.

Caching, which is the backbone of persistent performance benefits, can also have its downside. It's possible to cache too much information; quite simply, the size of any cache is limited to the size of available memory. As a result, Web applications have to choose what information to cache and what information not to cache, and the choice is not always an obvious one. In some cases, the choice isn't even a conscious one— some data structures create unwanted copies of themselves that hang around until they are specifically disposed of. These structures are rare, thankfully, and keeping track of them simply requires a little diligence.

Nested Subroutines and Scoped Variables

The structure of a persistent Perl program is slightly different from a stand-alone program, whether it is created automatically by a system such as Apache::Registry or written specifically for an environment such as FastCGI. One major difference between persistent and single-use environments is the treatment of global variables. Fortunately, the my keyword provides a way to alter the scope of these variables to make them behave consistently in any environment.

Of course, this use of lexical scoping has its own caveats. Because persistence is usually achieved by turning Perl programs into subroutines of other Perl programs, the structure of the compiled program might be noticeably different from that which was originally written. Fortunately, even these errors can be caught by using the strict and warnings pragma modules to check program code for odd behavior at runtime. Because these modules are compiled in with the final version of the program, they are likely to catch errors that would slip by a manual inspection of the source code.

The *my* Keyword

Global variables are likely to behave strangely in a persistent context. The scope of most variables defaults to the entire program environment. Thus, many existing Perl CGI or command-line applications contain many global variables. Listing 11.1 is an example of these in a simple program.

Listing 11.1   **Global Variable Example**

```
01 #!/usr/bin/perl
02
03 require 5.6.0;
04
05 $word = $ARGV[0];
06 count_and_reverse();
07
08
```

```
09 sub count_and_reverse
10 {
11   print "\nNow evaluating '$word'.\n";
12
13   foreach $letter (split '', $word)
14   {
15     $count++;
16     $reverse = $letter . $reverse;
17   }
18
19   print "The word '$word' contains $count letters.\n";
20   print "The reverse of '$word' is $reverse.\n\n";
21 }
```

Listing 11.1 is a Perl command-line program that takes a single word as an argument, counts the letters in the word, and reverses the word. It's written in a style that separates the program's basic logic from functional blocks, which is common for Perl CGI programs. Line 05 takes the first argument from the command line (`$ARGV[0]`) and assigns it to the scalar variable `$word`. Line 06 then calls the `count_and_reverse` subroutine defined in the remainder of the program, starting with line 09. This subroutine is called in a void context with no arguments. Thus, its only access to program input is through the global `$word` variable. Line 11 prints this variable in context, and the word is split into component letters in line 13 and used as the basis for a `foreach` loop. Inside the loop, line 15 increments a counter variable (`$count`) and adds the current letter to the beginning of `$reverse`. The subroutine ends by printing the final letter count and the reverse of the word, as stored in `$reverse`.

The output of Listing 11.1 should look similar to the following—assuming that a word like "foof" is given as input:

```
Now evaluating 'foof'.
The word 'foof' contains 4 letters.
The reverse of 'foof' is foof.
```

This result isn't particularly exciting from a Perl point of view. The important thing to notice about this program is that it operates consistently from one instance to the next and that it provides a correct count and reversal of the input argument. This is analogous to the execution pattern seen with CGI programs, which proceed only once through the main functional block.

In contrast, Listing 11.2 is an analog of how the program might look in a persistent context. For simplicity, the persistent event handler is replaced here with a simple loop operating over the array of provided arguments. Otherwise, the program has the same structure. Lines that have changed are emphasized in bold text.

Listing 11.2 **Global Variables in Persistent Context**

```perl
01 #!/usr/bin/perl
02
03 require 5.6.0;
04
05 foreach (@ARGV)
06 {
07   $word = $_;
08   count_and_reverse();
09 }
10
11 sub count_and_reverse
12 {
13   print "\nNow evaluating '$word'.\n";
14
15   foreach $letter (split '', $word)
16   {
17     $count++;
18     $reverse = $letter . $reverse;
19   }
20
21   print "The word '$word' contains $count letters.\n";
22   print "The reverse of '$word' is $reverse.\n\n";
23 }
```

Lines 05–09 of Listing 11.2 set up a `foreach` loop that loops through the command-line arguments provided by `@ARGV`. Line 07 updates the global variable `$word` with each argument, and line 08 calls the `count_and_reverse` subroutine. Because `$word` is being updated before each call to the subroutine, the expected behavior of the program would be identical to that of Listing 11.2. However, providing the program with a list of arguments such as "foof hershey kahlua" would produce a result similar to the following:

```
Now evaluating 'foof'.
The word 'foof' contains 4 letters.
The reverse of 'foof' is foof.


Now evaluating 'hershey'.
The word 'hershey' contains 11 letters.
The reverse of 'hershey' is yehsrehfoof.


Now evaluating 'kahlua'.
The word 'kahlua' contains 17 letters.
The reverse of 'kahlua' is aulhakyehsrehfoof.
```

Whoops! The behavior of this program is different from what you would expect. It evaluates the first argument correctly, but subsequent iterations of the count_and_reverse subroutine produce a count larger than expected and a $reverse value that includes previous values. This happens despite the fact that the value of $word is correct for each iteration of the subroutine.

If the functional part of this program were operating in a true persistent Perl environment rather than this simulation, the results would be the same. Each subsequent call to the program would include leftover values from previous iterations, and the result of the program would be inconsistent. In practice, the inconsistencies are harder to spot than they are in this simple program, and the resulting confusion can be much more damaging to a Web application's effectiveness. In these cases, using the strict and warnings pragma modules (see Listing 11.3 for a usage example) points out the culprits:

```
Global symbol "$word" requires explicit package name at line 9.
Global symbol "$word" requires explicit package name at line 15.
Global symbol "$letter" requires explicit package name at line 17.
...
Global symbol "$reverse" requires explicit package name at line 24.
Execution of ./listing11-03a.pl aborted due to compilation errors.
```

For this program, the problem lies in the global variables used inside the count_and_reverse subroutine, as the error messages from the strict pragma point out. These variables are created inherently the first time the subroutine is called, but no indication is given by the programmer that they should be limited in scope. As a result, they are defined as global in scope (the default), and their values are kept from one iteration of the subroutine to the next. Because no code is used to explicitly initialize the variables before they are used, new values are simply added to old ones for each iteration.

The solution is simple in this case: use the my keyword to confine the scope of the variable to the subroutine. Complete documentation on the use of the my keyword (and its newer sibling, our, which is used to explicitly create global variables) is available in the Perl documentation. For our purposes, it suffices to say that my declares the scope of a variable to be limited to the enclosing block. This enables Perl to remove the variable after the program leaves its defined scope and reinitialize it when it appears again. Listing 11.3 uses the my keyword to fix the persistence problems in Listing 11.2. Once again, differences are listed in bold text.

Listing 11.3 **File-Scoped Variables**

```
01 #!/usr/bin/perl
02
03 require 5.6.0;
04 use strict;
05 use warnings;
06
```

continues

Listing 11.3   **Continued**

```
07 my $word;
08
09 foreach (@ARGV)
10 {
11    $word = $_;
12    count_and_reverse();
13 }
14
15 sub count_and_reverse
16 {
17    print "\nNow evaluating '$word'.\n";
18
19    my $count = 0;
20    my $reverse = '';
21
22    foreach my $letter (split '', $word)
23    {
24       $count++;
25       $reverse = $letter . $reverse;
26    }
27
28    print "The word '$word' contains $count letters.\n";
29    print "The reverse of '$word' is $reverse.\n\n";
30 }
```

Lines 04 and 05 of Listing 11.3 add the strict and warnings pragmas to require
variable scoping and raise warnings at potential trouble spots, respectively. Line 07 has
been added to declare the scope of $word to be the outermost block of the program—
in this case, the entire file. This won't affect the way the program behaves in this
instance, but it becomes important if the program becomes incorporated into yet
another program. ("There's always a bigger fish.")

Lines 19 and 20 have a more immediate effect. Line 19 declares the scope of
$count and gives it an initial value of zero. It could be argued that either of these
would take care of the unusual behavior seen when Listing 11.2 is run, but both are
necessary to make sure that the variable has both a known initial value and a defined
scope within the program. The former is helpful to Perl when determining how to
handle the variable in later interactions, and the latter is necessary to let Perl know
when it can free the memory allocated to the variable. If the my keyword wasn't used
to confine the variable's scope to the subroutine block, the memory used by $count
would not be freed after the subroutine ended. In a Web context where the subroutine
(or persistent program) might not receive a request again for hours, this creates unnecessary inefficiency that's easily avoidable.

With these three my declarations, all global variables in the program are accounted for and their scope is limited to the smallest area possible. As a result, the output of this program should be identical to that of the original in Listing 11.1. This principle can be extended to any program developed for use in a persistent environment: Use the my declaration as each variable is initially used to avoid unusual behavior caused by the persistence of the program.

"Variable Will Not Stay Shared" Errors

Global variables aren't always easy to spot, however. In fact, some variables are global only in a persistent context—even when they would not be in a CGI context. This usually is caused by the automatic modifications made to individual CGI-style programs as they are incorporated into a persistent environment. Because each program is redefined as a subroutine, Perl might treat parts of the program differently.

For instance, Listing 11.4 is an example of a CGI-style program that would not seem to have any global variables. In fact, it's a minor modification of the program in Listing 11.3 that was corrected specifically to get rid of global variables. Only the basic structure of a CGI program has been added to account for Web form variable input and simple HTML output. As a result, Listing 11.4 can be used in a CGI environment or a persistent environment.

Listing 11.4 **CGI-Style Program with File-Scoped Variables**

```
01 #!/usr/bin/perl
02
03 require 5.6.0;
04 use strict;
05 use warnings;
06
07 use CGI;
08
09 my $word;
10 my $q = CGI->new();
11
12 print $q->header;
13 print "<pre>\n";
14
15 foreach ($q->param('word'))
16 {
17   $word = $_;
18   count_and_reverse();
19 }
20
21 print "</pre>\n";
22
23 sub count_and_reverse
24 {
```

continues

Listing 11.4 **Continued**

```
25    print "\nNow evaluating '$word'.\n";
26
27    my $count = 0;
28    my $reverse = '';
29
30    foreach my $letter (split '', $word)
31    {
32      $count++;
33      $reverse = $letter . $reverse;
34    }
35
36    print "The word '$word' contains $count letters.\n";
37    print "The reverse of '$word' is $reverse.\n\n";
38 }
```

In a CGI environment, the program in Listing 11.4 would produce output similar to that of Listing 11.3. Line 07 includes the CGI module to provide form variable processing and simplified HTML output. Line 10 creates a new CGI object $q and limits its scope to this file. Lines 12 and 13 output the basic structure of an HTML response, using a <pre> tag to display the rest of the output as preformatted text. Line 15 has been modified to get a list of input words from the word form variable as processed by the CGI module, but the rest of the foreach loop stays the same, as does the count_and_reverse subroutine. After each form variable is processed, line 21 prints a closing </pre> tag to end the HTML output. Because the core of this program hasn't changed significantly, the result of a CGI request to the program would be consistent with that which is found at the command line.

However, in a persistent context, this program produces a warning, and if the program is called again it produces inconsistent results. (It would produce inconsistent results without notice if warnings were not enabled, of course.) The warning, which might appear in a number of ways, depending on the environment, should appear essentially like the following:

```
Variable "$word" will not stay shared at (eval 83) line 25.
Subroutine count_and_reverse redefined at (eval 83) line 24.
```

In this case, the warning is not as helpful as the messages from the strict pragma in Listing 11.2, and it provides only vague clues as to the problem. Although stated cryptically, the effect is listed in the first warning, and the cause is listed in the second warning. The cause is explored in the next section of this chapter, "Subroutines and Trickery Revisited," but the problem can be addressed solely in terms of effect. In this case, line 25 is the first instance of $word in the subroutine. Thus, it would appear that something unusual is happening to it after the subroutine is called. The warning "will not stay shared" is Perl's way of indicating that the my declaration outside the subroutine is causing the variable to fall out of scope inside the subroutine, which is a situation brought on by persistence trickery that would normally not occur. As a result, the first instance of $word inside the subroutine causes a new global variable to be declared that does not share the value of the intended $word variable. In short, Perl understands that we mean the same variable. Thus, it's warning us that it won't be the same.

To overcome this error with a work-alike that keeps the my declaration outside the subroutine, the variable can be explicitly shared inside the subroutine by providing the value we want as an argument and creating a new variable to store it. Listing 11.5 illustrates the solution.

Listing 11.5   **Persistent-Style Program with File-Scoped Variables**

```
01 #!/usr/bin/perl
02
03 require 5.6.0;
04 use strict;
05 use warnings;
06
07 use CGI;
08
09 my $word;
10 my $q = CGI->new();
11
12 print $q->header;
13 print "<pre>\n";
14
15 foreach ($q->param('word'))
16 {
17   $word = $_;
18   count_and_reverse($word);
19 }
20
21 print "</pre>\n";
22
23 sub count_and_reverse
24 {
25   my $word = shift;
26   print "\nNow evaluating '$word'.\n";
27
28   my $count = 0;
29   my $reverse = '';
30
31   foreach my $letter (split '', $word)
32   {
33     $count++;
34     $reverse = $letter . $reverse;
35   }
36
37   print "The word '$word' contains $count letters.\n";
38   print "The reverse of '$word' is $reverse.\n\n";
39 }
```

Lines 18 and 25 of listing 11.5 add the structure necessary to explicitly pass the value of $word to the subroutine each time it is called. Line 18 calls count_and_reverse with the file-scoped $word as the argument, and line 25 assigns it to a new variable (also called $word), which is limited in scope to the subroutine itself. This variable could be called something other than $word, but when troubleshooting existing CGI programs, it's usually easier to keep the same variable names if there's little chance of confusion. This avoids potential mismatches.

Again, the general idea behind this specific solution is to explicitly declare the relationship between the variable in the subroutine and the variable in the main program. In this case, the relationship was a simple copy, but other relationships are possible as well. If $word needed to be modified by the subroutine for use with the main program, it might have been better to pass a reference to the variable rather than a copy. In addition, if a variable is likely to be common to many subroutines (such as the CGI object $q in Listing 11.5), it is sometimes less cumbersome to explicitly declare the variable as global using the our keyword instead. Take care with our, though, because it creates a global variable that is shared not only with subsequent instances of this persistent program, but also with all other persistent Perl programs running within the same application engine.

Subroutines and Trickery Revisited

To understand the mechanism behind the "variable will not stay shared" error, it's important to know how Perl handles nested subroutines. Perl performs its own compile-time trickery by modifying the program to extract subroutines from other subroutines and by promoting them to the top level of their namespace. This is done to provide a simpler list of subroutines with which the Perl compiler has to deal. As a result, the general form of the program in Perl is changed from a nested subroutine like this:

```
namespace
  sub foo {
    sub bar {
      sub baz {}
    }
  }
  sub bah {}
```

to a more manageable list of subroutines like this:

```
namespace
  sub foo {}
  sub bar {}
  sub baz {}
  sub bah {}
```

Normally this works without a problem because the subroutines are called when global variables are set correctly or when they are passed arguments that can be assigned to variables with local scope. Even in the case in which variables are scoped to the namespace or file by using my, the subroutines inherit that scope because they are a level below the namespace. Thus, the example in Listing 11.4 works fine in a CGI context because the subroutine is run from the main namespace, and $word is scoped to that namespace.

However, in the case in which variables are scoped to one subroutine and run within another, the scope is not inherited. For instance, a variable defined in subroutine foo using my would not be in scope within subroutine bar because bar is extracted from foo at compile time. This makes perfect sense in reverse: a variable scoped within bar should fall out of scope within foo. Because both subroutines are effectively at the same level after the compile-time switch, variables scoped to either are off limits to the other.

As an example, Listings 11.6 and 11.7 are equivalent programs in Perl. Listing 11.6 embeds the program from Listing 11.5 in a subroutine and calls it repeatedly from within the surrounding program. Listing 11.7 shows equivalent code after the inherent translation at compile time.

Listing 11.6   **Nested Subroutine Example**

```
01 #!/usr/bin/perl
02
03 require 5.6.0;
04 use strict;
05 use warnings;
06
07 handler('foof','hershey','kahlua');
08 handler('merlin','callie','elfie','xena');
09
10 sub handler
11 {
12   my $word;
13
14   foreach (@_)
15   {
16     $word = $_;
17     count_and_reverse($word);
18   }
19
20   sub count_and_reverse
21   {
22     my $word = shift;
23     print "\nNow evaluating '$word'.\n";
24
25     my $count = 0;
26     my $reverse = '';
```

continues

Listing 11.6 **Continued**

```
27
28    foreach my $letter (split '', $word)
29    {
30      $count++;
31      $reverse = $letter . $reverse;
32    }
33
34    print "The word '$word' contains $count letters.\n";
35    print "The reverse of '$word' is $reverse.\n\n";
36  }
37 }
```

Listing 11.7 **Equivalent Example**

```
01 #!/usr/bin/perl
02
03 require 5.6.0;
04 use strict;
05 use warnings;
06
07 handler('foof','hershey','kahlua');
08 handler('merlin','callie','elfie','xena');
09
10 sub handler
11 {
12   my $word;
13
14   foreach (@_)
15   {
16     $word = $_;
17     count_and_reverse($word);
18   }
19 }
20
21 sub count_and_reverse
22 {
23   my $word = shift;
24   print "\nNow evaluating '$word'.\n";
25
26   my $count = 0;
27   my $reverse = '';
28
29   foreach my $letter (split '', $word)
30   {
31     $count++;
32     $reverse = $letter . $reverse;
33   }
34
35   print "The word '$word' contains $count letters.\n";
36   print "The reverse of '$word' is $reverse.\n\n";
37 }
```

Although the cause of the "variable will not stay shared" warning isn't obvious in Listing 11.6, it should be clearer when seen in the equivalent Listing 11.7. Line 12 of Listing 11.7 limits the scope of $word to the handler subroutine. Thus, the variable would be out of scope when used in the count_and_reverse subroutine. Only by scoping each variable separately and passing its values explicitly can the relationship be defined.

The hint leading to this discovery was that the error message for Listing 11.4 in a persistent environment was "subroutine redefined." As noted before, each program segment of a Web application—which would be a separate program in a CGI context—is incorporated into the larger whole by creating a subroutine with its code. Because a program segment might itself contain subroutines, these subroutines are dealt with in a manner that is similar to the nested subroutine in Listing 11.6. Because of this chain of events, global variables were created where none were anticipated.

Use Warnings to Catch Unusual Behavior

Again, the value of using the strict and warnings pragma modules to catch potential pitfalls can't be overstated. In these cases and many others, odd behavior can be caught—or at least hinted to—by errors and warnings generated by these two modules. As shown in Listing 11.4, sometimes the cause of unusual behavior would be next to impossible to track down without the hints given by the warnings pragma module.

It's also important to keep warnings in use even after the Web application is put into production. It would seem to be better for performance to remove the pragmas when the code is no longer likely to change, but the performance benefits are slight and the danger of unchecked changes to the code is too great in a Web development environment. Simple changes to the environment, such as shifting from CGI to a persistent context, can cause minor changes in the way code is handled by Perl. It's better to find out that problems exist by seeing warnings in development rather than by seeing peculiar behavior from a live site.

Fork, Backticks, and Speed Killers

Global variables and scoping aren't the only problems encountered when translating CGI-style programs for persistent use. Although variable issues can cause unusual behavior, another class of issues affects performance directly. The problem arises when the application engine process needs to *fork*, or start another process to perform work. The forked subprocess is usually transitory. Thus, it is started and stopped within the span of one request from the Web server. This counteracts the performance benefits of keeping a persistent application engine in the first place.

Fortunately, there are usually ways to get around forked processes within a Web application. In Perl, it's almost always possible to modify the application to use a native Perl function or module rather than an external process. Even when the external process can't be replicated by native Perl code, a persistent interface to it probably can be created without the need to fork additional processes. Sometimes, the necessary changes are difficult to spot within legacy code because the fork isn't explicit, but most cases of forking code fall into a few categories that can be found and replaced with native code fairly easily.

Backticks and Forked Processes

For Web application programmers, forking is most likely to be used inherently when accessing system utilities or other programs external to the Perl application. The usual method for accessing these programs is to enclose a command in backticks and assign the output to a variable. Listing 11.8 is an example of a simple program that uses the UNIX system utility ls to list files in a directory.

Listing 11.8 **Backticks Example**

```
01 #!/usr/bin/perl
02
03 require 5.6.0;
04 use strict;
05 use warnings;
06
07 use CGI;
08
09 my $q = CGI->new;
10 print $q->start_html;
11
12 my $listing = `ls /tmp/perlfiles/`;
13
14 foreach my $file (split /\n/, $listing)
15 {
16   next unless $file =~ /.pl$/;
17   chomp($file);
18   print $q->p($file);
19 }
20
21 print $q->end_html;
```

Listing 11.8 creates a simple HTML page with a listing of the Perl programs in the /tmp/perlfiles/ directory. Lines 07–10 set up the CGI module and start the HTML page. The backticks in line 12 run the ls command in the default shell and return the output, which is assigned to the $listing variable. Line 14 splits the result into individual filenames and loops over the list. Line 16 excludes any filename that doesn't end in .pl, and lines 17 and 18 clean up the filename and print it as an HTML paragraph. At the end, line 21 caps off the HTML page.

Behind the scenes, most of the overhead incurred by this program is caused by line 12. Specifically, a command-line shell is opened by using backticks to process a command. Because this shell is an external program, it has to be started and restarted with each request, regardless of whether the program is running in a persistent context. As a result, one line of code slows the entire program to CGI speeds. If the command invoked within the backticks was yet another program as opposed to a shell command, the additional overhead of starting that program would slow the Web application down further.

The best way to avoid this kind of speed killer is to use native Perl functions to perform the same task as the system utility. This provides two benefits:

- The performance of the Web applications is no longer hampered by the external program.

- The Web application becomes more portable because it relies less on a specific environment.

Perl provides built-in functions that give equivalent functionality to most system utilities, and more esoteric programs usually have specific Perl interfaces defined to address this problem. Listing 11.9 is an example of how Listing 11.8 could be implemented using only native Perl.

Listing 11.9 **Native Perl Example**

```
01 #!/usr/bin/perl
02
03 require 5.6.0;
04 use strict;
05 use warnings;
06
07 use CGI;
08
09 my $q = CGI->new;
10 print $q->start_html;
11
12 opendir DIR, "/tmp/perlfiles/";
13
14 while (my $file = readdir DIR)
15 {
16   next unless $file =~ /.pl/;
17   chomp($file);
18   print $q->p($file);
19 }
20
21 closedir DIR;
22
23 print $q->end_html;
```

The main difference between Listings 11.8 and 11.9 is the function used to open a directory listing. Line 12 of Listing 11.9 uses the `opendir` function provided by Perl to open a directory in a fashion similar to the `open` function. Line 14 loops over individual filenames in a slightly different fashion, but the rest of the loop operates identically to Listing 11.8 and the results are the same. Line 21 is added to close the directory handle DIR that was created in line 12. These simple changes relieve the need to start an external process and open up the application to the full performance benefits of persistence.

Processes That Fork Unintentionally

Not all external processes are started by an explicit fork keyword or a command enclosed in backticks. Many common Web applications fork processes unintentionally by calling command-line programs indirectly. This can occur in two ways: A file handle might be opened to a forked process by specifying a pipe symbol in the open function, or a module might be used that performs its own fork. The latter case can be avoided only by knowing which modules are all-native (including those that use XS) and which modules use external processes. The former case, however, can be fixed by replacing pipes to external programs with Perl-native functions or modules.

Listing 11.10 is an example that uses one of the most common speed killers in a persistent Web application. Many programs send email based on Web application events, such as a new user sign-up or a successful e-commerce transaction. Because many of these programs initially are written for CGI or based on CGI applications, this problem often is inherited without realizing it is a problem.

Listing 11.10   **Common CGI Emailer Using Sendmail**

```
01 #!/usr/bin/perl
02
03 require 5.6.0;
04 use strict;
05 use warnings;
06
07 use CGI;
08
09 my $q = CGI->new;
10 print $q->start_html;
11
12 my $to = $q->param('to');
13 my $from = $q->param('from');
14 my $subject = $q->param('subject');
15 my $body = $q->param('body');
16
17 open MAIL, "| /usr/sbin/sendmail -t";
18
19 print MAIL "From: $from\n";
20 print MAIL "To: $to\n";
21 print MAIL "Subject: $subject\n\n";
22
23 print MAIL "$body\n";
24
```

```
25 close MAIL;
26
27 print $q->p("From: $from");
28 print $q->p("To: $to");
29 print $q->p("Subject: $subject");
30
31 print $q->p("$body");
32
33
34 print $q->end_html;
```

The problem with Listing 11.10 lies in line 17. Even though no backticks or fork functions are used, the pipe symbol in the open argument calls sendmail as a command line program and pipes the MAIL file handle to it. The rest of the program is perfectly ordinary. Lines 09–15 set up the CGI environment and retrieve the form variables to, from, subject, and body, which are used to determine the contents of the mail message. Lines 19–23 print the contents to the Sendmail program, and lines 27–31 print the same contents to the HTML output. Line 25 closes the sendmail pipe opened in line 17.

Of course, opening a pipe to sendmail involves more than just a pipe. A shell has to be started to process the command line from line 17, and that shell starts the sendmail process to set up the pipe. Again, these two events occur for each request, and the resulting overhead slows the Web application down to CGI speeds. The solution is to avoid starting a shell or an external program in the first place. Luckily this is possible by sending mail through the Net::SMTP module, which opens a socket to the mail server without the need for any new processes. Listing 11.11 incorporates the change.

Listing 11.11 **Native Perl Emailer Using Net::SMTP**

```
01 #!/usr/bin/perl
02
03 require 5.6.0;
04 use strict;
05 use warnings;
06
07 use CGI;
08 use Net::SMTP;
09
10 my $q = CGI->new;
11 print $q->start_html;
12
13 my $to = $q->param('to');
14 my $from = $q->param('from');
15 my $subject = $q->param('subject');
16 my $body = $q->param('body');
17
18 my $smtp = Net::SMTP->new('localhost');
```

continues

Listing 11.11   **Continued**

```
19
20 $smtp->mail($from);
21 $smtp->to($to);
22
23 $smtp->data();
24 $smtp->datasend("To: $to\n");
25 $smtp->datasend("Subject: $subject\n\n");
26 $smtp->datasend("$body\n");
27 $smtp->dataend();
28
29 $smtp->quit;
30
31 print $q->p("From: $from");
32 print $q->p("To: $to");
33 print $q->p("Subject: $subject");
34
35 print $q->p("$body");
36
37
38 print $q->end_html;
```

In this case, the code difference is a little more significant due to the differences between the piped file handle and the Net::SMTP module functions. Line 08 includes the Net::SMTP module itself, and line 18 opens a connection to the SMTP mail server on the local machine. Lines 20–27 pass the data to the server using functions provided by the `$smtp` connection object, and line 29 finally closes the connection to the server. Because the entire transaction is carried out using native Perl networking libraries and modules, no additional overhead is incurred. In addition, using a network connection might provide opportunities for further performance enhancements because the connection can be opened once and kept persistent depending on the Web application environment.

Discovering Speed Killers

As mentioned, it's difficult to find the true nature of a performance bottleneck—especially when the cause of the problem is architectural rather than programmatic. Luckily, most speed killers in a Perl Web application environment can be found in the few classes mentioned in this chapter. By following the style guidelines outlined, it's possible to avoid the majority of Web application speed killers.

However, the possibility still exists that a bottleneck is present that doesn't fall into one of these categories. As time goes on, that possibility becomes a certainty as new technologies are incorporated into the Web application framework. As a result, it's necessary to develop a more general way to pinpoint the source of a performance bottleneck—if not necessarily its nature. More information on evaluating the performance of a site and its parts can be found in Chapter 15, "Testing Site Performance."

Caching

Although some persistence problems are noticeable immediately, others can be caused by cumulative effects that won't be noticed until the Web application has been operating persistently for a considerable amount of time. These kinds of problems can be the most difficult to detect because the only obvious signs will be slow performance degradation, with a possibility of server crashes or unusual behavior after a prolonged slowdown. In some cases, though, the problems seem to fix themselves on a periodic basis because their causes are linked to the life cycles of the Web application engines themselves.

Caching provides most of the performance improvements seen by persistent Web applications because caching eliminates the overhead due to loading files off disk and processing them for use in the application. As shown in previous chapters, this holds true for compiling applications, processing simple files, or loading complex files into data structures. As a result, the usual response to any file, connection, or data structure in a persistent environment is to keep it around as long as possible in case some other part of the application might be able to benefit from its presence.

Caching comes at a price, however. The price usually isn't high, but it can be prohibitive if caching is used indiscriminately. Each cached variable, file, or data structure takes up an additional amount of memory, and over time, these cached structures can overwhelm the rest of an application engine and force it either to restart or to slow down the entire Web server machine. Luckily, most Web application environments rely on Perl to make the decision whether to keep a cached structure in memory, so many data structures are cached only if they are specifically marked as important within the application. Unfortunately, some complex data structures can escape Perl's scrutiny and stay in memory indefinitely, regardless of whether they can be used.

The main cause of unwanted caching is Perl's openness when it comes to the assignment of references. Perl cleans up memory based on the current activity of a data structure, but it is altogether too easy to convince Perl that a data structure is still active, even though its only references come from itself. Worse yet, it's sometimes necessary to set up these circular references to model a data structure properly. The solution is to manually walk through the data structure and remove circular references, which luckily is handled by some modules themselves and offered as an object method.

Circular References

In Perl, the main reason that unanticipated caching occurs is because Perl frees memory taken up by variables when the variables are no longer being used. Perl determines this by keeping tabs on the *reference count* of a variable, the number of currently active variables, and the program sections that refer to it. Perl knows to keep a variable in memory as long as the reference count for the variable is not zero, and it can safely remove the variable from memory when the reference count reaches zero because there is no longer any way for the program to access the variable.

The problem with reference counts is that Perl enables references to be assigned programmatically instead of handling them all inherently. In fact, most of Perl's object-oriented programming structure is based on the assignment of variable references. This kind of caching can be considered a memory leak in this context because the amount of memory used by the program increases over time as each request adds more unused objects to memory.

Most Perl modules do not create circular references, though, and many that do clean up the circular references. Thus, circular references are not a reason to avoid object-oriented modules as a matter of course. However, modules that create complex hierarchical data structures can be subject to intractable circular references. This is more likely to occur when the module enables individual parts of the hierarchies to be manipulated by offering subclassed objects as containers for other objects.

Example: XML::DOM Objects

One module that creates intractable circular references as a matter of course is the XML::DOM module. XML::DOM provides a legion of subclass objects that can be linked in a containment hierarchy to provide flexible access to any part of an XML document's structure. The XML::DOM::Element object, for instance, represents a tagged element in the document's hierarchy. This object can contain references to other Element objects, as well as references to the XML::DOM::Document object that the Element is part of and to the Element that is its parent. (More details on the XML::DOM module can be found in Chapter 16, "XML and Content Management.")

These connections between objects can easily become too complex for Perl to sort out automatically, which makes it difficult for Perl to determine when the object has gone out of scope. As a result, methods need to be invoked to dispose of objects manually, or the objects will stay in memory long after the request that created them has been fulfilled and closed.

Listing 11.12 provides an example of XML::DOM code that could produce unwanted cached objects if the objects were not disposed of manually. It processes the XML file in Listing 11.13 and displays a simple list of nodes and their values.

Listing 11.12 **DOM Object Processor Example**

```
01 #!/usr/bin/perl
02
03 require 5.6.0;
04 use strict;
05 use warnings;
06
07 use CGI;
08 use XML::DOM;
09
10 my $q = CGI->new;
```

```
11 print $q->start_html;
12
13 my $parser = XML::DOM::Parser->new;
14
15 my $doc = $parser->parsefile('/tmp/listing11-13.xml');
16
17 my $root = $doc->getDocumentElement;
18
19 foreach my $node ($root->getChildNodes)
20 {
21   next unless $node->getNodeType == 1;
22
23   my $tag_name = $node->getTagName;
24   my $value = $node->getFirstChild->getData;
25
26   print $q->p("\u$value is a $tag_name.");
27 }
28
29 print $q->end_html;
30
31 $doc->dispose;
```

Listing 11.13   **Sample XML File**

```
01 <test>
02 <food>tofu</food>
03 <food>ham</food>
04 <food>stuff</food>
05 </test>
```

For our purposes, the two most important lines in Listing 11.12 are line 15 and line 31, which create and dispose of the XML::DOM document, respectively. In addition, line 13 creates an XML::DOM::Parser object to parse the XML file into a hierarchy of XML::DOM objects. Lines 17–27 use various object methods from the XML::DOM objects to retrieve and manipulate the data contained in the XML document. These lines show some of the connections made between the objects and their hierarchical relationship. The creation of the main document object in line 15 is the cause of all these objects and connections, however. If not disposed, each request would generate a new document object from the parsed XML file, which stayed in memory despite its last real reference ($doc) going out of scope at the end of the program. Over time, the memory used by these objects would bloat the size of the application engine to fill available memory, slowing the Web server to a crawl and eventually crashing the machine. By calling the dispose method in line 31, the program lets XML::DOM know that it should look through its own set of objects and remove any circular references to ease Perl's cleanup job.

Even though this technique relies on removing a data structure from memory at the end of every request, adding a more useful layer of controlled caching is still possible. The key is to make a master copy of the cached object when it is first processed and then provide copies of the object to be used by the actual program. Because there's always one untouched copy of the object in a separate cache, the programmer doesn't have to worry about modifications to a cached object being carried on to other requests. In addition, the master copy can be stored along with a file date so that the master can be updated if the file changes on disk. This kind of deliberate caching isn't likely to incur nearly the memory penalty of uncontrolled caching, and the resulting object copies behave consistently no matter how often they are used in any circumstance.

Summary

Adapting Perl Web applications for a persistent environment can invoke some daunting issues, but persistence problems fall into a few well-defined classes. In addition, the problems usually can be overcome with a combination of good Perl programming style and reliance on the built-in tools Perl provides for checking code for problems at runtime. Common persistence problems include variable scoping issues, which can usually be dealt with by using the my keyword correctly and watching for warnings. Performance problems can occur when external processes cause additional overhead, but these situations can be avoided by using native Perl modules and functions for system interaction. Unwanted caching due to the persistent environment can present its own problems, but the solutions usually can be found within the same modules causing the trouble. One thing is true no matter what the problem or solution: The benefits of persistence are worth the effort.

12

Environments for Reducing Development Time

INCREASING THE PERFORMANCE OF PERL CODE AS it executes is one thing, but there are aspects of a Web application that can't be sped up automatically. However, a change in architecture—and the resultant development environment—can do for development overhead what persistence does for execution time. A new approach can also pave the way for more robust applications that keep the final product fixed firmly in mind.

The first step to improving the development process for Web applications in Perl is to move from a Perl-centric approach to a Web-centric approach. This is done by setting up an environment that enables Perl code to be embedded in HTML, instead of the other way around. At first blush, it would seem to be an equivalent situation, but the difference in perspective can make the difference between a Web-savvy developer and a developer who can't make the leap from Perl to the Web.

Embedding Perl in HTML or XML

To put it simply, embedding Perl in Hypertext Markup Language (HTML) (or Extensible Markup Language [XML], eventually) avoids simplistic application designs. If the focus of an application is what the Perl code is doing rather than how the result is presented to the user, that result is likely to be too simple to convey the full meaning of the data being presented. In an HTML environment, the end product is everything because it's the only thing the user sees.

Basing a program on HTML makes it more Web-like and takes advantage of Web techniques. For instance, a Web application has the capability to reference parts of the same application (other pages) or parts of other Web applications indiscriminately. The point of a hypertext system is to link all possible applications (or pages) in a web of nodes that have no boundaries. If a Web application is designed as a monolithic structure, it's less likely to take advantage of these links to communicate with anything but itself.

After the focus is shifted from traditional applications to Web-centric applications, it's possible to ease development further by adding template mechanisms and convenience methods. The need for reusable components becomes much more acute when hundreds of programs with minor differences are being created to operate as a whole within a coherent environment. Because Web users value consistency from one site to the next and insist on consistency within a site, it makes perfect sense to separate out those parts of a site that stay constant and reference them indirectly within each individual program. From there, it's only a short hop to writing the programs themselves as components that are referenced indirectly by a user's actions as he or she moves through a dynamic site.

"Hello World" Syndrome

The first Web application learned by most Common Gateway Interface (CGI)-style developers is nearly identical to the first application learned by any other programmer— "Hello World." Listing 12.1 is an example of how the Hello World program might be created by a Web programmer who is beginning to learn Perl CGI.

Listing 12.1 **Hello World**

```perl
01 #!/usr/bin/perl
02
03 # include libraries
04 require 5.6.0;
05 use strict;
06 use warnings;
07 use CGI;
08
09 # initiate CGI parser object
10 my $q = CGI->new;
11
12 # begin the page
13 print $q->header,
14      $q->start_html('Hello World');
15
16 print $q->p("Hello, World!");
17
18 print $q->end_html;
```

This program might look pretty impressive from a Perl point of view. In a Web context, though, it's one line of relevant information and 17 lines of telling us what we already know—we're using Perl, we're writing a Web application, and it's creating HTML. Its output probably would inspire no one:

```
Hello, World!
```

As it's written, the program produces a very simple page. It doesn't take advantage of HTML's more advanced features. However, the simple case still is difficult enough that more complex tasks (such as the compilation of information from around the Web by a page like My Yahoo!) seem daunting in comparison to their HTML output. In fact, as the program gets more complex, it still finds no room for the frills, color, and ease of use users have come to expect on the Web. As a result, too many mature applications on the Web show the same blandness from which Hello World suffers.

Worse yet, future Web applications written in the same style have to start from Hello World all over again because none of the code developed for one application is exported into the environment for other applications to use. This provides no continuity at all over the course of a site, and it relegates usability concerns to the few Web programmers who have successfully slogged through the reams of code necessary to get the programs working in the first place.

Embracing Web Style

The Web is based on HTML pages for a very good reason. Back when the Web was invented, a simple page markup and hypertext description language was also developed. It was designed to be simpler to understand—and therefore more likely to be used—than page description languages, such as PostScript, or programming languages, such as C. The result (HTML) became one of the handful of reasons why the Web became phenomenally popular in the ensuing years. Suddenly, the distance between source code and final product was shorter than ever before. It was short enough that ordinary tinkerers could take a look at the workings of a multi-million-dollar site and discover its secrets in a matter of hours.

The core of Web style is that HTML pages have a certain look and feel that comes about from the kind of markup HTML enables. This creates pages that flow from top to bottom in (generally) one column of text with frequent breaks in the text caused by headers, images, and hyperlinks. Viewing an HTML source file gives the same impression—a single flow broken by a few different types of text. Images might surround the core information stream, but their meaning usually fades to the background as the central focus of the page is concentrated on. The application logic sometimes can obfuscate that by being more abstract. For designers who are used to seeing the content of a page in terms of a flow with some breaks, it might be difficult to get a handle on how a page flows when it is listed as nested subroutines or abstract function calls. The flow is further impeded when the page itself is buried in a mound of print statements and environment declarations.

Web-like programming can give rise to stronger Web pages and more intuitive Web applications. Because the Web style is so easy to grasp, Web applications written in a similar style would seem to benefit from the same easy-to-understand logic. As it turns out, this is often the case when developing Web applications in a Web-centric style. The applications match their final output so closely that simply viewing the end result indicates the source of any discord or flawed program logic. Additional componentization of the application spreads this vision further by enabling the programmer or designer to separate the program out by visual section. After a program is fully Web-centric, it becomes easy for a Web programmer to focus on a section of code by addressing just the output of that section, without giving any thought to the sections around it—on the page or on other unseen pages.

Templates and Code Separation

Templates defining the overall look and behavior of a site are a natural extension of the idea of embedding Perl code in HTML. Templates can be viewed as HTML-centric pages with smaller Perl snippets, which stand for abstract parts of the Web application interface. In fact, there's no better way to think of them—because Perl and HTML are both known quantities, viewing a template system as Perl-in-HTML makes it much easier to implement. The details can be tricky, however; see Chapter 13, "Using Templates with Perl Applications," for more information on templates.

Code separation also is a tricky topic because the code part of an application can't be completely separate from the display part of the application. It's possible to create abstractions of each in the arena of the other, but there's no complete way to separate the two because there always has to be a connection point. Embedding code in HTML provides a good interface that doesn't have to give up either the robustness of code or the simplicity of HTML. In addition, it takes away the need to create an artificial third layer that might not have the strengths of either.

Comparisons with CGI.pm Style

Before talking about embedded solutions, you need to get a better understanding of CGI.pm style. It's a style that grew out of the standard Perl programming style, with the addition of the conventions of CGI.pm, which is the most prominent CGI interaction library in use. CGI.pm offers a host of functions for accessing environment and form variables and controlling output. By controlling the way that the Perl program interacts with these interfaces, CGI.pm emphasizes the Perlish nature of a Web application and hides much of the HTML code that eventually results.

The CGI.pm style usually is overkill when creating a Web application. Functions are present that are just Perl translations of HTML text. Thus, it's often easier just to print the HTML directly instead of calling a Perl function that might be less familiar to a Web designer. In addition, the style of HTML tags is not fully compatible with a linear programming method such as the one Perl uses. Trying to compose a complex document with these functions becomes awkward and unreadable, while the equivalent HTML would be trivial to compose. In addition, using CGI.pm to access form variables for Web application communication can be cumbersome and repetitive. In short, CGI.pm has its place, but it usually is much more useful in an inherent context instead of being used explicitly.

SQL Query Processor Revisited

The SQL query processor example from Chapter 7, "Perl for the Web," reprinted here as Listing 12.2, is written using the CGI style. This program is self-contained, relying on multiple requests to the same program to provide a complete Web application. It incorporates no other files aside from Perl modules. Its coding style is overwhelmingly Perl-centric with very few intimations that the output of the program is actually HTML. It also assumes only the barest of execution environments. Thus, every aspect of Perl initialization is present and necessary.

Listing 12.2 **SQL Query Processor**

```
001 #!/usr/bin/perl
002
003 #----------------------------------------
004 #
005 # sql_query.pl - CGI application example
006 #
007 #----------------------------------------
008
009 # include libraries
010 require 5.6.0;
011 use strict;
012 use warnings;
013 use CGI;
014 use DBI;
015
016 # declare some variables
017 my ($q, $dbh, $sth, $query, $datasource, $user, $password, $error,
    ➥$field, $result, $results);
018 my (@datasources);
019
020 # initiate CGI parser object
021 $q = CGI->new;
022
023 # begin the page
024 print $q->header,
025     $q->start_html('SQL Database Viewer'),
026     $q->h2('SQL Database Viewer');
027
028 # build a (safe) list of data sources
029 foreach (DBI->available_drivers)
```

continues

Listing 12.2   **Continued**

```
030 {
031   eval {
032     foreach (DBI->data_sources($_))
033     {
034       push @datasources, $_;
035     }
036   };
037 }
038
039
040 # display the entry form
041 print $q->start_form;
042
043 print qq{<p>Choose a datasource:</p>\n};
044 print $q->popup_menu(-name => 'datasource',
045                      -values => \@datasources);
046
047 print qq{<p>Specify username/password:</p>\n};
048 print $q->textfield(-name => 'user',
049                     -size => 10);
050 print $q->password_field(-name => 'password',
051                          -size => 10);
052
053 print qq{<p>Enter a SELECT query:</p>\n};
054 print $q->textarea(-name => 'query',
055                    -rows => '5',
056                    -cols => '40',
057                    -wrap => 'virtual');
058
059 print $q->p, $q->submit;
060 print $q->end_form;
061
062 # get form variables
063 $datasource = $q->param('datasource');
064 $user = $q->param('user');
065 $password = $q->param('password');
066 $query = $q->param('query');
067
068 # check form variables
069 if ($query)
070 {
071   $error = "Improper datasource specified" unless ($datasource =~
        / ^dbi/i);
072   $error = "Query should start with SELECT" unless ($query =~
        / ^select/i);
073 }
074
075 # if a query is specified and form variables are OK,
076 if ($query and !$error)
```

```
077 {
078   # connect to the database
079   $dbh = DBI->connect($datasource, $user, $password)
080          or $error = "Connection failed: $DBI::errstr";
081
082   # if the database connection worked, send the query
083   unless ($error)
084   {
085     $sth = $dbh->prepare($query)
086            or $error = "Query failed: $DBI::errstr";
087     $sth->execute or $error = "Query failed: $DBI::errstr";
088   }
089 }
090
091 # if any errors are present, display the error and exit
092 if ($error) {print $q->p("Error: $error"), $q->end_html and exit;}
093
094 # if the query produced an output,
095 if ($query and $sth->{NAME})
096 {
097   # start a data table
098   print qq{<table border="1">\n};
099   print qq{<tr>\n};
100
101   # display the fields as table headers
102   foreach $field (@{$sth->{NAME}})
103   {
104     print qq{<th>$field</th>\n};
105   }
106   print qq{</tr>\n};
107
108   # display the results in a table
109   while ($results = $sth->fetchrow_arrayref)
110   {
111     print qq{<tr>\n};
112     foreach $result (@$results)
113     {
114       print qq{<td>$result</td>\n};
115     }
116     print qq{</tr>\n};
117   }
118
119   # finish the data table
120   print qq{</table>\n};
121 }
122
123 # finish the page
124 print $q->end_html;
125
126 # disconnect from the database
127 $dbh->disconnect if $dbh;
```

Incidentally, Listing 12.2 should run in CGI as it would in persistent environments. This is made possible by using the my keyword in lines 17 and 18 to restrict the scope of program variables. It's also helped by using the strict and warnings pragma modules to check the code as it is compiled. Otherwise, the listing doesn't require any stylistic changes to make it executable in a persistent environment.

This emphasizes the difference between CGI *style* and the CGI *environment*. The CGI environment already has been exposed in previous chapters as a performance drain, which can be overcome by using a persistent environment, as described in Chapter 9, "The Power of Persistence," and Chapter 10, "Tools for Perl Persistence." CGI style, however, is the style of Web application programming encouraged by the limitations of that environment. This includes the following:

- The overall style and look of the code listing. CGI-style code looks like a Perl program from beginning to end because it runs with few assumptions about its environment.

- The code used to perform basic program functions. This includes both standard Perl code sections and code used specifically for CGI functions.

- Whether those functions are needed at all. CGI-style code assumes that all program functions must be performed explicitly. With persistence, some functions can be performed implicitly within the Web server environment.

Process Form Variables

Form variables are the main means of explicit communication between the client browser and Web applications. They usually result from a user filling in information in HTML form fields. An example of this is a username typed into an HTML text field. After it is submitted, the names and values of all form variables are sent along with the page request. These variables then become the parameters used by the Web application to respond to the request appropriately.

Processing form variables can be a difficult task for CGI beginners, but after the form variable problem is solved, there's very little reason to vary the solution. The CGI protocol provides the names and values of all form variables to any CGI program, but the format of these variables is not conducive to easy Perl programming. For example, Listing 12.2 might produce form values in this format:

```
datasource=dbi:null&user=poppy&password=f8ntom&query=SELECT+*+FROM+dual
```

The format is standardized and parsible, but writing a parser to split out variables and their values would be too complex a task for most beginner Web applications. Luckily, the problem has been solved in a general way and incorporated into the CGI module. CGI.pm provides form variable access through a set of object methods—one of which is the param method used to retrieve an individual form variable by name. Lines 063–066 of Listing 12.2 retrieve the necessary form variables for the rest of the application.

In Listing 12.2, only a few form variables need be brought into the program. Thus, they are assigned individually using the `param` method. To enable the variables to contain a wide range of values, very little checking is performed. The only exceptions are the data source—which should start with `DBI`—and the SQL query itself, which is limited to `SELECT` statements to reduce the potential for unanticipated changes to the database. Most Web applications require much more variable checking than this example. For instance, an order form would need more stringent checks on the format of a credit card number or zip code.

Query a Database

Although database access isn't central to most programming languages, it has become central to Web application programming. As a result, it should be a central part of any embedded Perl programming environment. A database often is used as the central place where a Web application can store and retrieve information. Providing access to this kind of data should be as seamless as possible. In addition, many Web applications are designed to provide a browseable interface to data stored in a database. These applications require a seamless interface between Perl and the database.

Listing 12.2 is devoted to database access. Thus, it makes sense that database methods should be common throughout the program. In addition, the program is designed to accept a wide variety of `SELECT` queries and display a wide variety of results from those queries. Therefore, the methods it uses to process the queries are more generic than would be found in most Web applications. For instance, line 085 of Listing 12.2 simply passes the SQL query as it is provided by the input form, but most Web applications would compose the database query from a number of form variables based on a SQL template.

It should be noted that database access and CGI.pm do not overlap at all. CGI.pm doesn't provide any convenience methods for accessing a database in a Web-friendly fashion, nor does it provide shortcuts for handling or displaying the resultant data from queries. As a result, the methods used in Listing 12.2 to interact with the database are provided directly by the DBI module, which is discussed in greater detail in Chapter 14, "Database-Backed Web Sites."

Format Data in HTML

Another core aspect of Web applications is the need to generate HTML-formatted text from data sources. Often the format of the data being presented is known when the application is being designed so that the data can be placed within an HTML context with a fine grain of control over presentation. In some cases, though, the data being displayed can vary widely from one request to the next. In these cases, it's more important to provide a flexible framework in which all possible results are displayed in an understandable fashion, even though some control over formatting layout might be given up. The SQL query processor is one of these programs, as illustrated by the data table generation code in lines 109–117.

The HTML generated in Listing 12.2 largely depends on the results of the SQL query provided. As a result, the exact number of table cells in each row is not known, and it's not possible to present the table in its entirety. Rather, parts of the table are abstracted out and governed by `foreach` loops. The result of the code ends up looking like the following:

```
<tr>
<th>id</th>
<th>username</th>
<th>realname</th>
</tr>
<tr>
<td>12</td>
<td>cmonster</td>
<td>Chris Radcliff</td>
</tr>
```

Note that CGI.pm object methods aren't being used to generate the table tags. It would be possible to do so, but very little abstraction would be gained, and the code would have to be more awkward. The CGI module does provide some assistance with creating form fields from data structures, but the majority of other CGI methods seem to be simple copies of the HTML tags they generate. For instance, line 114 could be rewritten as follows:

```
# the original line:
#     print qq{<td>$result</td>\n};
# is replaced by:
      print $q->td($result), "\n";
```

Although the resulting line is more Perlish, the change doesn't add much abstraction because the function name is the same as the resulting HTML tag name. Any additional styles or formatting have to be added to the Perl explicitly to appear in the HTML. For instance, setting the contents of each table cell in bold would require as much Perl as HTML:

```
# the original line:
#     print qq{<td><b>$result</b></td>\n};
# is replaced by:
      print $q->td($q->b($result)), "\n";
```

It is important to note that the CGI.pm style buries HTML formatting in the Perl code. This makes the job of both site designers and programmers even more difficult because an explicit translation step has to be performed between the HTML the site designer expects and the CGI methods the programmer produces. Because there's no intrinsic benefit to making the translation in most cases, it's more likely that the CGI methods for HTML creation will go unused.

HTML::Mason

One of the most common Perl embedding environments is HTML::Mason
(http://www.masonhq.com). HTML::Mason is also one of the most robust Perl development environments for the Web at the time this book was being written. In fact,
HTML::Mason can be considered on par with commercial efforts, such as Perl Server
Pages (PSP), and dedicated Web languages, such as PHP.

Mason is presented as a programming environment for reusable Web application
segments. It enables Perl to be embedded in HTML pages, and it also enables other
pages to be included in the page by invoking them as components. These components
can be pure HTML, pure Perl, or a mix of the two, and the interface between the
calling component and the called component is defined robustly.

HTML::Mason is best implemented in a persistent environment, but it has few
dependencies on platform or architecture. Mason usually is used in conjunction with
mod_perl, for instance, but it can just as easily be used in a FastCGI application or as a
CGI process. Details of installing and configuring HTML::Mason for a specific platform are subject to change, but instructions can be found at the Mason Web site.

Query Processor Application Changes

The syntax used by HTML::Mason is similar to many other Perl embedding environments, but it is different from CGI.pm style in many important respects. Listing 12.3 is
an example of modifications that could be made to the SQL query processor from
Listing 12.2 to adapt it for use within the HTML::Mason framework.

Listing 12.3   **SQL Processor in HTML::Mason**

```
001 <%args>
002 $query=>''
003 $datasource=>''
004 $user=>''
005 $pass=>''
006 </%args>
007
008 <%perl>
009 # declare some variables
010 my ($dbh, $sth, $error, $field, $result, $results);
011 my (@datasources);
012
013 # build a (safe) list of data sources
014 foreach (DBI->available_drivers)
015 {
016   eval {
017     foreach (DBI->data_sources($_))
018     {
019       push @datasources, $_;
020     }
```

continues

Listing 12.3 **Continued**

```
021   };
022 }
023 </%perl>
024
025 <html>
026 <head>
027 <title>SQL Query Browser</title>
028 </head>
029 <body>
030
031 <h3>SQL Query Browser</h3>
032
033 <form method="post">
034 <p>Choose a datasource:</p>
035
036 <select name="datasource">
037 %foreach my $source (@datasources) {
038 %  if ($source eq $datasource) {
039 <option selected="selected"><%$source%></option>
040 %  } else {
041 <option><%$source%></option>
042 %  }
043 %}
044 </select>
045
046 <p>Specify username/password:</p>
047
048 <input type="text" name="user" size="10" value="<%$user%>" />
049  
050 <input type="password" name="password" size="10"
    ⇒value="<%$password%>" />
051
052 <p>Enter a SELECT query:</p>
053
054 <textarea name="query" rows="5" cols="40"
055  wrap="virtual"><%$query%></textarea>
056
057 <p><input type="submit" /></p>
058 </form>
059
060 <%perl>
061 if ($query)
062 {
063   # check form variables
064   $error = "Improper datasource specified" unless ($datasource =~
      /^dbi/i);
065   $error = "Query should start with SELECT" unless ($query =~
      /^select/i);
066
067   unless ($error)
068   {
```

```
069     # connect to the database
070     $dbh = DBI->connect($datasource, $user, $password)
071             or $error = "Connection failed: $✦✛✧✦✚✦✳☐☐▲▼☐";
072
073     # if the database connection worked, send the query
074     unless ($error)
075     {
076       $sth = $dbh->prepare($query)
077             or $error = "Query failed: $DBI::errstr";
078       $sth->execute or $error = "Query failed: $DBI::errstr";
079     }
080   }
081
082   # if any errors are present, display the error
083   if ($error)
084   {
085     print qq{<p><font color="red"><b>Error: $error</b></font></p>};
086   }
087
088   # if the query produced an output,
089   if (!$error and $sth->{NAME})
090   {
091     # start a data table
092     print qq{<table border="1">\n};
093     print qq{<tr>\n};
094
095     # display the fields as table headers
096     foreach $field (@{$sth->{NAME}})
097     {
098       print qq{<th>$field</th>\n};
099     }
100     print qq{</tr>\n};
101
102     # display the results in a table
103     while ($results = $sth->fetchrow_arrayref)
104     {
105       print qq{<tr>\n};
106       foreach $result (@$results)
107       {
108         print qq{<td>$result</td>\n};
109       }
110       print qq{</tr>\n};
111     }
112
113     # finish the data table
114     print qq{</table>\n};
115   }
116 }
117 </%perl>
118 </body>
119 </html>
```

From a structural point of view, Listing 12.3 isn't much different from Listing 12.2. This is due in part to the fact that the SQL query Web application is of medium complexity with a mix of both HTML-heavy and Perl-heavy sections. In contrast, an application with only a few short sections of Perl mixed in with a large amount of HTML would look significantly different from a CGI version of the program, whereas an application with mostly Perl and little HTML would look nearly identical. Because most pages on a complete Web site are more like the former than the latter, stylistic differences between CGI and HTML::Mason are likely to be more noticeable in practice. The SQL query application also is self-contained instead of spread across a number of pages. This deemphasizes one of the strengths of HTML::Mason—the capability to share program components easily among a number of pages.

One stylistic aspect of Mason—and of all the other embedded environments in this chapter—that should be immediately noticeable is the lack of Perl initialization code at the beginning of the program. In fact, the first 13 lines of Listing 12.2 have no counterpart in Listing 12.3 or subsequent examples. This is an acknowledgment of the persistent environment of which these programs are likely to be a part. A program such as this isn't going to be run from a shell. Therefore, there's no `#!/usr/bin/perl` to indicate where the Perl executable is. Likewise, the page is part of an environment in which DBI and other supporting Perl modules already have been declared and loaded. Thus, there's no need to include modules explicitly at this point. With HTML::Mason specifically, this program is considered to be only one part of a whole Web application that can be called from any other part as easily as from the Web server directly. This shift in thinking does more than save a few lines of initialization at the beginning of each program; it breaks Web applications free of the restraints of the `cgi-bin` directory and promotes them to first-class citizens that are integrated with the rest of the Web site.

Demarcating Perl Segments

The simplest way to embed Perl in an HTML::Mason page is by enclosing it in a section delimited by `<%perl>` at the beginning and `</%perl>` at the end. An embedded Perl section such as this is evaluated as though it were a short Perl program. It then is replaced in the HTML page with the printed results of the section. In addition, the Perl section has access to any variables defined before it that are still in scope (based on `my` declarations), and variables defined within the section are available to subsequent sections and other embedded structures. This type of embedded Perl segment is common to all environments listed in this chapter, and they all provide roughly the same functionality. Each environment has its own way of evaluating the Perl sections and other embedded structures as the program is executed, but the resultant output is similar enough to be equivalent.

In a Mason page, this kind of segment is most useful when evaluating multiple lines of Perl, as in lines 008–023 of Listing 12.3. These lines are nearly identical to the corresponding section in Listing 12.2. In both cases, they declare the scope of variables used throughout the rest of the program. They then create a list of data sources and store it in `@datasources`. Because the Perl code isn't creating or affecting any HTML output directly, it's best to keep this code separated in its own section—as opposed to the HTML-centric sections that follow it. Lines 060–117 of Listing 12.3 also are enclosed in a `<%perl>` block, but the reasoning is a little less direct. The number of `print` statements producing HTML would seem to indicate that lines 091–114 at least could be written in an HTML-centric style, but the need for Perl conditionals and loops on practically every other line would make the code confusing as the style shifted back and forth. With so many nested loops, confusing code could make unmatched-bracket errors difficult to trace.

For cases in which a minimal amount of Perl is needed in a section to provide conditionals or loops, individual lines of Perl can be indicated with a percent symbol at the beginning of the line. For instance, lines 036–044 of Listing 12.3 use a number of single Perl statements to provide a list of data source options by looping through the `@datasources` array.

Although this mix of Perl and HTML is slightly more confusing than would be optimal in most cases, it actually provides one of the simplest ways to directly populate a drop-down list from a Perl variable with a preselected, specified value. Drop-down form elements are particularly difficult to code directly while providing the functionality that site users expect. If a site is likely to use many of them, it's generally advised to create a custom component that handles the specifics of creating the list box. (See the next section, "Using External Program Components.")

As a trivial case, it also would be possible to simply enclose the entire contents of Listing 12.2 in an embedded Perl segment instead of separating out the Perl-centric and HTML-centric sections. This wouldn't provide any of the benefits of embedded Perl, however, and would incur the overhead of parsing the document as though the HTML sections were present. However, there are some cases when it's necessary to write pages using this style. For instance, if a page already is available as a CGI program, it's sometimes easiest to copy the entire program into an embedded Perl segment to offer it quickly. After the environment has been changed, it's possible to adapt smaller program sections to embedded code over time without compromising usability. It's also easier to merge an existing CGI program into a new site style using this process.

Using External Program Components

In HTML::Mason, every page is a component. The Web server calls the first page—known as the *top-level component*—which then calls any additional Mason components through a tag in the form `<& component &>`. (HTML::Mason provides other ways to call components, including automatically-called components inserted before the top-level component, but variations on that theme are outside the scope of this book.) For instance, a component file named `listbox` in the same directory might be called with the following syntax:

```
<& listbox &>
```

The `listbox` component would then be executed and its result included in place. This can be useful for defining common ways to handle difficult constructs, such as the `<select>` form widget discussed in the previous section. In that case, lines 036–044 of Listing 12.3 could be replaced with the following call to the `listbox` component:

```
<& listbox, items=>[@datasource], selected=>$source &>
```

In this case, the relevant data are passed to the component as the named arguments, which are `items` and `selected`. The array of items to be listed is passed through reference as `items`, and the value of the selected item is passed as `selected`. Naming the arguments this way enables Mason to name them correctly within the component. It's also possible to pass arguments anonymously by simply listing them, but that method is discouraged for the sake of readability and uniformity.

After passing, arguments can be accessed within other Mason components in a few different ways. If named arguments are passed, they can be imported into the component by way of the `<%args>` block. For instance, the `listbox` component, as called in the previous example, might contain an `<%args>` block, which introduces the `@items` and `$selected` named arguments like this:

```
<%args>
@items
$selected=>''
</%args>

<select name="datasource">
%foreach my $item (@items) {
%  if ($item eq $selected) {
<option selected="selected"><%$item%></option>
%  } else {
<option><%$item%></option>
%  }
%}
</select>
```

This same syntax is used whether arguments are being passed from other components or from the Web server itself. For instance, in Listing 12.3, lines 001–006 make up the <%args> block that defines incoming form variables. The variables are each assigned a default of an empty string to avoid error messages if there are no values present. These variables then are used as normal in the rest of Listing 12.3. For instance, lines 063 and 064 check the `$datasource` and `$query` variables, respectively. Alternately, the %ARGS hash contains all named arguments passed to the component, regardless of whether they have been assigned to variables. For instance, line 064 could access the `datasource` named argument from this hash directly as `$ARGS{datasource}`. The choice between declaring named variables or accessing the hash is a matter of style; the former usually is more readable, but the latter serves as a reminder that the values come from an external source. In some cases, it's useful to make a distinction between the raw arguments stored in %ARGS when the local variables might have been modified.

HTML::Mason also provides the `$m` request object for object-oriented access to all aspects of the Mason environment. Most functions of `$m` are more customizable versions of standard Mason functions, such as the calling of components or the accessing of arguments. In addition, though, the `$m` object offers a fine grain of control over data caching, session management, and other architectural workings of Mason. The HTML::Mason documentation provides a complete listing of the methods provided by the `$m` object.

Displaying Inline Variables

It's sometimes useful to include variable values in a block of HTML text. The full syntax of a `<%perl>print $value</%perl>` block would be cumbersome in these cases. Therefore, Mason provides an alternate syntax specifically for evaluating expressions. Any Perl expression is evaluated inline when enclosed in a block of the form <% expression %>. This kind of block can be used to display a variable, such as `$query`, or to evaluate and display an expression, such as `localtime()` or `"moo"x3`.

In Listing 12.3, lines 046—055 use inline variables to display the default values of each form field as given by the form variable arguments defined in <%args>. Note that this syntax is used only when the variable is included in an HTML block, not when the variable is used in a `<%perl>` block or other sections of Perl code.

Benefits and Limitations

Mason's emphasis on components makes writing robust template systems much easier because much of the work inherent in combining HTML templates with program segments is handled by HTML::Mason itself. HTML-compatible templates can be incorporated very easily by making the template an automatic top-level component for every Mason file in a directory. Sections of the template page then can be filled in with other shared components, including the original page requested. Further discussion of templates can be found in Chapter 13.

Mason's biggest problem might be one of overabundance. With so many ways to create reusable components, templates, preprocessors, and post-fixers, it's tempting to overengineer a site so that every possible aspect of HTML::Mason is used. The result of such an endeavor by a component novice, however, is likely to be a big mess. Mason provides much more than the average dynamic Web site needs, especially when the site has only recently made the leap from CGI to persistent Perl—let alone embedded Perl. This problem can be overcome by using restraint and implementing new Mason features only when they are called for and well thought out. However, restraint isn't the hallmark of a Web designer. Thus, additional care should be taken when developing a style guide for Mason programmers.

EmbPerl

EmbPerl is another embedded Perl environment for use with mod_perl and other persistent environments. As this book was written, EmbPerl development was headed in the direction of a Mason-style component model called EmbPerl Objects, even though historically EmbPerl was designed for use with simpler, single-page Web application embedding. The older style is reviewed here because EmbPerl Objects still are in a state of flux.

EmbPerl's syntax overall is very similar to HTML::Mason and other embedding systems. Blocks of Perl code are set apart from HTML text with identifiers, and inline variables are displayed using another set of identifiers. EmbPerl has a few more sets of identifiers, however, because it has additional limitations on the type of code each block can contain. This adds complexity that can result in some awkwardness when developing Web applications that need to use different block styles in conjunction with them.

Query Processor Application Changes

The syntax used by EmbPerl is analogous to HTML::Mason, albeit with a different set of block identifiers and a simplified interface to form variables. Listing 12.4 is an example of modifications that could be made to the SQL query processor from Listing 12.2 to adapt it for use within the EmbPerl framework.

Listing 12.4 **SQL Processor in EmbPerl**

```
001 [-
002 # declare some variables
003 my ($dbh, $sth, $error, $field, $result, $results, $head, $dat);
004 my (@datasources);
005
006 # build a (safe) list of data sources
007 foreach (DBI->available_drivers)
008 {
009   eval {
```

```
010     foreach (DBI->data_sources($_))
011     {
012        push @datasources, $_;
013     }
014   };
015 }
016 -]
017
018 <html>
019 <head>
020 <title>SQL Query Browser</title>
021 </head>
022 <body>
023
024 <h3>SQL Query Browser</h3>
025
026 <form method="post">
027 <p>Choose a datasource:</p>
028
029 <select name="datasource">
030 [-
031 foreach my $source (@datasources)
032 {
033   if ($source eq $fvar{datasource})
034   {
035     print qq{<option selected="selected">$source</option>\n};
036   }
037   else
038   {
039     print qq{<option>$source</option>\n};
040   }
041 }
042 -]
043 </select>
044
045 <p>Specify username/password:</p>
046
047 <input type="text" name="user" size="10" value="[+$fvar{user}+]" />
048  
049 <input type="password" name="password"
050  size="10" value="[+$fvar{password}-]" />
051
052 <p>Enter a SELECT query:</p>
053
054 <textarea name="query" rows="5" cols="40"
055  wrap="virtual">[+$fvar{query}+]</textarea>
056
057 <p><input type="submit" /></p>
058 </form>
059
060 [-
```

continues

Listing 12.4 **Continued**

```
061 if ($fvar{query})
062 {
063   # check form variables
064   $error = "Improper datasource specified"
065           unless ($fvar{datasource} =~ /^dbi/i);
066   $error = "Query should start with SELECT"
067           unless ($fvar{query} =~ /^select/i);
068
069   unless ($error)
070   {
071     # connect to the database
072     $dbh = DBI->connect($fvar{datasource}, $fvar{user},
        ➥$fvar{password})
073             or $error = "Connection failed: $DBI::errstr";
074
075     # if the database connection worked, send the query
076     unless ($error)
077     {
078       $sth = $dbh->prepare($fvar{query})
079               or $error = "Query failed: $DBI::errstr";
080       $sth->execute or $error = "Query failed: $DBI::errstr";
081       $head = $sth->{NAME};
082       $dat = $sth->fetchall_arrayref;
083     }
084   }
085 }
086 -]
087
088 [$ if ($error) $]
089 <p><font color="red"><b>Error: [+ $error +] </b></font></p>
090 [$ endif $]
091
092 [$ if (!$error and $head) $]
093 <table border="1">
094   <tr><th>[+ $head->[$col] +]</th></tr>
095   <tr><td>[+ $dat->[$row][$col] +]</td></tr>
096 </table>
097 [$ endif $]
098
099 </body>
100 </html>
```

Again, the major difference between EmbPerl and CGI style is the beginning of the program because using Perl and including common modules are assumed. In addition, Listing 12.2 could have been rewritten in EmbPerl simply by enclosing the entire listing in [- and -] block identifiers with additional native EmbPerl syntax added to the program as it became necessary. EmbPerl style is noticeably different from HTML::Mason toward the end of Listing 12.4, which shows both EmbPerl's limitations due to the way the pages are processed as well as its built-in database handling features.

Demarcating Perl Segments

Embedded Perl sections are denoted a few different ways in EmbPerl, depending on how they should be treated. Complete Perl segments that can be executed independently are set apart by enclosing them in [- and -] identifiers. Lines 060–086 of Listing 12.4, for instance, make up a block that checks form variables, creates a database connection, and sends the specified query to the database. Unlike blocks in HTML::Mason and the other environments discussed in this chapter, these blocks must be complete blocks of Perl code. This means that loops, conditional blocks, eval blocks, and subroutines can't contain a mix of these Perl blocks and HTML sections.

EmbPerl does provide a way to mix conditional and loop code with HTML sections. Blocks denoted by [$ $] are used for program structures such as if, for, and while, which are called *meta commands* by EmbPerl. Unfortunately, the code used within these blocks is not Perl, but a Perl-like command language used specifically for these purposes. For instance, in Listing 12.4, lines 088–090 comprise a conditional block with the value of the variable $error as the condition. Conditional blocks of this nature start with the usual if, but they aren't ended by closing brackets. Instead, a shell-like endif command is used.

Like HTML::Mason, EmbPerl provides a simplified syntax to evaluate an expression. The [+ +] block denotes a program segment, which should be evaluated as an expression with the result displayed in place. For example, line 089 of Listing 12.4 displays an error message inline as defined by the variable $error. This syntax enables the variable to be set apart from surrounding HTML in an unobtrusive manner.

One of EmbPerl's strengths is the automated table-creation features that it includes. When provided with an array reference called $head and a reference to an array of arrays called $dat, EmbPerl can use the inherent variables $row and $col to iterate over an entire data set and display it in a formatted table. For example, lines 093–096 of Listing 12.4 create a data table consisting of the results of the specified SQL query, including column headers with the names of the result fields. This short block of HTML—and the EmbPerl automation behind it—does the work of a large chunk of Listing 12.2, replacing over 20 lines of Perl code to accomplish the same result. Although the cases to which this facility applies are few, Web application designers could use more shortcuts of this nature.

Form Variables

Form variables are provided by EmbPerl through the %fvar hash variable. Similar to Mason's %ARGS variable, %fvar holds one named entry for each form variable provided. You access the variables the same way as you do any other hash values. As a result, form variables can be used either in place (such as the way they are in lines 063–068 of Listing 12.4) or by assigning them to other variables before use, as shown in the following code:

```
# check form variables
$error = "Improper datasource specified"
        unless ($fvar{datasource} =~ /^dbi/i);
$error = "Query should start with SELECT"
        unless ($fvar{query} =~ /^select/i);
```

In these lines, the form variables are accessed directly by reading them from the `%fvar` hash each time they are needed. This is sometimes used to set form variables apart from internal program variables such as `$error`. Some Web applications assign form variables to internal variables only after the values have been modified to keep a copy of the form variable values in their original state. Note that no additional steps need be taken to import the form variables—as opposed to CGI-style programs that have to parse the variables explicitly.

Benefits and Limitations

EmbPerl serves well its purpose as a simple Perl-embedding environment. It provides persistent execution for Perl code embedded in HTML pages. It also provides convenient access to form variables. One of the most useful aspects of EmbPerl is the table autocreation facility, which shows off the capability of an environment to truly reduce the lines of code necessary to perform a common Web application task.

EmbPerl's biggest limitation is the awkward nature of its embedded Perl blocks. Different types of blocks have to be used for different types of code, and the program structure block—probably the most common type to use on a Web site—is implemented in meta-code, not Perl itself. Although this problem is slated to be addressed in version 2.0 of EmbPerl, the solution is yet another type of block with new syntax and uncertain applications. Remembering the usage differences between all these varieties of blocks is difficult, and the resultant mix of block types with similar delimiters can cause confusion and lead to unnecessary errors.

Apache::ASP

Apache::ASP is an embedding environment that is designed to provide an Apache version of the PerlScript syntax of Active Server Pages (ASP), which is an environment used with the Internet Information Server (IIS) under Windows operating systems.

The syntax used by Apache::ASP is again very similar to Mason and EmbPerl, with Perl code sections set apart from HTML text by delimiters and inline variables and expressions denoted by a similar set of delimiters. The delimiter symbols used by Apache::ASP are identical to those used in ASP under IIS. Thus, the format should be very familiar to programmers who are used to ASP-style code. In addition, interface objects for Web server interaction—including form variable access and result header declarations—are very similar to the objects used in ASP under IIS.

Apache::ASP has the benefit of wide acceptance among graphic HTML editors and Web application development environments. The ASP style likely is recognized by a wide variety of client-side tools (mostly in Windows environments), including graphic editors. Therefore, editors that produce valid Apache::ASP code without damaging the underlying Perl code are more common than with some lesser-known embedding styles.

Query Processor Application Changes

The CGI-style query processor in Listing 12.2 would have many of the same changes made to it in order to use it with Apache::ASP as Listing 12.3 did to make it compatible with HTML::Mason. There are a few noticeable differences, however, which are outlined in Listing 12.5.

Listing 12.5   **SQL Processor in Apache::ASP**

```
001 <%
002 # declare some variables
003 my ($dbh, $sth, $error, $field, $result, $results);
004 my (@datasources);
005 my %QUERY = %{$Request->Form};
006
007 # build a (safe) list of data sources
008 foreach (DBI->available_drivers)
009 {
010   eval {
011     foreach (DBI->data_sources($_))
012     {
013       push @datasources, $_;
014     }
015   };
016 }
017 %>
018
019 <html>
020 <head>
021 <title>SQL Query Browser</title>
022 </head>
023 <body>
024
025 <h3>SQL Query Browser</h3>
026
027 <form method="post">
028 <p>Choose a datasource:</p>
029
```

continues

Listing 12.5   **Continued**

```
030 <select name="datasource">
031 <%
032 foreach my $source (@datasources)
033 {
034   if ($source eq $QUERY{datasource})
035   {
036     print qq{<option selected="selected">$source</option>\n};
037   }
038   else
039   {
040     print qq{<option>$source</option>\n};
041   }
042 }
043 %>
044 </select>
045
046 <p>Specify username/password:</p>
047
048 <input type="text" name="user" size="10" value="<%=$QUERY{user}%>" />
049  
050 <input type="password" name="password" size="10"value="
    ↪<%=$QUERY{password}%>" />
051
052 <p>Enter a SELECT query:</p>
053
054 <textarea name="query" rows="5" cols="40" wrap="virtual">
    ↪<%=$QUERY{query}%> </textarea>
055
056 <p><input type="submit" /></p>
057 </form>
058
059 <%
060 if ($QUERY{query})
061 {
062   # check form variables
063   $error = "Improper datasource specified" unless
064   (($QUERY{datasource}=~ /^dbi/i);
065   $error = "Query should start with SELECT" unless ($QUERY{query} =~/
    ↪^select/i);
066
067   unless ($error)
068   {
069     # connect to the database
070     $dbh = DBI->connect($QUERY{datasource}, $QUERY{user},
       ↪$QUERY{password})
071             or $error = "Connection failed: $DBI::errstr";
072
```

```
073    # if the database connection worked, send the query
074    unless ($error)
075    {
076      $sth = $dbh->prepare($QUERY{query})
077            or $error = "Query failed: $DBI::errstr";
078      $sth->execute or $error = "Query failed: $DBI::errstr";
079    }
080  }
081
082  # if any errors are present, display the error
083  if ($error)
084  {
085    print qq{<p><font color="red"><b>Error: $error</b></font></p>};
086  }
087
088  # if the query produced an output,
089  if (!$error and $sth->{NAME})
090  {
091    # start a data table
092    print qq{<table border="1">\n};
093    print qq{<tr>\n};
094
095    # display the fields as table headers
096    foreach $field (@{$sth->{NAME}})
097    {
098      print qq{<th>$field</th>\n};
099    }
100    print qq{</tr>\n};
101
102    # display the results in a table
103    while ($results = $sth->fetchrow_arrayref)
104    {
105      print qq{<tr>\n};
106      foreach $result (@$results)
107      {
108        print qq{<td>$result</td>\n};
109      }
110      print qq{</tr>\n};
111    }
112
113    # finish the data table
114    print qq{</table>\n};
115  }
116 }
117 %>
118 </body>
119 </html>
```

The simplicity of the ASP style provides a clean way to embed all sorts of Perl code into an HTML page. However, Listing 12.5 shows that very little appreciable difference exists between Apache::ASP style and CGI style because of that same simplicity. Apache::ASP doesn't provide much in the way of additional Web application abstraction or componentization. Thus, the biggest difference between ASP-style and CGI-style code would be seen in pages that consist mostly of HTML with only a few Perl segments.

Demarcating Perl Segments

Perl segments are noted in Apache::ASP using the `<% %>` delimiters. As with HTML::Mason or EmbPerl, any Perl code placed within the delimiters is evaluated by Apache::ASP as though it were a Perl program. Unlike EmbPerl, though, any kind of Perl code is valid within the delimiters, and only one kind of delimiter is used for most code sections. For instance, lines 031–043 of Listing 12.5 (which display a drop-down list of data sources based on the `@datasources` array) could be listed as they are or rewritten as the following:

```
<%
foreach my $source (@datasources)
{
  if ($source eq $QUERY{datasource})
  {
%>
<option selected="selected"><%= $source %></option>
<%
  }
  else
  {
%>
<option><%= $source %></option>
<%
  }
}
%>
```

This version of the code would be perfectly valid even though it breaks up a Perl loop between delineated blocks. (It doesn't add much readability, though.) For inline variables, Apache::ASP provides the `<%= %>` delimiter syntax, which evaluates the expression within the block and displays the result inline. Line 048 of Listing 12.5 (which displays an input text box for the username) uses the inline display notation to show the existing value of the `user` form variable.

Form Variables

Because of Apache::ASP's inheritance of the ASP programming style, form variables are only accessible from the $Request object through the Form method. The method provides a single form variable value if provided a variable name, or it provides a hash of all the form variables if not. Unfortunately, there's no direct access to form variables. Thus, the usual way to access the variables would have to involve CGI-style statements assigning each variable in turn.

A different approach was taken in Listing 12.5. Because the Form method provides a hash of form variables and their values if no variable name is specified, line 005 creates a hash called %QUERY to store all the form variables for direct access. This hash then can be used in the same manner as those provided by Mason or EmbPerl, as seen in line 048 and onward. This also provides a general means by which the behavior of one embedding environment can be modified to simulate others—the hash could just as easily be called %fvar, %ARGS, or a combination of these if there were already code using one style or another.

Benefits and Limitations

The ASP syntax is simple and familiar to many Web programmers. Because ASP is a common format, many Web application editors provide additional features for ASP. These features include syntax highlighting and code previews that are unavailable for other embedded Perl styles. This familiarity of ASP data structures also means that Web programmers might have an easier time adapting existing ASP skill sets to Apache::ASP. In the other direction, writing pages in an ASP style enables the pages to be ported to PerlScript for IIS, if that becomes necessary.

The utility of Apache::ASP is limited by its need to be similar to the VBScript or PerlScript implementations of ASP. As an example, form variables are accessible by two different methods on the $Request object—one works only for POST requests and one works only for GET requests. Because many Web applications need to enable both types of requests, this creates a difficult hurdle for application developers where none is necessary.

Perl Server Pages (PSP)

PSP is a format originally designed for use with Version 3 of the VelociGen application environment. It is an extension of the original embedded mode of VelociGen, which was similar to Mason, EmbPerl, and Apache::ASP in that it enabled Perl segments to be set in HTML pages by surrounding the code in delimiters. The original environment also provided simple program components and automated form variable parsing.

PSP extends the original embedding concept by providing an intermediate language, which looks more like ColdFusion or Java Server Pages (JSP) than embedded Perl. This templating language consists of HTML-like tags that perform functions based on definitions written in Perl, HTML, or the PSP language itself. This results in an abstracted language that can be further abstracted and customized as necessary using either inline definitions or external definition files.

Coinciding with the release of this book, VelociGen has kindly agreed to release a reference implementation of PSP for the Apache server as open source software under the Artistic License.

Query Processor Application Changes

At its core, the PSP style is very similar to the style used with HTML::Mason, EmbPerl, and Apache::ASP. As a result, it's possible to make the PSP version of the SQL query processor in Listing 12.2 look very similar to the other listing styles in this chapter. Listing 12.6 is one example of this style.

Listing 12.6 **SQL Processor in PSP**

```
001 <perl>
002 # declare some variables
003 my ($dbh, $sth, $error, $field, $result, $results);
004 my (@datasources);
005
006 # build a (safe) list of data sources
007 foreach (DBI->available_drivers)
008 {
009   eval {
010     foreach (DBI->data_sources($_))
011     {
012       push @datasources, $_;
013     }
014   };
015 }
016 </perl>
017
018 <include file="$ENV{DOCUMENT_ROOT}/page.psp" />
019 <template title="SQL Query Browser" section="Admin">
020
021 <form method="post">
022 <output>
023 <p>Choose a datasource:</p>
024
025 <select name="datasource">
026 <loop name="source" list="@datasources">
027 <if cond="$source eq $QUERY{datasource}">
028 <option selected="selected">$source</option>
029 <else />
```

```
030 <option>$source</option>
031 </if>
032 </loop>
033 </select>
034
035 <p>Specify username/password:</p>
036
037 <input type="text" name="user" size="10" value="$QUERY{user}" />
038  
039 <input type="password" name="password" size="10"
    ↬value="$QUERY{password}" />
040
041 <p>Enter a SELECT query:</p>
042
043 <textarea name="query" rows="5" cols="40" wrap="virtual">$QUERY{query}
    ↬</textarea>
044
045 <p><input type="submit" /></p>
046 </output>
047 </form>
048
049 <perl>
050 if ($QUERY{query})
051 {
052   # check form variables
053   $error = "Improper datasource specified" unless ($QUERY{datasource}
      ↬=~ /^dbi/i);
054   $error = "Query should start with SELECT" unless ($QUERY{query} =~
      ↬/^select/i);
055
056   unless ($error)
057   {
058     # connect to the database
059     $dbh = DBI->connect($QUERY{datasource}, $QUERY{user},
      ↬$QUERY{password})
060             or $error = "Connection failed: $DBI::errstr";
061
062     # if the database connection worked, send the query
063     unless ($error)
064     {
065       $sth = $dbh->prepare($QUERY{query})
066               or $error = "Query failed: $DBI::errstr";
067       $sth->execute or $error = "Query failed: $DBI::errstr";
068     }
069   }
070
071   # if any errors are present, display the error
072   if ($error)
073   {
074     print qq{<p><font color="red"><b>Error: $error</b></font></p>};
075   }
```

continues

Listing 12.6 **Continued**

```
076
077   # if the query produced an output,
078   if (!$error and $sth->{NAME})
079   {
080     # start a data table
081     print qq{<table border="1">\n};
082     print qq{<tr>\n};
083
084     # display the fields as table headers
085     foreach $field (@{$sth->{NAME}})
086     {
087       print qq{<th>$field</th>\n};
088     }
089     print qq{</tr>\n};
090
091     # display the results in a table
092     while ($results = $sth->fetchrow_arrayref)
093     {
094       print qq{<tr>\n};
095       foreach $result (@$results)
096       {
097         print qq{<td>$result</td>\n};
098       }
099       print qq{</tr>\n};
100     }
101
102     # finish the data table
103     print qq{</table>\n};
104   }
105 }
106 </perl>
107 </template>
```

Much in the way that a CGI program could be copied verbatim into an embedded page and used as the starting point for further tuning and abstraction, Listing 12.6 could be used as a starting point for further abstraction using PSP. The PSP tag style requires some planning to define a reasonable set of tags for the right level of abstraction, though. Thus, the real benefit of increased abstraction comes when a large group of Web application pages on a site are developed using a core set of custom tags.

One tag used in this listing—the <template> tag—isn't be mentioned until Chapter 13. For now, suffice it to say that this template provides the basic structure of an HTML page in which the rest of the printed HTML is set before returning the combined result.

Demarcating Perl Segments

Perl segments in PSP pages are enclosed using the `<perl>` tag. This method is similar to the segment styles of Mason, EmbPerl, and Apache::ASP. However, there's only one type of Perl segment within a PSP page, which is used for any kind of Perl statements, including portions of loops and other blocks.

The `%COOKIE`, `%QUERY`, and `%ENV` hashes are provided automatically as interfaces to the environment. The `%ENV` hash is an augmented version of the environment variables provided by Perl and the Web server, with additional entries for the location of the document root directory and similar PSP-centric information. The `%QUERY` hash provides access to form variables in a way that is similar to the way in which the `%ARGS` hash in Mason or the `%fvar` hash in EmbPerl works. Form variables are used directly in lines 053 and 054 of Listing 12.6, for example. In addition, the `%COOKIE` hash provides access to data stored in client-side cookies, which can be useful for state management and automatic user recognition.

Displaying Inline Variables

Inline variable display is handled differently in PSP than in most other embedded Perl environments. PSP takes the approach that variables are likely to be used only in certain sections of the page. In that case, it might be better to treat the sections as a whole rather than separating out individual program statements.

For this purpose, PSP provides the `<output>` tag. Text within the `<output>` tag is treated in a way that is similar to the way Perl treats a double-quoted string: variables in the text are replaced by the values of the variables as defined. In contrast, if a variable name is present outside the `<output>` tag, it is printed just as listed. Lines 037 and 039 of Listing 12.6, for instance, use the values of form variables as the default values for input text boxes. This is made possible by the `<output>` tag started on line 022 and ended on line 046, just inside the `<form>` tag.

The `<output>` tag treats undefined variables differently than does a Perl double-quoted string. If a variable is used within an `<output>` tag that hasn't been defined (as opposed to one that is empty or that holds a value), it is displayed as though there were no `<output>` tag in effect. This makes it easier to display a dollar sign in normal contexts without having to escape it.

Using Standard PSP Tags

A host of standard PSP tags are provided with the reference implementation. Most of these tags are defined within a central tag library also written as a PSP page, but some—like the `<tag>` tag and other fundamental tags—are implemented within the PSP parser. The standard tags provide a library of functions likely to be needed for common Web applications, including loop and conditional processing, database connectivity, client access to the Web, and basic XML processing.

For example, lines 025–033 of Listing 12.6 create a drop-down list of data sources based on the `@datasources` array with the chosen data source highlighted. Line 027 uses the `<loop>` tag to start a loop over the values of the `@datasources` array, setting the `$source` variable to the current loop value. Line 027 starts a conditional block with the `<if>` tag, and line 029 partitions the results of a true condition from the result of a false condition with an `<else>` tag.

Obviously, database-oriented tags would be useful for Listing 12.6 as well. They are omitted here only because the database tags included with the PSP reference implementation are better suited to a specific data source instead of the drop-down choice given by the `datasource` query variable. Translating the DBI-format datasource given by this variable into the database and data source variables needed by the `<sql>` tag would require additional steps that are unnecessary when the existing code works just as well. For examples of the `<sql>` tag and database access with PSP pages, see Chapter 14.

Declaring New PSP Tags

PSP provides the `<tag>` tag to enable the definition of new tags. This isn't used within Listing 12.6, but a custom tag could easily have been defined within the page. For instance, a tag could be defined to produce the drop-down box in lines 025–033 in a more readable fashion. The page would use the `<tag>` tag to provide a tag definition, and it would then use the tag itself in place of the larger code block, as shown in the following code:

```
<tag name="dropdown" accepts="name, values, default">
<perl>my @values = @{$values}</perl>
<select name="$name">
<loop name="item" list="@values">
<if cond="$item eq $default">
<option selected="selected">$item</option>
<else />
<option>$item</option>
</if>
</loop>
</select>
</tag>

<perl>my $datasources = \@datasources</perl>
<dropdown name="datasource" values="$datasources" default="$datasource"
/>
```

The `<tag>` tag itself takes the two attributes, `name` and `accepts`, among others. The `name` attribute specifies the name of the tag being defined ("dropdown" in this case), and the `accepts` attribute defines the attributes that can be passed from the tag for use as variables within the definition. In this case, the `<dropdown>` tag can have attributes called `name`, `values`, and `default`, each of which is assigned to a scalar variable of the same name for use within the definition. After being defined, the tag can be used immediately to create the drop-down box, just as the block of code in Listing 12.6

does. Of course, this kind of tag definition wouldn't save any time, effort, or space in this one program. However, if the definition were placed in a library file with other useful definitions and used throughout the site, the resulting abstraction would make each page more readable in the long run.

It's possible to override existing HTML tags with custom tags, but it is not advised. Conflicts and unwanted parsing loops can occur when the HTML tags are used within their custom counterparts. For instance, it might seem reasonable to override the <td> HTML tag with a PSP tag of the same name that automatically sets the font style within the table cell. However, after that tag is defined, there's no way to specify a <td> tag without that formatting because it always is interpreted by the PSP page parser. It would be more advisable to create a tag with a different name—such as <mytd>—to provide access to the original tag definition.

Using External Components

PSP provides the <include> tag for parsing and including other PSP pages. These pages are handled more like server-side includes than HTML::Mason components because the page doesn't take any arguments when it is being included. (Tags themselves handle that aspect of componentization instead.) For instance, line 018 of Listing 12.6 includes a file called page.psp that contains the definition of a <template> tag:

```
<include file="$ENV{DOCUMENT_ROOT}/page.psp" />
```

The file attribute indicates the absolute or relative path to the file to include, which could be either a PSP file or another type of text file. In the case of a PSP file, the file is compiled in place of the <include> tag and incorporated into the main program. As shown with the <template> tag and the page.psp file, the <include> tag can be used to create simple site templates. More templating ideas can be found in Chapter 13.

The <include> tag also can be used to create libraries of PSP tags. One such library is the default library included with the PSP parser. These libraries are simply collections of PSP tag definitions using the <tag> tag, which define a set of custom tags for use in other PSP pages on the site. Tag libraries can be included explicitly in each file that uses them, or each tag can be defined as global to all PSP pages by setting a global attribute in the tag definition. The library then only has to be loaded once as the application engine starts to be accessible by all other pages.

Benefits and Limitations

The PSP syntax is very close to HTML syntax, which makes it a good choice for a templating and high-level Web application language. In addition, the capability to create custom tags makes the tag system infinitely customizable. Tag sets can be created for a Web application as the application is being defined, and the resulting code can be cleaned up considerably as a result.

A limitation of the PSP style comes from the HTML-style tag syntax, in which it can be awkward to express programmatic constructs. For instance, the `<if>` `<else/>` `</if>` construct is a bit awkward because the `else` block is started by an empty tag while the `if` tag extends beyond the end of its corresponding block. HTML-style syntax also can cause code to become less distinguishable from straight HTML, making it more difficult to get a sense of the program flow from the structure of the listing.

In addition, the way PSP pages are parsed casts some uncertainty on the execution order of program segments because it's possible that tags will be evaluated from the interior out, instead of from first to last. This becomes most apparent when errors occur, which shows less-than-informative messages. These messages reference the program that was generated from the PSP code, which usually has little relation to the PSP code itself.

Performance Issues with Embedding

Embedding is a good choice for most Web application needs, but it isn't always the best choice. For one, embedding Perl code in HTML can incur additional overhead. Usually this comes from the increased time taken when compiling an embedded page into a Perl application. It also comes from the increased memory usage created by the page parser and related code.

Additionally, developing a complex application in embedded mode often requires additional work to decipher error messages generated by Perl. Because the embedded Perl code is interspersed with HTML, it's sometimes difficult to use standard code-scanning techniques to get a sense of how the program is supposed to operate and where the error comes from. Occasionally, these concerns can outweigh the benefits of embedding code in Web pages.

Increased Overhead

Embedded Perl code isn't necessarily as efficient overall as more traditional persistent Perl. This is due to a number of factors, which are not all applicable to every embedding environment. For one, not all embedded code is processed the same way. Some environments translate the embedded pages into pure-Perl code before compiling. Other environments compile Perl blocks individually and then treat them more like server-side includes when composing a page in response to a request. The result of these behind-the-scenes changes are rarely controllable and can sometimes result in fundamentally less efficient code than would be produced by hand.

Another source of overhead with embedding is the parser itself. No matter how it's implemented, the parser used to separate program segments out from HTML has to invoke some overhead. It might take additional time to parse a page before each request, or it might just take up additional memory while it waits for new pages to be parsed into pure-Perl programs. The resultant overhead is sometimes large enough to make the use of embedding prohibitive, although in most mixed-code Web applications, this isn't the case.

Error messages also can be difficult to decipher due to translations occurring behind the scenes. Perl normally identifies errors based on the line number of the offending code and (in the case of a syntax error) the code surrounding it for context. Unfortunately, both clues correspond to the post-translated code rather than the pre-translated embedded file. Thus, it might be difficult to match up the error to its location and circumstance. In addition, errors can be introduced by the parsing step itself, especially in the case in which a Perl block was not properly delineated.

When Not to Embed

Two types of pages should probably be avoided when embedding Perl code. The first is obvious: Pages that contain only HTML and need no code are poor candidates for embedding. Parsing these pages takes time, and the performance of an embedded Perl page never exceeds the performance of the corresponding pure-HTML page. Oddly enough, this unusual situation often can occur when a site goes through repeated redesigns. A site that contains mostly embedded Perl can be replaced with pages that are pure HTML but that require the same filenames to preserve links from outside sources. In this case, it's often a good idea to declare those pages as a form of HTML within the Web server configuration to save the overhead of parsing them through a Perl environment.

On the other end of the spectrum, code that doesn't produce HTML at all is usually a poor candidate for embedding as well. Such code usually ends up as a single Perl block delimiter surrounding an otherwise pure Perl program. In this case, it's generally better to avoid the overhead of parsing the page by implementing the program directly in persistent Perl. Of course, this might require adding additional code to handle common aspects of CGI-style programs, such as form variable processing and environment initialization, so the performance trade-off might not be worth the additional work of developing in a CGI style. Embedding Perl in HTML might also make it difficult to use standard Perl development tools for syntax checking and debugging. This can impede the development of complex programs in an embedded environment. However, this might be a blessing in disguise if it encourages complex sections of Perl code to be abstracted out of embedded pages and into reusable modules. These modules then can be checked and debugged using all the usual tools.

Evangelizing Web Usability

One of my hidden motives behind encouraging embedded programming style is its impact on the Web usability testing cycle. By forcing Web programs to conform more closely to the structure of their output, embedded programming makes it much easier to see the effects of stylistic and structural changes to a Web application. Combined with template programming, embedded Perl can break programmers of the Hello World habit and encourage a little bit more thought about the relationship between the code we write and the way the application behaves on site.

Of course, the other requirement is an understanding of the mechanics of Web usability, a subject that is outside the scope of this book entirely. Fortunately, it's the sole subject of an excellent book, *Designing Web Usability*, by Jakob Nielsen. This book is published under the New Riders banner and is pure distilled Web wisdom. After you've read this book, read his next, *Homepage Usability* (Fall 2001).

Evangelizing these aspects of good Web design is as important as designing the applications in the first place. As Dr. Nielsen's work has shown time and time again, programmers ignore usability concerns at their own peril. Thus, it's important to lock onto good usability practices and principles and stick to them. Luckily, most Web designers are copycats. If they see a good design getting lots of attention, they won't hesitate to copy the good design for their own uses. If that happened more often, the Web would become a wonderful place to surf.

Summary

Web application development can be made more Web-centric and componentized by embedding Perl in HTML pages, which helps programmers break out of the Hello World frame of mind. Many embedding environments are available. HTML::Mason provides a robust framework for creating reusable program components. EmbPerl provides a simpler environment with helpful table generation features. Apache::ASP brings ASP PerlScript support to the Apache server. PSP enables HTML-style tags to be created using a combination of HTML and Perl code. Any of these environments is likely to promote new development using a Web-centric model, but it's also good to consider times when embedding incurs too much overhead. In cases when the page is likely to contain all static HTML or no HTML at all, performance can be improved by using only HTML or only Perl.

13

Using Templates with
Perl Applications

AFTER PERL CODE CAN BE EMBEDDED IN HTML pages, the next logical step is to make the process of writing Web-centric programs easier. The embedding environments listed in Chapter 12, "Environments for Reducing Development Time," have the raw capabilities that enable Web-centric programming to be automated to some degree. One way to accomplish this is by incorporating templates into Perl Web applications.

The idea behind a template is to separate formatting information and program structure to keep the development of each part separate. The template itself is a document that contains formatting instructions that are used by the program to create a final product—in this case, an HTML page. It is usually hoped that the separation can be accomplished in a generalized form to enable one template to be used for all programs in a given group.

Generalized templating also gives designers the freedom to create a template without the need to know anything about the programs that will use it. Thus, a template language usually is created to enable program features to be indicated in an abstract form. For instance, a template language designed for a news site could have defined placeholders for the title and body of a story, as well as for story images and related links. Because any number of stories share these basic elements, it's possible to write a template that could be used across all of them. In addition, because the code that displays the stories might change (for example, drawing story data from an Extensible Markup Language [XML] file rather than from a database), it's better to create templates with abstracted sections than with specific code.

At its simplest, a templating system involves two files, the template and the program to which it is applied. In practice, there are likely many template files and even more application files using the templates. The programs usually handle their interaction with the template files on their own using a template library or custom code. In addition, some template systems use a third type of file, a program that manages the relationship between templates and templated applications. This template manager might be incorporated into the Perl embedding environment itself, or it might be written as a Web application preprocessor to be executed before embedded applications.

Template HTML and Graphic Editors

The primary goal of a template system is to give site designers a representative document they can create and edit with ordinary HTML tools. This means that the template document should be as close to standard HTML as possible, even when it contains the indicators that indicate where application segments fill in parts of the template. As a result, template HTML can't be radically different from standard HTML because it might not render correctly in its raw form within graphic HTML editing software.

On the other hand, templates are useful only as long as the tools used by site designers don't interfere with the template language itself. Sometimes, the abstracted code included in a template document can be removed or altered by the graphic HTML editors used by designers. If this happens, unexpected results can occur when using the template document in a Web application. Luckily, this can be avoided somewhat by using template syntax that is unlikely to be modified by common HTML editors. In addition, preferences in the editing programs themselves can sometimes be changed to accommodate the templating language.

Of course, there's only so far that the software can go to make a designer's life easier. It's also necessary to develop good guidelines for designers to follow so that they will maintain good template structure. If designers have a good grasp of the template language and how it looks and is treated in their favorite HTML editing software, it's much more likely that Web applications will end up looking as expected.

HTML That Doesn't Interfere

A good way to accommodate graphic editors with a template system is to incorporate the template information into valid HTML segments that are either represented in a visual way or ignored completely. The goal behind this idea is to affect the formatting of the template HTML in one of two ways:

- Not at all. Template code is either rendered using a nonobtrusive symbol or coloring on the page or completely ignored by the page previewer. This usually occurs when template code uses comment-style code or custom HTML tags.

- Exactly as the final Web application would. This could be as simple as displaying variable names for information that will be filled in by the application or using entire blocks of representative data that is excised later. This includes text-like placeholders for text and image-like placeholders for images as well as entire sections that might be filled in by the Web application.

With HTML 4.0, a number of new tags and structures were introduced to make this process much easier. The `<span>` tag, for instance, provides a way to declare the style of a specific area of an HTML document. In a template context, it also can be used to denote the location of a section to be filled in by a Web application. The following template code segment could be used to fill in a news story:

```
...
<span class="newsblock">
<h2><span name="app.headline">Headline</span></h2>
<p><span name="app.abstract">This is where the story would be.</span></p>
</span>
...
```

The template contains two sections to be removed by the templating application and replaced by generated text. The first section denoted by the `<span>` tag, `app.headline`, is removed and replaced by headline text generated by the application. The second section, `app.abstract`, is removed and replaced by another text segment generated by the application. The resultant text might look like the following:

```
...
<span class="newsblock">
<h2>Damian Conway Wins Honors</h2>
<p>Conway won the White Camel award Tuesday for most awards received.</p>
</span>
...
```

Note that the `<span>` tag is used for two purposes within this template section. It is used to provide placeholders for the replaced text, but it's also used within its original HTML context to denote a style class called `newsblock`. Differentiation between the two uses is possible by using the `name` attribute on template sections and the `class` attribute on standard HTML spans. This is possible because most HTML editing software treats both types of `<span>` tags as valid; it simply ignores the ones without `class` attributes. The Web application then can pick out only those `<span>` tags with the `name` attribute to use as template sections.

Another common way to set template information apart is to use comment-style sections that are ignored by even the oldest browsers and graphic editors. These sections can be extracted by the template processing code in a fashion similar to `<span>` sections. The comment-style version of the previous example might look like the following:

```
...
<span class="newsblock">
<h2><!-- start app.headline -->Headline<!-- end app.headline --></h2>
<p><!-- start app.abstract -->This is where the story would be.<!-- end
app.abstract --></p>
</span>
...
```

A third way to indicate template sections is to use Perlish variables in a style similar to double-quoted strings. This kind of template is sometimes much more efficient to process because it can be dealt with in a native Perl fashion. Perl-style variables are also more likely to fit into HTML templates in which tag-style sections wouldn't fit, such as the following example:

```
...
<span class="newsblock">
<h2>$headline</h2>
<img src="$story_image_url" align="right" />
<p>$story_text</p>
</span>
...
```

Here, the variable `$story_image_url` is used to denote the image URL text to be filled in by the Web application. This section is used to fill in part of an HTML tag rather than a plain text section or a complete HTML tag. Therefore, HTML editors have less trouble rendering it than they would have rendering an invalid HTML tag with another HTML-like tag nested inside it. In practice, a combination of variable-like section identifiers and tag-like section identifiers combines the best aspects of both systems.

Effects of Graphic Editors on Templates

No matter what the templating system is, it's possible that an unaware HTML editing program will remove or modify the template information. Many graphic editors take a "smart" approach to HTML similar to the approach Word takes to word processing— they make changes to the document based on internal rules instead of expecting the user to make them manually. This usually saves time and produces better output when dealing with pure HTML, but even minor changes to templating code can upset the result of a Web application.

For instance, the template document in Listing 13.2 later in this chapter would be modified automatically by graphic HTML editors like Netscape Composer because the file doesn't follow traditional HTML format. The file has the following general format:

```
<tag name="template" accepts="title, section" body="1">
<output>
<html>
<head>
<title>VeloMeter - $title</title>
</head>

<body bgcolor="white">
...
</body>
</html>
</output>
</tag>
```

Because the file doesn't start with `<html>` and end with `</html>`, Composer assumes that the user has made a mistake. As a result, it moves the `<html>` and `<head>` elements of the page so that they start before the `<tag>` and `<output>` elements, assuming that the latter actually are supposed to surround the `<body>` element instead. The result ends up looking something like this:

```
<html>
<head>
<title>VeloMeter - $title</title>
</head>

<tag name="template" accepts="title, section" body="1">
<output>
<body bgcolor="white">
...
</body>
</output>
</tag>
</html>
```

Unfortunately, this causes the template code to behave differently than expected. This particular template requires all elements of the resultant page to be contained within the `<tag>` element, for instance. Thus, it ends up excluding the `<html>` and `<head>` elements from the template as it's processed. Even worse, in this case, all text outside the `<tag>` element is printed as soon as the file is included. Therefore, the resulting output would both start and end the `<html>` element before the `<body>` element was reached.

In addition, some graphic HTML editors see template tags that they don't understand as extraneous formatting information, and the HTML editors remove the tags entirely. Others automatically modify the template information to suit the page design as it exists. This is more likely to happen when repurposing standard HTML tags, such as `<span>`, as mentioned in the previous chapter. This also is more likely to happen when the editing application takes a more active role in creating the formatting, styles, and accompanying HTML of a document.

Even in the case of HTML comment syntax, graphic editors might automatically remove the comment as superfluous. Because there is no visual evidence that the tag has been removed, it's sometimes difficult to tell if this has even happened without viewing the source of the page every so often to check. On the other hand, some editors display commented code as an obtrusive icon that disrupts the flow of the page and encourages manual deleting. The icon sometimes can be a good indicator of where template sections are located, but designers with little knowledge of the visual effect of template codes still might remove the codes inadvertently when polishing the page.

The Best Defense: Social Engineering

In many cases, the only way to ensure that template information won't be excluded or modified by a graphic editor is to raise awareness of the template syntax among site designers. The tools being used to edit HTML are known best by the designers themselves. Therefore, it makes sense to foster an awareness of the general format of template code and the specific effects that might be seen in HTML editors. Of course, these same designers are also the people using the template language to indicate Web application sections within a template, so it's not too much to ask for a general knowledge of the language and its effects.

This is another reason to keep the template language simple and understandable. The more complex a templating language is, the more likely it is that designers will have difficulty learning all its possible permutations. If the language is too difficult to figure out, designers have a hard time even figuring out the relationship between the template and the output of the Web application. With a simpler set of codes and a more uniform method for denoting template sections, designers are more likely to absorb the full range of identifiers and determine how best to use them within standard HTML tools.

The complexity of template interactions also gives weight to the idea of a staging area for site designers to use when testing templates against live information. There's no better test of a template's interaction with Web applications than actually using it with an application in the correct environment. The staging area can be tailored to the templating needs with a set of sample pages generated using the new template and representative site data. However, the data and applications only need to be representative. It shouldn't be necessary to keep a complete copy of the live site up to date for staging use. Formatting can be checked against similar pages just as easily, and mirroring a live site might be more trouble than a staging area would justify.

Applying Templates Across a Site

The core reason for developing a template is to apply a uniform look and feel across an entire site or group of sites. Developing the template is the first step in this direction, but it's also necessary to modify other pages and applications on the site to adopt the template as well. A site template won't help uniformity much if the component applications and pages don't reflect changes made in the template document. As a result, it's necessary to set up a general way for all site documents to access the same template, no matter how it changes.

Templates can be applied across a site in a number of ways. The main difference between these methods is the complexity of the site and the corresponding complexity of the template system used. Simple sites usually need only one template document, which then can be referred to directly in all other documents and applications on the site. More complex sites—those with sections that look and feel different from each other—usually can be served by a group of similar template documents in a central location with a consistent naming scheme or a template manager providing access. Very complex sites—ones with issues such as user access control and personalized content—can be served by a dynamic template that changes depending on the application from which it's being called.

No matter how templates are implemented for a site, some thought should be given to future applications of the templates. Will applications a few years down the road be able to take advantage of the same templates designed today? Conversely, will applications written today be able to use templates that are designed for a radically different site in the future? If not, is there a way that the old templates can be adapted for the new applications, or vice versa? These questions should be kept in mind when designing template languages or putting template systems into place.

Single-Template Case

For many sites, a single site template suffices for all pages on the site, both dynamic and static. This template should be stored in a single file that is updated by the site designer directly. This avoids any derivative work caused by the artificial need for site administrators to modify the template for use with applications. Keeping a single copy also provides a central place for essential edits to be made by all site personnel. Thus, site designers have a current snapshot of the site design with which to work, no matter what changes have been made.

Of course, a staging area for template design might also be a good idea so that the effects of site modifications aren't instant and irretrievable. If that is the case, the same rules apply to the staging area copy of the template that would apply to a single copy of the template. The production copy then can be taken as a regular snapshot of the staging area template with no changes made directly to the production copy. Even more complex systems of distributed design can be used—including CVS and other content management systems—but the core idea remains the same: Use a single central copy (or repository) that is accessible by all site personnel.

The first aspect of a single template to consider is where to put the template so that it is accessible to all pages and applications on the site. This location needn't be in the site document tree because the template is likely to be processed by a Web application that has a longer reach into the Web server's file system. However, the template should be in an area from which the Web server user—the user the Web server is running as—has permission to read. In addition, if a Web application is used to create and manage the template files, the Web server user also should have write and create access to the template file and directory where it resides. (Create access is necessary because some template managers remove old templates before creating new ones.) It's also advisable that the template location be easy to remember and easy to type—the combination saves headaches down the line when page creators and Web application programmers need to reference the template in their files. For instance, a file path such as /web/templates/page.txt is reasonably resistant to typos and misspelling and easy enough for site designers to memorize.

After a suitable template location is determined, pages and applications on the site can be modified to use the template. For static pages, this might involve translating pure HTML pages into a format that can be handled by a template manager or embedded Perl processor. It also might involve changing the extension or content type of the static HTML pages so that they are automatically recognized and processed by the template manager application. However, in some cases, it's possible to define a preprocessor to add the template to the static files without modifying their content types or adding code to the pages themselves. Either way, modifications to all the pages and applications should have to occur only once to bring them into the template system. After that occurs, changes should be made solely within the template system itself.

When applying a template to site elements, care should be taken to leave no part of the site out of the core template system. Some applications might present problems when adding template processing code, but modifying the application for templating is worth any effort required. It might be tempting to simply copy the template into the application and adapt it for use within the program, but the simplicity of such an approach is deceptive. Any process that is required when translating a template for use with an odd application has to be repeated each time the template changes, which could be every week or every day, depending on the activity of site designers. Eventually, either the work required to continually update the template copy outstrips the work required to add templating, or the template copy stored in the application falls out of date and site unity suffers as a result. It is more robust in the long run to adapt all applications to use the central template from the start.

Multiple Templates

Sites with a more complex structure might need multiple templates to provide a different style for each section of the site. As an example, a site might need multiple templates if the home page of the site and other overview pages have a fundamentally different structure than pages that display a specific bit of data—a news story or a product description, for example. The need for multiple templates also can occur when a site uses pop-up windows for some types of pages—a shipping table displayed when a customer is using an e-commerce application, for instance. Multiple templates also can reduce the complexity of any individual template by enabling more variation in page design with less variation within the template itself.

A group of template files can be set up in a fashion similar to the single template case. In fact, a single template can be viewed as a special case of a multiple-template system. A template location should be determined and a template-naming scheme defined. In this case, the naming scheme also should involve a descriptive name that indicates the site section to which the template corresponds. Then, the templates themselves can be added using the defined naming scheme. Template code then should be added to every static and dynamic page on the site, with special attention paid to generalizing the template code so that new templates can be used as they appear, without modifying the code again.

After multiple templates are defined, there should be some way to distinguish between templates within applications and static files. The simplest way to distinguish between templates in most template systems is by specifying the filename directly within the code that calls the template. If this isn't possible within the bounds of the template system, it's also possible to specify the template file as an attribute of the template being called. For instance, a Web application being used in the `forum` section of a Web site might call a template file called `forum.txt`. The translation between section names and filenames can be handled by the template manager application. A concern here is the use of templates within preprocessor code. If a template location is hard-coded into the preprocessor program, that single template is used for all static pages, no matter which section of the site they are part of. One solution to this situation is to define site sections in terms of their URL locations so that the preprocessor can call different templates accordingly. For instance, every file in the `/forum/` subdirectory of the Web document directory might use the `forum.txt` template file. This kind of inherent template specification might create limitations on the relation between the structure of a site and its file locations. However, many site designers already use site directories to organize the content of a site so the change won't necessarily be a burden.

Dynamic Templates

For sites with structure that varies based on user preferences and permissions, a dynamic template enables page structure to be generated interactively. This comes in handy mostly in situations in which site content has to change based directly on the user that is accessing it. For instance, a site governed by user access control lists might show different content to different users depending on their access levels and areas of interest. A site also might generate page structure based on themes and choices specified by user preferences. In any case, the structure of the page is no longer a simple matter of the designer's wish, but more a matter of the combined choices and authorization of the user making the request.

Simple dynamic templates are made possible by embedding Perl within the template itself—assuming that the template manager enables embedded Perl. Sections of the template can be filled in by executing code based on the incoming request, just as in the Web application itself. For instance, conditional code can be added to a site menu that displays only certain menu choices to certain users. Other aspects of a dynamic template can be retrieved from a database or processed from an XML data file. The possibilities are as wide as with any Web application, but the result is open to all pages across a site. Because the template can be made available to a site preprocessor, a dynamic template can be used by static HTML pages *and* dynamic Web applications.

More robust dynamic templates can be created by developing a Perl module that provides methods to create page structure. Because the pages calling the template usually are embedding Perl into HTML, calling object methods from a template module can be just as simple as calling other kinds of template functions. A dedicated template module enables more control to be exercised over fundamental aspects of the Web application interface, including access control, session management, and user preferences. Module-based templates also enable nonembedded Perl code to access and use templates. This overcomes a hurdle that most simple template systems have trouble addressing: If the template document is written in an embedded-Perl style, programs written in a Common Gateway Interface (CGI) style might not have access to it. Any Perl program can access a Perl module template, so all programs benefit equally.

Of course, creating templates dynamically can invalidate one strength of template design—the ability to edit the templates in standard HTML editors. Because any Perl code is likely to throw off a graphic HTML editor, this is true regardless of whether the template is an HTML page with a little embedded Perl code or a full-blown Perl module. Luckily, the solution here is the same as the original template solution—separate the representative HTML out from the dynamic template as well. At this point, the resulting HTML is more a convenient construct than a working template for the look and feel of the completed site, but even a construct can provide enough information for site designers to create a coherent look and feel across the site.

A Simple Template Using Perl Server Pages (PSP)

Returning to the simple template case, it might be helpful to see an example of a template system fully realized. The system developed in this section is reduced to the simplest case possible: one template and one application using it. The system can be extended easily to use multiple templates and many templated applications, but the principles for that case are identical to this one.

I've chosen PSP as the environment for this template system simply because it's the environment with which I'm most familiar. A similar system could be created using HTML::Mason or a dozen other environments. PSP was chosen also because it's the server environment for VeloMeter.com, a handy site to which I have access and over which I have editorial control. PSP also has the basic requirements for a simple templating system built into its abstracted language—I can create a template tag within PSP with a minimum of extraneous work. This kind of reasoning is important when choosing an environment that enables templates to be designed easily.

In addition to the template system created here—or any custom template system created for a specific site—a number of existing template systems exist that work perfectly well for the purposes of a simple site like this. Those systems are covered later in this chapter, in the "Template Modules on CPAN" section.

Using the *<template>* Tag

The core of the template system developed here is a PSP tag called `<template>`. This tag performs the work of joining the output of a Web application to the site template. A few additional parameters are specified to provide a more integrated page style, but the core purpose of the `<template>` tag simply is to wrap a Web application in a predefined template shell. Listing 13.1 shows an example of this kind of templated application.

Listing 13.1   **VeloMeter Page with Template** *(register.psp)*

```
01 <include file="$ENV{DOCUMENT_ROOT}/page.psp" />
02 <template title="Load Testing Forum - Register" section="forum">
03
04 <p>Registration with the VeloMeter forum isn't necessary to post or
   ➡view messages, but it does allow others to recognize messages posted
   ➡by you as yours alone. As a result, we've tried to make registration
   ➡as painless as possible.</p>
05
06 <p>We also respect your privacy. Your email address won't be posted on
   ➡the site or used for any marketing purposes. The email is only
   ➡required in order to provide a basic check of your identity.</p>
07
08 <form action="do_register.pperl" method="post">
09 <output>
```

continues

Listing 13.1 **Continued**

```
10 <p style="color: red;font-weight: bold">$QUERY{error}</p>
11
12 <p>Your name:<br />
13 <input type="text" name="fullname" size="30" maxlength="50"
   ↪value="$QUERY{fullname}" /></p>
14
15 <p>Email address:<br />
16 <input type="text" name="email" size="40" maxlength="200"
   ↪value="$QUERY{email}" /></p>
17
18 <p>Username/Password:<br />
19 <input type="text" name="username" size="20" value="$QUERY{username}"
   ↪/> 
20 <input type="password" name="password" size="20"
   ↪value="$QUERY{password}" />
21 </p>
22
23 <p><input type="submit" value="Register" /></p>
24
25 <p>Once you register, you will recieve an email with confirmation
   ↪instructions. You will be able to post messages immediately after
   ↪confirmation.</p>
26
27 </output>
28 </form>
29
30 </template>
```

One thing that might be noticed about this page right away is its striking similarity to a simple HTML page. In fact, the page itself is close enough to pure HTML that it would be rendered just fine by itself in a browser, as shown in Figure 13.1.

There are a few differences in the page due to the templating environment, though. Line 01 of Listing 13.1 contains an <include> tag that loads the template from its assigned location. In this case, the template is stored in a file called page.psp, which is located in the document root directory of the Web server (as specified in the DOCUMENT_ROOT environment variable), but it also might be found in an absolute directory, which contains only templates. In addition, different templates can be used in different applications by changing the file referenced in the <include> tag because the syntax of the rest of the file can stay the same.

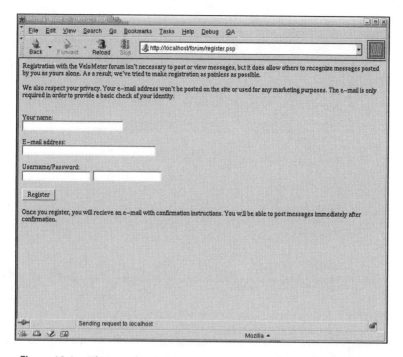

Figure 13.1   This templated application can be viewed directly in a browser.

The next alteration to the templated page is the `<template>` tag itself. This element encompasses the entire page to be displayed. It starts on line 02 with the first tag after the `<include>` tag and ends on line 30 at the end of the file. The contents within the tag are considered the body of the page to be inserted into the template, as specified in the next section of this chapter, "The `<tag>` Tag and `page.psp` Template." The `<template>` tag also has two possible attributes, `title` and `section`. The `title` attribute simply specifies the title of this page to be displayed in the appropriate parts of the template. The `section` attribute isn't actually used by the template example in the next section, but it might be used in the future to alter a dynamic template based on the section specified. Extra attributes, such as `section`, are good to add as soon as they are conceived to avoid editing the page again after the template is given additional functionality.

Other PSP tags are used in Listing 13.2, but they all are part of the Web application itself, not the template system. The end result of the `<template>` tag is a page that merges the template included by line 01 with the contents of the `<template>` tag. When combined with the template defined in the next section, the resulting page looks similar to Figure 13.2 in a Web browser.

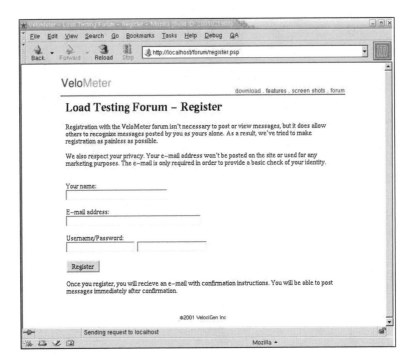

Figure 13.2 The result after the template is applied.

The difference between the two pages is subtle, but the template provided a definite look and feel to the Web application page. The contents of the page are centered within a defined area on a white background, and a logo and navigation for the site have been added before the beginning of the page. In addition, the title provided to the `<template>` tag now is listed both as the HTML page title (as seen in the title bar of the browser window) and within the page as a more obvious heading.

The *<tag>* Tag and *page.psp* Template

The template used by Listing 13.1 has to define the `<template>` tag as well as provide the template HTML to complete the page. An example of a template that does both is shown in Listing 13.2, which provides some simple structure to the page and defines basic navigation as well. Note again that this page has to be viewable as HTML in a standard Web browser or in graphic HTML tools. As a result, extra care has been taken to make sure that the template logic doesn't interfere with the basic structure of the HTML in the template.

Listing 13.2 **Template Definition** (*page.psp*)

```
01 <tag name="template" accepts="title, section" body="1">
02 <output>
03 <html>
04 <head>
05 <title>VeloMeter - $title</title>
06 </head>
07
08 <body bgcolor="white">
09 <table width="80%" align="Center" cellspacing="0" cellpadding="0"
   ➥border="0">
10 <tr>
11 <td colspan="3"><a href="/"><img src="/images/logo-velometer-200.png"
   ➥alt="VeloMeter" border="0" /=""></a></td>
12 </tr>
13 <tr>
14 <td colspan="3" align="Right"><font face="Arial, Helvetica"
   ➥size="2"><a href="/download.psp">download</a> . <a
   ➥href="/features.psp">features</a> . <a href="/screenshots.psp">
15 screen shots</a> . <a href="/forum/">forum</a></font></td>
16 </tr>
17 <tr>
18 <td colspan="3" bgcolor="#333399"><font face="Helvetica, Arial, sans-
   ➥serif"><img src="/images/dot-black.gif" width="2" height="2"
   ➥border="0" /=""></font></td>
19 </tr>
20 <tr>
21 <td valign="top" colspan="3">
22 <table width="100%" cellpadding="10" cellspacing="0" border="0">
23 <tr>
24 <td>
25 <h2>$title</h2>
26 $body
27 </td>
28 </tr>
29
30 </table>
31 </td>
32 </tr>
33 </table>
34
35 <p align="center"><font face="Arial, Helvetica" size="1">&copy;2001
36 <a href="http://www.velocigen.com/">VelociGen Inc</a></font></p>
37 </body>
38 </html>
39 </output>
40 </tag>
```

In PSP, a custom HTML tag is defined by using another custom tag, called `<tag>`. This tag can contain any valid PSP page content, which then is executed after the tag is used. In Listing 13.2, the `<tag>` tag is used in line 01 to define a tag called `template` by specifying the name of the tag in the `name` attribute of the `<tag>` tag. This name could be any valid XML string, but a good rule of thumb is to avoid names already used by HTML elements. Another attribute of the `<tag>` tag is `accepts`, which defines a list of variables that the tag defines in terms of specified attributes. In this case, the `<template>` tag accepts attributes called `title` and `section` that are assigned to variables with the same names. These variables are lexically scoped to their assigned tag, so multiple tags can use the same variable/attribute name without causing overlap or unusual behavior. The last attribute of `<tag>` is `body`, which indicates that the contents of the `<template>` element should be accessible within a special variable called `$body`. The `<tag>` tag ends on line 40, the last line of the template.

The variables defined within the scope of the `<template>` tag—`$title`, `$body`, and `$section`—can be called directly within the template text by using the `<output>` tag in lines 02 and 39. Everything within `<output>` then is treated like a double-quoted string in Perl. Lines 05 and 25 use the `$title` variable to display the specified title, for instance, and line 27 places the `$body` variable in context. That single line represents the entire result of any Web application or static file that invokes the `<template>` tag, just as the `<template>` tag itself represents this template in those files. These two constructs provide the abstracted interface between templates and Web applications that then can be extended across the site.

Enhancing Templates

A system like this could support multiple templates of the same format by simply varying the name of the file being included with the initial `<include>` tag. For instance, a different template could be used for each section of the site. The syntax of the `<template>` tag would stay exactly the same because the format of the tag being defined wouldn't vary at all.

Additionally, templates could incorporate other pages with headlines, news, or other section filler. This works particularly well when adding dynamic listings to a template that are common to the entire site but still generated by Perl code. An `<include>` tag could be used to load these sections into the template, further abstracting them away from the formatting of the page. This is similar to the component model used by HTML::Mason, which could be used to provide a modular template in the same fashion.

This kind of template file also can support dynamic features that change the format of the page based on attributes passed along with the `<template>` tag. The `section` attribute, for example, could be used to choose navigation features. This could be incorporated by adding a conditional using either Perl code or PSP tags. Additional dynamic page elements could be added as needed, but most of them would compromise the ability of site designers to view the page in an HTML editor.

Automating Template Updates

The ability to use templates is one thing, but it's not worth much without giving designers a way to update the site template automatically without needing to involve technical staff. Site designers need a way to update the look of a site in real time, even if they are only updating a staging site that is separate from the live site. It's also helpful to provide a Web interface to site updates because secure Web access is common to many platforms and requires a minimum of special software. In contrast, secure FTP or shell access requires software that is unlikely to be found by default on systems used by Web designers.

The simplest way to provide Web-based access to template updates is by creating a Web application to accept and track template uploads. This application can be written using the same framework that is used by all other Web applications on the site. The application even can use the template itself to provide a uniform interface with little extra work. A simple template management application is illustrated in Listing 13.3 through Listing 13.6 in this section.

A Template Upload Application

Listing 13.3 is a simple upload form that uses HTTP upload to provide a common interface to transferring files onto the server. The listing uses the same template as Listing 13.1, so the resulting page has the same look and feel as the rest of the site.

Listing 13.3 **Template Upload in PSP** *(upload.psp)*

```
01 <include file="$ENV{DOCUMENT_ROOT}/page.psp" />
02 <template title="Upload a new template">
03
04 <p>This page allows you to send a new template to the server.
05 Choose a file to send using this form, then click "Send file"
06 to check the integrity of the file and assign it a name using
07 the next page.</p>
08
09 <form action="do_upload.pperl" method="post"
   ➥enctype="multipart/form-data">
10 <output>
11 <p style="color: red;font-weight: bold">$QUERY{error}</p>
12
13 <p>Template file to upload:<br />
14 <input name="template" type="file" /></p>
15
16 <p><input type="submit" value="Send file" /></p>
17
18 <p>Once the template is received, it will be previewed using a
19 test page. If the page loads correctly, use the form shown to
20 complete the template installation. If the page does not display
21 correctly, return to this page and upload the corrected file.</p>
22
```

continues

Listing 13.3   **Continued**

```
23 </output>
24 </form>
25
26 </template>
```

One important feature of this Web application to notice from the start is the lack of
Perl code in Listing 13.3, which simply displays the form and passes the result to
another file. The idea here is to separate the display application from the application
that does work. A PSP page handles the front end, while the persistent Perl page handles the back end. When used as a general principle, this method avoids some of the
most common—and most dangerous—pitfalls of Web application design. Specifically, it
avoids unusual effects if a particular page is reloaded, printed, or opened in a new
window. If the page was performing work as well as displaying HTML, these actions
would cause it to perform the work again. The results of this duplication range from
additional load on the server to duplicate entries made in backend databases for
orders, messages, and other submitted items. Because the page is only displaying a
result instead of acting on server systems, however, it can be reloaded any number of
times and provide the exact same visual result. That result is seen in Figure 13.3.

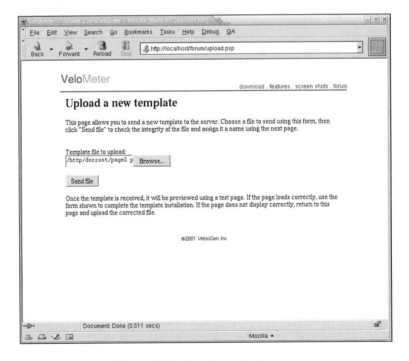

Figure 13.3   Template upload page.

The important parts of Listing 13.3 are contained in lines 09 and 14. Line 09 starts the <form> element, which points to the backend file do_upload.pperl and declares the encoding type to be multipart/form-data. This means that the resulting request can contain an uploaded file as well as other form variables. Line 09 follows through on that promise by using an <input> tag of type file. This results in the text box pictured in Figure 13.3 with the "Browse..." button next to it. A file path can be typed into the text box manually, or the button can be used to invoke a file selection dialog box with which the user can fill the text box automatically. The file specified in this box is sent to the backend application, along with its filename and other form variables.

Accepting File Uploads

After a file is uploaded to the server, it's necessary to retrieve the file and store it. Listing 13.4 provides a backend application that performs this task by saving the file to a temporary location and forwarding the user on to a page that displays a confirmation page.

Listing 13.4 **Template Upload Back-End** *(do_upload.pperl)*

```
01 use 5.6.0;
02 use strict;
03 use warnings;
04
05 use CGI ();
06
07 my $q = CGI->new();
08
09 # get the uploaded file
10 my $fh = $q->upload('template');
11
12 # if no file is uploaded,
13 unless ($fh) {error("No file was sent. Please select a file to
   ↪upload.")};
14
15 # place the uploaded file in a temporary directory
16 open(TEST, ">$ENV{DOCUMENT_ROOT}/templates/test.psp")
17     or error("Can't write temporary file: $!");
18 while (<$fh>)
19 {
20   print TEST;
21 }
22 close TEST;
23
24 # redirect the user to the naming page
25 print qq{Location: set_name.psp\n\n};
26
27 sub error ($)
28 {
29   my $error = shift;
```

continues

Listing 13.4   **Continued**

```
30   $error =~ s/\s/+/g;
31
32   # redirect the user to the upload page with an error
33   print qq{Location: upload.psp?error=$error\n\n};
34   exit;
35 }
```

Listing 13.4 is written in a persistent Perl style, which is similar to the CGI style, except that it assumes it is running in a persistent environment. Lines 01–03 initialize the environment to ensure that persistent-compatible code is being written. Line 05 invokes the CGI.pm module—CGI.pm provides methods for reading uploaded files. Line 07 creates the CGI object $q, and line 10 assigns the $fh file handle to the uploaded file provided by the upload method of the CGI object. Line 13 checks whether a file has actually been uploaded and sends an error to be displayed in the upload page, if necessary.

After the file has been received, lines 16–22 open a temporary location for the uploaded file and write it to disk. This location should be standard enough to enable the test page (as outlined in the next section of this chapter) to access it consistently each time. For this example, a fixed filename is used to store all test pages. Some systems might want to store each uploaded template in a separate file to provide accountability and backup.

After the file is uploaded and saved, line 25 redirects the user to a page that tests the new template and enables a permanent place to be assigned. An error subroutine is defined in lines 27–35 to provide a generic way to pass errors back to the original upload page for display and reentry.

Checking the New Template

The best way to test a new template is to use it in a sample page. Because a successful template needs to be assigned a name on the server, it makes sense to make the test page a form that accepts the template's name as well. Listing 13.5 is an example of a test page that also serves as a completion form.

Listing 13.5   **Template Preview Page** *(set_name.psp)*

```
01 <include file="$ENV{DOCUMENT_ROOT}/templates/test.psp" />
02 <template title="Name this template">
03
04 <p>Check this template for validity, then choose a name
05 for the template and click "Install template."</p>
06
07 <form action="do_set_name.pperl" method="post">
08 <output>
09 <p style="color: red;font-weight: bold">$QUERY{error}</p>
```

```
10
11 <p>Template name:<br />
12 <input name="template" type="text" size="30" value="$QUERY{template}"
   ⮑ /></p>
13
14 <p><input type="submit" value="Install template" /></p>
15
16
17 </output>
18 </form>
19
20 </template>
```

Listing 13.5 is a form that is similar to the upload form in Listing 13.3. The main difference in this listing is the template used to display this page—it should be the same
one that was just saved by the backend application in Listing 13.4. Line 01 of Listing
13.5 loads the new template and its associated <template> tag; then it applies the
template to the form HTML. The result, assuming all goes correctly, should look
somewhat similar to Figure 13.4.

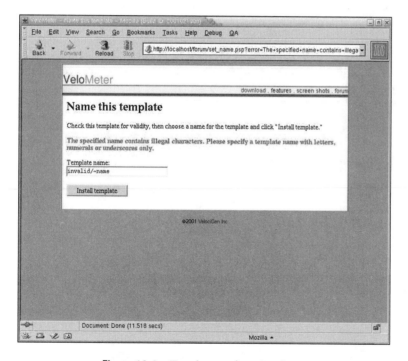

Figure 13.4 Template confirmation form.

The page in Figure 13.4 is shown using a template that differs slightly from the template in Listing 13.2. This is done to show how differences appear in the confirmation form. This page serves as a simple staging area for template design. Templates can be uploaded here repeatedly to check their performance and appearance and then saved to the live server when they are approved. If the template doesn't work for some reason or causes an error on the server, that also appears on this page. If another template needs to be uploaded, the user can access the upload form by returning to the previous page.

After it has been determined that the new template is satisfactory, the form can be used to determine the name assigned to the new template. In this case, the name is kept simple, but any naming convention can be used. Figure 13.4 also shows the error result of some simple checking performed by the naming backend application. Template names are restricted in this case to a single string consisting of letters, numbers, or underscores.

New Template Notification

If the new template is satisfactory, it is saved to the specified filename. Additionally, it might be wise to notify site personnel that the template has changed. Listing 13.6 provides a persistent Perl program to carry this out.

Listing 13.6 **Template Naming and Notification** *(do_set_name.pperl)*

```
01 use 5.6.0;
02 use strict;
03 use warnings;
04
05 use CGI ();
06 use Net::SMTP ();
07
08 my $q = CGI->new();
09
10 # get the template name
11 our $template = $q->param('template');
12
13 # remove the trailing ".psp" if present
14 $template =~ s/\.psp$//;
15
16 # check the assigned name
17 unless ($template)
18 {
19   error("Please specify a template name.");
20 };
21
22 if ($template =~ /[^A-Za-z0-9_]/)
23 {
24   error("The specified name contains illegal characters. "
```

```perl
25            ."Please specify a template name with letters, "
26            ."numerals or underscores only.");
27 }
28
29 my $filename = "$ENV{DOCUMENT_ROOT}/templates/$template.psp";
30
31 # write the temporary template file to the n
32 open(NEWFILE, ">$filename") or error("Can't write $filename: $!");
33 open(OLDFILE, "$ENV{DOCUMENT_ROOT}/templates/test.psp")
34      or error("Can't open temporary template file: $!");
35 print NEWFILE while (<OLDFILE>);
36 close OLDFILE;
37 close NEWFILE;
38
39 # send an email notification
40 my $smtp = Net::SMTP->new('mail.server.com');
41
42 $smtp->mail('user@company.com');
43 $smtp->to('user@company.com');
44
45 $smtp->data();
46 $smtp->datasend("To: user\@company.com\n");
47 $smtp->datasend("Subject: Template '$template' has been updated.\n");
48 $smtp->datasend("\n");
49 $smtp->datasend("The template named '$template' has been updated\n");
50 $smtp->datasend("and added as $filename.\n\n");
51 $smtp->dataend();
52
53 $smtp->quit;
54
55
56 # redirect the user to the upload page
57 print qq{Location: upload.psp\n\n};
58
59 undef $template;
60
61 sub error ($)
62 {
63   my $error = shift;
64   $error =~ s/\s/+/g;
65
66   # redirect the user to the naming page with an error
67   print qq{Location:
   ➥set_name.psp?error=$error&template=$template\n\n};
68   exit;
69 }
```

Like Listing 13.4, Listing 13.6 is written in a persistent style, as declared in lines 01–03. Lines 05 and 06 load the CGI.pm and Net::SMTP modules, respectively. Net::SMTP provides a pure-Perl interface to email servers. Line 08 creates the $q CGI object for form variable interaction. Line 11 then assigns the template form variable to the $template global variable declared using the our keyword.

> **A Note About *our***
>
> Using the our keyword in a persistent context usually isn't advised because it overrides the protections offered by the strict pragma. In some cases, it's necessary to use global variables to simplify subroutine interaction, however. As long as the our declaration is combined with variable clean-up code (as used in Listing 13.6 in line 59), it is possible to use it in a persistent context without unexpected behavior.

After the $template variable is defined, it needs to be checked for a legitimate value to be used as the filename for the saved template. Line 14 removes any .psp extension added by the user to standardize the naming format. Line 17 makes sure the result actually contains a filename—on the odd chance that the user specified the name .psp or nothing at all. The template format then is checked by line 22 for any characters not allowed in the template filename. If illegal characters are found, the user is directed back to the entry form with an error message. Note at this point that the template name sent back to the entry form is the processed version (without any .psp extension) instead of the raw form variable. In most cases, it's better to provide the user with the original entered values if an error occurs, but in this case, the modified name is preferred because it indicates to the user one aspect of the proper format for further reference.

After the filename has been verified, lines 29–37 write the new template to the file specified. It also would be possible to delete the temporary file using the unlink command after line 37, but in this case, it is left in place until the next uploaded template overwrites it.

After the file has been written correctly, lines 40–53 send an email notification with the new template name and its saved location. This section of the program could just as easily log the action to a file, save the uploaded template to an archive, or perform any other action required after a template has been uploaded. After notification has been sent, the program redirects the user to the original upload page.

Template Modules on CPAN

In addition to the custom template managers made possible with embedded programming environments such as PSP and HTML::Mason, a number of template management modules are available on the Comprehensive Perl Archive Network (CPAN). These modules vary from simple variable interpolation modules to full-blown HTML document management systems with more variations introduced regularly. As this book was written, only a few of the template modules were available in released versions greater than 1.0.

One common aspect of the Perl templating modules available on CPAN is their Perl-centric design. This design contrasts with the Web-centric design of systems such as HTML::Mason and PSP. Many of the modules assume a usage that is similar to the CGI.pm module, with object methods to handle variable assignment and section definition. This approach doesn't mesh well with the embedded programming model, but it does enable templates to be used with persistent Perl code written in a CGI style.

Two of the common templating modules available on CPAN are HTML::Template and Text::Template. They take different approaches to the template language they implement—HTML::Template abstracts Perl completely away from the template language, whereas Text::Template uses Perl segments directly as the template language. In addition, Text::Template is designed for use with any text template, whereas HTML::Template is geared toward HTML specifically. However, the basic idea behind both is to provide a programmatic interface to filling templates with information stored in Perl data structures.

HTML::Template

The HTML::Template model is separated into two parts:

- Templates with a custom template language
- Program code that loads and manipulates the templates

The template language uses HTML-like tags to specify template sections and variables to interpolate. When templates are processed, the programming interface to HTML::Template provides a group of methods that act on the HTML::Template object created by loading the template into the Perl program.

Templates in this system consist of any valid HTML file with extra HTML::Template tags specifying sections to interpolate programmatically. The most basic tag used to interpolate values is <TMPL_VAR>, which specifies a variable to be replaced with the value specified in a Perl program that loads the template. For instance, the following code section would replace the variable fullname with a name provided by the Perl program:

```
<p>The officer in charge was <TMPL_VAR NAME="fullname">.</p>
```

With the appropriate code in the persistent application, the <TMPL_VAR> tag would be replaced by a full name. The code for this uses the param method of the template object created by loading the template into HTML::Template. To replace the <TMPL_VAR> tag with the full name value and display the result, for instance, the code might look like the following:

```
my $template = HTML::Template->new(filename => 'officer.tmpl');
$template->param( fullname => $full_name );
print $template->output;
```

The main difficulty with HTML::Template arises from its oversimplified template language and CGI-style module interface. The module interface is too complex to provide a simple templating system to HTML-style documents and the template language is too simple to be a dynamic template manager. An indicator of this tension comes from the other tags used by the templating language: `<TMPL_LOOP>`, `<TMPL_IF>`, and `<TMPL_ELSE>`. These tags are included to provide Perl-like constructs for complex templates, but they work only somewhat like their Perl counterparts. To use the template constructs the way the analogous structures in a Perl program would be used, the Perl code in the main application has to become more complex and, potentially, more difficult to maintain. Similarly, HTML::Template provides no facility for creating tags other than the core set provided, so Perl-generated sections of the template can't be included without first assigning their output to a variable and interpolating the variable through the `param` method.

Text::Template

Another approach to template processing in Perl is exemplified by the Text::Template module. This module is designed for use with any sort of text document, HTML or otherwise. The module could just as easily be used to fill names into an automated email system or any other generated text document. To assist this process, the module provides an interface to load templates from most sources of text, including files, file handles, and Perl variables.

Text::Template is similar to embedded Perl solutions on the surface. Rather than use a special syntax for the template language, Text::Template uses Perl sections enclosed in curly braces. When the template is processed, the Perl sections are evaluated and replaced with their values. The current values of variables in the calling program are used to interpolate any variables listed in the template, and other Perl code in the template is executed as listed. For instance, this template segment would replace the specified Perl section with the contents of the `$full_name` variable:

```
<p>The officer in charge was {$fullname}.</p>
```

However, Text::Template is implemented in a manner that is different from embedded Perl environments. Rather than being invoked directly and interpolated inherently by the invoking environment, a Text::Template template is loaded explicitly by Perl code that resembles CGI style more than an embedded Perl environment. For instance, replacing the `$fullname` variable with its value would require a code segment like the following:

```
my $template = Text::Template->new(TYPE => FILE, SOURCE =>
'officer.tmpl');
my $full_name = 'Officer Krupke';
my $text = $template->fill_in();
print $text;
```

This subtle difference between embedding systems and Text::Template means that templates written for Text:Template potentially could be used by CGI-style programs as well as embedded Perl programs. In addition, templates could be created for any number of page sections and then evaluated one at a time by the Web application to create a complete HTML page. This makes Text::Template a good basic toolkit for creating customized template systems, if not a complete template manager.

The major advantage to using Text::Template also is its biggest drawback. Using Perl as the template language provides a robust language that's fully compatible with the underlying Web application code. However, the main point of abstracting code out of a template is to provide template access to site designers who don't know—or wish to learn—Perl. In addition, the Perl segments in the template have no additional structure or syntax added to enable abstraction of Perl constructs beyond simple variables. This is likely to lead to more Perl in the template than site designers would prefer. It also leads to less abstraction, which is contrary to the goal of templates.

Other Template Modules

CPAN is full of other Perl modules that provide the same type templating features in various implementations. Modules such as CGI:FastTemplate, HTML::FormTemplate, HTML::DynamicTemplate, the Template Toolkit, and others all provide some subset or superset of the functions required to create a templating system, and many more are likely on the way. This profusion of template interfaces probably is due to the highly custom nature of template systems—no one templating approach is good for every circumstance, so finding the right approach to templating always requires some searching and evaluation.

Performance Issues with Templates

As can be expected with any system that saves programming time and does real work, most template systems involve additional processing overhead. The types and amount of overhead vary depending on the template manager and Perl environments used, but most template systems use a bit more CPU time to process and interpolate a template and a little more memory to store the data structures used to store templates. Some template managers can add considerable overhead if templates are being interpolated inefficiently, however. Testing the performance of a few candidate template systems against a suitably complex template and Web application is generally recommended.

Caching templates is the most important performance improvement a template manager can provide. Performance can suffer significantly if templates are loaded off disk with each request, just as CGI programs lose performance if they are loaded and processed with each request. Some template managers cache templates automatically, but others are not designed for a persistent environment. In the latter case, it's sometimes necessary to implement a caching mechanism that stores processed template objects and reuses them with each request.

Scheduled Publishing with LWP

Although templates are useful even on a purely static site, the overhead of template processing might be high relative to simply serving static HTML pages. For high traffic sites where overhead due to template processing is prohibitive, a good alternative is scheduled publishing.

Not all pages need to be generated dynamically for each request. Following the rule of caching information whenever possible, it might be a good idea to precache dynamic pages as HTML instead. Depending on the frequency of updates to the underlying information, pages can be published on a schedule that can reduce processing overhead by a few orders of magnitude. For instance, a news site that gets a hundred home page requests per second might update its headline database only every five minutes. Instead of accessing the database to generate a home page with headlines for each request, the site can publish the page to HTML once a minute. The resulting overhead would drop by a factor of 6000.

Publishing dynamic pages to HTML from a Perl program is made possible by the LWP module. LWP provides an interface to Web client operations, including retrieving a Web page over the network. A simple program can be written to access the dynamic Web page as a browser and save the result to disk as a static HTML file. This kind of program then can be scheduled to run at regular intervals to provide a relatively current snapshot of the page being generated.

Incidentally, most embedded Perl environments provide a method of caching the result of dynamic pages on an individual basis. This enables the pages to be accessed with a dynamic naming scheme instead of publishing some pages to HTML in new locations and keeping others in their original locations. These cached pages usually incur minor overhead because the Perl environment can't cache the pages as efficiently as the Web server can, but the resulting flexibility usually is worth this minor performance difference.

Summary

Templates are a natural extension of embedded program that enable HTML formatting to be abstracted away from Perl code. The resulting interface gives both site designers and Web application developers the freedom to design their respective parts of Web applications without requiring input from the other group. Templates can be implemented in a number of ways, but the common approach is to create an HTML-like syntax for the template document, which then is interpolated by code residing in the Web application or a separate template management system. Simple systems can involve a single template document for all Web applications or static files, while more complex template systems use many dynamic templates that customize their output to suit requests. A simple template system can be written trivially in embedded environments such as PSP and HTML::Mason, or any number of existing template modules can be downloaded from CPAN for use with embedded or CGI-style programs. Templates likely are to incur a minor performance penalty, but the resulting flexibility in site design usually is more than worth the overhead.

Templates for the Lazy

Before I became aware of these fancy templating methods—in fact, before any of them were developed—I was faced with the task of implementing something that would offer all the benefits of a template without the work involved in creating a real template system.

My first solution was a distressingly simple one, implemented in the heady Web days of 1996 when dynamic sites were new and I had too much free time at work. The acute problem at that time was how to write as little HTML by hand as possible while still creating a commercial-quality site. Most sites at the time were composed entirely by hand, but that meant lots of tedious cutting and pasting whenever a menu or a background color was changed. I was keen on simplifying this process down to a few clicks and a Perl script. Compounding the problem was the need to do some of my work remotely from a terminal that had only basic Web access.

The solution I developed was dubbed Wackel, and it was a simple solution indeed. A repository of HTML fragments was kept that could be edited individually from an HTML form. These fragments—which consisted of a header file, a footer file, and the core segment from each existing Web page—could be compiled in real time to test the resulting HTML for completeness. This virtual site also could be used as a staging area for new designs and page modifications. After modifications to the staging site were approved, it then was possible to publish the compiled HTML files to the live site in their completed form. Note that none of the files was actually dynamic in nature—the whole system was designed simply to administer a static site.

Later, I discovered VelociGen (the software, not the company) and a little gem of a function called `vepload`, which did the work of Wackel in real time and with half the lines of code. Pages could be broken into their header, core, and footer sections, and the header and footer could be called from each core page directly through the `vepload` function embedded in a `<perl>` block. This also opened up the possibilities of embedded Perl code in HTML, and I was off and running. This technique still is a valid way to implement templates, even if the resulting template files aren't quite valid HTML, and I still use a variation of it to create the pages on my own site. (Of course, I'm bound to start using the newer templating methods Real Soon Now.)

14

Database-Backed Web Sites

THE UTILITY OF THE WEB TOOK A GIANT LEAP FORWARD when databases started being used as backend repositories for Web applications. Databases provide a flexible, dynamic way to store information for use on the Web, and existing databases provide treasure troves of data to be presented and extended by Web applications.

Databases, however, are used differently than are Web applications. A database user is usually accessing it through a continuous programmatic interface that makes one SQL query at a time with progress indicators and partial results available to mask the time taken by large queries. Fortunately, the utility of databases in Web application design has led to a number of solutions—both within Perl and within the database systems themselves—that enable databases to be used in a Web-centric fashion. They are used without sacrificing the data integrity, availability, and performance that are their greatest strengths.

Examples of this chapter's principles are offered for MySQL and Oracle, but the same ideas apply to any relational database management system (RDBMS), including commercial systems such as SQL Server, Informix, or DB2, as well as open-source systems such as PostgreSQL.

Accelerating DBI for the Web

When a Web site is using persistent Perl connections, as described in Chapter 10, "Tools for Perl Persistence," improving database access time isn't difficult. The persistent environment provides a new layer of continuity between Web server requests, and this layer can be used to maintain database connections and other cached information about the database.

Performance blocks can be removed from Web applications at many levels:

- The database connection architecture can be made more efficient using Apache::DBI.

- Database query preparing and execution can be streamlined using placeholders and cached statements.

- Perl's internal representation of the resultant data can be reduced and accelerated by using references.

Using Apache::DBI

The Apache::DBI module has few features, but the most important is the simple redefinition of DBI's `connect` method, which can improve Web application performance immensely. Normally, a database connection is opened by DBI each time the `connect` method is called, and the connection is closed when the `disconnect` method is called, usually at the end of a program or module. In Web Common Gateway Interface (CGI) context, this means that database connections are opened and closed every time a CGI program is run, which could be hundreds of times per second. Because a database connection takes up to ten seconds to be established, this means that the database connection time is a thousand times too slow to be acceptable.

In a persistent environment, the same effect occurs. Even though the Web application persists across many requests, `connect` and `disconnect` still are being called during each request, and a new database connection is being made and broken each time. Again, this increases the application runtime to an unacceptable level.

Apache::DBI works by caching open database connections based on the database accessed and the database user specified when connecting. The `connect` method within DBI defers to the same method within Apache::DBI if the environment is persistent, which enables the Apache::DBI `connect` method to keep track of open connections and to return them to the caller program as needed. The `connect` method also checks connections before returning them to ensure that a particular connection has not been closed by the database or some external process.

Apache::DBI also overloads the `disconnect` method to keep open database connections from being closed inadvertently by programs that are written without Apache::DBI in mind. Because of this, no programs need be modified and no tables need be restructured to use Apache::DBI. In fact, it's better to invoke Apache::DBI outside the body of your program code to ensure that it is used by all Web applications across the board. This can be done by including a directive in the `httpd.conf` configuration for Apache or the startup scripts for mod_perl, VelociGen, and other persistent Perl environments, as shown in Listing 14.1.

Listing 14.1 **Load Apache::DBI for all Applications**

```
01 # add one to httpd.conf file for
02 # Apache-based servers with mod_perl
03 PerlModule Apache::DBI
04 PerlRequire Apache/DBI.pm
05
06 # add one to startup.pl, vep_startup.pl
07 # or similar Perl engine startup scripts
08 use Apache::DBI;
09 require Apache::DBI;
10
11 # add a connect string to startup.pl, etc.
12 # to open a connection when the server starts
13 Apache::DBI->connect_on_init($datasource, $user, $pass);
```

Because of the unique relationship between DBI and Apache::DBI, the DBI module checks when it is loaded to see if Apache::DBI is already in use. Thus, if Apache::DBI is loaded before all occurrences of DBI in a Web application, database connections are cached regardless of whether an individual script uses Apache::DBI.

Lines 03 and 04 of Listing 14.1 illustrate two possible ways to invoke Apache::DBI at server startup when using mod_perl. The `PerlModule` or `PerlRequire` directive in `httpd.conf` corresponds to a `use` or `require` directive in a Perl program, respectively. Alternately, line 08 or 09 could be used in the startup script executed when the Perl engine starts, as long as Apache::DBI is called before DBI in that script. Either method ensures that any connection made by DBI in persistent programs is cached by Apache::DBI.

Additional performance gains can be achieved by creating a database connection when the server starts each Perl engine. This is done by calling the `connect_on_init` method in the startup script with the same parameters that are used in the Web application, as in line 13 of Listing 14.1. When doing this, make sure that the arguments passed to `connect_on_init` are exactly the same as those used in the Web application, including preference arguments such as `AutoCommit` or `RaiseError`. Otherwise, Apache::DBI assumes that the connections are different, and the initial connection are cached but never used.

Note that Apache::DBI does not require the Apache server to be used. Any Web server that supports a persistent Perl environment (see Chapter 10) can use Apache::DBI by placing the `use` statement in the Perl engine's startup script.

There is one case in which Apache::DBI is not advised. When site users are accessing the database with individual database user names and passwords, it is better to forego Apache::DBI because the module would cache each user's connection separately. Additionally, Apache::DBI can't share database connections across Perl engines. As a result, each user's connection would be held open and cached across multiple Perl interpreters, and the number of open connections would soon grow to a point at which the database would refuse connections or otherwise behave erratically.

An additional case to watch for is when Apache, mod_perl, and Apache::DBI are used together in a high-transaction environment. Because Apache::DBI can't share database connections across Perl engines, at least one connection is opened for each engine, which translates to one open connection per httpd process started by Apache. On a high-transaction server, this could mean that hundreds of database connections are open at all times. Although this might not cause problems for most database systems, small sites might find that the database begins to behave erratically when Web applications are scaled to higher volumes of traffic.

Preparing Statements with Placeholders

When using DBI for database access, a query generally is passed to the database in two steps with a separate process used to return the result. The query is first sent to the database with a `prepare` method, which instructs the database to make an execution plan for the query and which returns a statement handle representing the prepared plan. Then, an `execute` method is called on the statement handle, which instructs the database to execute the plan and return the results to DBI. After DBI has the results, a variety of methods can be called on the statement handle to extract the data for use by the program. This process might seem cumbersome to database developers who are accustomed to instant results returned from a single query entered at the command line or through a graphic interface, but DBI is designed this way to match the steps performed internally by the database when a query is executed. This enables each step of the process to be optimized by the program based on the type and frequency of queries that are expected and the process by which the result will be used.

One way to optimize database-to-Web performance is by using placeholders to stand in for data in an SQL query. When a query is prepared by DBI, the database creates a plan of the best way to access the data needed to fulfill the query. This is another example of the one-user, continuous-access database model that assumes that the user is performing a unique query and waiting for the results. The plan is simply thrown away after it is executed, leaving the database to create another plan from scratch. Unfortunately, a Web application is likely to make a similar query hundreds of times per second, so the database spends much of its time generating the same plan repeatedly.

Placeholders help this situation by giving the database a uniform template of the type of query that will be used in a number of executed statements. The placeholders themselves—demarcated by a question mark—can indicate any value that would ordinarily be assigned to or compared against a data field. For instance, in this SQL query:

```
SELECT *
FROM foof
WHERE foo = 'bar'
```

the SQL subclause WHERE foo = 'bar' could be rewritten as WHERE foo = ?, with the value 'bar' being represented by a placeholder. It could not be written as WHERE ? = 'bar' because foo is a field name, not a value. The database accepts the placeholder in a template and makes a plan around it—thereby creating a more generic plan that then can be reused.

After a template has been sent through the DBI prepare method and an execution plan has been generated by the database, the DBI execute method can be called against the prepared plan that's stored in the DBI statement handle $sth (see Listing 14.2). This can be done as many times as needed without generating a new plan. The values specified by placeholders in the prepared template are passed as arguments to the execute method each time it is called. These values are analyzed by DBI to determine their data type if it hasn't previously been specified.

Listings 14.2 and 14.3 provide a comparison between a standard way of invoking DBI for a stand-alone (or CGI) Perl application and an accelerated example that assumes Apache::DBI is being used in a persistent environment. The listing is part of the forum application in Listing 14.7, which is found in the "MySQL Example" section later this chapter.

Listing 14.2 **Standard DBI Example**

```
01 # show all the responses to this message
02 my ($childid, $title, $username, $created);
03 $sth = $dbh->prepare(q{SELECT m.msgid, m.title, u.username,
04              DATE_FORMAT(m.created, '%d %M %Y') as created
05              FROM messages m, users u
06              WHERE m.authorid = u.userid
07              AND m.parentid = $msgid
08              ORDER BY msgid DESC});
09 $sth->execute;
10
11 while (($childid, $title, $username, $created) = $sth->fetchrow_array)
12 {
13   print qq{<li><a href="tree.psp?msgid=$childid">$title</a>};
14   print qq{ by $username on $created</li>\n};
15 }
16 $sth->finish;
```

Listing 14.3   **Accelerated DBI Example**

```
01 # show all the responses to this message
02 my ($childid, $title, $username, $created);
03 $sth = $dbh->prepare_cached(q{SELECT m.msgid, m.title, u.username,
04                 DATE_FORMAT(m.created, '%d %M %Y') as created
05                 FROM messages m, users u
06                 WHERE m.authorid = u.userid
07                 AND m.parentid = ?
08                 ORDER BY msgid DESC});
09 $sth->execute($msgid);
10 $sth->bind_columns(\($childid, $title, $username, $created));
11
12 while ($sth->fetch)
13 {
14   print qq{<li><a href="tree.psp?msgid=$childid">$title</a>};
15   print qq{ by $username on $created</li>\n};
16 }
17 $sth->finish;
```

In terms of placeholders, the differences between Listing 14.2 and Listing 14.3 are minor compared to the performance improvements achieved. The statement being prepared is almost identical with only one value in line 07 ($msgid) replaced by a placeholder. The rest of the statement is the same, no matter which arguments are passed to the program, so it can be left unchanged.

The only other placeholder-related change between the two listings is in the execute statement at line 09. The value that was originally used within the statement at line 07 now is being passed as an argument to the execute method, which fills the placeholder in the prepared execution plan with the value provided. DBI also determines the data type of the value provided by checking if the value is a number. Because the value is being passed through a method call instead of within an SQL query string, the value does not have to be quoted, even if it is a string. In this case, $msgid always is a number, and DBI has no difficulty determining its data type and passing the value.

Placeholders can be made more convenient by binding variables to the input placeholders using the bind_param method. The example could be changed as shown in Listing 14.4 by adding a bind_param statement at line 07, which would enable the execute method in line 08 to be called without arguments, as it was originally. The placeholder is specified by number in the first argument, and then by the value to be used. The data type of the value can optionally be provided in case DBI would have a difficult time determining the type automatically. Additional values could be bound by adding a similar statement for each placeholder.

Listing 14.4 **DBI Example with *bind_param***

```
01 # show all the responses to this message
02 my ($childid, $title, $username, $created);
03 $sth = $dbh->prepare_cached(q{SELECT m.msgid, m.title, u.username,
04                 DATE_FORMAT(m.created, '%d %M %Y') as created
05                 FROM messages m, users u
06                 WHERE m.authorid = u.userid
07                 AND m.parentid = ?
08                 ORDER BY msgid DESC});
09 $sth->bind_param(1, $msgid, SQL_INTEGER);
10 $sth->execute;
11 $sth->bind_columns(\($childid, $title, $username, $created));
12
13 while ($sth->fetch)
14 {
15   print qq{<li><a href="tree.psp?msgid=$childid">$title</a>};
16   print qq{ by $username on $created</li>\n};
17 }
18 $sth->finish;
```

It is important to note that not all databases and DBI drivers support placeholders, and some drivers support placeholders differently than others. The examples in this chapter should work with most databases, but check the relevant driver documentation for specific examples of how to use placeholders with a particular database.

Preparing Cached Statements

Cached statements can improve performance for queries that are likely to be used frequently across multiple instances of the same program. Like statements with placeholders, cached statements relieve the database from having to generate execution plans for similar queries.

DBI caches statements only when explicitly instructed to do so by using the `prepare_cached` method, as seen on line 03 of Listing 14.4. This keeps DBI from caching all statements, regardless of whether they would be reused, by forcing the application developer to specify which statements are likely to be reused.

The example in Listing 14.4 uses `prepare_cached` to indicate that the execution plan generated for the statement being prepared is applicable to all instances of this statement. This is only true if the statement as prepared is identical each time; if any aspect of the statement changes from one instance of the program to the next, the statement is not reused after it is cached. For example, the statement in Listing 14.2 should not be cached because the value of `$msgid` changes from one instance of the application to the next as different messages are requested. The statement in Listing 14.4, although it returns the same result, can be cached because it uses a placeholder to represent the value that changes. Because the statement as prepared does not change, the plan created for that statement can be cached and reused.

Thought should be given to instances in which cached statements would be useful. In most cases, a statement should be prepared using `prepare_cached` only if it can be represented as a single-quoted string, that is, only if no values are interpolated by Perl at runtime. Conversely, a statement should not be cached if it is being composed at runtime. This would occur when a search statement adds a line to the WHERE clause for each search parameter because the potential exists for having too many statements cached overall. However, some interpolated values can be cached if the number of possibilities is severely limited; for example, a query that is chosen from two or three possibilities through an `if` statement also could be cached because the total number of statements cached overall is small and fixed.

Retrieving Data Sets as References

Although savings in connection and query time improve the efficiency of all Web application database queries, some queries benefit additionally from increased efficiency in retrieving the result data. Large result sets with many rows can be returned more quickly by retrieving the values through references.

A common way to retrieve the results of a database query is by calling the `fetchrow_array` method on the statement handle, as illustrated in line 11 of Listing 14.2. This method returns one row's worth of data as a list of values that can be assigned to an array or individual variables, as in this example. Because DBI already stores the returned values internally, this requires those values to be copied to the new variables created for each row returned. For small result sets with few rows, the time required to copy the result values is minimal, so this method is still acceptable for queries that return only one row of data. For larger sets of query results, however, the overhead of creating variables and reassigning values can be expensive. In the case of Listing 14.2, the overhead of copying `$title`, `$username`, and `$created` would become noticeable with result sets as small as a few dozen rows. The effect would become more obvious if the much larger `body` field were also returned each time.

DBI provides methods for retrieving results as references to the existing database driver (DBD) data structures, which removes the extra overhead caused by copying data to the application's own variables. The references are standard Perl structures that can be de-referenced within the application to use the associated values. Take care not to assign the de-referenced values to variables within the `while` block, however, because it invalidate the savings by performing the copy operation anyway.

Line 13 in Listing 14.4 uses the `fetch` synonym for the `fetchrow_arrayref` method, which is the fastest way to retrieve data from a statement handle. (Incidentally, `fetchrow_hashref` is provided for similar situations, but the performance improvements are not as great due to the overhead of creating the hash to reference.) Although Listing 14.4 doesn't assign the returned references to any values, it does use them inherently as described in the next section, "Binding Result Columns." Because `fetch` incurs no overhead in terms of returning values or assigning variables, it serves perfectly as a row increment method for the `while` loop in this case.

Binding Result Columns

For convenience, result values can be bound to variables in a manner similar to binding placeholder values. Binding result columns also can bring a slight performance improvement by removing the overhead of repeated variable creation. DBI provides the `bind_columns` method, which enables predefined variables to be associated through reference to values returned from a statement handle. By making the connection between returned values and variables only once for a given statement, `bind_columns` gives the convenience of using custom variables with the performance of using references.

Binding columns is best for data sets that return many rows at a time, although it gives no performance loss in any case. The `bind_columns` method is best used in combination with returned references (using `fetch` or `fetchrow_arrayref` as mentioned in the previous section, "Retrieving Data Sets as References") to provide the best performance for large data sets. A statement that returns just one row would probably not benefit from using `bind_columns`, however; the additional statements required to file-scope variables, bind them as references, and return them through `fetch` would give little performance benefit over a simple assignment through a `fetchrow_array` statement.

In Listing 14.4, line 11 binds the result columns to the `$childid`, `$title`, `$username`, and `$created` variables. The variables are file-scoped through the `my` keyword in line 02, and then passed to `bind_columns` as references in the order in which their values are returned from the query prepared in line 03. With each call to `$sth->fetch` in line 13, the variables passed in line 11 are assigned the values of the next result row.

Bound results can be useful for substituting data for variables placed in template text, as mentioned in Chapter 13, "Using Templates with Perl Applications." If a program such as Listing 14.4 were used to fill values in a provided template with Perl-style variables embedded, the text could be evaluated by using an `eval` statement within the `while` loop, as follows:

```
my $template = q{<li><a href="tree.psp?msgid=$childid">$title</a>};
while ($sth->fetch)
{
  eval "print $template";
}
```

This type of automated variable substitution provides improved performance in a situation where it's most needed. Templates are usually used in situations in which processing them shouldn't incur overhead over a custom-coded application. Therefore, everything that can be done to limit processing time should be done. Luckily, the abstraction afforded by a template provides the opportunity to tune statements such as these without affecting the way the application behaves.

Web-Modeled SQL Statements

Architectural efficiency improvements can go a long way in reducing the time and CPU load a Web application requires, but even the best Web application architecture still grinds to a halt if the SQL queries aren't optimized for Web performance. A poorly written Perl program can make even persistent environments slow by causing each request to reopen files from disk or start programs each time. In addition, a poorly written SQL statement can make a persistent connection to the database slow by causing each query to do a full table scan or transfer much more data than is necessary. Fortunately, there are some simple principles to use when checking SQL statements for Web appropriateness, so it isn't very difficult to improve the performance of a bad SQL statement. Even more fortunate would be the presence of a database programmer or database administrator to write the SQL statement for us.

As mentioned before, the structure of database systems assumes that a single user waits the few seconds (or minutes) required to process a query and return results. This is a reasonable assumption when the user base is a fixed number of known users because a database user usually understands that there is a database involved and knows what to expect from previous queries. Database front-ends also have a number of ways to let the user know that data is on its way; the hourglass spins, partial data is displayed, and database-specific messages are sometimes made available to gauge the remaining query time. Therefore, a performance loss of a dozen seconds per query is no cause for concern; the users wait until prompted to do otherwise.

On the Web, however, those assumptions are all false. The user is accessing a page, not processing a database query, and the same icon (that spinning globe, glowing N, or throbbing dinosaur) is used to indicate page response delays due to any reason. The user might cause a dozen database queries to execute on each page visited without ever knowing that a database is involved at all. No special database messages are displayed, and usually, no partial data is made available for users while other data is delivered. Confronted by a page that just doesn't respond after eight seconds, the user assumes that the page isn't going to respond at all. He or she stops the page from loading and goes elsewhere.

Queries can be improved significantly without modifying the underlying database structures by modifying the queries to suit a Web model more closely. A Web application presents a lot of data in a single page, but it also provides the capability to spread data out through a series of hyperlinked views. Web applications also might need to present data that is timely, but often times, "timely" just as easily can mean twenty minutes as twenty seconds. A Web query also can be improved by restricting the ways that data is accessed. A little flexibility is lost, but users might not realize it is missing if the interface compensates for it and masks the edges.

Inner and Outer Joins

Two of the most common query types—inner and outer joins—are some of the most expensive queries in terms of the time required to plan and process them. Joins are a necessary part of relational databases—the "relational" part, to be precise—but by their very nature, they require two distinct sets of data to be matched in some specified way to return results that are common between them. If done correctly, it can be a powerful way to make connections in data that otherwise would have to be handled programmatically. If done poorly, though, a join or two can slow the response time of a Web database to a crawl.

The basic idea behind a join is that two tables have at least one field in common, so records can be matched up in terms of the correlation of the fields. In the case of the tables in Figure 14.1, each table has a field or set of fields that can be matched up to other fields to provide combined records with information from each table.

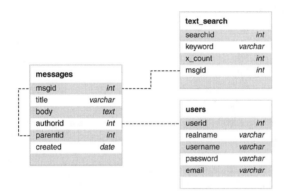

Figure 14.1   Relational Table Schema from VeloMeter.com.

The tables used for the VeloMeter forum contain fields that are used to identify relationships between records. The `msgid` field in the `messages` table, for instance, is related to the same field in the `text_search` table. When a query is prepared against this schema, related fields from both `messages` and `text_search` can be included in the same result. In this case, it enables the body of a message from `messages` to be returned by searching for a keyword in `text_search`.

Joins are such a common occurrence in relational database design that they're generally taken for granted. It's considered good schema design to separate out data that would otherwise be repeated from record to record. If the name stored in the realname field of the users table in Figure 14.1 were repeated for every associated message in the messages table, for instance, it would waste space by repeating a long string more times than necessary. It also would make it necessary to change every record in the messages table whenever the user made changes or corrections to his or her name. This won't happen often in the case of a name, but for more transient data—for instance, phone numbers or email addresses—it becomes more of an issue.

A join can be expensive because the tables being joined are sometimes searched in their entirety for records that match before the requested records are returned. This process is called a full table scan, and it makes a real dent in performance whenever it has to be performed.

Joins can be improved greatly by improving the design and implementation of the table schema, but some performance gains can be seen by changing the design of a joined query to take advantage of the Web application paradigm. For instance, instead of joining the users and messages tables on the userid field and searching through the username field for a listing of messages created by the user currently logged in, it might be possible to pass the userid field and related information along through a session manager and select from only the messages table based on the parentid field and avoid the join entirely. It's also possible to rely on the hyperlinked nature of a Web application to provide information without selecting it all at once. In a listing of messages with a particular keyword, for instance, it would be possible to join only the text_search and messages tables to provide the titles and creation dates of the returned results with the knowledge that user information from the users table would be provided for each message through a details page.

Queries with joins also can be made faster by making sure that the fields being joined are indexed. A database administrator knows which fields in a table are indexed and which are not, so when given a choice, it's better to join indexed fields. A more detailed discussion of indexed fields is offered in the "Index Joined Fields" section later in this chapter.

Other Expensive Queries

Other SQL keywords—such as UNION and INTERSECT—can turn an otherwise efficient query into a very expensive one. They usually occur in queries that are both complex and that stretch the boundaries of what is possible within the framework of a relational database. One example would be performing aggregations on data from groups of tables that contain overlapping data, which might or might not correspond. For instance, it might be desirable to get a count of the unique email addresses contained in both a table of survey respondents and a table of registered users. The normal approach would be to count the number of unique email addresses in one table, and then add that number to the count from the other table. Unfortunately, email addresses that are present in both tables would be counted twice. One way to get a count of unique addresses could be the query in Listing 14.5.

Listing 14.5 **Expensive *UNION* Query**

```
01 SELECT COUNT(DISTINCT email)
02 FROM
03 (
04   SELECT DISTINCT email
05   FROM users
06   WHERE email IS NOT NULL
07   UNION
08   SELECT DISTINCT emailaddr as email
09   FROM survey
10   WHERE emailaddr IS NOT NULL
11 )
```

The performance of the query in Listing 14.5 is hampered solely by the UNION keyword. Other components of the query are perfectly fast on their own. The SELECT DISTINCT statements are both as fast as they can be, and the COUNT(DISTINCT email) statement would be very fast if performed on each table individually. When the UNION keyword is used in the subquery, however, it requires the database to compile the entire contents of both queries and then scan the combined contents of those queries before sending them to the outer query. This outer query in turn has to scan the entire result for duplicates before returning the count. These full result scans are the least optimized way to return data and can cause an order of magnitude increase in the time needed to perform the query.

In fact, most queries that require the full result set to be returned cause performance to degrade with results getting worse as the data set increases in size. These queries can be deceptively fast when running them against small data sets, though, so simulating much larger data sets is good practice when testing application performance. Application performance testing is covered in detail in Chapter 15, "Testing Site Performance."

The query in Listing 14.5 could be improved by rewriting it by joining the users and survey tables or by using a subquery. This won't remove the need for a full-table scan in all cases, but the database's execution optimizer is more likely to figure out an optimized plan with either of those options. Higher performance can be gained by additionally indexing the email and emailaddr fields if possible, as discussed in the "Index Joined Fields" section later in this chapter.

On the other hand, aggregate queries processed within the database—using keywords such as MAX, SUM, and GROUP BY—can be much faster overall than retrieving the raw data and aggregating it within Perl. For instance, selecting the average age of registered site users as listed in an age field would take much less time if selected using the AVG keyword within the database than if computed within Perl by selecting all the ages, adding them, and then dividing. This is usually due to the overhead resulting from retrieving large data sets and then processing them a record at a time within Perl. The database server has much greater optimization for arithmetic functions such as these, and sometimes greater processing power to boot. In addition, queries executed within the database can be cached using snapshots and materialized views, as discussed in the "Views Versus Snapshots" section later in this chapter.

Text Searches

The text search is another common query type used in Web applications, with good reason. Web users prefer to have simple interfaces to complete search facilities, and backend search techniques have to be very flexible as a result. Web application users are familiar with the simple interface offered by Web search engines such as Google or AltaVista, so it's necessary to offer them an interface that behaves as expected when given a wide range of possible search terms. It also helps to automate the process of full-text searching because it's not always possible to hand-code keywords for every text item on a Web site, especially when the data being searched is dynamically generated from a database.

Text searching of this type is usually implemented in a database with the LIKE keyword, which enables search fields to be matched against partial text strings. LIKE uses the percent symbol to indicate that arbitrary text could match in its place, as Listing 14.6 illustrates.

Listing 14.6   **Full-Text Search Through an Expensive *LIKE* Query**

```
01 <sql name="search" dbtype="mysql" db="test" action="query">
02 <output>
03 SELECT DISTINCT m.msgid, m.title,
04   DATE_FORMAT(m.created, '%d %M %Y') as created
05 FROM messages m
06 WHERE m.body LIKE '%$keyword%'
07 </output>
08 </sql>
```

The query in Listing 14.6, which is a modified part of the VeloMeter.com forum application described in the "MySQL Example" section later in this chapter, matches a provided keyword stored in the $keyword variable against the body of messages stored in the messages table. When the keyword provided is 'bob', for example, line 06 evaluates to WHERE m.body LIKE '%bob%', which scans the entire table for a body field that contains the substring 'bob'. This is a fairly common use of LIKE, which approximates the behavior of a Web search engine pretty closely.

Unfortunately, the need for a full table scan each time the query is run would make the query in Listing 14.6 prohibitive in a Web context with even a few hundred rows in the table. The database can't optimize a LIKE query such as this one the way it would a simple match because every possible substring of each `body` field has to be checked, and indexing the fields by substring would be prohibitive. Fortunately, the efficiency of queries using `LIKE` can be improved in a few ways:

- The search can be narrowed to field values that start with the search keyword using `WHERE m.body LIKE '$keyword%'`. This removes the need for a full-table scan, but it also reduces the utility of a full-text search in this context. This kind of query would be better suited to matching names in an address book, where 'John', 'john', and 'John Q.' would all be matched by `LIKE 'John%'`.

- The search can be narrowed further to field values that match the length, if not the case, of the keyword using `WHERE m.body LIKE '$keyword'`. This improves performance greatly by enabling field indexes to be used more frequently, but completely invalidates the full-text search above. This kind of query would be best for matching values, such as user names, Canadian postal codes, or MS-DOS file names, that have indeterminate case.

- The search can be completely replaced with a query that doesn't use `LIKE`, by modifying the database to include a hash table or other convenience data structure. This method keeps all the utility of the application with very few changes to the query itself, but requires a modification to the structure of the database. These modifications are discussed in greater detail in the "Full-Text Searching" section of this chapter.

Although modifications to SQL queries in Web applications might require more effort than the architectural changes mentioned in the previous section, the work done to optimize the most expensive ten percent of a Web application's queries might free up ninety percent of the database server's resources for additional use. Because database servers are the most difficult Web application resources to scale, the extra work can be worthwhile.

Managing Databases For Web Performance

Although many improvements to database performance can be accomplished within the scope of Web applications, the performance of SQL queries also can be improved by changing the structure of the database involved.

Many databases are designed using optimizations for individual users, with little regard for the special needs a Web application has. Web applications are likely to make frequent, simple requests for small data sets with many similar requests varying only in the specific data requested. The data structures used in a Web application aren't likely to change dramatically, and when they do, it's usually due to a complete application redesign. As a result, flexibility in data storage is not as important as simplicity and performance.

By modifying a complex or slow database schema and adding convenience structures for Web use, it's possible to wring more performance out of a database. It's best if
a database administrator with Web experience does the optimization, but any Web
application developer with sufficient database knowledge can make basic changes that
have a dramatic effect on performance.

Denormalize Data Tables

Normalization is one approach to the design of relational databases that is usually
taken to ensure flexibility in the structure of the database that the database server itself
does not provide. For instance, the inability of the Oracle database server to drop fields
from a table after it contains data is a common reason to implement the schema of an
Oracle database in a normalized fashion.

Normalized data structures rely on the relational nature of database systems to build
virtual table structures from groups of tables that contain both information and related
metadata about the type of information stored. For instance, the tables shown in
Figure 14.2 and 14.3 store similar information, but the table in Figure 14.3 has been
normalized to provide a more flexible structure for storing data.

username	email	realname
debra	debra@ax.com	Debra Dell
kerrigan	queen@yahoo.com	Pirate Queen
chris	chris@globalspin.com	Chris Radcliff
bob	brt2104@aol.com	Bob Robertson
freep	thefreep@aol.com	Tony Freep
jaime	big_guy@net.net	Jaime Ryan

Figure 14.2   Standard user table structure.

username	field	data
debra	email	debra@ax.com
debra	email	debra@yahoo.com
debra	realname	Debra Dell
kerrigan	email	queen@yahoo.com
kerrigan	realname	Pirate Queen
kerrigan	realname	Mary Kerrigan

Figure 14.3   Normalized user table structure.

The table in Figure 14.2 contains the kind of data that is reasonable within any Web
application. The `username`, `email`, and `realname` fields are likely to be encountered over
and over when dealing with people in a multiuser system. Each field corresponds to
the data stored within it, and the queries used to extract data from this table would be
pretty straightforward. The table in Figure 14.3 contains the same data, but that data

has been normalized into a structure that remains the same no matter which fields are associated with each record. A record in the virtual table implied by the data now spans multiple real records, and the names of the fields are now stored the same way the data is stored. Note that this enables something that a standard table otherwise would not support. A single "record" in the normalized table can store an arbitrary number of values for each field, as opposed to a single value per field in the standard approach.

Normalized data is very useful for recording arbitrary data structures that would otherwise be encumbered by the spreadsheet-like nature of database tables. If records are likely to contain an arbitrary number of fields with arbitrary types that might change depending on the record itself, normalized tables might be the solution in use.

However, normalized tables are not always desired when providing a database for a Web-based application. Web applications are much more sensitive to performance degradation. Because normalized table structures implement much of the structure of a table independently of the underlying table structure itself, a database server is less likely to be able to optimize a query against normalized tables. In addition, normalized tables are much more likely to require the expensive queries mentioned in the previous section, "Web-Modeled SQL Statements," because the structure of a normalized table is less conducive to SQL queries than the traditional row-and-column style (also called *denormalized* tables).

Fortunately, Web applications can overcome the same limitations in database design that normalized tables overcome by using program logic to mask some of the irregularities found in a standard table. Benefits of the normalized table in Figure 14.3, for example, could be replicated by modifying the table in Figure 14.2 to include multiple fields for each type of information. The `email` field could be replaced by enumerated fields such as `email1`, `email2`, and `email3`, each of which is considered an equivalent field by the Web application. The application would then use a `WHERE` clause such as the following to search for an individual email:

```
WHERE email1 = '$email'
OR email2 = '$email'
OR email3 = '$email'
```

Another way to replicate this feature is by parsing the field before processing `INSERT` and `UPDATE` statements and after processing `SELECT` statements within a Web application. The `realname` field in Figure 14.2, for instance, could be filled with a comma-delimited string to represent multiple equivalent values. This method enables an arbitrary number of values to be assigned to a single field as long as the total length of the values doesn't exceed the field's maximum. This method should not be used for fields that are searched, however, because of the performance hit that substring queries incur. See the "Text Searches" section earlier in this chapter for more information.

Although restructuring the schema can bring significant performance benefits over normalized data, it is sometimes not possible to represent the source data in a flat structure. This can happen when the database is mainly used by another application, with the Web application used only to summarize some data from the application's data structures. In that case, it can be more helpful to add additional database structures to repurpose the existing data for Web use. See the following section for information about creating snapshots for quick access to data from normalized structures.

Index Joined Fields

When inner and outer joins are necessary, their performance can be helped significantly by choosing an efficient set of fields to join, and then indexing them. These might be data fields that have some meaning within the context of the record, or generated fields that are used specifically because they can be indexed easily. Either way, it's important to make sure that the fields used to join tables are indexed whenever possible. This gives the database as much information as it can get to provide suitable optimizations for a query when an execution plan is being generated.

Without an index on joined fields, the database usually has to perform at least one sort on the table, which requires a full table scan. Although this varies from database to database, an equivalent process usually occurs in any database when joined fields are not indexed. This occurs if the field from either table being joined is not indexed; the greatest performance loss occurs if neither field is indexed, but joining an indexed field to an unindexed one still incurs a significant performance loss. When joining a pair of indexed fields, however, the database can usually optimize the query to scan only those records that are applicable to the query, leaving the bulk of records untouched and saving a great deal of time.

Some fields are not good choices for an index—and therefore a join—because they contain data that is too costly to index on a regular basis. For instance, a 4000-character VARCHAR field that stores message titles would be a bad choice for an index because the size of the index necessary to index such a field would be very large. Additionally, each insert into such a table would require the message title to be added to both the field itself and the index of the field, potentially doubling the overhead of an INSERT or UPDATE query.

Good indexed fields are usually numeric fields with automatically generated values or small text or numeric data fields that are unlikely to change over the life of the record. A phone number field would be a bad choice for a join, for instance, because the number is likely to change and corresponding fields in other tables would have to be located and updated along with it. It's usually best in a Web setting to use automatically generated numbers for record identifiers (or primary keys), and then carry the key values over to related records in other tables as foreign keys. The reason for this is simple; because Web users are likely to have frequent interaction with the database without understanding its structure or having direct access to it, it's always possible that a Web user will want to change any value that is apparent—such as a username or message title—without regard for other fields in other tables that reference that value.

By providing a layer of abstraction to the Web user where the database joins arbitrary-numbered fields that are never seen in the Web interface, the application is never limited in terms of the type of data it enables the user to change at any time. Figure 14.4 provides an example of this principle.

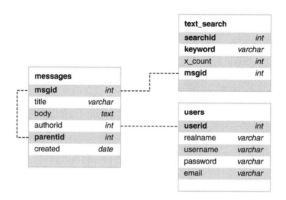

Figure 14.4   VeloMeter forum tables revisited.

Figure 14.4 shows the VeloMeter.com forum table example again, this time with indexed fields highlighted and the relationships between joined fields specified explicitly. Note that each joined field has "id" at the end, and the keyword field (which is indexed but not used in a join) does not. This is a style used to help differentiate between primary and foreign keys when mixed among data fields in a query. Each ID field is an autonumbered integer, chosen as such because of the quick indexing and small storage size allowed by integers.

Create Snapshots

If a query is still slow and expensive after optimization, it sometimes can help to create snapshots of the data on a regular basis. *Snapshots* are copies of the state of a query at a given moment that can be updated automatically by the database server on a scheduled basis. Snapshots provide faster access to data in some circumstances by precomputing the results of a query and storing them in a separate table that can be read from more quickly.

Snapshots are created by providing a SELECT statement to use when creating or updating the snapshot, as well as a set of database directives describing update frequency, storage limits, and other snapshot accounting parameters. This query is saved by the database for use in updating the snapshot at regular intervals. The query can be changed if needed, but otherwise, it's not necessary to reexecute the query whenever a snapshot update is necessary.

Not all databases support snapshots—Oracle, Microsoft SQL Server and Informix do, but MySQL and PostgreSQL don't—but it is possible to create data snapshots using a stand-alone Perl application run by a scheduler. The details of how to create a table using the results of a query vary widely from database to database, but the general steps involved are similar:

- Start with the query that is being optimized by the snapshot. If at all possible, write a single query that creates a table based on the output of this query. SQL syntax such as `CREATE TABLE foo AS ...` enables this, but database implementations vary widely. Other possibilities are insert statements with subqueries to select data or stored procedures that select and insert data programmatically.

- If a single query is not possible, write a set of queries that perform the same actions: create a table or clear out the values from an old table, select the data as needed, and insert a result row into the database with the selected values.

- Write a simple Perl application that processes the snapshot creation query or queries. If it is possible to create the snapshot in a single query, the program logic should be very simple and program execution time should be only as long as the original `SELECT` query takes. If a set of queries is necessary, create the table first, and then select the data and insert it a row at a time using a `foreach` loop and the DBI `prepare_cached` and `bind_columns` methods with placeholders. This method takes longer than a single query, but the DBI efficiency methods help keep execution time down.

After the Perl application is written, schedule it using `cron` or a similar system scheduler so that it runs as often as the data warrants. Be sure not to run the application so often that it is unable to complete the snapshot before the next scheduled snapshot; for instance, if the application takes six minutes to complete a snapshot, scheduling it every five minutes results in unusual behavior. Similarly, make sure the application continues to run in a reasonable time as the data set it's selecting gets larger. An application that takes seconds to run on a small data set might take much longer to run once more data is made available to it.

Views Versus Snapshots

It is important to note the difference between the Oracle view table and a snapshot. The two constructs sometimes can be used interchangeably with standard database applications, but there can be a marked difference in performance between an Oracle view and an analogous snapshot.

A *view* is a convenience table that links to the underlying data through a `SELECT` statement. The view is created to provide a layer of abstraction to the underlying tables involved, usually to make subsequent queries easier to write by database users. However, a view is not designed to improve the performance of the query it represents. A query against the view is translated into the equivalent query against the original data tables, which provides a continuously up-to-date result without the need for regular external updates. However, in most cases, a plan has to be created both for the view and the query it represents, which causes extra overhead and reduces performance, even when compared to the original query.

On the other hand, a snapshot actually creates a temporary table and copies the results of the specified query into it. As described in the last section, a snapshot provides a simplified set of fields the way a view does, but it is designed also to improve the performance of SELECT queries run against the snapshot. When accessed, a query against the snapshot only has to have a simple plan created, and no interaction has to take place with the tables that supplied data for the snapshot. The snapshot requires regular updates to maintain a reasonably recent copy of the data, but query performance is improved considerably versus the original query or a corresponding view.

In version 8i and later, Oracle provides "materialized" views, which create their own snapshot-like tables to provide a cached version of the view on a scheduled basis. These views are more like snapshots than the original views, so they are useful in providing the same query optimization that a snapshot would provide. One notable aspect of materialized views is the capability to use them implicitly in queries that would otherwise use the original tables. By specifying ENABLE QUERY REWRITE when the materialized view is created, it is allowed to circumvent the normal plan created by a similar query and provide precomputed values from the materialized view instead. Therefore, a new query doesn't have to be created when a materialized view is used to optimize table performance the way it would if a snapshot were being used. This can come in handy when optimizing performance after a query is already in wide use throughout a Web application.

MySQL Example

Database systems can vary significantly in terms of their support of ANSI SQL and proprietary additions to it.

The examples in this chapter are written for a common database, MySQL. MySQL is likely to be used in simple Web applications because of its ubiquity in low-cost efficient operating systems such as Linux and FreeBSD. A MySQL installation is easy to set up, has mild system requirements, and provides incredible performance for most Web applications. Oracle, another database system found in Web installments, is likely to be found in large-scale information systems that require performance on high-end hardware with complete data reliability and security. Oracle has stricter hardware requirements and a steeper learning curve, but it provides a rock-solid base for mission-critical Web application databases.

MySQL provides impressive speed for Web applications because of its light-weight implementation and its concentration on simple data storage and retrieval. MySQL is open-source software, which has made it more widely available than most other database systems. (As of early 2001, PostgreSQL is starting to look like an open-source challenger to MySQL's speed and ease of use while offering full transaction support, but most installations are still likely to find MySQL first.) MySQL also provides a simplified security model, which enables operating system security to be used in place of a dedicated password scheme and remote connections to the database to take place without a specialized network interface.

However, MySQL gets incredible performance at the expense of important database features, such as transaction processing and rollback. MySQL does not have the capability to gracefully recover from problems that occur when the state of the database is undetermined, for instance, in the middle of a query that adds 100 to the salary field for every record in an employee table. In the case of an error in the midst of such a query, databases that support transactions would simply roll back to the state the database was in before the query started. MySQL, on the other hand, would leave the database partially modified by the query.

Transactions also are important because of the possibility that two queries will act on the same data at the same time, causing one or the other to use incorrect values when inserting into the table. MySQL provides the capability to lock access to a table, but this requires special programming techniques and still doesn't provide the full robustness of a transaction model.

For many Web applications, though, the speed provided by MySQL is more a concern than transaction support. For the example in this section, integrity of the data being stored is not nearly as important as the speed with which it is accessed.

Database-Backed Web Forum

One compelling use for a database-driven Web application is the forum, a place where site viewers can become contributors by adding their own voice to the site's content. Forums are especially useful on sites with changing content that need to stay abreast of recent developments. VeloMeter, an open-source load testing tool, needed a forum for its site to enable users to answer each others questions about installation, new versions, and tips on using VeloMeter effectively.

The forum's setup is simple, which enables flexibility in programming the application as well as ease-of-use for site visitors posting to or reading from the forum. The forum is based around simple text messages that can be searched, viewed, or replied to with a few administrative pages that enable users to identify themselves to the system. The messages are stored in a table called messages, as are users and associated information, as described in Figures 14.1 and 14.4 earlier in this chapter. Any message then can be displayed in the format shown in Figure 14.5. (The program used to display this page is described in greater detail in the next section of this chapter.)

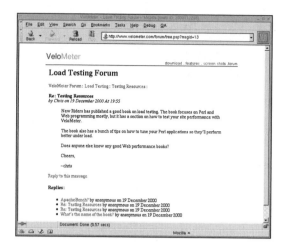

Figure 14.5 The VeloMeter forum displays a message with parents and replies.

The forum enables any number of messages to be posted with effectively infinite levels of replies and threads possible. This design is desirable because it's impossible to tell how many levels of replies a given message will have. So, any arbitrary limit placed on the number of levels for the ease of database design would likely restrict the possible uses of the forum. It also would limit programming possibilities down the road.

Arbitrary levels of replies are made possible by a self-join, which connects rows in the `messages` table with other rows in the same table in a parent-child relationship. To do this, the table includes a `parentid` field that references the `msgid` field of another row. This one added field enables a message to be related (in one direction only) to any number of messages designated as replies to it by joining those two fields. With the right query, a full hierarchy of parents and children could be produced, although that kind of query is generally too expensive for a simple forum application. The self-join also enables a list of parents to be compiled with little effort, which helps users to navigate through all the possible levels of replies.

Cached Display Query with Placeholders

The display query page in Listing 14.7 is one of many Perl Server Pages (PSP) that make up the entire VeloMeter forum application. (PSP pages are described in greater detail with complete implementation instructions in Chapter 12, "Environments For Reducing Development Time.") It's the most commonly accessed page because it displays any message with all its parents and replies. Most links from this page refer back to it, with only the message to display changing from request to request.

Listing 14.7 **Forum Message Display** (*tree.psp*)

```
01 <perl>
02 # determine which message to focus on
03 my $msgid = $QUERY{msgid} || 1;
04
05 # build a hierarchy for this message's parents
06 my $parents = '';
07 my $dbh = DBI->connect('dbi:mysql:test','','',{RaiseError => 1});
08 my $sth = $dbh->prepare('SELECT title, parentid FROM messages where
   ➥msgid = ?');
09 $sth->execute($msgid);
10 my ($p_title, $parentid) = $sth->fetchrow_array;
11 $sth->finish;
12 while ($parentid)
13 {
14   $sth->execute($parentid);
15   my $msgid = $parentid;
16   ($p_title, $parentid) = $sth->fetchrow_array;
17   $parents = qq{<a href="tree.psp?msgid=$msgid">$p_title</a> :
     ➥$parents};
18   $sth->finish;
19 }
20 </perl>
21
22 <sql name="msg_info" dbtype="mysql" db="test" action="query">
23 <output>
24 SELECT m.title, m.body,
25   DATE_FORMAT(m.created, '%d %M %Y At %H:%i') as created,
26   u.username
27 FROM messages m, users u
28 WHERE m.authorid = u.userid
29 AND m.msgid = $msgid
30 </output>
31 </sql>
32
33 <include file="$ENV{DOCUMENT_ROOT}/page.psp" />
34 <template title="Load Testing Forum" section="Forum">
35
36 <fetch query="msg_info" fetch="title, body, created, username"
   ➥type="sql">
37 <output>
38 <p>$parents</p>
39 <p><b>$title</b><br />
40 <i>by $username on $created</i></p>
41 <blockquote>$body</blockquote>
42 <p><a href="add_msg.psp?parentid=$msgid">Reply to this message</a> |
   ➥<a href="add_msg.psp?parentid=1">Post a new message</a> |
43 <a href="search.psp">Search messages</a> | <a
   ➥href="register.psp">Register as a user</a></p>
44 </output>
```

```
45 </fetch>
46
47 <h4>Replies:</h4>
48 <ul>
49 <perl>
50 # show all the responses to this message
51 my ($childid, $title, $username, $created);
52 $sth = $dbh->prepare_cached(q{SELECT m.msgid, m.title, u.username,
53                 DATE_FORMAT(m.created, '%d %M %Y') as created
54                 FROM messages m, users u
55                 WHERE m.authorid = u.userid
56                 AND m.parentid = ?
57                 ORDER BY msgid DESC});
58 $sth->execute($msgid);
59 $sth->bind_columns(\($childid, $title, $username, $created));
60
61 while ($sth->fetch)
62 {
63   print qq{<li><a href="tree.psp?msgid=$childid">$title</a>};
64   print qq{ by $username on $created</li>\n};
65 }
66 $sth->finish;
67 </perl>
68 </ul>
69
70 </template>
```

As complex as the page might look at first glance, its structure is simple. The page is broken into three logical sections, each of which is filled from an appropriate set of database information. The first section, queried by lines 05 to 19 of Listing 14.7 and displayed in line 36, consists of a list of links to the current message's parent messages, traced back to the original message used to start the forum. The second section of the page, displayed by lines 22 through 46 of the listing, contains the title and body of the current message with additional information about its creation time and author. The third section of the page, displayed by lines 48 to 66 of the listing, is a list of the replies to date that this message has received, with general information about the date and author of each message. Each section uses a different method to retrieve its contents from the database, and each has been optimized to take advantage of the persistent environment and Web application design.

The first section starts out by connecting to the database in line 07—using Apache::DBI, which has been loaded elsewhere—and preparing a statement in line 08 that retrieves the `title` and `parentid` fields from the record corresponding to a given message. The message in question is replaced by a placeholder because this query is going to be used repeatedly in this section. This happens first in line 09 when the query is executed for the current message; the data returned is assigned to the variables

$p_title and $parent_id in line 10 using the standard fetchrow_array method provided by DBI. Line 11 makes sure the query is explicitly finished to avoid warning messages or unusual behavior.

Line 12 starts a while loop that is used to build the list of parents starting from the immediate parent of the current message. In each iteration, line 14 executes the query for the parent of the previous message, and then line 16 assigns the new $p_title and $parentid values over the old. The title of the parent message and a link to that message are then added to the beginning of the list (stored in $parents) in line 17, and the process starts over again. The loop continues adding parent messages to the list until the parentid field returns a false value, in this case, zero. At that point, all parents in the chain (back to the original message) are part of the list. Recursive queries like this almost always benefit from using the same prepared query repeatedly; recursive queries tend to have few changes from iteration to iteration, and the changing elements can be represented easily by placeholders. In this case, no matter how many levels of parents are found, the query has to be prepared only once.

The second section of the page in Listing 14.7 is much simpler and requires little optimization beyond the use of Apache::DBI. The result fields returned by the query are more likely to undergo more cosmetic changes because they are the focus of the page. Because of these considerations, the ease of representing the query in tag format outweighed the need to eke out every last drop of performance. The query won't be slow by any means; the joined fields specified in line 28 are both indexed, as is the $msgid field in line 29. The fetch tag used to display the result in lines 36 through 45 is optimized behind the scenes to use bound columns and the fetchrow_arrayref method, so data retrieval won't lack for performance either. The majority of the displayed text in lines 38 to 43 is HTML, which makes the tag-based functions more suited to this part of the page.

The third section of the page is optimized in a few ways, both within the page and across all possible pages. In this case, it's useful to optimize the query as much as possible because it stands to be executed dozens of times per page request with little variation in the structure of the query or the values returned. Line 52 prepares the query using prepare_cached and a placeholder to save the cost of preparing an execution plan for this potentially expensive query even once per page. Line 59 binds the return results to a set of variables to improve readability later on and save the overhead of variable creation and data copying. Lines 61 through 65 then print a list item and link for each message returned by the query, and line 66 finishes off the query after completion.

Individually, the optimizations made to Listing 14.7 might seem insignificant, but these changes can make the difference between overloading a database server (or not) when added across hundreds of requests per second.

Full-Text Searching

A full-text search can be the most valuable part of a forum application because it enables readers to find messages of interest to them among all the messages available in the forum. A full-text search is even more useful in this case than it would be for an entire Web site—a site is likely to have navigational aids based on content grouping, but it would be impractical to offer the same kinds of grouping in a user-contributed forum. Queries to do direct text searching of a database can be prohibitive, however. So, special means are sometimes necessary to provide the ability to search through a large amount of text quickly.

The example in Listing 14.8 implements the simplest of search aids, a hash table containing keywords and the messages in which they can be found. The table itself is very simple, as shown in Figure 14.4 earlier in this chapter. The simplicity enables the hash table to do its job while being optimized as much as possible. This avoids performance penalties that would potentially invalidate the main reason for using a search aid in the first place. The program is designed to be run as a stand-alone application from the command line or a scheduler, but it just as easily could be changed to work within a persistent environment, if needed. In this way, it could be triggered by a system event, such as the addition of a new message.

Listing 14.8   **Build a Hash Table (*build_hash.pl*)**

```
01 #----------------------------------------
02 #
03 # build_hash.pperl - search optimization
04 #
05 #----------------------------------------
06
07 use 5.6.0;
08 use strict;
09 use warnings;
10 use DBI;
11
12 # connect to the database
13 my $dbh = DBI->connect('dbi:mysql:test','','',{RaiseError => 1});
14
15 # clear out the old hash table values
16 my $sth = $dbh->prepare('delete from text_search');
17 $sth->execute;
18
19 # get all the messages
20 $sth = $dbh->prepare('SELECT msgid, title, body
21                       FROM messages');
22 $sth->execute;
23 my ($msgid, $title, $body);
24 $sth->bind_columns(\($msgid, $title, $body));
25
26 # pre-cache the insert statement for later
```

continues

Listing 14.8   **Continued**

```
27 my $sti = $dbh->prepare(qq{INSERT INTO text_search
28                              (keyword, msgid, x_count)
29                              VALUES (?,?,?)});
30
31 # for each message,
32 while ($sth->fetch)
33 {
34   # create a key count hash
35   my %key_count;
36
37   # break the message into keywords
38   my $keyword;
39   foreach $keyword (split(/[^A-Za-z-']/,$title." ".$body))
40   {
41     # increment the hash entry for that keyword
42     $key_count{lc($keyword)}++ if (length($keyword) > 2);
43   }
44
45   # insert a row for each key_counthash entry
46   my $q_keyword;
47   foreach $keyword (keys %key_count)
48   {
49     $sti->execute($keyword, $msgid, $key_count{$keyword});
50   }
51 }
52 $sth->finish;
53
54 $dbh->disconnect;
```

Lines 13 through 17 of the example connect to the database and remove any previous
hash table entries. This is a simplistic way of removing the previous data from such a
large table, but it works for the purposes of a small forum like this one. If this were a
banking application or a high-traffic news site, the table would probably need to be
cleared one group at a time with each group being cleared and reinserted in a single
transaction to reduce the possibility of incorrect results being returned by a query due
to incomplete hash data.

Lines 20 through 29 prepare both a SELECT query and an INSERT query, passing the
resultant plan to $sth and $sti, respectively. The $sti handle is used repeatedly as the
program loops through data returned by the $sth handle, so the associated query is
prepared only once to reduce the load it places on the database. This becomes increas-
ingly important as the number of messages being indexed increases because the insert
query likely is to be executed dozens of times for each message and making a new
execution plan for each query could quickly take the lion's share of the program's
allotted processing time.

The rest of the program also is simple in design. Line 39 breaks each message into a set of keywords, and then loops through them to produce a count of the number of instances of each keyword in the message. This provides a basic way to weight the relevance of a message to any given keyword, as will be shown in the search display page. Line 42 makes sure that keywords are greater than two characters long to avoid a glut of tiny words; this process could be made more intelligent by specifically weeding out a list of common words such as "if," "the," and "or." Line 49 then inserts a database entry for each keyword in the message, along with the message id and the incidence count generated earlier. This one block is likely to be executed more frequently than any other part of the program, so it is kept as minimal as possible.

The hash table can be regenerated on a schedule by using a system scheduler, such as `cron`, to invoke the table generation program at regular intervals. It's important to check how long the program takes to finish on a regular basis to avoid the chaos caused when a new instance of the program starts to generate a new hash table before the previous program finishes. In the case of the VeloMeter forum, the hash table is regenerated once an hour. This provides a reasonably timely search because the forum isn't very busy—few new messages are posted over the course of an hour because most visitors are content to read the postings of others.

Note that many database systems come with internal utilities for creating full-text hash tables on a scheduled basis that might be far superior to a cron-scheduled Perl program. See the documentation for your RDBMS to test the possibilities.

After a hash table is available, keyword-based search queries can be used, as in Listing 14.9. This search is as simple as the rest of the forum, but the possibilities for keyword searches are endless. Searches can use various methods to emphasize the potential relevance of a match or the keywords found within the match, and additional processing power can be devoted to finding related keywords as well as those specified, including synonyms and misspelled words. The basis of this simple search, however, is a simple text match between the keywords given and those listed in the database.

Listing 14.9 **Search Query Display** (*search.psp*)

```
01 <include file="$ENV{DOCUMENT_ROOT}/page.psp" />
02 <template title="Search - Load Testing Forum" section="Forum">
03
04 <form action="search.psp" method="get">
05 <output>
06 <p>Search: 
07 <input type="text" name="search" size="30" value="$QUERY{search}" />
08  
09 <input type="submit" value="Search" /></p>
10 </output>
11 </form>
12
13 <if cond="$QUERY{search}">
14 <perl>
```

continues

Listing 14.9   **Continued**

```
15 # break the search up into keywords
16 my $search_where;
17 foreach $keyword (split(/[^A-Za-z-']/o,$QUERY{search}))
18 {
19   # add an OR for each keyword
20   next unless (length($keyword) > 2);
21   $search_where .= "OR t.keyword = '$keyword'\n";
22 }
23
24 # replace the first OR with an AND
25 if ($search_where)
26 {
27   substr($search_where,0,2) = 'AND (';
28   $search_where .= ")";
29 }
30 else
31 {
32   $search_where = "AND t.keyword = ''";
33 }
34 </perl>
35
36 <sql name="search" dbtype="mysql" db="test" action="query">
37 <output>
38 SELECT DISTINCT m.msgid, m.title,
39   DATE_FORMAT(m.created, '%d %M %Y') as created
40 FROM messages m, text_search t
41 WHERE m.msgid = t.msgid
42 $search_where
43 </output>
44 </sql>
45 <h4>Results:</h4>
46 <ul>
47 <fetch query="search" fetch="msgid, title, created" type="sql">
48 <output>
49 <li><a href="tree.psp?msgid=$msgid">$title</a> from $created</li>
50 </output>
51 </fetch>
52 </ul>
53 </if>
54 </template>
```

Lines 04 through 11 of the page display a simple search entry box, as is found on most other search engines. The same page is used to display both the search box and the results page to preserve the search keywords as they are entered. This makes correcting typos and adding keywords much easier for the user—without adding too much code.

Line 13 checks whether keywords have been submitted to the form. It then displays the rest of the page only if the form variable search contains any values. If keywords have been submitted, line 17 splits them into a list of individual keywords and composes the `WHERE` clause of a `SELECT` query with all keywords searched individually. This particular implementation finds any message with any of the keywords specified, but more advanced queries could be created that give weight to messages that contain more than one of the keywords. Lines 25 through 29 change the query to separate the keyword clause from other clauses, and line 32 covers the case in which no valid keywords are submitted.

The `<sql>` tag in line 36 prepares the query, including the prepared `WHERE` clause in line 42, and then the `<fetch>` tag in line 47 displays a list item for each search result. The results displayed are minimal, to enable quick scanning of all possible results for a descriptive title that might provide more information. This listing also leaves out the author's name to avoid a query that joins three tables, but a quick click to any message listed gives that information and more. The complete list looks something like the result in Figure 14.6, which provides surprisingly useful results considering the sparse simplicity of the search being performed.

Figure 14.6   A full-text search with results.

When a Database is Too Much

A database provides a flexible way to store Web-created and Web-accessible data, but it isn't always necessary to use one for all data presented by a Web site. Databases incur overhead simply by being designed to handle random access to large quantities of codified data. Databases could potentially store any kind of data. Thus, the facilities present in all cases have to be capable of handling queries of arbitrary complexity against any table. This overhead can sometimes be circumvented by using a simpler hierarchical storage method, such as an internal data structure or a file system, which gains speed by eschewing the flexibility of random access.

A perfect example of this principle is the Web site itself. If a database were the perfect repository for text data, the files that make up a Web site would be stored in the database and all Web server access would go directly to it. Instead, however, pages are usually stored as files and managed by the Web server because the Web server is capable of providing text files more quickly and reliably when accessed in Web-fashion. This is because a Web access is usually very specific, referencing a single file in the hierarchy by use of the URL and complete path. It also helps that this is the only way to access a file; there are no facilities for accessing a file based on its last modified date, size, or contents. These restrictions also enable the Web server to cache Web pages without having to replicate the entire structure of the file system; if the Web server needed to cache records in a database, it would be necessary to cache all the relationships between records as well as the indexes used to provide faster access.

When a database causes too much overhead, other resources are available to store the data used by a Web application. User preferences can be stored outside a database, as can document-based data that could be accessed through the file system. Session-based data, which is used to maintain state, also is a good candidate for storage outside the database—at least on a temporary basis.

User Preferences

Although user preferences could be used to customize an experience for every visitor, sites seldom change their format to suit a specific user. The reason is simple—there are too many user interface possibilities to test, and it is more efficient to concentrate on improving the usability of one user interface that customizing the interface for all possible tastes. Also, Web site visitors are likely to see a site only once and might never have the chance to express preferences, which invalidates all the work involved in customizing.

This reasoning shouldn't be ignored when providing some customization for users who are likely to visit a site repeatedly. The temptation might be to provide a whole host of user-defined attributes, such as colors, fonts, and navigation placement, but the truth is that most users don't care about this fine a grain of customization, and those who do won't necessarily make the best choices anyway. This level of customization would almost certainly require a database for implementation, and the overhead of accessing a database—usually a large set of joined tables due to the nature and number of options—for each Web request is extreme.

Customization can be simulated by providing a few versions of the site for different user tastes. This avoids both the problem of overhead and the problem of inexperienced users who don't understand how to customize the environment. By offering the user some choice, a site can accommodate the most likely variations requested by users while limiting those variations to ones that are both compatible with the site's design and aesthetically pleasing.

Templates and multihomed documents can be used to automate the process of providing different user interfaces on the same site. Each variation can be implemented as a template page—with one chosen as the default—and the user then can select which template he or she prefers, perhaps by trying each on a sample page (or the preferences selector itself.) After it is selected, the only user preference that has to be remembered is the name of the template page, which is an easy task for a session manager. Multihomed documents could enable the same to hold true without requiring any user preferences to be saved at all. Different themes could be specified by accessing different directories, which enables the user to pick a theme by bookmarking the resultant URL. (Multihomed documents and their uses are described in more detail in Chapter 17, "Publishing XML for the Wireless Devices.")

Document-Based Data

Although a database can be a good repository for some document-based data, as mentioned earlier, a file system might be much more efficient when delivering the data through a Web application. This holds true for more than just Web pages; other text data, such as XML files or Word documents, also are good candidates for file-system storage. Because these documents can easily be organized within a hierarchical system—for instance, by year, month, and day for news stories or press releases—storing them through the file system enables faster access as well as easier browsing. With XML files, it's also possible to post-process the files as they are being served. This is covered in Chapter 16, "XML and Content Management," and Chapter 17.

Databases can be good for text searching, though, so it might be worthwhile to store a version of the document-based data in the database for this purpose. It's also possible to store just the URL or another file-based link to the document in the database with any meta-information. This makes retrieval of the document a two-step process when accessing it through the database, but it saves a lot of effort when accessing the file directly. This also gets around the problem of storing binary documents—such as PNG graphics files or MP3 music files—in a database, which can involve a less-than-intuitive process as well.

User State Management

Maintaining user state while an application is being accessed is a major concern when designing programs for the Web. The HTTP access model is stateless by design; it was understood that a document should be served without regard to previous documents accessed or further document access. Unfortunately, this means that Web applications can't rely on the programming environment to provide a complete picture of the user's state. State information usually includes important data such as the last function executed or the current items of a shopping cart, which usually can't be expressed in terms of simple requests and responses from a Web browser.

User state can be recorded in a database, but state information also can be stored in other forms. The most widely known is the *cookie*, a persistent value that is set by the Web server but stored on the client for a specified period of time. Cookies are good for storing small amounts of data that are not crucial to an application's performance, especially when the data needs to persist from session to session no matter how much time passes between visits. Cookies can be problematic when storing information that needs to be reliably accessible, so it's not advised to use cookies alone to track application state. Also, many browsers are configured to reject cookies entirely, so it's usually necessary to provide alternate state management facilities in case cookies aren't available.

Document-based state management is useful when the application is operating on a text file, which can be stored temporarily while the user acts on it. This is best suited to Web applications with a fixed number of users, such as an intranet application or fee-based service. Document-based state also is suited to applications that are document-centric with a single document being acted on by a number of processes that happen sequentially or recursively. The basic idea is to write applications that derive their entire state by reading the relevant document with all actions operating on the same document. An example is generating an XML purchase order by filling in sections of it through Web forms. Any existing values can be used to prefill form fields, so a user could return to any form in the sequence and change information as necessary. After it is completed, the purchase order document can be reviewed and finalized, which might involve storing a copy in the database for indexing and meta-information.

Session managers also can be used to track user state and provide simple information about the user's activities. A session manager stores an arbitrary set of data associated with a single value—the session ID. Session ID values then can be passed through client-side cookies, as part of the page URL, or by sending hidden form variables with standard queries. When a new page is requested, the session ID is read by the application and all associated state information is recovered quickly from the session management daemon.

Apache::Session

The name Apache::Session is probably a misnomer because the module doesn't require Apache and doesn't provide a complete session manager, either client or server. Rather, Apache::Session is a persistence framework that provides a generic way to store session-type data structures, which enables more specific session managers to be built on top of the Apache::Session architecture.

Apache::Session provides data persistence by connecting to databases (through DBI), flat files (similar to the document-based model described in the "User State Management" section earlier in this chapter), or shared memory. Shared memory provides the best performance in most applications, but it is the most volatile storage method of the three. The module also provides lock management for all the connection types, using the built-in locking facilities of the data source if available or implementing it internally, if necessary. The module also handles ID generation, which otherwise would be a difficult aspect of session management to implement due to the need for values that are both secure and unique.

If the existing session managers do not suit the needs of a specific project, it's possible to subclass Apache::Session directly to implement a custom session management system. Similarly, existing implementations, such as the well-documented MySQL subclass, can be modified to suit a custom configuration, which enables only the additional features to be implemented in custom code. This is done without the need to reinvent useful parts of the existing implementation.

What a Good Database Administrator (DBA) is Worth

As a Webmaster and a Web application programmer, I've generally had to wear as many hats as there are jobs to do. Graphic design, programming, page layout, systems integration, and project management all have to be covered because I'm a one-man team. There's no one else to turn to for assistance, so I've had to learn new technologies as they were incorporated into each application. In time, I started to seek out new technologies and techniques just to see what was possible. It's part of what drives me to learn.

There's one aspect of Web application design that I've never relished learning, though: database design and implementation. Databases are big ugly beasts, and as soon as I think I've learned something fundamental about their personalities, they change into completely different beings (new and improved!), and I have to start from scratch again. It gets worse when I try to keep track of more than one member of the bestiary—Oracle, Informix, and MySQL, for example. At that point, all the quirks of the different systems start to run together. So, it's hard to remember which optimization goes with which version of which RDBMS.

Fortunately, I've found one technology and one person who make the job a lot easier. I've talked about the technology already; DBI makes my job much easier by hiding as many of the implementation differences from me as possible while exploiting them behind the scenes. I fell in love with DBI as soon as it hit release 0.93, and it's been invisibly stabilizing and optimizing my code ever since. Tim Bunce, DBI's lead developer, is to thank for much of the amazing work done on this software, but he's not the person I'm referring to.

The person that makes my job a lot easier is more of an abstraction instantiated by people I've worked with: the DBA. I've worked with quite a few, and they're generally the type of people who can look at a nightmarishly long query with self-joins, subqueries, and every expensive construct mentioned in this chapter and visualize not only the execution plan, but also the optimizations necessary to remove 90 percent of the performance-killing inefficiencies. This also is the person who can pick out the two or three changes to a database schema that make subsequent queries ten times faster, and he or she is the person who keeps track of the infinite configuration minutiae that need to be tweaked to keep the beast purring. This isn't the person who fiddled with MySQL the other day and got a sample database working; a good DBA has had years to collect the mountains of implementation trivia that make up the real working knowledge of an RDBMS.

continues

continued

The benefit of a good DBA is immeasurable, but the monetary benefits of a well-tuned database—the queries and schema as well as the system itself—can be calculated as easily as any performance improvements. The "Evaluating the Cost of Down Time" section in Chapter 1 gives a good indication of the money that can be saved by improving performance even a little; an efficient database design can earn the salary of a good DBA ten times over. The DBAs I've known have earned their keep and then some, not just by improving the performance of Web applications, but also by improving the productivity of Web programmers by freeing them from the burden of optimizing both their applications and the underlying data structures they're accessing. In short, love your DBA and your applications will run faster. Believe me—it's worth any expense.

Summary

There are many areas where a database can be optimized for Web use, and the overall utility of using databases as storage areas for dynamic data makes performance a pressing concern for most Web applications. Fortunately, database interactions can be optimized at the application level by using Apache::DBI persistence and DBI's optimization facilities. This can be done at the query level by avoiding expensive query constructs and using the strengths of the Web to simplify queries, or it can be done at the database architecture level with a little care in schema construction. Sometimes, though, the best way to improve the performance of a Web application is by sidestepping the database entirely with session managers, cumulative documents, or cookies.

15

Testing Site Performance

I T'S NOT ENOUGH TO WRITE THE FASTEST WEB applications imaginable and develop the most efficient architecture to host them. In a real-world situation, a Web site also should be tested to see just how fast those applications perform. It's also nice to know just where the architecture might break down under heavy load. A good start to performance testing comes from simply acknowledging that performance is a factor that can be measured and compared against real-world situations. After this idea is firmly in place, it's possible to design a series of repeatable tests that produce results that can be used to predict the future performance of the site under any condition.

Performance testing tools make it possible to test the response of a site to a variety of traffic levels before it is put into production. A number of testing applications exist, and some are made freely available either independently or in conjunction with Web server software. However, most of these tools are designed to provide only basic performance information for simple areas of a Web site, with little support for the complex paths taken by real-world site visitors. These tools generally require some outside assistance to provide understandable data based on realistic tests. Fortunately, Perl provides a good framework for automating tools and creating more complex tests without much extra work. Perl also enables analysis to be incorporated into the automation program and customized to provide specific performance results.

Creating a Useful Test

As I mentioned in Chapter 5, "Architecture-Based Performance Loss," a poorly conceived test can be worse than no site testing at all. The best way to start a site performance test is to gather the data necessary to make the test realistic and representative. This usually involves discovering the usage patterns of current site visitors or using a proxy to capture a log of a few representative visits. This data then can be used to provide a more robust test of all parts of the site in the combinations likely to be seen with real usage. Testing also requires a good grasp of the amount of traffic currently experienced by the site or expected after the site goes live. The combination of realistic usage patterns and traffic estimates enables testers to produce a baseline figure for site traffic, which then can be used to determine the effects of both incremental and exponential increases of traffic.

For most sites, determining site usage or predicting site patterns in exhaustive detail won't be necessary. The data need be complete only to the extent that it affects the test results. Besides, real-world usage on a live site is likely to vary greatly from day to day and over the life of the site, so only a representative average of site usage is necessary. "Representative data" can be loosely defined and still provide valuable insights into the state of site performance and future trends.

Discovering Usage Patterns

For a good test that's representative of real-world site traffic, a realistic set of requests to the site is necessary. There's no better source for these sets than real-world data collected from existing traffic to a Web site. This data indicates how actual visitors are using the site as it exists. Thus, it can be assumed that additional visitors to the site will probably use the site in the same way. Usage data can provide insight into the relative popularity of site sections and functions, which translates to the relative use of static files and Perl programs. For instance, a site with ten static HTML files and two search programs might see much heavier use of the search programs. Site usage analysis would indicate that the search programs should be weighted more heavily in testing.

The best source of existing site usage information also is the most commonly available: server logs. Most Web servers take copious notes on every incoming request in a server access log. Server access logs usually contain an entry for each request that includes the client address, a time stamp, the URL being requested, the referring page, and the status of the request. With this information, analogous site requests can be generated easily by a server load testing application, in essence recreating the traffic from any given time period. These blocks of requests can be valuable when testing site performance because they contain a mix of files—including static HTML, programs, and graphic files—that otherwise might be overlooked during performance testing.

In addition, server log information usually is all that's necessary to recreate an individual user's complete path through the site, which is called a *visit* or *session*. Session information usually is valuable when testing a Web application that requires multiple requests to perform a coherent action. For example, an e-commerce application that makes a flight reservation might require four or five pages to complete the transaction. Because later pages in the transaction rely on the results of the previous pages, it's necessary to generate simulated requests in the correct order.

Session information can be extracted from an access log fairly easily. If one client IP address is selected and lines containing the address are extracted from the log file, the result is a list of every URL visited by a single user over time. That list can be further narrowed to a single session by choosing only one connected set of URLs from the entire record. The start and end of a session usually can be identified by finding a common entry page—a login page, for example—and extracting entries from that point until a likely exit page is reached. (A page displaying the results of a transaction is an example of an exit page.) Finding the start and end of a session is easier for sites, such as Google, that serve a single purpose from a common starting point, and determining entry and exit pages can be difficult for diffuse sites, such as Yahoo!, that have multiple points of entry. In general, though, a Web application transaction already has some identifier—a user login or session ID, for instance—that separates out a single session.

Using Proxy Data

Server access logs aren't always an ideal source of usage information for a site in development. Logs are sometimes unavailable for the site being tested, or existing server logs might refer to pages and applications on a current site that aren't representative of the new site being created. In some cases, only a specific part of the site is being tested—exclusive of the rest of the site. In these cases, acquiring and processing existing usage data from server logs becomes a problem. In other cases, access logs don't contain all the information necessary to recreate a complete user session. Data stored in cookies or sent through POST requests usually is not recorded in access logs. Thus, requests that rely on this data for session state information or program flow can't be recreated from log data alone.

When server access logs aren't viable for testing, it's possible to generate a representative set of user sessions by using a *Web proxy*. A Web proxy is a server that accepts all Web requests from a client and passes them along to the Web server and then accepts the response from the server and passes it back to the client. Web proxies usually are used to provide caching or additional security for Web requests, but for server testing, a proxy needs to log only the requests and their associated POST and cookie information as they pass through. In addition, because a proxy for this purpose is concerned more with accurate logging than with throughput, the proxy can be implemented either within the load testing application or with available tools such as Perl. (A proxy implementation in Perl is left as an exercise for the reader. A simple proxy is included with VeloMeter, as mentioned later in this chapter.)

One of the strong points of using a Web proxy to capture client requests is ubiquity. Almost all Web clients—including browsers, file updaters, and custom Web clients—can be configured to use a proxy to process all Web requests. The Web client handles the connection to the proxy automatically, and the rest of the user interface behaves identically, regardless of whether a proxy is used. For instance, specifying a proxy in the Netscape Web browser requires only a simple change to the preferences. After the change has been made, any interaction between Netscape and the Web sites is filtered through the proxy transparently. (I've been known to spend hours diagnosing a "network problem" because I've forgotten to change my Netscape preferences back after demonstrating a proxy during tutorials. Transparency can have its pitfalls.)

Estimating Site Traffic

When interpreting the results of performance testing, it's important to compare them to a current benchmark using the same metrics. It might make sense to find that a Web application has a response time of 0.02 seconds in a test environment, but that value provides little insight into the response time of that application in the future—or the total number of requests the application can process in a given time period. A better result would be a comparison between the current performance of the application and the maximum performance the application can sustain under heavy load. In addition, an idea of current traffic estimates usually provides a framework for evaluating testing results. Determining current traffic levels has the added benefit of forcing the tester to think in terms of traffic units (for example, requests per second [RPS]) rather than in terms of response times.

Site traffic can be estimated in a number of ways, but the easiest source of traffic data comes from log analysis software. In fact, some log analysis programs produce traffic figures as a matter of course—any figures listed as requests (or hits) per a specified time period can be converted to the commonly used RPS. If precalculated figures aren't available, a figure in RPS can be attained easily by taking any listing of the number of requests in a time period and dividing it by the number of seconds in that period. In addition, log analysis figures might also include the minimum and maximum number of hits in a given time period. These values, especially the maximum, can give hints about future traffic levels and periodic traffic increases.

When determining site traffic in terms of a simple unit (such as RPS), keep in mind that not all requests are equal in terms of server load and response times. Requests for static HTML, for instance, are likely to enjoy higher throughput than requests to a Web application. As a result, site traffic that's composed of mostly dynamic requests might cause the same load as a much larger number of static requests. Thus, the ratio of the two can be an important number to determine as well. Don't discount static requests entirely. They do contribute to overall load and play a part in perceived performance, but be sure to reduce their significance in load analysis because they are unlikely to be the cause of a performance bottleneck.

Basic Load Simulation with ApacheBench

After representative site usage data has been collected, the next step in testing site performance is to simulate site traffic using a load testing application. At its core, a load testing application simply generates Web requests based on input, times the responses, and records or displays the results. Many applications are available, but a few are more likely to be encountered by Perl programmers in standard Web environments.

ApacheBench is a tool included with most distributions of the Apache Web server. It's a simple load testing application designed to take a single URL and a few configuration parameters and produce a report based on the requests sent by the application. The application is very efficient as a result, so ApacheBench can simulate a heavy load without much CPU or memory impact. This can come in handy when simulating thousands of simultaneous users with a single client machine.

ApacheBench doesn't provide a user-friendly interface, and the tests it performs generally are simplistic when used in the default configuration. However, it is possible to write a Perl program that controls ApacheBench to automate more complex simulations, including dynamic requests from a server or proxy log. The result of this kind of automation more closely resembles a full-featured load testing application suite, and a good deal of input customization and report generation can be built in.

Configuring ApacheBench

ApacheBench is a command-line program, usually found under the name `ab` in the Apache binary directory or in a system utilities directory. Each execution of ApacheBench corresponds to a load test performed on a single URL—the program simply accesses the URL repeatedly until the test is completed. Testing parameters are specified by command-line arguments, including the total time spent testing and the number of concurrent users to simulate. Additional parameters, such as POST request data (for simulating Web forms) and cookie values, can be specified as well. A sample test performed on a local server with a time limit of 30 seconds and a simulated load of 20 users might be configured like this:

```
ab -t 30 -c 20 http://localhost/perl/foodle.pl
```

The `-t` parameter specifies the total test time in seconds; with the `-n` parameter, the duration of the test can be limited by the number of requests. Concurrency is specified by the `-c` parameter, which sets the number of simultaneous users (or threads, in this case) accessing the URL at the same time. If concurrency were set to 1, for instance, ApacheBench would always wait for a response before initiating the next request. Setting higher values for the `-c` parameter generally increases the load experienced by the server, up to a limit imposed by client capabilities. The result of a typical ApacheBench test might look like the following:

```
This is ApacheBench, Version 1.3c <$Revision: 1.41 $> apache-1.3
Copyright (c) 1996 Adam Twiss, Zeus Technology Ltd, http://www.zeustech.net/
Copyright (c) 1998-1999 The Apache Group, http://www.apache.org/
```

```
Benchmarking localhost (be patient)...

Server Software:        Apache/1.3.14
Server Hostname:        localhost
Server Port:            80

Document Path:          /perl/foodle.pl
Document Length:        2511 bytes

Concurrency Level:      20
Time taken for tests:   30.004 seconds
Complete requests:      19989
Failed requests:        0
Total transferred:      55991990 bytes
HTML transferred:       50194890 bytes
Requests per second:    666.21
Transfer rate:          1866.15 kb/s received

Connnection Times (ms)
              min   avg   max
Connect:        0     3   128
Processing:     4    25   810
Total:          4    28   938
```

Of the values reported by ApacheBench, the few that are most interesting for site performance testing are complete requests, failed requests, and RPS. Complete requests gives the total number of requests that came back in a successful form, which is divided by the time taken for tests to calculate the RPS value. The RPS value might be faulty in some situations, however. Some valid responses might be listed as failed requests due to assumptions on the part of ApacheBench. For the purposes of the test, a complete request is one that receives a response with a status of 200 OK that is the same length as the initial response. If a page is dynamically generated from a Web application, it might return a different status code or have a different length and therefore be classified as a failed request. These requests should be added to the total to compute the true RPS value.

Simulating a Simple Path

Performing a robust performance test can be difficult given the basic command-line interface to ApacheBench. Simulating even a simple path through the site is difficult when URLs have to be entered one at a time, and the result is unlikely to be representative of the mixed requests received by a live site. Fortunately, a Perl interface to the ApacheBench application was developed to facilitate more complex paths than are enabled by the command-line interface. The HTTPD::Bench::ApacheBench module provides an object interface based around test runs and URL sets that makes it possible to create repeatable performance tests based on real-world data.

Listing 15.1 is a test set example using a single usage path encoded in a command-line Perl program. The program uses HTTPD::Bench::ApacheBench to test the response rate of a set of URLs at various concurrency values. Results of the test are displayed to the console.

Listing 15.1   **Simple ApacheBench Automation**

```perl
01 #!/usr/bin/perl
02
03 use 5.6.0;
04 use strict;
05 use warnings;
06
07 use HTTPD::Bench::ApacheBench;
08
09 # create and configure the ApacheBench object
10 my $b = HTTPD::Bench::ApacheBench->new;
11 $b->priority("run_priority");
12 $b->repeat(1000);
13
14 # add the URL list
15 my $list = HTTPD::Bench::ApacheBench::Run->new();
16 $list->order('depth_first');
17 $list->urls([
18              "http://localhost/index.html",
19              "http://localhost/thing.html",
20              "http://localhost/perl/foodle.pl",
21              ] );
22 $b->add_run($list);
23
24
25 # run the load test and return the result
26 foreach my $number_of_users (5,10,15,20)
27 {
28   $b->concurrency($number_of_users);
29   my $ro = $b->execute;
30
31   # calculate requests per second
32   print "$number_of_users users, ", $b->total_requests, " total
      ↪requests:\n";
33   my $rps = sprintf('%2.2f', (1000*$b->total_requests / $b-
      ↪>total_time));
34   print "$rps requests per second\n\n";
35 }
```

Lines 01–07 of Listing 15.1 set up the environment and load the HTTPD::Bench::ApacheBench module. Line 10 creates a benchmarking object that provides both configuration methods and regression methods for the test. Line 11 sets the priority of the test runs, which would affect only this program if it used more than one test path.

Line 12 sets the number of times to repeat the test; this value should be set to keep the test running at least 30 seconds. Shorter tests are likely to produce erratic results because the server doesn't have time to adjust to a sustained load.

Lines 15–22 add a list of URLs as a single test run. Line 16 specifies that the list should be ordered *depth-first*, or completed in full before starting the next repetition, as opposed to *breadth-first*, which would loop over each URL individually. Line 22 adds the test run object created in line 15 to the complete test. Multiple tests can be added this way, allowing a more varied set of user interactions to be simulated.

Lines 26–35 perform a test once for each value of $number_of_users, which varies the concurrency value starting at 5 users and ending with 20 simultaneous users. These values should be determined interactively during testing; settings used in practice are likely to be much higher than these defaults. Line 28 applies the current concurrency value to the test, and line 29 starts the test itself. Lines 32–34 display a selection of the test results, concentrating on the RPS values for each level of concurrency. The output of a typical run might look like the following:

```
5 users, 3000 total requests:
345.94 requests per second

10 users, 3000 total requests:
301.08 requests per second

15 users, 3000 total requests:
301.02 requests per second

20 users, 3000 total requests:
301.17 requests per second
```

Note that the number of total requests doesn't vary based on the number of users. That number is based solely on the number of URLs given in the test path times the number of repetitions. Note also that the total number of requests for this particular run isn't enough to carry the test for more than 10 seconds; results from an initial run should be used to modify the number of repetitions or the number of URLs to provide a longer test. Three URLs isn't a very robust sample of site usage. Thus, this test could be augmented by using more data from site access logs to fill out the test path.

Comparing Multiple Simple Paths

Listing 15.2 provides a more general way to configure site paths. It also produces output that is more amenable to automated comparisons using spreadsheet software and other numeric tools. The example is a similar command-line Perl program that reads URLs for a test path from a log file specified on the command line, saves the results to a comma-separated values (CSV) file, and displays the results to the console.

Listing 15.2 **Log-Based ApacheBench Automation**

```perl
01 #!/usr/bin/perl
02
03 use 5.6.0;
04 use strict;
05 use warnings;
06
07 use HTTPD::Bench::ApacheBench;
08
09 # create and configure the ApacheBench object
10 my $b = HTTPD::Bench::ApacheBench->new;
11 $b->priority("run_priority");
12 $b->repeat(1000);
13
14 # get a URL list from the specified file
15 my $filename = $ARGV[0];
16 unless ($filename)
17 {
18   print "Please specify a filename.\n\n";
19   exit;
20 }
21 open URLFILE, "$filename" or die "Can't open $filename: $!";
22 my @urls = <URLFILE>;
23 close URLFILE;
24
25 print "Simulating load from path:\n";
26 print @urls, "\n";
27
28 # add the URL list
29 my $list = HTTPD::Bench::ApacheBench::Run->new();
30 $list->order('depth_first');
31 $list->urls(\@urls);
32 $b->add_run($list);
33
34 my $csvfile = $ARGV[1] || "$filename.csv";
35 open CSV, ">$csvfile" or die "Can't open $csvfile for writing: $!";
36 print CSV "Test path, users, total requests, total time, RPS,\n";
37
38 # run the load test and return the result
39 foreach my $number_of_users (5,10,15,20)
40 {
41   $b->concurrency($number_of_users);
42   my $ro = $b->execute;
43
44   print "$number_of_users users, ", $b->total_requests, " total
     requests:\n";
45
46   # calculate and display requests per second
47   my $rps = sprintf('%2.2f', (1000*$b->total_requests
     / $b->total_time));
```

continues

Listing 15.2 **Continued**

```
48   print "$rps requests per second\n\n";
49
50   # log run results to CSV file
51   print CSV "$filename, ";
52   print CSV "$number_of_users, ";
53   print CSV $b->total_requests, ", ";
54   print CSV $b->total_time, ", ";
55   print CSV "$rps, ";
56   print CSV "\n";
57 }
58 close CSV;
```

Lines 15–23 open the file specified as a command-line argument and read in a list of URLs to use as the test path. Line 15 gets the file name from $ARGV[0], and lines 16–20 display an error and exit if no file name is provided. Lines 21–23 open the file and assign each line of the file as an element in the @urls array. Line 31 assigns the list of URLs to a test run. As a result, the input file for Listing 15.2 is formatted with one URL per line, as in the following example:

```
http://localhost/index.html
http://localhost/perl/foodle.pl
http://localhost/thing.html
```

A list of URLs in this format easily can be extracted from site access logs or custom proxy logs. Lines 25 and 26 of the program print the list of URLs being used in the test run for verification. The console output of Listing 15.2 looks like the following:

```
Simulating load from path:
http://localhost/index.html
http://localhost/perl/foodle.pl
http://localhost/thing.html

5 users, 3000 total requests:
329.20 requests per second

10 users, 3000 total requests:
300.93 requests per second

15 users, 3000 total requests:
301.69 requests per second

20 users, 3000 total requests:
300.63 requests per second
```

Lines 34–36 open and label a CSV file that is used to save the test results in a format readable by other programs for further analysis. Line 34 tries to read the file name from the second command-line argument; if none is provided, it uses the name of the input file with a .csv extension appended. The labels printed by line 36 are optional and should correspond directly with the values printed to the file in lines 51–56 for each test run. Again, the emphasis in this example is on the number of RPS for each run, but other data is provided by the HTTPD::Bench::ApacheBench module if needed. A file produced using the format in Listing 15.2 would look like the following:

```
Test path, users, total requests, total time, RPS,
first-set, 5, 3000, 9113, 329.20,
first-set, 10, 3000, 9969, 300.93,
first-set, 15, 3000, 9944, 301.69,
first-set, 20, 3000, 9979, 300.63,
```

The CSV output can be used to compare the results from multiple sets by importing the files into a spreadsheet program or database. These results also can be used to compare the performance of a Web application at baseline and after changes have been made to the application. Additional analysis can be performed within the Perl program, as well; the only limiting factors are the complexity of the file that specifies URLs for test runs and the format of the CSV file produced as output. This kind of program also can be used to produce Web-friendly graphs and tables from the results, although care should be taken in making the program itself available as a dynamic Web application. Such an application could easily be turned into a site from which distributed denial of service attacks could be carried out.

Comparing Multiple Complex Paths

The capability to pass complex requests to the server would make Listing 15.2 a more robust performance-testing tool. URLs can encode some kinds of form data, but most Web applications require POST data or cookie values to operate correctly. Listing 15.3 is a Perl program that reads paths with POST data from a more complex log file and provides results similar to those from Listing 15.2.

Listing 15.3 **Complex ApacheBench Automation**

```
01 #!/usr/bin/perl
02
03 use 5.6.0;
04 use strict;
05 use warnings;
06
07 use HTTPD::Bench::ApacheBench;
08
09 # create and configure the ApacheBench object
10 my $b = HTTPD::Bench::ApacheBench->new;
11 $b->priority("run_priority");
12 $b->repeat(1000);
13
14 # get a URL list from the specified file
15 my $filename = $ARGV[0];
16 unless ($filename)
```

continues

Listing 15.3   **Continued**

```
17 {
18   print "Please specify a filename.\n\n";
19   exit;
20 }
21 open URLFILE, "$filename" or die "Can't open $filename: $!";
22 my @urls;
23 my @post_data;
24 while (my $line = <URLFILE>)
25 {
26   my ($url, $post) = split "\t", $line;
27   $post = '' unless ($post =~ tr/=//);
28   push @urls, "$url\n";
29   push @post_data, $post;
30 }
31 close URLFILE;
32
33 print "Simulating load from path:\n";
34 print @urls, "\n";
35
36 # add the URL list
37 my $list = HTTPD::Bench::ApacheBench::Run->new();
38 $list->order('depth_first');
39 $list->urls(\@urls);
40 $list->postdata(\@post_data);
41 $b->add_run($list);
42
43 my $csvfile = $ARGV[1] || "$filename.csv";
44 open CSV, ">$csvfile" or die "Can't open $csvfile for writing: $!";
45 print CSV "Test path, users, total requests, total time, RPS,\n";
46
47 # run the load test and return the result
48 foreach my $number_of_users (5,10,15,20)
49 {
50   $b->concurrency($number_of_users);
51   my $ro = $b->execute;
52
53   print "$number_of_users users, ", $b->total_requests, " total
     ⟿requests:\n";
54
55   # calculate and display requests per second
56   my $rps = sprintf('%2.2f', (1000*$b->total_requests
     ⟿/ $b->total_time));
57   print "$rps requests per second\n\n";
58
59   # log run results to CSV file
60   print CSV "$filename, ";
61   print CSV "$number_of_users, ";
62   print CSV $b->total_requests, ", ";
63   print CSV $b->total_time, ", ";
```

```
64   print CSV "$rps, ";
65   print CSV "\n";
66 }
67 close CSV;
```

HTTPD::Bench::ApacheBench enables POST data to be specified for each request in a test series. Lines 21–31 open the file specified as a command-line argument and populate an array of URLs as well as a corresponding array of POST data. Line 26 splits each line of the file into a URL and POST data segment. The input file format for Listing 15.3 is slightly different from the one for Listing 15.2; each line contains a URL and its associated post information separated by a tab character:

```
http://localhost/index.html
http://localhost/perl/foodle.pl        id=1234&name=fred
http://localhost/thing.html
```

Not all requests have associated POST data, although each line has a tab character after the URL. To handle the difference, line 27 checks for lines without POST data—identifiable by the lack of an = character—and creates an empty entry in the @post_data array for each one. The array of POST data is then added to the test run in line 40. URLs with no corresponding POST data are sent through GET requests by HTTPD::Bench::ApacheBench, and the rest are sent using POST requests. In the sample file, the first and third URLs would be processed using GET requests, and the second URL would be sent through a POST request with the supplied POST data.

These programs only hint at the scriptability of an ApacheBench setup, of course. Cookie data could be added to the mix, or session information could be generated using new POST data for each request. HTTPD::Bench::ApacheBench also provides more detailed data about the result of each test. Thus, values provided in the response could be used to generate new requests that mimic the cycle of a client browser more closely.

Graphic Comparisons with VeloMeter

Of course, after a site performance analysis tool is written to handle robust test sets and produce graphable results, a logical option is to combine the application with a user-friendly interface and graphing tools. The result would rival high-end performance analysis packages while retaining the capability to be customized. VeloMeter is an application that followed just such a path. Originally developed by VelociGen as an in-house tool for testing the performance of client sites, VeloMeter eventually gained features such as a graphing library and a built-in proxy server for generating usage logs interactively.

VeloMeter is written in Java, so the application can run under any Java environment. In addition to a short run as a commercial application, VeloMeter was offered as a free download from the VelociGen Web site. Starting with version 3.0, VeloMeter is offered as open source software under the GNU General Public License (GPL), which gives anyone permission to use, modify, and redistribute the program. It is available in Java source form or as a binary package for Linux or Windows environments.

Proxy Configuration

A VeloMeter testing session is organized around test sets, which are single site paths that consist of a list of URLs with associated POST and cookie data. A test set can be entered manually one URL at a time, or it can be generated using the built-in proxy server and a standard Web browser. The latter method is considerably easier and more likely to produce complete test sets, including graphic file requests and POST data that might be overlooked otherwise. The dialog box in Figure 15.1 provides an example of the proxy configuration process and results.

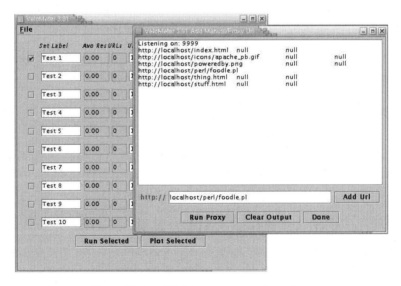

Figure 15.1   VeloMeter proxy configuration.

When activated, the VeloMeter proxy indicates which port it is using (usually 9999). This port should be specified when configuring the proxy settings of the browser being used to generate test sets. After the browser is configured, a user can browse through the site to be tested as normal, and the interactions between the browser and the Web server are recorded in the proxy window. Each URL is listed on its own line with accompanying POST or cookie values (or `null`, if none). After the session is complete, the test set can be saved by stopping the proxy with the Done button. Any number of test sets can be generated this way, and additional URLs can be added to any test set by using the same process.

Log File Configuration

Test sets can be saved to or loaded from VeloMeter-format test set files. Each file can contain one or more test sets in a format similar to the following:

```
# 5 users Set (6 urls, 5 users, 100 times)
[name]
5 users

[users]
5

[times]
100

[urls]
http://localhost:80/thing.html          null    null
http://localhost:80/index.html          null    null
http://localhost:80/icons/apache_pb.gif         null    null
http://localhost:80/poweredby.png       null    null
http://localhost:80/perl/foodle.pl      null    null
http://localhost:80/stuff.html          null    null
[end set]
# End 5 users Set
```

The core of a test set is the list of URLs in the [urls] section. This list follows a simple format, with one URL per line followed by POST and cookie value strings, separated by a tab character. The list of URLs easily can be extracted from a site access log, with POST and cookie data added by hand if necessary. Conversely, lists generated by the VeloMeter proxy server can be adapted for use with other load testing applications, including Listing 15.3 earlier in this chapter. In VeloMeter 3.0, test sets from files in the VeloMeter format can be imported into the comparison form using the File menu.

Comparison Settings

After test sets have been generated or imported, each set can be run individually to generate a performance test and save the results. A useful baseline test can be created by importing the same test set repeatedly and then assigning an incremental number of users to each set. For example, Figure 15.2 shows a test set that has been imported four times and assigned levels of concurrency in increments of five users. Note that the total number of requests is derived by multiplying the number of URLs by both the number of users and the number of repeated runs.

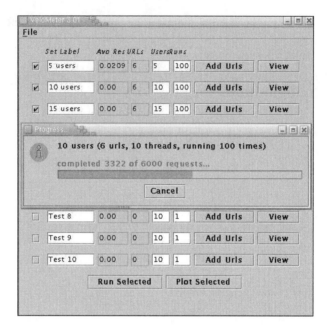

Figure 15.2 Running a VeloMeter test.

Test runs can be repeated individually or in groups, if necessary, but VeloMeter saves only the results of the most recent test. Results from each set can be compared either by saving the result data or by plotting the results on a common graph. A table of result data can be viewed individually for each test set and saved in CSV format from the display dialog if desired. Results also can be plotted individually or in groups on a graph that displays the average response times for each URL in a set. When used in conjunction with the testing method shown in Figure 15.2, this type of URL-by-URL comparison might provide insights into the source of bottlenecks at various concurrency levels. The graph of response times can be overlaid by a bar chart showing the average response time and RPS value for each test run, which gives a more-is-better indicator of which run performed the best.

VeloMeter is undergoing continuous development as this book is being written; you will likely see significant changes due to its open-source nature. Check the Web site for this book for current updates of the VeloMeter software.

Simulating Site Overload

The most common test performed on a site is an *overload test*, which sends requests to a site as fast as the site can handle them. As usually conducted, however, an overload test is good only for comparisons between configurations that have been subjected to the same overload test. The comparison might be between different configurations of a site, different iterations of a Web application, or even different times when a site is active. An overload test doesn't provide any relationship between its results and the current traffic experienced by a site, however. As a result, site testing should be carried out with the idea that any one test is incomplete by itself and that it requires a comparison test to put it into perspective.

All these tests assume that the site being tested is a development site, not a live site. *Under no circumstances should overload testing be performed on a live site.* Sites are expected to behave erratically when put under these conditions, and requests might be dropped or incorrect data returned if a user accesses a live site while testing is performed. If a live site needs to be tested, make a copy of the site solely for testing or use the procedures in the "Testing a Live Site" section of this chapter.

Checking Baseline Performance

When testing a site to determine the maximum traffic it can support, it's good to start with a reasonable amount of load that produces response times and server activity similar to the current load. This value can take some fine tuning to achieve, but site usage data from access logs and site analysis software can provide some insights into the amount of traffic the site currently receives. Add additional load gradually, checking response times and server monitors to gauge the server's reaction. With tools such as ApacheBench and VeloMeter, load can be added by increasing the number of users (or concurrent threads) accessing the site simultaneously.

At some point during testing, the server should encounter a bottleneck that causes response times to change noticeably. When this happens, the load being generated at that point can be considered the maximum baseline traffic that can be handled gracefully by the server. That load then can be used in more robust site tests to determine site response in terms of RPS and total response time for each URL being tested. For instance, a concurrency value of 2,000 users might produce results of 200 RPS and an average response time of 0.5 seconds. These values won't relate directly. Thus, the important numbers to consider are the RPSs—especially compared to current traffic values—and the response times, which can be used to determine the overall response time perceived by visitors. If a site that is currently receiving 50 RPS can achieve a baseline of 200 RPS, for example, traffic to the site can grow by 400 percent without losing significant performance.

In addition, a test can be performed to see how the server responds when it is completely overloaded. This usually can be simulated by generating as much traffic as the client machine can produce and then adding in as many client machines as necessary to cause the server to overload. The point of overload can be gauged by checking the load test application for dropped requests or by accessing the server with a normal Web browser to see if it returns the `500 Server Busy` error or stops responding to Web requests entirely.

Finding Points of Failure

One of the most difficult parts of performance testing is determining the root cause of a bottleneck. When a server is overloaded by testing, the resultant performance disruption to different parts of the server could be either the cause of the slowdown or a result of it. For instance, a server bottleneck due to Perl processing might use all available processing power and tie up every Web server process, which slows down any other Web request. Overall Web server slowness might lead a site tester to incorrectly determine that the Web server itself was the cause of the bottleneck, while the real culprit goes undetected.

The cause of a bottleneck sometimes can be determined by repeating the test multiple times and watching the condition of each system involved to catch unusual behavior. For instance, the `top` program can be run in a UNIX environment to determine memory and CPU usage of processes in real time. A test can be performed while the `top` program is running to check if any particular process (such as the Web server, the application engines, or the database) is taking up an unusual amount of memory or processor time. Additionally, the conditions that cause overload can be throttled back a bit to catch conditions that are close to failure but that haven't yet gone over the top.

Retesting After Fixes

After performance data is collected and potential bottlenecks have been identified, work usually is done to fix the root of the problem and overcome the bottlenecks. (If not, work *should* be done to fix the problem.) This isn't the end of the process, however. After performance bottlenecks seem to be solved, it's important to retest the site using the original test sets. This will indicate if a real performance improvement has been realized, and it will provide numbers that can be used to calculate a percentage improvement. Then the improvement can be compared to estimated traffic growth in order to determine whether the time spent finding a solution allowed the site to handle traffic growth from the same time period. For example, a 10% improvement that took six weeks to implement didn't meet its goal if site traffic increased 20% over the same period.

The performance testing process might have any number of these iterations, as many as the development timeline allows. As a result, it's good to plan for as many testing cycles as possible, starting as early as possible in the timeline to allow time for fixes and retesting. One good place to which performance testing can be added is regression and acceptance test cycles. When load testing is considered a regular part of the Web application evaluation process, the work done in designing performance test sets can be combined with usability tests and other standard testing practices.

Testing a Live Site

Sometimes a site is already in production before it can be tested. Unfortunately, testing the performance of a live site is trickier than testing a site in development. Even when a site has been load tested during development, it's important to continue testing a site after it is put in production.

A repetition of the baseline test described earlier in this section can provide valuable data for a live site. Using data determined from the development site—or similar data determined indirectly from usage patterns—you can test the live site using the baseline testing configuration. Of course, the last thing a busy site needs is to be inundated by load testing requests while it also is handling real user traffic. Therefore, extra care needs to be taken to restrict the test set to a percentage of current traffic that is well within the graceful maximum.

It also is important to exclude any usage information that alters or adds data to the site. User requests that post information to forums, e-commerce forms, and other site input applications should not be duplicated because their effects are duplicated as well. For instance, it's not a good idea to use a forum-posting request as the template for a thousand similar requests because each adds a new message to the forum. Similarly, any request that is likely to alter the site indirectly—for instance, a user login that alters the "last logged in" date—should be avoided as well. These exclusions might reduce the accuracy of the representative requests, but the alternative is a site with erroneous data created whenever testing occurs.

Interpreting Test Results

Web site performance indicators have had a rough history. They started out as an offshoot of the infamous hit counter graphic, and in most cases, they've gone downhill from there. The industry never quite got the idea of "hits" out of its collective consciousness, and site log analysis tools have been crippled as a result. I usually have to go to great pains to eradicate any mention of hits when configuring a new analysis tool, but the result is worth it. Web applications, HTML files, and sundry files such as graphics and PDFs should be treated differently when judging performance, and analysis tools that lump them together provide analyses of marginal utility at best.

With load testing tools, the opposite is true—there isn't nearly enough synthesis being performed within the application. ApacheBench, for instance, produces a result that means more to the hit-counter crowd than anyone; the assumption is that I'd like to see only the absolute best transfer rate possible for a single file being tested. There's no way for me to get what I really want—the time I have before my Web server collapses under the strain of traffic increases—without having to do lots of work massaging the results into a format that makes sense. I'm not alone: I have yet to see any real-world performance test—in a magazine or on the Web—provide the results in a format directly produced by any load-testing application. I'm much more likely to see results displayed as a graph produced by Excel from hand-entered data. This isn't the kind of environment that encourages Web administrators to test their sites more often.

Closer to home, VeloMeter is no exception to this rule. The initial release of VeloMeter created exciting color graphs, but the data in those graphs was nearly useless for anything but raw comparisons. Gleaning any sort of useful information from the VeloMeter data required hours of configuration and reconfiguration and meticulous notes of both the conditions and the results of each test. The current iteration has made some progress in the right direction, but it still produces results that are more closely related to the hit counter than to the kind of usage I'm liable to see from a real site over time. It still doesn't take connection speeds or varying numbers of realistic users into account.

Summary

Web application performance testing can be difficult to understand, but the results of a well-designed test are usually worth the effort. The first step to a successful load test is designing the test with real-world data and a realistic expectation of the results that are needed to prepare the site for future traffic. After a testing plan is in place and representative data are collected, load generators such as ApacheBench or VeloMeter can be used to simulate high request volumes and to gauge the response times and throughput of the server. Using these tools, a tester can check baseline performance levels, simulate the SlashDot effect, or overload a development site to determine potential bottlenecks. Data gleaned from these tests can be used to fix potential performance problems, evaluate new hardware and software, and provide assurance that the site can perform efficiently under any expected load.

Solutions for the Future

16

XML and Content Management

THE EXTENSIBLE MARKUP LANGUAGE (XML) IS USUALLY THE first technology invoked when talking about the future of the Web. An offshoot of the Hypertext Markup Language (HTML) and the Standard Generalized Markup Language (SGML) standards, XML was developed as a way to create platform-neutral data representation languages. XML languages for common data needs have already started to appear, and many more are in development. In addition, a major strength of XML is the capability to encode XML data without needing to explicitly declare a language. Because the rules of valid XML formatting are strictly defined, any XML document can be parsed using the same tools, regardless of whether the language is known beforehand.

A number of robust XML interfaces have been developed for Perl, and more are likely to be developed in the future. The proliferation of such interfaces is made possible by the standardized accessibility of XML, combined with Perl's excellent text-handling capabilities. Perl's interfaces to XML documents range from the simple and direct to the robust and complex, but so far no clear favorite has emerged. It's possible that a cross-language standard, such as the Document Object Model (DOM), will become a Perl favorite as well. It's just as likely that a specifically Perlish XML interface will emerge the way DBI did as a database interface.

There are many applications for XML interfaces on the Web, but the first wide use of XML might be Web content management. XML fits well into the document-centric Web model, and much of the data currently available on the Web can be translated easily into XML documents. In addition, XML provides a finer grain of control over the way a document is expressed. The same data can be formatted in an infinite number of ways, and alternate views of a single XML file can be created to enable users to exercise control over the way in which they view the data.

XML Now With XML::Simple

XML::Simple is a module that provides a lightweight interface to XML files that is implemented in a Perlish fashion. XML::Simple parses XML files into native Perl data structures that can be accessed using standard Perl functions and operators. The structures then can be altered or updated and translated back to XML files. The XML::Simple module provides a good way to access XML documents that have a simple, predefined structure. Configuration files, database results, and other simple data files are good candidates for translation into XML and for use with XML::Simple.

Unfortunately, not all XML interface situations can be covered by using XML::Simple. The module's reliance on native Perl data types limits its representation of XML structures to those that make sense in a Perlish context. The results of parsing XML files with XML::Simple can be variable, even with files that are well suited to it. Structures that are distinct in XML syntax might map to the same Perl data types, creating ambiguity when the parsed structures are translated back to XML. For simple cases with regular XML structure, however, XML::Simple provides a good way to start accessing XML documents as quickly as possible.

Simple XML Parsing

In most cases, XML is used to store existing data in a platform-independent format. Data is well-suited for storage in XML if it can be stored hierarchically. Listing 16.1 is an example of a hierarchy—a table of contents—that translates well into XML.

Listing 16.1 **Table of Contents File**

```
01 <book>
02 <title>Perl for the Web</title>
03 <author>Chris Radcliff</author>
04 <chapter>
05 <number>0</number>
06 <title>Introduction</title>
07 <section>About this book</section>
08 <section>Conventions</section>
09 </chapter>
10 <chapter>
11 <number>1</number>
```

```
12 <title>Foobar chapter</title>
13 <section>How to Foobar</section>
14 <section>How to Foobaz</section>
15 </chapter>
16 <chapter>
17 <number>2</number>
18 <title>Barbaz chapter</title>
19 <section>How to Barbaz</section>
20 <section>When not to Barbaz</section>
21 </chapter>
22 <appendix>
23 <number>A</number>
24 <title>Alphabet Soup: Reference and Glossary</title>
25 <section>XML Bestiary</section>
26 <section>Specifications and Organizations</section>
27 </appendix>
28 </book>
```

Similarly, XML-encoded data that can be represented as a Perl data structure is well-suited for processing by XML::Simple. Because Perl deals in scalars, arrays, and hashes, XML structures that can be meaningfully mapped onto these variables are easier to access using XML::Simple than are structures that are more complex. For instance, an HTML-like document is likely to map awkwardly onto Perl data structures because the tags in such a file are mixed within the values of container tags. A structure such as the following is trivial to represent in Perl:

```
<cats>
  <name>Hershey</name>
  <name>Kahlua</name>
  <name>Merlin</name>
</cats>
```

An array of name values can be created that mimics the structure directly. However, a mixed structure such as the following would be awkward to represent in Perl:

```
<discussion>
  <statement>
    Cats are often given odd names like
    <name>Hershey</name>, <name>Kahlua</name>, or
    <name>Merlin</name>.
  </statement>
</discussion>
```

The latter structure, although it's valid XML, mixes unnamed text elements and tagged elements within the <statement> tag, which makes it difficult to create a Perl structure containing all the elements. A simple array of all the elements under <statement> might be created, but it would include all elements in order with no distinction between the text elements and the <name> values. Parsing such a file would require a more robust interface such as XML::DOM. Listing 16.1 is a good candidate for using XML::Simple because the data is stored in a format that can be represented as name/value pairs—a hash, in other words.

The file in Listing 16.1 also is very regular in its structure. Values are stored in elements that are named consistently, which helps when retrieving values programmatically. For instance, all chapter numbers are stored in the element path /book/chapter/number, which is both regular and easily identifiable. Even duplicate data is stored in identifiable sections that can be turned into array structures in Perl. Chapters are found in the element path /book/chapter, for instance, and sections are found through the element path /book/chapter/section. Storing multiples uniformly as arrays makes it possible to access all the values with a foreach loop or use standard array functions such as grep or map.

Accessing a value in an XML::Simple structure is handled through Perl's standard methods for processing variables and references. An object interface is provided for creating the structures, but no object methods are necessary to get values. For instance, retrieving the value of the <title> element from the document in Listing 16.1 could be performed in the following way:

```
$book->{title}
```

The result would be a scalar value containing the title. More complex values are returned as array references or hash references, which in turn can be accessed using standard Perl operators. The end result of any accessed path is always the scalar value of the tag or attribute.

XML Without the XML

One good reason to use XML::Simple is that it provides many of the benefits of XML—named access to data and platform independent data files among them—without requiring much knowledge of XML arcana. A Perl program can be written that accesses all parts of an XML file without having to know parsing details or file formatting. For instance, Listing 16.2 is a Web application written in Perl Server Pages (PSP) that uses XML::Simple to display the table of contents in Listing 16.1 as HTML. (A modified version of this program can be used as an entry point for the publishing system mentioned later in this chapter.)

Listing 16.2   **Table of Contents Display Program**

```
01 <html>
02
03 <perl>
04 use XML::Simple ();
05
06 my $xs = XML::Simple->new(forcearray => ['section', 'appendix',
   'chapter'],
07                            memshare => 1);
08 my $book = $xs->XMLin("$ENV{DOCUMENT_ROOT}/thebook/toc.xml");
```

```
09 </perl>
10
11 <output>
12 <head>
13 <title>$book->{title}</title>
14 </head>
15
16 <body bgcolor="white">
17 <h3>$book->{title}</h3>
18 <p>by $book->{author}</p>
19
20 <loop name="chapter" list="@{$book->{chapter}}">
21 <p>Chapter $chapter->{number}: $chapter->{title}</p>
22 <ul>
23 <loop name="section" list="@{$chapter->{section}}">
24 <li>$section</li>
25 </loop>
26 </ul>
27 </loop>
28
29 <loop name="appendix" list="@{$book->{appendix}}">
30 <p>Appendix $appendix->{number}: $appendix->{title}</p>
31 <ul>
32 <loop name="section" list="@{$appendix->{section}}">
33 <li>$section</li>
34 </loop>
35 </ul>
36 </loop>
37
38 </body>
39 </output>
40 </html>
```

Lines 04–08 of Listing 16.2 set up XML::Simple and parse the XML document into a Perl data structure. Line 06 creates an XML::Simple parser object and stores it in $xs. The forcearray parameter is specified to standardize the way XML::Simple translates the <section>, <appendix>, and <chapter> elements into arrays. The memcache parameter is set to cache parsed XML documents in memory for the life of the Perl interpreter. Line 08 invokes the XMLin method to load and parse the toc.xml file from Listing 16.1 and store the result in $book. The rest of Listing 16.2 doesn't reference XML::Simple; all further interaction is with the Perl data structures referenced by $book.

Lines 11–39 use the PSP <output> tag to mix HTML and Perl variables. Lines 13 and 17 display the book title, and line 18 displays the book author. Lines 20–27 create a new paragraph for each chapter stored in the array reference $book->{chapter}, and lines 23–25 loop through the sections of each chapter and create a bulleted list accordingly. Lines 29–36 do the same for each appendix stored in $book->{appendix}. The end result is an HTML-formatted list, as shown in Figure 16.1.

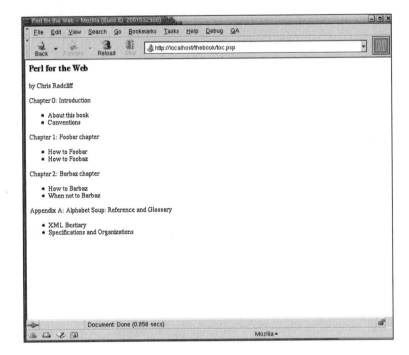

Figure 16.1 Table of contents display.

Another bonus to using XML to store the table of contents becomes apparent when the displayed result needs to be changed. For instance, adding a link to each section of the table of contents would be a simple matter of changing line 24 of Listing 16.2 to the following:

```
<li><a href="show.psp?section=$section">$section</a></li>
```

The change automatically would be applied to all sections in the table of contents. Similarly, if the underlying data needs to be changed, the changes can be made without the need to alter formatting as well. In fact, changes can be made to the data without any knowledge of the eventual formatting at all. This provides an additional layer of separation for systems using templates—the result is independent data storage, program logic, and display formatting.

XML::Simple Caveats

An XML interface this simple has to have its faults, though. With XML::Simple, the problem lies in the way in which it translates XML structures into Perl variables. To provide an interface without the need for many object methods and complex data types, XML::Simple has to gloss over some of the distinctions between XML structures. The resulting ambiguity between similar structures can cause the XML coming out of XML::Simple to be considerably different from the XML that went in. An example of this effect can be seen by running the XML document from Listing 16.1 through XML::Simple and viewing the result. Listing 16.3 performs the transformation on any XML file specified.

Listing 16.3 **XML Simplifier**

```
01 #!/usr/bin/perl
02
03 require 5.6.0;
04 use strict;
05 use warnings;
06
07 use XML::Simple ();
08
09 my $xs = XML::Simple->new();
10
11 my $file_in = $ARGV[0]
12   or die "Please specify a file to simplify.\n";
13
14 print $xs->XMLout($xs->XMLin($file_in));
```

Line 14 of Listing 16.3 is the one that does all the work. It reads the file specified in $ARGV[0] into the XML::Simple parser created in line 09. It then translates the result back into an XML document and prints it. Because XML::Simple doesn't retain all the distinctions between XML elements and attributes, the XML document displayed looks considerably different, as shown in Listing 16.4.

Listing 16.4 **Simplified Result**

```
01 <opt title="Perl for the Web" author="Chris Radcliff">
02   <appendix title="Alphabet Soup: Reference and Glossary" number="A">
03     <section>XML Bestiary</section>
04     <section>Specifications and Organizations</section>
05   </appendix>
06   <chapter title="Introduction" number="0">
07     <section>About this book</section>
08     <section>Conventions</section>
09   </chapter>
10   <chapter title="Foobar chapter" number="1">
11     <section>How to Foobar</section>
12     <section>How to Foobaz</section>
13   </chapter>
14   <chapter title="Barbaz chapter" number="2">
15     <section>How to Barbaz</section>
16     <section>When not to Barbaz</section>
17   </chapter>
18 </opt>
```

At first glance, the "simplified" XML file in Listing 16.4 would seem to have been modified for the better. The module decided that some aspects of the file were better suited to attributes and changed the format accordingly. The result is a clearer visual representation of the relationship between chapters and sections, with titles and related attributes moved to secondary roles. However, the differences become apparent at closer inspection. The root element has been changed from <book> to <opt>, and the appendix has moved from the end of the table of contents to the front.

These changes wouldn't affect the way XML::Simple represents the XML document, but they would definitely change the way that most other XML parsers would represent the document. In turn, any program that relied on reading the document in the original form might be unable to find information that has been restructured, even though the structure still makes sense from a human standpoint. For instance, a program written using the DOM interface might look for the title of a chapter in the second child node of the <chapter> element, based on the file in Listing 16.1. In the modified file, though, the second child element of a chapter is likely to be a section title.

In addition, XML::Simple can be sensitive to changes in a document's structure—changes that wouldn't seem to make a difference at first glance. For instance, if the document in Listing 16.1 had only one section listed under one of the chapters, the internal representation of that section would have changed from an array reference to a scalar by default. The only way to avoid breaking a program in the way that Listing 16.3 has done is to force every instance of the <section> element to be treated as an array. Unfortunately, these problems might not show up with the documents used to test an application. Therefore, other documents assumed to be in the same format might break an application that worked initially. The solution is to test XML::Simple programs with a wide array of sample documents to ferret out potential problems.

Tools for Creating XML Interfaces

After the limits of XML::Simple are reached, a more robust interface to XML documents becomes necessary. Fortunately, many already have been developed for use with Perl. Unfortunately, each has its own strengths and weaknesses, and some have more of the latter than the former. However, it's usually possible to find a good general-purpose XML interface that is well suited to a particular project, whether the XML needs to be processed as a stream, parsed into a tree structure for random access, or translated into another document directly.

XML::Parser and Expat

The core of most XML interfaces in Perl is the XML::Parser module. XML::Parser was originally written as an interface to the expat parser written in C by James Clark. The module provides an event-based approach to XML parsing—custom Perl subroutines are executed for each element encountered during parsing. For a time, it was Perl's only interface to XML, but other interfaces were soon implemented by writing modules for use as the subroutines XML::Parser calls as it parses the document.

XML::Parser provides a low-level interface to XML processing, one that makes few assumptions about the structure of the XML file or the methods used to access it. It's for this reason that most XML interfaces are built on top of XML::Parser. However, the same reason makes XML::Parser a poor fit for most Web applications, especially in a Perl context. XML::Parser provides few shortcuts to extracting a particular piece of data from an XML file. Thus, even simple XML document access requires a custom parser to be developed. This approach also is less forgiving because adding support for new tags usually requires additional custom subroutines.

XML::DOM

One interface to XML that Perl shares with other languages is the DOM. Perl implements the DOM by way of the XML::DOM module. XML documents are parsed into a structure made up of *nodes*, where each node is an XML element, attribute, or text value. Nodes can be accessed through DOM-standard object methods such as getDocumentElement and getData. The DOM interface enables the creation of XML structures as well—nodes can be created, copied, or relocated through additional object methods.

The existing DOM parser, XML::DOM::Parser, uses XML::Parser to create a native Perl data structure made up of objects and their methods. As the time this book was being written, efforts were underway to provide a faster DOM interface for Perl. A number of candidates written in C have been proposed, including a DOM version of the Sablotron processor and the Xerces parser, and Perl interfaces to them are in development. Just as XML::Parser eventually gave rise to a profusion of robust XML interfaces, XML::DOM will probably lend its interface to a long succession of modules with improved performance.

Other XML Tools

The list of XML tools developed for Perl is long and rapidly expanding. A wide array of parsers, organizers, filters, and object models have been developed in the quest for the ultimate Perl XML interface. An exhaustive list would be impossible to keep current, but a number of projects are worth noting. Check the Comprehensive Perl Archive Network (CPAN) for a more complete list, for documentation, and for download information.

XML::Grove and its newer relative, Orchard, provide a different object model than the DOM, but with the same intent: to represent XML structures in an unambiguous way that enables consistent access to any data within the structures. SAX filters take a different approach, using an event-handler model to process XML files as a series of data events. XSLT processors, such as Sablotron, provide a special subset of functionality based on XSLT. The intent of XSLT isn't to represent the XML structures, but to provide a standard way to specify the translation of XML documents into other documents, including HTML documents and other XML formats. Each interface has already found its niche, and early exploration of the XML space by these modules has paved the way for evolving versions and new modules to come.

A Sample XML–Based Publishing System

Publishing document-based information to multiple targets is a good use for XML on the Web. Often times, XML data can be used to distinguish infrequently changing data from the often-updated formatting that helps display it to a wide audience. The data can live much longer than its original Web site or any other displayed instance of it. Thus, XML provides a standard format that can be used and reused to publish the information.

As an example, what better to publish in a book about Perl for the Web but the book itself? The goal is to publish all chapters from the book on the Web in HTML and other useful forms, as illustrated in Figure 16.2.

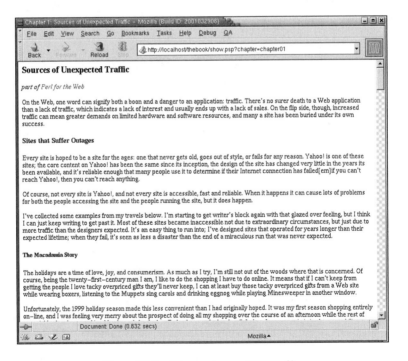

Figure 16.2   Chapter 1 as an HTML file.

The first step in publishing chapters to the Web is to encode the chapters in a format that is resistant to change over time. The chapters and their associated files are long, and any changes made across the board would take an inordinate amount of time to implement. This makes XML a natural choice for the chapters—they can be stored in a format that specifies only the basic structure of each chapter, with reasonable assurance that the format is usable by a wide variety of display programs. If all else fails, the files themselves should be human-readable to enable hand editing and transcription, if necessary.

After the chapters are available in an XML format, the next step is to write a display application to add the desired formatting. Because the primary target is the Web, an embedded application using templates is a good choice. These templates then can be modified for other formatting situations. Display isn't the only goal, though, so an additional application should be written to facilitate searching through the chapters and displaying only the relevant results. This type of add-on shows the flexibility of the XML approach and sets the stage for more exciting applications of the data in the future.

Simple Book Format

This book consists of a number of chapters that are divided into sections, most of which have titles. The sections are in turn divided into subsections. This pattern is repeated for at least four levels of sections. At any level, the fundamental block of text used in the book is a paragraph, which might be a text paragraph or a block of code. With these aspects of a chapter in mind, the Simple Book Format (SBF) file in Listing 16.5 can be constructed as an outline of a sample chapter.

Listing 16.5 **Sample SBF File**

```
01 <chapter>
02 <number>15</number>
03 <title>Sample Chapter</title>
04 <paragraph type="normal">This is some introductory text.</paragraph>
05 <paragraph type="normal">Multiple &lt;b&gt;paragraphs&lt;/b&gt; are
   ↪possible here.</paragraph>
06 <section>
07 <title>I'm a c-level section</title>
08 <paragraph type="normal">This is the body of the c-level
   ↪section.</paragraph>
09 <paragraph type="normal">Multiple paragraphs are possible here as
   ↪well.</paragraph>
10 <section>
11 <title>I'm a d-level section</title>
```

continues

Listing 16.5   **Continued**

```
12 <paragraph type="normal">This is the body of the d-level
   ➥section.</paragraph>
13 <paragraph type="listing" number="1" title="Sample code">
14 my $foo = "bar";
15 print "Let's raise the $foo a little.\n";
16 </paragraph>
17 </section>
18 <section>
19 <title>I'm another d-level section</title>
20 <paragraph type="normal">This is the body of the second d-level
   ➥section.</paragraph>
21 </section>
22 </section>
23 <section>
24 <title>I'm another c-level section</title>
25 <paragraph type="normal">This is the body of the second c-level
   ➥section.</paragraph>
26 </section>
27 </chapter>
```

The file in Listing 16.5 contains examples of a few notable structures. The chapter number and title are stored in corresponding elements in lines 02 and 03. Opening paragraphs (which would come right after the chapter title in the printed book) are listed without any containing structures on lines 04 and 05. Both paragraphs are given the attribute `type="normal"`, as are most paragraphs in the sample chapter. One exception is the code listing from line 13 to line 16, which is given the attribute `type="listing"` as well as `number` and `title` attributes. Other types of paragraphs—including figures and untitled code segments—could be specified in this way as well. Note also that line 05 contains escaped characters, which will be expanded into the more-familiar `<b>` and `</b>` used by HTML. Embedding formatting codes into the data this way breaks the separation a little, but it makes processing a little easier and won't incur a penalty in our Web-centric applications.

One element in the document can be nested within others of its type. The `<section>` element might be found under the `<chapter>` element or another `<section>` element. This kind of recursion makes processing the document a little more complex, but in this case, the structure of the underlying data demanded it. A beneficial side effect of recursion is the equivalent tags used for a top-level section and all its subsections. This equivalence enables any section to be cut and pasted into another section as needed, without changing the name of its tags.

XML::Simple Templates

After the file format has been determined, a display application is needed to translate the XML data into a format usable by Web browsers. It's hoped that eventually this kind of translation will be handled automatically by the browser using the Extensible Style Language (XSL), but until that occurs, it's good to develop a server-side translator that produces HTML. Listing 16.6 is an example of a display application that uses PSP templates and XML::Simple to translate any file in the SBF format for Web viewing.

Listing 16.6 **Templates with XML::Simple**

```
01 <perl>
02 use XML::Simple ();
03
04 my $xs = XML::Simple->new(forcearray => ['section', 'paragraph'],
05                                memshare => 1);
06 my $chapter = $xs->
   ➥XMLin("$ENV{DOCUMENT_ROOT}/thebook/$QUERY{chapter}.xml");
07 </perl>
08
09 <include file="$ENV{DOCUMENT_ROOT}/templates/chapter.psp" />
10
11 <template chapter="$chapter" />
```

Listing 16.6 might seem unnaturally short, but that's because most of the work is being handled by the display template included in line 09 and called in line 11. The $chapter variable populated in line 06 contains the entire parsed contents of the XML file specified in the chapter query variable, so no other information has to be passed to the template.

Publishing to HTML

If the contents of the data file are provided in an easily accessible format, creating a template for the data becomes simple as well. Some aspects of the template are non-trivial because some of the data is stored recursively, but the rest can be handled with a simple substitution template. Listing 16.7 is a template that displays an entire SBF chapter in HTML (as seen in Figure 16.2).

Listing 16.7 **SBF to HTML Full-Chapter Template**

```
01 <tag name="template" accepts="chapter">
02 <output>
03 <html>
04 <head>
05 <title>Chapter $chapter->{number}: $chapter->{title}</title>
06 </head>
```

continues

Listing 16.7 **Continued**

```
07
08 <body bgcolor="white">
09 <h3>$chapter->{title}</h3>
10 <p><i>part of <a href="/thebook/">Perl for the Web</a></i></p>
11
12 <loop name="paragraph" list="@{$chapter->{paragraph}}">
13 <p>$paragraph->{content}</p>
14 </loop>
15
16 <loop name="section" list="@{$chapter->{section}}">
17 <h4>$section->{title}</h4>
18 <loop name="paragraph" list="@{$section->{paragraph}}">
19 <p>$paragraph->{content}</p>
20 </loop>
21 <loop name="section" list="@{$section->{section}}">
22 <h5>$section->{title}</h5>
23 <loop name="paragraph" list="@{$section->{paragraph}}">
24 <if cond="$paragraph->{type} eq 'listing'">
25 <p><b><i>Listing $chapter->{number}.$paragraph->{number}
   ⇒$paragraph->{title}</i></b></p>
26 <p><font color="green"><pre>$paragraph->{content}</pre></font></p>
27 <else />
28 <p>$paragraph->{content}</p>
29 </if>
30 </loop>
31 </loop>
32 </loop>
33 </body>
34 </html>
35 </output>
36 </tag>
```

The template in Listing 16.7 uses the same template principles outlined in Chapter 13, "Using Templates with Perl Applications." The entire template is enclosed in a <tag> tag on lines 02 and 36. The template accepts the $chapter variable, which contains the XML::Simple parsed SBF file. Parts of that variable are incorporated into HTML using the <output> tag on lines 03 and 35. The loop in lines 12–14 displays the opening paragraphs, and the larger loop in lines 16–32 handles the rest of the recursive sections and their paragraphs. Line 24 creates a special case for paragraphs that are code listings, displaying the title of the listing and formatting the code with a <pre> tag to preserve spacing.

As complex as the template in Listing 16.7 might seem, it still is a valid HTML file that renders correctly in a Web browser. Graphic HTML editors might have varying success in editing the formatting of the file without disturbing the <loop> tags, however, and the use of loops and Perlish variable references blurs the line between text templates and program structure. A clearer distinction could be enforced in an application such as this, but it would probably involve increased complexity in Listing 16.6 without much reduced complexity or readability in the template.

Alternate Templates

Developing a template for simple HTML translation is only the beginning. Additional templates can be created to provide different windows on the same data. Formatting can be altered significantly by simply changing the HTML in the template, and segments of the chapter can be emphasized or excluded based on user selections. Listing 16.8 is a template that shows one section of the chapter at a time with enough context to provide navigation to other sections.

Listing 16.8   **SBF to HTML Single-Section Template**

```
01 <tag name="template" accepts="chapter, selection">
02 <output>
03 <html>
04 <head>
05 <title>Chapter $chapter->{number}: $chapter->{title}
   -$selection</title>
06 </head>
07
08 <body bgcolor="#9999FF">
09 <table width="80%" border="0" cellspacing="0" cellpadding="5"
   align="center">
10 <tr>
11 <td bgcolor="white">
12 <h3>$chapter->{title}</h3>
13 <p><i>part of <a href="/thebook/">Perl for the Web</a></i></p>
14
15 <loop name="paragraph" list="@{$chapter->{paragraph}}">
16 <p>$paragraph->{content}</p>
17 </loop>
18
19 <loop name="section" list="@{$chapter->{section}}">
20 <h4>$section->{title}</h4>
21 <if cond="$section->{title} eq $selection">
22 <loop name="paragraph" list="@{$section->{paragraph}}">
23 <p>$paragraph->{content}</p>
24 </loop>
25 <loop name="section" list="@{$section->{section}}">
26 <h5>$section->{title}</h5>
27 <loop name="paragraph" list="@{$section->{paragraph}}">
28 <if cond="$paragraph->{type} eq 'listing'">
29 <p><b><i>Listing $chapter->{number}.$paragraph->{number}
   $paragraph>{title}</i></b></p>
30 <p><font color="green"><pre>$paragraph->{content}</pre></font></p>
31 <else />
```

continues

Listing 16.8 **Continued**

```
32 <p>$paragraph->{content}</p>
33 </if>
34 </loop>
35 </loop>
36 <else />
37 <perl>my $trans = $section->{title}; $trans =~ s/\s/+/g;</perl>
38 <p><font size="2" face="Arial, Helvetica, sans-serif"><a
   ➥href="section.psp?chapter=$QUERY{chapter}&section=$trans">view this
   ➥section</a></font></p>
39 </if>
40 </loop>
41 </td>
42 </tr>
43 </table>
44 </body>
45 </html>
46 </output>
47 </tag>
```

The template in Listing 16.8 is different from Listing 16.7 only in a few respects. It accepts an additional parameter ($selection) in line 01, and it contains some additional formatting to center the text in a display table. The main difference lies in the <if> conditional in line 21, which checks the section title and displays it only if it's the specified selection. Otherwise, lines 31–33 display a link to the omitted section, as displayed by the same file. The code that utilizes this template can be built into the same application as Listing 16.6, or a separate page can be implemented, as in Listing 16.9.

Listing 16.9 **Section Display Page**

```
01 <perl>
02 use XML::Simple ();
03
04 my $xs = XML::Simple->new(forcearray => ['section', 'paragraph'],
05                           memshare => 1);
06 my $chapter =
   ➥$xs->XMLin("$ENV{DOCUMENT_ROOT}/thebook/$QUERY{chapter}.xml");
07 </perl>
08
09 <include file="$ENV{DOCUMENT_ROOT}/templates/section.psp" />
10
11 <template chapter="$chapter" selection="$QUERY{section}" />
```

Again, the differences are minor. Line 09 of Listing 16.9 includes the template from Listing 16.8, and line 11 calls the template with an additional attribute `selection`, as defined by the query variable `section`. The rest of the changes are handled by the template. The result is quite different, however, as shown in Figure 16.3.

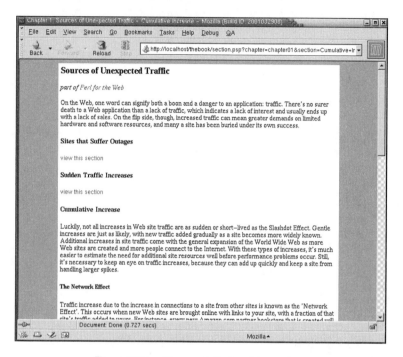

Figure 16.3   Chapter 1 displayed in sections.

One benefit to selectively displaying information from an XML file is the additional formatting that can be added to the result without needing to worry about file size or readability. Large files such as these chapters tend to overwhelm the formatting capabilities of browsers if displayed as anything more complex than a stream of text. A shorter page gives more freedom to the site designer to add navigation and white space to improve the aesthetics of the page. In addition, an important aspect of reading on the Web is the ability to scan a page for interesting information based on headers and links. Because a chapter in its raw form is simply long blocks of text, omitting the section text emphasizes the headers and enables the user to scan through them before content is selected for expansion.

Full-Text Searching

The capability to pinpoint a section within a chapter also provides a benefit for full-text searching applications. In general, search engines on the Web have to address data at the file level, with little knowledge of the structure of any given file. It's sometimes possible to point to a section within an HTML file, but the entire file still has to be downloaded and displayed before the section can be found. With an XML file, granularity can be set as small as needed. In Listing 16.10, for example, a hash table is created. It identifies the occurrence of keywords in named sections within chapter files.

Listing 16.10   **Creating a Full-Text Hash Table**

```perl
01 #!/usr/bin/perl
02
03 use 5.6.0;
04 use strict;
05 use warnings;
06
07 use DBI;
08 use XML::Simple ();
09
10 # connect to the database
11 my $dbh = DBI->connect('dbi:mysql:test','','',{RaiseError => 1});
12
13 # clear out the old hash table values
14 my $sth = $dbh->prepare('delete from book_search');
15 $sth->execute;
16
17 # pre-cache the insert statement for later
18 my $sti = $dbh->prepare(qq{INSERT INTO book_search
19                           (keyword, chapter, section, x_count)
20                           VALUES (?,?,?,?)});
21
22 # open each chapter
23 my $xs = XML::Simple->new(forcearray => ['section', 'paragraph']);
24 my $file = "chapter01";
25 my $chapter = $xs->XMLin("/http/docroot/thebook/$file.xml");
26
27 # load sections into a Perl hash
28 our %sections;
29 foreach my $paragraph (@{$chapter->{paragraph}})
30 {
31   next unless $paragraph->{type} eq 'normal';
32   $sections{'main'} .= $paragraph->{content};
33 }
34
35 foreach my $section (@{$chapter->{section}})
36 {
37   my $title = $section->{title};
38   add_paragraphs($title, $section);
39 }
40
```

```
41 # record keywords for each section
42 foreach my $section (keys %sections)
43 {
44   # create a key count hash
45   my %key_count;
46
47   # break the message into keywords
48   my $keyword;
49   foreach $keyword (split(/[^A-Za-z-_']/, $sections{$section}))
50   {
51     # increment the hash entry for that keyword
52     $key_count{lc($keyword)}++ if (length($keyword) > 2);
53   }
54
55   # insert a row for each key_counthash entry
56   my $q_keyword;
57   foreach $keyword (keys %key_count)
58   {
59     $sti->execute($keyword, $file, $section, $key_count{$keyword});
60   }
61 }
62 $sth->finish;
63
64
65 $dbh->disconnect;
66
67 sub add_paragraphs
68 {
69   my $title = shift;
70   my $section = shift;
71
72   foreach my $paragraph (@{$section->{paragraph}})
73   {
74     next unless $paragraph->{type} eq 'normal';
75     $sections{$title} .= $paragraph->{content};
76   }
77
78   foreach my $subsection (@{$section->{section}})
79   {
80     add_paragraphs($title, $subsection);
81   }
82 }
```

Listing 16.10 builds a hash table in a database to store the relationship between keywords and the sections in which they're found. Lines 34–37 open and parse a chapter file. Lines 40–45 use the %sections hash to associate the initial paragraphs in the chapter with a section called main that can be treated as the default section in display applications. Lines 17–51 do the same for each top-level section in the chapter, using the add_paragraphs subroutine to recurse through subsections and associate them with the same section. Lines 54–74 split each section into keywords and insert each keyword into the hash table. Note that the hash table is being built for the underlying data, instead of for any representation of it. The hash records only the chapter number and section name as identifiers, so search results can be used to display a section, regardless of its format.

The hash table can be used by a standard search page to quickly locate sections with requested keywords and generate links to the appropriate display pages. Listing 16.11 is an example of such a search page. It generates links to the display page from Listing 16.9.

Listing 16.11 **Search Page**

```
01 <include file="$ENV{DOCUMENT_ROOT}/templates/book.psp" />
02 <template title="Search">
03
04 <form action="search.psp" method="get">
05 <output>
06 <p>Search: 
07 <input type="text" name="search" size="30" value="$QUERY{search}" />
08  
09 <input type="submit" value="Search" /></p>
10 </output>
11 </form>
12
13 <if cond="$QUERY{search}">
14 <perl>
15 # break the search up into keywords
16 my $search_where;
17 foreach $keyword (split(/[^A-Za-z-']/,$QUERY{search}))
18 {
19   # add an OR for each keyword
20   next unless (length($keyword) > 2);
21   $search_where .= "OR keyword = '$keyword'\n";
22 }
23
24 # replace the first OR with an AND
25 if ($search_where)
26 {
27   substr($search_where,0,2) = 'AND (';
28   $search_where .= ")";
29 }
30 else
31 {
32   $search_where = "AND keyword = ''";
33 }
34 </perl>
35
36 <sql name="search" dbtype="mysql" db="test" action="query">
37 <output>
38 SELECT chapter, section, SUM(x_count) as x_count
39 FROM book_search
40 WHERE x_count IS NOT NULL
41 $search_where
42 GROUP BY chapter, section
```

```
43 ORDER BY 3 DESC, chapter
44 </output>
45 </sql>
46 <h4>Results:</h4>
47 <ul>
48 <fetch query="search" fetch="chapter, section, x_count" type="sql">
49 <perl>my $trans = $section; $trans =~ s/\s/+/g;</perl>
50 <output>
51 <li><a href="section.psp?chapter=$chapter&section=$trans">$section</a>
   ↪in $chapter</li>
52 </output>
53 </fetch>
54 </ul>
55 </if>
56 </template>
```

The form of Listing 16.11 is almost identical to the search page listed in Chapter 14, "Database-Backed Web Sites." The main difference lies in the SELECT statement in lines 38–43. This statement selects section identifiers from the book_search table, groups them by identifier to combine duplicate results, and orders the results based on the number of keyword occurrences. Other differences are found in lines 49 and 51, which format and display a link to each section specified in the search result. See the description of Listing 14.9 in Chapter 14 for a more complete description of the page. The results of a common search are shown in Figure 16.4.

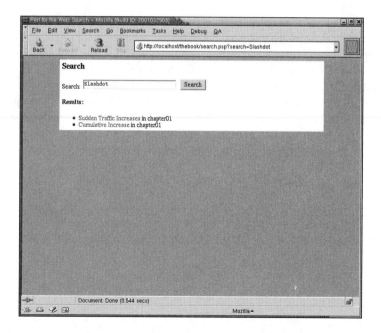

Figure 16.4 Full-text search result.

The Eminence of Paper

As useful as the Web is for retrieving information, and as useful as XML might be for storing it, paper still reigns supreme when it comes to the display of large amounts of data. Paper has high contrast, high resolution, and only as much flicker as the lighting used to illuminate it. These attributes probably will take decades to replicate with computer screens and other electronic display media. As a result, it should be expected that users will want to view text on paper for a long time to come.

If you're reading this in book format, sit down in front of a computer, pull up the Web site, and compare this to the same page on screen. (If you're reading this on the Web, by all means buy the book and make the same comparison.) Unless you have a huge screen with great resolution, you'll probably notice right off the bat that the page displays more of the book at one time than the screen does. The text also is easier to read; you'll read faster and with better comprehension out of the book than off the Web. (The Web users just skimmed past that, so they won't be offended.) On top of that, the book is more portable overall, uses less power, has a greater field of view and a higher range of operating temperatures. That's the key to paper's continued reign, and it's not likely to be beat for deep reading any time soon.

Whatever paper has in terms of readability, though, it loses when the contest is interactivity. It's not searchable. It doesn't have a place to ask questions or make comments. The code segments can't be cut and pasted into a text editor. Because of this, documents are more likely to come from an electronic source such as the Web, even though they might go straight to the printer as soon as they're found—or as soon as they're composed. The point of all this is that the same document is likely to show up both in electronic form and on paper, no matter how ephemeral the electronic form or old-fashioned the paper form. Keep this in mind when designing content for the Web, and you might end up with a site that's well-suited for both.

Summary

XML is a complex technology, but at its heart, it's just another text format for Perl to parse and represent in applications. A number of interfaces to XML have been written for Perl—from simple parsers such as XML::Simple to complex interfaces such as XML::DOM—and most are based on XML::Parser. On the Web, XML provides a solid format for content storage, and the flexible nature of XML documents enables a finer grain of control over how the content is expressed. A simple content management system can be created to provide multiple modes of expression for a given XML file, including full text searching of all or part of an XML document.

17

Publishing XML for Wireless Devices

Publishing content to wireless devices—including cell phones, Palm computers, and other personal digital assistants (PDAs)—is a good use of Extensible Markup Language (XML). Many of the data formats being adopted for these devices are defined as XML languages, and sharing document data between standard HTML-producing Web applications and new wireless applications is best done through a structured format such as XML. In addition, the data shared by these applications can be used to create new applications using much of the same code base.

Taking advantage of new content outlets requires a new way of presenting information on a site. For sites with underlying XML documents, one answer is to provide different views of the same data in a variety of formats. These views are easy to provide if a site is already using templates and persistent Perl programs. The key is to use the Web server to route incoming requests to the appropriate Web applications and to provide the full path to the requested information.

Wireless Markup Language (WML) Decks for the Wireless Web

Wireless devices would seem like a natural way to access the Web. Web-based directions, address books, and other mobile-friendly data often are needed when a computer isn't nearby, and wireless networks provide connections virtually anywhere. Unfortunately, Web access from the current generation of wireless devices is abysmal. Screens on most wireless devices are tiny, with poor resolution, no color, and few input methods. Wireless Web connections are slow, and the memory limitations of cell phones are extreme. As a result, Web pages written for display on large, colorful monitors with full keyboards and high-speed connections are likely to be unrecognizable and unusable on a wireless device.

An early answer to the wireless Web problem came in the form of the Wireless Access Protocol (WAP) and the Wireless Markup Language (WML). WAP was implemented as a low-bandwidth protocol for retrieving Web information from *WAP gateways* that provide bridges to the Web. WML is an XML language that emphasizes the tiny screen sizes and special navigation requirements of wireless devices by using a subset of the simpler formatting aspects of HTML combined with additional WAP-centric tags.

WML is set up like a deck of cards, where each *card* is an HTML-like page and cards are collected into *decks*, which are complete WML files. The cards are designed to carry screen-sized chunks of information, and decks collect related cards to reduce the wait associated with repeatedly accessing the wireless network. When accessed, each WML file is compiled into a stream of bytecode by the WAP gateway and delivered to the wireless device by the WAP protocol. The workings of the WAP protocol and the format of the bytecode are immaterial to WML site designers, however, because WAP gateways create the bridge from WAP to HTTP automatically.

WML and Future Standards

WML has had a difficult time gaining acceptance because of the restrictions imposed on it by devices and by design. For instance, WML documents are limited to a maximum size determined by the bytecode produced by the WAP gateway. In addition, because WML is an XML language, the syntax for WML files is strict. Site designers who are used to the forgiving nature of HTML browsers sometimes find it frustrating when a WAP gateway rejects their WML pages due to malformed syntax. In addition, no indication is given to the client or the server as to why the WML file was rejected, so fixing WML is usually a trial-and-error process. Listing 17.1 is a WML version of the XML table of contents in Listing 16.1 from Chapter 16, "XML and Content Management."

Listing 17.1 **Table of Contents in WML**

```
01 <?xml version="1.0"?>
02 <!DOCTYPE wml PUBLIC "-//WAPFORUM//DTD WML 1.1//EN"
03  "http://www.wapforum.org/DTD/wml_1.1.xml">
04 <wml>
05
06 <template>
07 <do type="prev" name="Prev" label="Prev">
08 <prev/>
09 </do>
10 </template>
11
12 <card id="index" title="Perl for the Web">
13 <p>Table of Contents:</p>
14 <p><a href="#c0">Introduction</a></p>
15 <p><a href="#c1">Foobar chapter</a></p>
16 <p><a href="#c2">Barbaz chapter</a></p>
17 <p><a href="#cA">Appendix A</a></p>
18 </card>
19
20 <card id="c0" title="Introduction">
21 <p><a href="c.psp/c0/s1/p0.wml">About this book</a></p>
22 <p><a href="c.psp/c0/s2/p0.wml">Conventions</a></p>
23 </card>
24
25 <card id="c1" title="Foobar chapter">
26 <p><a href="c.psp/c1/s1/p0.wml">How to Foobar</a></p>
27 <p><a href="c.psp/c1/s2/p0.wml">How to Foobaz</a></p>
28 </card>
29
30 <card id="c2" title="Barbaz chapter">
31 <p><a href="c.psp/c2/s1/p0.wml">How to Barbaz</a></p>
32 <p><a href="c.psp/c2/s2/p0.wml">When not to Barbaz</a></p>
33 </card>
34
35 <card id="cA" title="Alphabet Soup: Reference and Glossary">
36 <p><a href="c.psp/c3/s1/p0.wml">XML Bestiary</a></p>
37 <p><a href="c.psp/c3/s2/p0.wml">Specifications and
   ➥Organizations</a></p>
38 </card>
39
40 </wml>
```

The table of contents WML file in Listing 17.1 is laid out as a deck with five simple cards. The file starts by defining a template for all the cards in the deck with the <template> tag on line 06. (This <template> tag is valid WML, not a server-side tag.) The template defines a <do> tag in lines 07–09, which, in this case, sets a Prev menu option that sends the browser to the previous card viewed. The index card defined in lines 12–18 is the default card displayed and contains a top-level listing of the chapters in the table of contents. Each chapter listing is also a link to the card detailing the chapter. Line 14, for instance, is a listing named "Introduction," which points to the card named c0 that is defined in lines 20–23. Each chapter card contains a listing of chapter sections, which are hyperlinks to the associated WML files. The end result is a WML deck that enables wireless Web users to drill down through small sets of menu choices to find a specific section, as shown in Figure 17.1. In practice, this file would be generated from the original XML by a Perl script that keeps track of the relationships between cards in the deck.

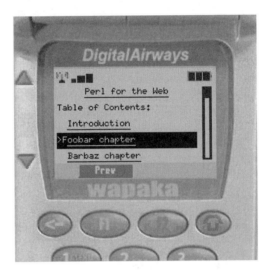

Figure 17.1 Table of contents viewed in a WAP simulator.

After WML was introduced, a competing language called iMode was developed by a NTT DoCoMo, a company that produces cell phone interfaces. Based on a subset of HTML, iMode takes a more lenient approach to wireless Web site design. iMode sites are very similar to HTML-based sites, with the caveat that iMode devices have small screens and tiny memories and only understand basic HTML tags. Unfortunately, iMode phones can't access WML sites and vice-versa; a site hoping to offer services to both would be forced to create a separate version of the service for each.

Recently, a new wireless markup standard based on the Extensible Hypertext Markup Language (XHTML) was developed and christened XHTML Basic. The idea behind XHTML Basic is to provide a language that has the familiar usage of HTML, the strict syntax of XML, and a reduced set of tags tailored to wireless devices.

XHTML Basic has already been agreed to as both the next version of iMode as well as the next version of WML. Therefore, content managers who convert site content to WML directly might find themselves with another conversion project very soon. Converting site content to an intermediate XML format might be a better choice because structured XML documents lend themselves to dynamic transformations. When used with templates, an intermediate XML format enables HTML, WML, and new standards to be presented simultaneously by the same site. See the "Multihomed Documents" section later in this chapter for more information.

Book Content for Wireless Devices

Although reading an entire book on a cell phone is not recommended, it's sometimes handy to have Web content in a form that is accessible anywhere at any time. For example, it might be useful to offer the book content from Chapter 16 in a wireless format. Luckily, the framework for this has already been set up; chapters already are segmented into individual sections and paragraphs, and a template system already has been created to provide access to the chapters through XML::Simple.

These same principles would apply for any site information from any data source offered in any text-like form, not just book content from XML files for the wireless Web. For instance, a news site such as SlashDot might want to offer headlines from its database as VoiceXML, which is an XML format used to provide voice interaction with text data. The use of templates and the persistent Perl processor still would be the same. In fact, after these techniques are developed for one XML format, very little additional work is required to adapt them to other formats over different channels.

Adding Templates for WML

As described in Chapter 16, chapters are stored in Simple Book Format (SBF) files. To produce WML files from the SBF file, a template can be used, just as it would to produce HTML output. In this case, using a template gives an additional benefit; the template can be tested on a wireless device, and all pages generated from the tested template can be assumed to work identically. Listing 17.2 is a template that sets a paragraph from the SBF chapter file into a WML card format with simple navigation. (See Listing 17.3 later in this chapter for the Perl program that processes this template.)

Listing 17.2   **SBF Paragraph to WML Template**

```
01 <tag name="wmltemplate" accepts="title, next, previous, paragraph">
02 <output>
03 <?xml version="1.0"?>
04 <!DOCTYPE wml PUBLIC "-//WAPFORUM//DTD WML 1.1//EN"
05   "http://www.wapforum.org/DTD/wml_1.1.xml">
06 <wml>
07 <card id="index" title="$title">
08
```

continues

Listing 17.2 **Continued**

```
09 <do type="prev" name="Prev" label="Prev">
10 <go href="p$previous.wml" />
11 </do>
12 <do type="options" name="Next" label="Next">
13 <go href="p$next.wml" />
14 </do>
15
16 <p>$paragraph->{content}</p>
17
18 </card>
19 </wml>
20 </output>
21 </tag>
```

The WML deck template in Listing 17.2 is laid out in a fashion similar to the table of contents deck in Listing 17.1. The template is set up using the `<tag>` tag in lines 01 and 21, which accepts variables set by the template processor. (This template also could be designed to accept the full parse tree, but processing the parse tree beforehand makes for a simpler, easier-to-test template.) Line 07 starts the card and sets the title. Lines 09–14 create two menu options for navigation, `Prev` and `Next`, which are hyperlinks to the paragraphs before and after the one displayed. Line 16 displays the paragraph contents as provided. The result is a WML file that contains a single paragraph of the book XML file, as shown in Figure 17.2.

Figure 17.2 Book paragraph viewed in a WAP simulator.

With this template and a coherent naming scheme, any chapter can be displayed paragraph by paragraph with paging provided by the `Prev` and `Next` buttons. Combined with the table of contents page and search page—which could be generated with similar templates—an entire book easily can be made available to any wireless device. Additional templates could be created after the transition to XHTML Basic is started, and updates to the underlying chapter files would be made available to all formats simultaneously.

Multihomed Documents

HTML, WML, VoiceXML, and other translations can be viewed as virtual versions of the underlying XML documents. As such, it's sometimes helpful to provide more coherent URL names to access the translated versions. A standard URL for a program-generated WML file might look like the following:

```
http://www.site.com/perl/wap.pl?file=chapter12&section=4
```

Unfortunately, the URL itself gives very little indication of the format of the resulting file. The program name `wap.pl` hints that the result might be in WML format, but it also might be in XHTML or another WAP format. In addition, the relationship between the parameter values and the result aren't easy to determine directly. If the same output came from a static file listed on the same site, it probably would have a more understandable URL:

```
http://www.site.com/wap/chapter12/section4.wml
```

This URL is both easier to decipher and easier to remember. Because site designers and some visitors use URLs to understand the structure of a site, providing a URL that resembles a static location is sometimes preferable. This becomes more prominent when different views of the same underlying data are presented via separate document URLs. Translating a URL such as this is possible using *multihomed documents*, which are documents that are processed differently based on the way they're accessed. For instance, the following URLs all access the same file:

```
http://www.site.com/thebook/chapter12.html
http://www.site.com/wap/c12/s4/p1.wml
http://www.site.com/xml/chapter12.xml
http://www.site.com/voice/chapter12/section4.vxml
```

Multihomed documents work well in situations in which data files are stored in a hierarchy that needs to be repeated in multiple formats. URL translation of this sort also enables underlying data sources to be changed while maintaining existing URLs. For instance, if a file is first offered as HTML and then changed to be generated from an XML source file, the transition can be eased by creating a multihomed document that responds to the original URL by generating the appropriate HTML output.

Uncoupling Document Names with *PATH_INFO*

Multihomed documents can be created in a number of ways, largely dependent on the Web server and Perl environment. In the simplest case, file information can be added to the end of a program URL as though the program were a directory. The additional information is passed to the program in the PATH_INFO environment variable. For instance, a program called c.psp that displays a WML file might be accessed by the following URL:

```
http://www.site.com/c.psp/c1/s1/p0.wml
```

The Web server would access the c.psp program and give it the PATH_INFO value of /c1/s1/p0.wml. This value then could be used to determine the file to process and other request information. Form variables sent through GET and POST requests still would be processed in the ordinary fashion, if present. PATH_INFO is often used to indicate an actual file on the Web server, but it can indicate any other dynamic information as well.

Book Publisher with *PATH_INFO*

To publish book contents using URL information provided through PATH_INFO, it is necessary to translate the path into a form that the program can use to locate the requested information. This might be a simple change when translating an HTML path to an XML filename, or it can require regular expressions to extract variables encoded into a readable URL. Listing 17.3 is an example of the latter and uses PATH_INFO to store the parameters for generating a WML file.

Listing 17.3   **WML Chapter Display Using *PATH_INFO***

```
01 <perl>
02 use XML::Simple ();
03
04 my ($c, $s, $p) = $ENV{PATH_INFO} =~ m{/c(.+?)/s(\d+)/p(\d+).wml};
05 $c = "0$c" unless (length($c) > 1);
06
07 my $xs = XML::Simple->new(forcearray => ['section', 'paragraph'],
08                            memshare => 1);
09 my $chapter = $xs->XMLin("$ENV{DOCUMENT_ROOT}/thebook/chapter$c.xml");
10 my ($section, $title, @paragraphs);
11
12 if ($s)
13 {
14   $section = $chapter->{section}->[$s -1];
15   $title = $section->{title};
16   @paragraphs = @{$section->{paragraph}};
17
18   add_paragraphs(\@paragraphs, $section);
19 }
20 else
```

```
21 {
22   $title = $chapter->{title};
23   @paragraphs = @{$chapter->{paragraph}};
24 }
25
26 my $paragraph = $paragraphs[$p];
27 my $next = ($p < $#paragraphs) ? ($p + 1) : 0;
28 my $previous = ($p > 0) ? ($p - 1) : $#paragraphs;
29
30 print "Content-type: text/vnd.wap.wml\n\n";
31 </perl>
32
33 <include file="$ENV{DOCUMENT_ROOT}/templates/wmlparagraph.psp" />
34
35 <output>
36 <wmltemplate title="$title" next="$next" previous="$previous"
   ⇒paragraph="$paragraph" />
37 </output>
38
39 <perl>
40 sub add_paragraphs
41 {
42   my $paragraphs = shift;
43   my $section = shift;
44
45   push (@{$paragraphs}, @{$section->{paragraph}});
46
47   foreach my $subsection (@{$section->{section}})
48   {
49     add_paragraphs($paragraphs, $subsection);
50   }
51 }
52 </perl>
```

The majority of the code in Listing 17.3 finds a specified paragraph within a specified section within a specified chapter. These specified values come from the PATH_INFO environment variable, as extracted in line 04. The regular expression in Line 04 searches for the numeric parts of the path information—preceded by c, s, and p designators—and assigns the values to the $c, $s, and $p variables, respectively. Line 05 makes sure that the number in $c is in the same format as those used to designate the chapter files. Line 09 parses the requested chapter file, and lines 12–24 load the requested section's paragraphs into the @paragraphs array. Line 26 chooses the requested paragraph, and lines 27 and 28 set the numbers of the previous and next paragraphs, wrapping around if necessary. Line 30 sets the proper content type for the WML file, and line 33 calls the template specified in Listing 17.2.

Adding Directory Processors

In most cases, using the URL of the program as the base URL of the multihomed document isn't an ideal solution. This is especially true when the program is being used to replace a set of static files with the output of dynamic translations. The solution in these cases is to make the program a *directory processor*, which is a program that handles all requests to a particular directory or file type. The Web server provides the file path as a `PATH_INFO` variable to the program specified as the processor for that directory. For instance, the following URLs would both receive the same response if the `/thebook/c.psp` program were defined as the processor for the `/wap` directory:

```
http://www.site.com/thebook/c.psp/wap/c1/s2/p0.wml
http://www.site.com/wap/c1/s2/p0.wml
```

The procedure for setting up directory processors varies depending on the Web server being used. Version 1.3 of Apache Server, for instance, uses the `Action` and `SetHandler` directives in the `httpd.conf` configuration file to specify a directory processor. For instance, to set up the relationship used in the URLs in the previous code example, the following could be added to the `httpd.conf` file:

```
Action wap-chapter /thebook/c.psp
<Location "/wap">
SetHandler wap-chapter
</Location>
```

The `Action` directive assigns the `wap-chapter` identifier to the program located at the `/thebook/c.psp` virtual file. Note that this location can be any kind of program, including persistent Common Gateway Interface (CGI)-style programs and templated programs using HTML::Mason or Perl Server Pages (PSP). The `SetHandler` directive then can be used in any new or existing Location or Directory block. The Location block is used for virtual locations and the Directory block is used for translated file paths within the file system.

WML Revisited

Multihomed documents suit WML and wireless devices for a number of reasons. First, multihomed documents make it possible to compress the URL identifier for a specific page down to the absolute minimum of characters. Because the WAP protocol defines an upper limit to page size, any effort to reduce the overall size of a page is worthwhile. With a multihomed document, the first hyperlink in the following code (from a file at `/wap/c12/s2/p0.wml`, for instance) can be replaced with the second hyperlink, which is a dramatic improvement over an already-short URL:

```
<go href="c.psp?c=12&s=2&p=1" />
<go href="p1.wml" />
```

In addition, WML presents a taste of the kind of challenges Web application developers will face in the future. Web programmers don't want to write the same applications over and over again for different types of browsers, so a facility that enables multiple views into the same data might provide a more reusable approach to application design. For wireless devices, a version of the site can be provided for WML 1.1, WML 1.2, iMode, and XHTML Basic without having to update each version separately. With such a simple change in focus comes a great deal more freedom from the vagaries of standards.

Summary

Wireless devices pose a special problem for Web application designers. Their requirements are strictly defined, but the standards to which they adhere are likely to change. The solution is to create an interface that can be decoupled from the underlying data so that it can be recreated as new standards come available. Templates, XML documents, and flexible Perl programs can be used to generate today's WML files using the same XML documents used by existing Web applications. Tomorrow's standards and more can be addressed by creating multiple windows into the same data in a variety of formats and adding templates as necessary to support more.

18

XML as a B2B Interface

BEYOND CONTENT MANAGEMENT, EXTENSIBLE MARKUP LANGUAGE (XML) has gained notoriety as a base protocol for business-to-business (B2B) integration efforts. XML enables business data to be encoded in a format that is both cross-platform and easily standardized. XML works well as a cross-platform protocol because it is a text format with Unicode support, which makes it readable by any platform with any character set. Standards can be created for languages based on XML by developing a Document Type Definition (DTD), an XML Schema, or a sample document for the specification. This enables businesses to describe their interfaces in terms of a named standard—the purchasing language cXML, for instance—instead of defining a custom interface for each business relationship.

Perl is an excellent language for implementing B2B interfaces because the process usually involves text processing, network interaction, and systems integration, which are three of Perl's strongest areas. Perl already connects to many common information systems, including most databases. Additional systems can be accessed by Perl programs through a number of local and network-based interfaces, including sockets and component layers such as COM and CORBA. In addition, existing Web interfaces are good candidates for B2B integration with Perl because most of the work of integrating back-end systems already has been done.

Early XML-based B2B interfaces were developed for specific partner relationships, but companies and organizations soon realized that the cost of implementing a new interface for each partner was prohibitive, even using XML. Custom interfaces are giving way to generalized interface protocols such as XML for Remote Process Calls (XML-RPC) and Simple Object Access Protocol (SOAP), which offer better integration with existing software models. These generic interfaces also hold the promise of true interface automation, which should lead to more robust interfaces.

B2B Examples

With all the hype surrounding the Internet, e-commerce, and the new economy, it's amazing how many businesses still interact using low-tech methods. High-tech companies on the cutting edge are no exception—many times the fulfillment process for e-commerce orders consists of an employee printing and faxing the order to a supplier. Automation tends to stop at the door. Therefore, many processes outside the core business still start with hand entry and end with a printed confirmation. Many of these processes could benefit from B2B integration, regardless of whether the relationship is between businesses, organizations, or private users. When implemented in a standardized way, B2B integration promises to be as great an improvement in automated partner interactions as the Web was for user interactions.

B2B interaction takes many forms. Standards have been developed for many B2B-related XML languages, and more are in development. Business processes can be connected to each other directly, or they can interact through a trading floor. Web content can be distributed through B2B-style interfaces, as can other syndicated content.

Trading Floors

Trading floors are centralized repositories of XML documents, usually designed to provide generic interactions between a number of trading partners at the same time. Trading floors might be run by a company such as Ariba, which consolidates connections between businesses and their suppliers, or they might be implemented by information consolidators such as SourceForge.

Connecting to a trading floor with Perl is a job that can be tackled using existing modules. Trading floors usually have a specific set of XML standards that they support. Thus, all interaction with the trading floor has to be conducted using those languages. When a language is provided, modules such as XML::DOM or Orchard can be used to create, read, or modify documents for the interface. Modules such as LWP can be used if the trading floor uses HTTP or FTP network protocols, or custom protocols can be implemented using the IO::Socket::INET module. Local information can be gathered from the DBI modules. For even easier integration, document samples provided by the trading floor can be imported into Document Object Model (DOM) or Orchard structures as templates and local data can be added to them.

Creating a trading floor in Perl can be done just as easily. In fact, a trading floor in XML can be handled using templates, embedded programming, and a persistent environment—just as a Web site would. Persistent Perl is capable of handling the high traffic necessary for automating interactions between all the clients of a trading floor. Templates also can be used to implement new interfaces that enable clients to use their preferred tools. Translation from one interface style to another—between the cXML and CBL purchasing languages, for instance—can be provided as an additional service. All the logging, security, and customer service issues that pertain to a robust Web site pertain to a trading floor as well. Thus, it makes sense for both to use similar tools.

Early trading floors have had mixed success. Many trading floor operators have found that their potential clients need technical assistance getting their own systems integrated, let alone integrated with their partners. XML is an ideal language for structured communication, but many businesses have little or no expertise in using XML tools. Fortunately, Perl can help with this. Trading floor proprietors can implement lightweight Perl servers at client sites to serve as a bridge between client systems and the trading floor. Costs can be kept down by using inexpensive hardware and the open-source LAMP architecture—Linux, Apache, MySQL, and Perl.

Web Site Content Mirrors

An application of B2B interfaces that might not be obvious is the mirroring of Web sites and other Internet content. Companies such as Akamai and Digital Island offer services that spread Web site content around the Internet so that a high-speed connection always is available between a site visitor and a content mirror. Similar mirroring systems are used to deliver popular software—the Comprehensive Perl Archive Network (CPAN) itself is mirrored around the world. Common to all mirroring systems is the capability to transfer as little data as possible to reduce the network load on the central server. To this end, mirroring systems usually break Web pages into sections that can be reconstituted on the mirrored site.

Because existing mirroring schemes usually require a specialized interface, some improvement might be gained by implementing a generic XML interface to mirror content on remote sites. If a site is designed to use a set of XML files as core data, the files can be transferred from a central server to mirrors around the world. The mirror sites then can use templates to localize the content and integrate it with other mirrored content. Using XML as a data transfer language also enables mirror sites to provide dynamic content, including searchable databases. Databases can be synchronized by using an XML interface to transfer records that have been modified since the last update.

Content Syndication

Mirrors aren't the only way in which content gets reused. Traditional content syndication services, such as Reuters and Associated Press, offer news feeds to news sites around the Web. In addition, Web sites such as Freshmeat, PlanetOut, and Space.com have syndicated their content feeds to other Web sites. Many additional types of Web sites would benefit greatly from syndicating their content, using the syndicated content from other sites, or both. For instance, a company that produces electric cars might benefit from syndicated news about its cars from news sites or reliability reports from consumer sites. Those sites might benefit from updated pricing, availability, and release information about the cars. In other cases, open syndication—providing raw XML versions of site content—might be preferred. For instance, SlashDot offers its latest headlines in an XML format to encourage the development of desktop applications that display its content. Any site looking to build consistent traffic streams might benefit from a similar approach.

Perl and XML make content syndication as easy as creating or using local XML files. XML from syndication servers can be transferred to local storage using a scheduled process, or it can be gathered in real time through the LWP module. Caching algorithms can be implemented on the target sites to provide near-real-time updates without the problem of local storage. Templates then can be created to provide a layer of abstraction between site design and the underlying network protocols.

The real key to widespread content syndication is standards. If a new interface to content doesn't have to be created for each relationship between source and target sites, more sites can syndicate content from a wider group of sources. Standardized XML formats for content distribution will give rise to specialized Perl modules for accessing the content in the same way that XML's standard structure gave rise to modules such as XML::Simple. If content syndication interfaces become common enough that they require little effort to implement, more Web sites will benefit from content that is already available.

Implementations with XML-RPC

In 1998, Dave Winer of Userland (http://www.userland.com) developed a method for calling procedures on remote machines and returning the results in an XML format. His idea was to use existing Internet protocols—TCP/IP, HTTP, and XML—to pass messages back and forth from the client to the server. The result was XML-RPC, which is a specification that enables arbitrary method calls to be invoked with a standard set of arguments. The specification covers message structures, standard data types, and error handling.

XML-RPC has seen limited use, as compared to the more robust SOAP protocol, mainly because of the third-party support SOAP has gained since the two were developed. SOAP is designed to be applicable to a wider array of circumstances, but it is a much more complex protocol as a result. XML-RPC has a simpler specification and a much narrower set of implementation possibilities. As a result, in many circumstances, it's possible to implement an equivalent XML-RPC interface with simpler tools and less expertise.

Remote Procedure Calls (RPC)

An RPC is a method that is called on a class residing on another server. It's directly analogous to the kinds of calls that can be made on Perl modules, including a named method that takes parameters and returns a simple result. For instance, a class called `headlines` might provide a method called `getHeadlineTitle`, which takes the name of a magazine as a string argument and returns an article title as a string result. In XML-RPC, the method request and its associated response might look like the following:

```
<methodCall>
 <methodName>headlines.getHeadlineTitle</methodName>
 <params>
  <param><value><string>PerlWeek</string></value></param>
 </params>
</methodCall>

<methodResponse>
 <params>
  <param><value><string>Sites that Bite</string></value></param>
 </params>
</methodResponse>
```

The method call is contained in a `<methodCall>` tag, which in turn contains a `<methodName>` tag containing the name of the class and method being invoked on the remote server. Arguments to the method are contained in a `<params>` tag, with each argument represented by a `<param>` tag containing a data type tag and the parameter value. In this case, the parameter is a string containing `PerlWeek`, but a parameter can be an arbitrarily complex construct made up of a number of data types.

The data types enabled by XML-RPC should be familiar to Perl programmers—with a few additions. The `string` and `int` data types correspond to most scalars that a Perl program uses. Perl doesn't distinguish between string variables and various possible classes of numeric variables, but variables can be processed to test whether they are the correct type, if necessary. The `array` data type corresponds directly to Perl arrays, and the `struct` data type in XML-RPC is like a hash variable in Perl. XML-RPC does not include data types for use as variable references, but both `struct` and `array` parameters can include recursive `struct` and `array` types as values.

The response to a method call is contained in a `<methodResponse>` tag, which contains a similar `<params>` tag to hold result values. The `<methodResponse>` tag also can contain a `<fault>` tag with an error definition if problems were encountered during processing.

Exposing XML-RPC Interfaces

The Frontier::RPC2 module, a Perl interface to the XML-RPC protocol, was developed by Ken MacLeod in response to the XML-RPC specification. (The "2" refers to the second iteration of the protocol—the first was developed for a server product called Frontier and simply labeled "RPC.") Frontier::RPC2 provides a number of methods for encoding Perl data structures into an XML-RPC request or response message. However, most interaction with the module occurs through the Client and Daemon modules included with the package.

An XML-RPC client can be implemented through the Frontier::Client module. Calls to Frontier::Client are simple and use an object-oriented structure. A client object is created with the URL of the XML-RPC server specified, and the `call` method is used to call a specified method with an array of arguments. Arguments might take the form of Perl scalars, arrays, or hashes, all of which are translated into the corresponding XML-RPC data types. Alternately, the arguments might be special XML-RPC data types, such as `boolean` or `double`, that can be created using Frontier::Client object methods of the same names. The response from a `call` method is returned as either an implicitly-translated Perl variable or a data type object that can be translated explicitly using a `value` method.

An XML-RPC server is implemented using the Frontier::Daemon module. The implementation is simple; XML-RPC methods are mapped to Perl subroutines using a hash specified when the Frontier::Daemon object is instantiated. The module converts incoming requests into subroutine calls with the appropriate parameters and converts the returned result into an XML-RPC response.

Implementations with SOAP

Another RPC interface that has seen widespread use is SOAP. SOAP was developed by Microsoft, IBM, Userland, and a host of other companies and organizations. SOAP was originally an offshoot of the same project that spawned XML-RPC, but it since has grown into a full World Wide Web Consortium (W3C) specification. Support for SOAP has either been developed, or is in development for, Java, C, Visual Basic, Python, and Perl.

Microsoft has enough faith in SOAP to make it a core part of its .NET initiative, which is hoped to become a platform for true distributed computing over the Internet. SOAP was originally a Microsoft project, but it has been adopted as a standard by so many other companies and organizations that it has taken on an independent meaning outside the .NET initiative. If standards are adhered to, SOAP clients and servers are likely to become the next big wave of Internet activity.

SOAP::Lite

Perl support for the SOAP protocol is provided by the SOAP::Lite module written by Paul Kulchenko. Like XML::Simple, SOAP::Lite provides an XML interface without the need to program around the peculiarities of XML. It translates Perl structures into SOAP *envelopes*, which are SOAP messages containing routing and format information as well as method calls and serialized data. SOAP::Lite also handles most aspects of SOAP network connections, including compatibility layers for the slight differences in current SOAP server implementations.

SOAP implements data types similar to those used by XML-RPC, and a slew of additional data types. SOAP data types come mostly from the XML Schema specification, which defines simple types, such as strings, as well as complex types. In addition, XML Schema provides a method for declaring custom SOAP data types for a specific request, which enables complex structures to be defined and reused throughout a collection of SOAP services.

A SOAP::Lite Server

Although SOAP messages are designed to be the same for both request and response, SOAP::Lite is implemented in two parts: a client and a server. The server accepts SOAP requests and creates a result based on Perl modules provided to the SOAP::Lite module. Listing 18.1 is an example of a SOAP-based headline server implemented using SOAP::Lite's Common Gateway Interface (CGI)-style server.

Listing 18.1   **Simple SOAP::Lite Headline Server**

```
01 #!/usr/bin/perl -w
02 use strict;
03 use SOAP::Transport::HTTP;
04
05 SOAP::Transport::HTTP::CGI
06  -> dispatch_to('Headlines')
07  -> handle;
08
09
10 package Headlines;
11
12 sub get_headline
13 {
14   my $class = shift;
15   my $source = shift;
16
17   my %headlines =
18   (
19     'Slashdot' => {title => 'Perl Causes Warts',
20           url => 'http://www.slashdot.org/',
21           synopsis => 'Jon Katz uncovers a Perl scandal.'},
22     'PerlWeek' => {title => 'SOAP and You',
```

continues

Listing 18.1   **Continued**

```
23          url  => 'http://www.perlweek.com/',
24          synopsis => 'An overview of the personal impact.'},
25  );
26
27  return $headlines{$source};
28 }
```

Lines 03–07 of Listing 18.1 are the core of the SOAP interface. Line 03 loads the
SOAP::Transport::HTTP module—a part of the SOAP::Lite bundle that implements
the HTTP interfaces. Line 05 starts the call to the SOAP::Transport::HTTP::CGI
class, line 06 calls the `dispatch_to` method, and line 07 calls the `handle` method to
handle the incoming request. `dispatch_to` is used to declare classes that are made
available to the SOAP::Lite server. In this case, the `Headlines` package defines all the
methods available to SOAP requests. Other packages and modules could be added to
the `dispatch_to` parameters to provide multiple classes, and package directories can be
specified as well.

Lines 10–28 of Listing 18.1 define the simple package `Headlines`, which has one
subroutine, `get_headline`. The `get_headline` subroutine takes one argument and
returns a hash reference with keys for the `title`, `url`, and `synopsis` of an article. When
the server receives a SOAP request destined for the program in Listing 18.1,
SOAP::Lite does the following:

- Deserializes the request from a SOAP envelope into a usable format
- Determines which class the request is being called against (`Headlines`)
- Calls the subroutine (`get_headline`) corresponding to the SOAP method
- Serializes the result (a reference to a hash containing article details) into a SOAP
  response envelope

SOAP is a protocol that can be used over many transports, including HTTP, FTP, and
POP3/SMTP. SOAP::Lite correspondingly provides a transport class for each transport. In addition, SOAP::Lite provides a number of different servers for use in a Web
context, including a mod_perl server, an Apache module, a CGI-style server, and a
standalone server that implements its own network daemon.

A SOAP::Lite Client

SOAP::Lite clients connect to SOAP servers and process server methods with Perl
data types given as arguments. Listing 18.2 is an example of a SOAP-based headline
display client designed to be incorporated into a dynamic Perl Server Pages (PSP) page.

Listing 18.2   **Simple SOAP::Lite Headline Client**

```
01 <tag name="headline" accepts="source">
02
03 <perl>
04 use SOAP::Lite +autodispatch =>
05   uri   => 'http://localhost/Headlines',
06   proxy => 'http://localhost/cgi-bin/headlines.cgi';
07
08 my $h = Headlines->get_headline($source);
09 </perl>
10
11 <output>
12 <p><b><a href="$h->{url}">$h->{title}</a></b>
13 <br />$h->{synopsis}</p>
14 </output>
15
16 </tag>
```

Line 01 of Listing 18.2 declares a PSP tag called `headlines` that accepts an attribute called `$source`. Lines 04–06 set up the SOAP::Lite interface. Line 04 invokes the `autodispatch` feature of SOAP::Lite, which treats remote classes as though they are local Perl modules. Line 05 declares the name of the object being called on the server, which generally is defined by the server itself. In this case, the namespace is `http://localhost/Headlines` because the `Headlines` class is being called from the server at `localhost`. Line 06 declares the endpoint of the SOAP server, which, in this case, is the URL at which the server program can be found.

Line 08 calls the `get_headline` method of the `Headlines` class from the server, which was defined in Listing 18.1. This class and method would be called in exactly the same way, no matter how it was implemented. The deserialized result of the `get_headline` method is saved to the variable `$h`. Lines 11–14 display the results as though `$h` were any other Perl hash reference. The tag created by this definition could then be called from any PSP page:

```
<headlines source="PerlWeek" />
```

As line 08 of Listing 18.2 illustrates, SOAP servers can be used in a Perl program as though they were repositories of Perl modules. For e-commerce systems, this provides a novel way to implement functions such as credit-card authorization, shipping calculations, and any other library functions that need a simple interface to remote systems. Eventually, interfaces to common services can be created by providers in the same way that Web sites are created. These *Web services* provide a standardized, distributed set of functions that can be incorporated into any network-enabled application. (See Chapter 19, "Web Services," for more applications of this idea.)

Paul Kulchenko

One of Perl's strongest aspects is the community that surrounds it, especially the many people who contribute updates, fixes, and new modules. The Perl community has shown time and again that it can write excellent software as a group without needing a controlling corporation to drive the process. If there's a single shining example of the community that makes Perl a robust language, it's Paul Kulchenko. In SOAP::Lite, Paul created a module that exemplifies the simplicity, flexibility, and intuitiveness of Perl. Above all, he wrote it single-handedly.

The SOAP interface originally developed for Perl was awful. It was complex, half-finished, and it didn't do its job. That's really the worst a Perl module can do. I first ran across it when I was tasked with adding SOAP capabilities to an XML product. I had looked over the SOAP protocol and was suitably confused by it. So, I was hoping for a simple, easy-to-implement SOAP module that would abstract away most of the extraneous aspects of SOAP so that I could concentrate on the connection to my server. Unfortunately, what I found was a module that was unusable—literally. It would fail when invoked with use SOAP. Ordinarily, this would be an excuse to dive under the hood and make my own fixes, but the code in the SOAP module was difficult to follow. I finally gave up on it and decided to write my own.

I was only a few days into my own SOAP module when I heard about SOAP::Lite. Paul Kulchenko had noticed the abysmal state of the SOAP module as well, and decided as I did to start fresh with a simpler implementation. Paul's module was truly simple to use, and I was able to implement the interface I needed using a very early version of it—version 0.36, I believe. Since then, Paul has added a host of new features—all of which work beautifully—in response to user requests. His module has been cited as the epitome of SOAP implementations, and it's given Perl a leg up on the SOAP-based landscape of the next generation Web. I just hope that Paul gets suitably rewarded for his efforts and that more Perl enthusiasts like him follow in his footsteps.

Summary

Perl and XML provide a good infrastructure for building B2B interfaces between business partners and other organizations. The possibilities for B2B integration are endless—purchase cycles, content mirrors, and content syndication are just three of them. Custom B2B interaction languages can be created, or a standard such as XML-RPC or SOAP can be used to integrate RPCs from remote machines as though they were local Perl modules.

19

Web Services

T HE NEXT GENERATION OF BUSINESS–TO–BUSINESS (B2B) interfaces will come with an improved set of standards and more automated development. As this book is being written, standards such as Simple Object Access Protocol (SOAP), Web Services Description Language (WSDL), and Universal Description, Discovery, and Integration (UDDI) promise to change the way automated transactions are performed. These particular standards might not be the ones that form the backbone of the next-generation Web, but the solution they represent definitely will. There's too much information on the Web to program interfaces by hand and create custom interfaces for each partnership. Automation for Web processes is needed, and the model that will make it happen is called *Web services*.

In fact, the Web services model extends past business interfaces to encompass all types of automated network interactions. Within the existing "Web browsing" model, Web sites are seen as distinct locations visited directly by users with the intent to browse through available documents. The assumption is that a user takes a single path through a single site; thus, no interactions between multiple paths or sites are necessary. It's also assumed that a site contains all the information needed to display the proper documents to the user. For instance, the Travelocity site might retain seat preference information for a particular user, but that information had to be entered by the user at that same site. The user can't indicate that the Travelocity Web site should visit the Expedia site to get the required information.

With a Web services model, all programs are given access to the documents and interfaces provided by a site, and both the parameters and the results are encoded in a way that programs can understand without human interaction. This means that both client and server programs can get the information they need from Web services, even if a server program is accessing a Web service to process a request to its own Web service. For example, the Travelocity Web site might indicate to a browser that it needs information about seat preference. The user could indicate that the information is accessible through the Expedia site's preferences Web service. Better yet, a personal travel agent program on the user's computer could contact the Travelocity Web service directly to book a flight and then provide information from an escrow agency's Web service as input. With automated services such as these, sites can be linked into chains to perform useful tasks with as little user input as possible. In fact, the process can be taken over by automated systems like in-dash Global Positioning System (GPS) computers, which have the computing power and network connections necessary to access simplified Web services.

A Traveler's Story

It's late, and you're tired. You've been driving all day and most of the night, and you're starting to lose track of exactly where you are. The GPS claims you're still heading in the right direction, but you don't know this stretch of road from any other stretch in this godforsaken backwater.

Trippy has been a busy boy. He's been monitoring the Driver's current position and speed, running up ahead to check road conditions, and sniffing around to see if there are any factoids about the countryside that the Driver is currently traversing. There isn't much on the Net about this area, and the few things he's been able to find come up empty after parsing them against the Driver's preferences. Oh well, there's always more to find.

Just a few hours more. You thought you'd make good time on this trip, but you haven't been driving for more than 14 hours and already you're tired. You even stopped for dinner, so make that 13 hours on the road. Still tired, though.

It's ten o'clock and your eyes are drooping. The road's getting blurry and you almost missed that last curve. You really should get some rest. "All right," you say, giving in at last. "Trippy, where's the nearest hotel with a vacancy?"

The Driver gave a command, and Trippy takes a few milliseconds to figure out what he might possibly mean. ALICE has a pretty narrow idea of the possibilities, so Trippy figures that the Driver would like a room according to his Travelocity profile in a hotel that resides somewhere within a few minutes' driving distance from the next half-hour stretch of his route. "I'll check," he responds to the Driver.

Trippy checks a directory site and the usual group of travel portals, compiles a list of hotels within the zip codes the Driver is currently approaching, and sorts them based on their distance from the route. He queries the first twenty hotel sites to check for vacancies and prices and rules out those that don't have available rooms in the Driver's price range. A few sites don't respond to Trippy at all, so he rules them out after a few seconds as well.

Trippy takes this new list and sorts the rooms by their ratings as listed on the Fodor's, Let's Go, and Lonely Planet sites. Unrated rooms drop off the list. Trippy creates a knowledge tree of the top five, plots the potential course changes, and updates the driver.

Three seconds after you asked, the GPS tells you it found something. "There's a Travelodge nearby with rooms available for $78 per night," it says in its Stephen Hawking voice. That sounds good, but you could swear you saw a sign for $69.95 a couple exits back. Or was that a couple hours ago?

You ask, "Is there anything cheaper?"

The smarmy GPS immediately fires back, "There's a U-Pay Moto Tel not far from here that has rooms available for $56 per night. Its reputation is poor."

Fine, whatever. "Reserve the Travelodge," you say. Anything that gets you out of this car and into a clean bed is just fine.

Trippy whirls into action again. The route is changed to reflect the new stop. He queries the Travelocity site to make sure it can reserve a room on short notice. It can, so he makes the reservation using the Driver's cryptocard identification and his default Travelocity profile.

You pull up to the Travelodge after an eternal fifteen minutes of drooping eyelids and loud music. "You are zero miles from your next stop," the GPS chimes happily. Duh.

The night desk clerk looks about as awake as you are, but he gives you a room key as soon as you show ID. You are about to go up to your room when your stomach grumbles. It's been a while. You go back to the lobby, past the night desk, and out the door. You can't help but feel a little dependent as you open the car door and start the engine.

"Anything to eat around here?"

Automation: The Holy Grail

A technology such as the Trippy GPS computer sounds like something out of the Jetsons, but all the information necessary to create the exchange is already present on today's World Wide Web (WWW). Travelocity and other travel sites keep profiles of customer preferences. Sites such as Yahoo! can search for a business by its location. Many hotel companies have sites for information and reservations, and even small bed-and-breakfast hotels are developing their own. In addition, all the client technologies—voice interaction, GPS navigation, and in-dash computing—are well-defined and in production use. A system could be put together using today's tools, such as IBM's ViaVoice, the ALICE natural-language interface, and standard car-computing hardware.

The only part of this picture that's truly lacking is the automation necessary to bring the information from the network into the client technologies. Clients to access the Web are plentiful, but most Web information is in a form that's suitable only for visual browsing by a human using one of a narrow set of browsers. Rendering most Web pages on an alternative browser is a difficult task, as is extracting relevant data from the Web programmatically. Trying to feed information from the current

Travelocity or Travelodge sites into a voice computer is hard enough—getting that system to automatically sort through possibilities and present the best option would be nearly impossible. The problem, of course, lies with HTML.

The Problem with HTML

HTML provides a good interface for human-computer interaction. It's a language originally designed to facilitate communication through documents that are easy to read and easy to compose. Since then, HTML has become the de facto interface description standard on the WWW. HTML-formatted interfaces have been developed for business applications, games, directories, and a host of other information systems.

Automating interactions with a Web site would seem like a trivial matter. These interfaces are available through standard Internet protocols, so any computer with TCP/IP networking would have the capability to connect. A multitude of Perl modules are available to help connect to sites, send requests, and retrieve results. As a result, it is trivial to write a Perl program that simulates a user when connecting to Web interfaces.

However, HTML as it's used by Web interfaces is a terrible way to encode data for automated use. Its structure is loosely defined and geared more toward the display of arbitrary text information than the storage of data. HTML is designed to be a formatting and display language, and it is modeled more on word processing document formats than data encoding formats. An HTML document can contain all the information relevant to a task, but it's likely to be stored in a format that is more readable by humans than programs. All a typical browser can do is display the text and graphics specified in the HTML file, so automated programs have no standard way of extracting the information that a Web interface might return.

Screen Scrapers

Extracting data encoded in HTML pages is a difficult and time-consuming task, even for a person sitting in front of a visual browser. Anyone who has tried to copy data from an HTML table or source code listing into another program has run across the problem—data displayed on screen isn't necessarily being represented the same way in the HTML file. Usually, the user ends up having to copy and paste individual parts of the browser display to arrange them properly in another application.

An automated program that performs the equivalent of these steps on an HTML file is called a screen scraper because it "scrapes" the important information out of the file based on how it would render to a visual browser on screen. Screen scrapers normally have to make educated guesses about where in the HTML file a particular piece of data might be. They often are coded by hand to specify the usual location of data in relation to surrounding text.

In Perl, screen scrapers usually are implemented using regular expressions. An HTML file in this situation is seen as simply a large text value to be searched for patterns. Any HTML formatting that might be present usually is ignored. A more structured interface such as HTML::Parser is rarely used because most Web pages don't contain enough valid structure to be parsed meaningfully by HTML::Parser, and the structure of the resulting document might vary widely depending on tags that are otherwise ignored by visual browsers. If HTML tags are taken into account, it's usually to provide an example of the text surrounding a value sought by the screen scraper. For instance, a screen scraper might want the values from the following HTML text:

```
<p><b>Eric Hedstrom</b> has a many fine desert panoramas at his
site, <a href="http://jacinto.yi.org/">Jacinto</a>.
```

The name of the site's owner would be searched for in an area bracketed by <b> and </b> tags, while the URL and name of the site would be found between the href attribute and the trailing </a> tag, separated by the characters ">. Writing a regular expression to gather these values requires the assumption that the basic formatting of the site will not change. Unfortunately, the format of a site normally changes almost as rapidly as screen scrapers can be developed. Thus, these information gatherers present only a temporary solution.

Beyond Screen Scrapers

Screen scrapers are only a stopgap designed to provide compatibility when no other means of gathering the same information is available. No business or organization could possibly build an information infrastructure on such an unstable and labor-intensive interface. In addition, the overhead of processing excess formatting to extract needed information can be extreme. In some cases, a program might need to search through HTML files hundreds of times larger than the information it ends up extracting. In addition, full-text searches of this nature tend to require the least efficient search methods.

Historically, the only alternatives to screen scrapers were customized interfaces that reduced the uncertainty of processing transmissions. Companies such as CyberCash that interacted with many e-commerce sites on a variety of platforms had to create custom software for each platform to interact with their servers. These systems were reliable after they were developed, but new development was difficult enough to discourage rapid adoption, and a different proprietary protocol had to be used for each service provider. In an effort to provide standards, formats such as the Electronic Data Interchange (EDI) were developed. They used a fixed and standardized file format. However, these formats tended to be tailored to screen-scraper-like processing, and new development was still difficult and labor-intensive.

With Extensible Markup Language (XML) and the wide adoption of Internet protocols, the idea of combining HTML-like formatting simplicity with robust Internet security and stock Web software began to emerge. XML provides the potential for data storage formats that are legible to humans and easily readable by programs. In addition, XML formats can be transported over any number of existing Internet networking protocols, which enables programmers to use all the security features and server software already available for those protocols. As XML-based automation standards such as XML for Remote Process Calls (XML-RPC) and SOAP take hold, the goal of truly automating network interactions gets even closer.

SOAP and Web Services

SOAP provides a good alternative to the cluttered, unstructured data returned by most Web sites. Aspects of the protocol specification that are unlikely to change from one interface to the next are rigidly defined, but the protocol still enables a wide range of data constructs to be passed in a SOAP envelope. With the SOAP protocol and existing Web architecture, it's possible to create interfaces to Web information systems that require little custom programming. Because these interfaces also can be described using the same framework and no outside negotiation, they are the closest yet to being truly automated.

These automated interfaces to networked systems are called Web services. The Web services model combines the easy implementations of Web servers with the structured XML data of the SOAP protocol. The idea is to provide a Web service interface for every aspect of a business or organization and then publish complete descriptions of the interface to directories of similar Web services. Clients wishing to use a Web service then can browse the directory, find Web services that match their needs, and implement the services automatically. Thus, custom interface programming and specific partnership agreements give way to a Web-wide infrastructure the same way that custom networks gave way to the Internet.

Existing Web Services

Many Web services already are available, and sites that collect them into coherent directories have started to appear. XMethods (`http://www.xmethods.com`) and XMLToday (`http://www.xmltoday.com`) are sites geared toward SOAP enthusiasts, so many of the Web services listed are of an experimental nature. These sites host the service description for each Web service, but they also offer details on how to use the Web service in a client application. Some services even include sample programs implementing the service description as a client—many written in Perl using SOAP::Lite. Adding these services to an existing program is likely to get even easier as description standards become more widely used. See the "WSDL and UDDI" section later in this chapter for more information.

In the future, many Internet-savvy businesses are likely to implement SOAP interfaces to their service offerings. Early candidates include shipping companies, such as FedEx and UPS, who probably will provide their shipping services through SOAP as well as their existing custom interfaces. Document consolidation services also are likely to be early adopters of the Web services model. Examples include job posting boards such as Monster.com and Dice.com that process thousands of job postings, resume listings, and match requests daily. A set of Web services for common functions—posting a resume or getting details about an available position—would be of use both to users of the site and other sites with similar data. An additional standard could be developed even on top of SOAP to specifically suit the types of Web services these sites would offer.

Exposing Systems as Web Services

The core of a Web service is the set of SOAP interfaces it implements. Each interface is defined in terms of an object to which it's attached, a method that it implements, and the parameters that it accepts and emits. For instance, a SOAP interface to log into a job posting site might be implemented as a method called `getLoginToken` attached to an object called `Jobs`. The `getLoginToken` method might accept parameters called `username` and `password` and return a parameter called `token`. The method would be one of many implemented as part of the `Jobs` object, which together would make up the full Web service.

In Perl, SOAP::Lite is the preferred tool for implementing SOAP interfaces. SOAP::Lite enables each SOAP method to be defined as a subroutine with either named or unnamed parameters used as the arguments for the method. SOAP objects are represented as Perl modules, so the process for creating a full Web service would follow the standard procedures for creating modules in Perl. For instance, the `Jobs` object mentioned could be created using SOAP::Lite and a module named `Jobs.pm`, with subroutines named `getLoginToken` and so on. SOAP::Lite handles most thorny data serialization problems, so object references, session variables, and authorization tokens all can be implemented in a Perlish fashion.

When deciding how to implement a Web service for an existing HTML-based project, consider the work that already has been performed. If existing Web interfaces can be wrapped in a set of subroutines, considerable effort can be avoided. Form variables can be serialized easily into method parameters, and method names can be derived from existing page names, if necessary. Most of the work then would lie in encoding the output in a SOAP-friendly format rather than in an HTML-formatted page.

After creation, Web services can be reused also as the back end of a standard Web site. Object methods created for use with SOAP::Lite can be used with local Perl programs as well, so it's possible to encapsulate all the logic of a site in the object modules and use them with both. This reduces the job of the Web site designers to simply translating form requests into method calls and formatting the results using HTML templates.

Clustering Methods Usefully

Of course, Web services shouldn't follow the same conventions as Perl object methods simply because the interfaces can be connected automatically. Many object methods are defined for use by programmers with intimate knowledge of the interfaces they define. Simply exposing these methods directly as Web services won't make for service descriptions that are easy to understand.

Instead, Web services should be designed to be as human-readable and understandable as possible. Methods should be given descriptive titles that reflect their intended functions, and all parameters should be given names that make sense within the service description. For instance, an object method implemented on the server as `getHeads` with the parameters `string`, `int`, and `bool` probably won't illuminate the purpose of the function very well. However, a SOAP method definition such as the following would make it clearer:

```
<getNewsHeadlinesRequest>
  <siteName xsi:type="xsd:string" />
  <numberOfHeadlines xsi:type="xsd:int" />
  <provideSynopsis xsi:type="xsd:boolean" />
</getNewsHeadlinesRequest>
```

In addition, Web service methods should be clustered into SOAP objects that reflect a single overall purpose, however those methods are implemented on the server. In practice, this means that functions usually separated in Perl code—such as database access, session handlers, and search algorithms—shouldn't be presented as individual SOAP objects. Instead, methods should be clustered into objects based on their purpose within the Web service, such as retrieving shipping information or placing a customer service request.

WSDL and UDDI

The automation of Web interfaces is a noble goal, but it won't save much effort if the description of such services is left to traditional means. The current way to describe Web services involves pages of text devoted to values programmers must use when writing a special-purpose program to access the service. Because the goal of these services is complete automation, it would be wise to use the same standards—XML and network protocols—to define the interface descriptions as well as the interfaces. Thus, an automated Web services client also can automate the way it accesses services.

WSDL and UDDI standards were developed to do just this. Between the two, they promise to automate the description and discovery of Web services.

The WSDL Specification

WSDL is an XML language used to describe Web services, no matter how they are implemented. In current practice, a WSDL file describes a single SOAP object and all the methods it makes available. WSDL files consist of a series of declarations, each of which describes an aspect of the Web service to be defined. Sections declared include the endpoint location and the name of the object described in the specification. Additional sections cover a list of object methods defined, the encoding type used for requests and responses, and the protocol (for example, SOAP) used for communications.

A major part of any WSDL service specification is the structure of the request and response message accepted and emitted by the server for any given object method. This structure might be expressed in any notation that is itself valid XML. Initially, this means that messages can be described in terms of a basic array of parameters, where each parameter is of a known data type. As the standard progresses and gains better implementations, the XML Schema language also is used to describe more complex structures with custom data types. The end result is the capability to transmit full XML document types such as cXML or Extensible HTML (XHTML) through SOAP and describe the transactions automatically using WSDL and XML Schema.

WSDL files can be created by hand for each Web service, or they can be generated automatically for services that share a common set of attributes. The basic structure of a WSDL file can be specified as a template, which then is filled in with the appropriate values from the SOAP server and defined Web services. These values might be difficult to ascertain for systems that use SOAP::Lite or similar automated abstraction layers, but these same layers end up being the best way to implement WSDL automation anyway. Using templates to generate these files enables Web service descriptions to be defined consistently, even when the WSDL specification changes. Changes to the format from one revision of the specification to another simply require a change in the structure of the template because the underlying data to be described isn't likely to change much.

UDDI Directories

After a WSDL file is available for a Web service, it can be published to a UDDI directory. UDDI directories are Yahoo!-style listings of businesses and the services they offer. The services listed won't be limited to Web services using the SOAP protocol, but a major use of UDDI directories will be to store Web service descriptions and provide a standard way to find an appropriate Web service for a particular application. UDDI directories are initially being developed and deployed by Microsoft and IBM, the major backers of the UDDI standard, but additional directories are slated to go online as the standard gets more firmly defined.

A UDDI directory can be searched by business type, business name, or the type of service being offered. Initial UDDI directories can be accessed either through a dynamic HTML interface or an automated SOAP interface. The SOAP interface actually is being touted as the primary interface to UDDI data, in keeping with the Web services model. The SOAP interface also will enable UDDI directories to be kept synchronized with each other, thus forming a virtual directory that can be accessed through any individual implementation with consistent results. Eventually, it's likely that modules such as SOAP::Lite will use the same SOAP interfaces to publish WSDL files to UDDI directories automatically as Web services are being deployed.

The Changing Face of Standards

UDDI, WSDL, and SOAP are just the latest round of standards created to answer the same set of nagging problems. However, they aren't likely to be the last. Over the course of writing a SOAP interface to a generic XML server, I encountered no less than four iterations of the UDDI specification with various names and three iterations of WSDL under its parade of acronyms. SOAP itself is no exception. If it keeps up with the early pace of the HTML standard, the standard likely is to "officially" change faster than most client implementations can keep up. Such a disparity opens up the threat of fragmentation and implementation-specific features.

I hold one ray of hope, though, based on the fact that XML itself has been relatively resistant to change since the 1.0 standard was put in place. Because XML is the basis for the other standards, it provides a fixed set of boundaries within which all future standards can be expected to stay. Plus, because XML is regular enough to be programmable at the base level, much of the work that goes into supporting the derivative standards will apply no matter how they change. Who knows if any of the Web services standards will last very long, but the idea behind Web services is here to stay.

Summary

A new idea in B2B integration is encapsulated in the Web services model, which uses XML and Internet protocols to provide truly automated interfaces. Existing HTML interfaces have the advantage of wide use, but the work involved in automating them is prohibitive and prone to instability. SOAP provides a better interface language for implementing automated Web services because it's cross-platform and easy to implement in Perl. Exposing interfaces as Web services involves more than a simple translation from Perl modules to SOAP objects; however, much of the work that already has been done to create Web interfaces can be reused to add Web services. After services are available, they can be described using WSDL files and posted to UDDI directories, where they can be discovered and implemented without any custom programming at all.

20

Scaling a Perl Solution

VISITOR INTEREST, WHICH IS MEASURED IN TERMS of the overall traffic to a site, is the primary goal of most sites, but success can be as overwhelming as it is beneficial. Even with the most efficient architecture and hardware with the highest performance, a site can grow in popularity until it is deluged with requests. For some sites—such as the Internet Archive (http://www.archive.org), which stores gigabytes of archived video and Web content—the content of the site can stress hardware and network connections with even minimal amounts of traffic.

Web applications create their own special concerns. A Web application is likely to use more system resources per request to deliver data than would a static Web page. At the same time, dynamic pages are less likely to be cached by proxy servers and client browsers. As a result, sites that increase their focus on Web applications might see server load increases even when the overall traffic to the site is not increasing. Ironically, this usually means that sites start to perform poorly just as they are starting to provide essential services to their clients.

Adopting a more efficient architecture can provide a marked improvement in performance, but traffic might eventually use up any performance gains realized. The next line of defense is *scaling*, which increases the performance of a single Web server machine. Faster processors, more memory, and more storage media can be installed to improve the performance of server software without a change in architecture or configuration. However, the performance gains from such changes are only incremental. In addition, there's a fixed limit to the pace of these improvements, which is governed by the fastest available hardware and software. A more practical limit is enforced by the fact that hardware with the highest performance comes at a premium. These limits create an arbitrary ceiling to the traffic a system can support, so, eventually, traffic levels might call for higher performance than a single Web server can provide.

Load Balancing Versus Clustering

Load balancing is based on the idea that duplicated Web server machines scale linearly. In other words, if one machine processes a certain number of requests per second, two machines can process twice as many and ten machines can process ten times as many. In simple cases, this idea works well. For example, a Web site comprised mostly of static HTML pages and other static files scales linearly, so additional traffic can be served by adding duplicate Web server machines and then routing traffic to all machines equally.

Clustering, on the other hand, is based on separating a Web server into functional units and shifting the burden of each unit to a different machine. Clustering works well for sites that have a clear dividing line between functions, either as implemented or as viewed by site visitors. For instance, a site might have four distinct Web applications, each of which uses a database and a session manager. Such a site could be divided across six machines, one for each application and one each for the database and the session manager. The hope is that resource conflicts between applications are eliminated by giving each application its own server. In addition, clustering hopefully enables the applications to scale on their own machines without the need for synchronization between duplicate servers.

External Load Balancing

When balancing traffic across Web servers, one common solution is to implement an external system to route incoming traffic. A simple approach involves changing the DNS entry for a server so that requests for the IP address of a given machine name are given one address out of a group of identical machines. For instance, the name www.site.com might be assigned to machine numbers 2, 3, 4, and 5 on a given class C network. When a specific client requests the IP address for www.site.com, it would be given just one of these addresses, which it would interact with over the course of a visit. The hope is that the random assignment of addresses averages out and that each machine on the list receives an equal amount of traffic. Unfortunately, proxy servers for networks such as America Online and RoadRunner might cache only one address, thereby skewing the amount of traffic that that server receives for a given time period.

Load balancing products, such as F5's BigIP, are designed to serve as gateways to the network where a group of Web servers resides. These systems route requests dynamically to a specific server from a list of available Web servers. To a client machine, each request goes to the same machine name and IP address. However, the requests might actually be served by any number of equivalent Web servers. These tools also provide fail-over support—a Web server is taken off the list if it stops responding correctly to incoming requests. This type of load balancing provides more control over the distribution of traffic over servers.

The main difficulty inherent in a symmetric load-balancing situation is keeping a synchronized copy of all Web applications and their associated data on each Web server. This might not seem like a problem early in the development cycle because the content on all servers is simply copied from a central server. However, the lax development style used when dealing with a single Web server won't work for a dozen Web servers. If a change is made to application code on one server and not copied to the others, applications can quickly become so far out of synchronization that they have to be completely recopied. The same holds true for configuration, especially in Perl. Installing a module or upgrading to a new version becomes a more difficult problem when it has to be performed on all servers simultaneously.

Another concern lies with aspects of a Web application that can't be split into symmetric parts. Session managers, for instance, need to keep a list of open sessions, usually in memory. If each user request within a session is sent to a different server, all servers must have access to an identical copy of the session information. This usually is implemented by keeping a single session server to enable network connections. The same situation occurs with database servers and other system applications that can't be duplicated easily. Unfortunately, this means that not all parts of the Web application are being scaled at the same rate, so system application servers can easily get overwhelmed with Web application server requests.

Perl-Based Load Balancing

Load balancing also can be implemented solely at the application-engine level. Perl processing architectures such as FastCGI and VelociGen enable processing to be distributed over a group of machines. A single Web server then can be used to handle static requests, route application processing requests, and return the results to the client. Each set of application engines sits on an identically configured application server machine, which is devoted solely to responding to dynamic requests. Routing can be handled by a two-tiered application—the first program layer resides on the Web server and passes requests to the actual Web applications. It does this by consulting a routing table and choosing an application engine that is not currently processing another request.

As with other load balancing solutions, each application server in a balanced set must have an identical configuration with identical data. New servers can be added by copying the configuration of existing servers, but any changes to the server configuration can cause the applications to get out of synchronization and to produce unwanted results. Perl-based load balancing also suffers from the other problems inherent in symmetric load balancing. These problems include increased stress on databases due to additional application engines accessing the same system resource. In addition, load balancing at the application-engine level requires a single Web server to be used as a gateway, which might become an arbitrary bottleneck. Adding additional gateways increases the potential complexity of the system by requiring all copies of the routing layer application to share information about the disposition of application engines.

Perl-Based Clustering

With FastCGI, VelociGen, and other network-enabled Perl environments, it's also possible to cluster servers into functional groups. Each group can be configured to handle a designated portion of Web application traffic. Apache Web server configuration of FastCGI, for instance, enables individual applications to be assigned to directories, file types, or other URL masks. An additional layer of clustering can be implemented using a two-tiered approach that is similar to a load-balancing solution. The balancing application could check an incoming request against a list of servers that are equipped to handle that type of request and then route the request to an open application engine on one of those servers.

Some parts of a Web application can be clustered easily without any help from Perl. For instance, a database server that resides on the same machine as the Web server usually can be reimplemented on another machine and connected to over the network. Session servers, mail processors, and other system applications also can be moved to machines separate from the Web server with minimal changes to the Web application code. Clustering in this fashion can be a way to solve the problem of system applications that don't scale well. For instance, balancing a database server symmetrically over several machines is difficult because it requires each copy of the database to synchronize updates and inserts with other copies continuously. However, breaking a database into functional parts is considerably easier. Tables specific to each application can reside on different database servers, reducing the overall number of queries to each database as well as the number of application engines with cached connections open.

Unfortunately, clustering also can reach an inherent limit because Web applications only have a finite number of functional parts. After a point, it's no longer feasible to break an application into smaller components because the component functions and modules overlap. When that happens, it's usually necessary to implement a combination of load balancing and clustering techniques to increase capacity even further. However, this kind of combination is likely to increase the performance of a cluster more than either technique would individually. This happens because the limitations of each are overcome to some degree by the use of the other.

Perl-Based Synchronization

Aside from performing the work of application engines, Perl can help synchronize content over a balanced set of servers. Content is likely to be stored as text files, which makes a text-centric language such as Perl a good choice for copying files to a group of servers based on whether they have been changed. Perl also can be used to develop a staged application development environment consisting of a development server and a publishing tool. All changes are made and tested on the development server, and the publishing tool copies the resulting changes to the appropriate balanced or clustered servers as necessary. The publishing tool can use standard file copying tools such as scp more quickly than they can be used by hand, so the possibility for inconsistent results from different servers in a cluster is reduced significantly. Implementing a publishing tool also can reduce a developer's desire to implement "minor changes" on the production servers by making the update process simpler and more automatic.

Perl can be used to update the server configuration on multiple servers simultaneously or in controlled shifts. Software can be installed using predefined scripts, Perl modules can be added automatically, and server processes can be restarted automatically when necessary. In addition, each server can be removed from a load balancing rotation for the duration of the update. It then can be returned to duty before starting on the next server, thereby reducing the chance that normal loads will overload the servers still available. Designing and implementing such an administration tool in Perl can help define configuration procedures explicitly. Update processes can be codified in working code, and the results of each procedure can be recorded to a central log.

Perl is an excellent choice for creating these administrative tools because it can use existing system tools to carry out the process. After all, Perl was originally developed as a system administration language. Rather than reinvent revision control, an administrative tool can use CVS functions to carry out updates. Instead of compiling Perl modules from the command line, an administrative tool can use the Comprehensive Perl Archive Network (CPAN) module to automate and log the process. Configuration hooks even can be written into servers such as Apache to provide a finer grain of control over the state of each Web server process.

DBI and Advanced Data Sets

Perl's DBI module provides a common interface to all databases that use the structured query language (SQL). However, DBI takes a literal approach to database access. It includes only those access methods that are common to SQL databases, without taking into account applications that need to access the database in a way that's awkward in standard SQL. For instance, applications that need to page through a large data set or access multiple databases won't get any inherent support from DBI. It's possible to write abstraction layers on top of DBI that accomplish these types of tasks, but a more satisfying solution would be to implement generic layers that suit a wide variety of these needs with the potential for greater efficiency.

The area of database access will probably gain more attention as the modules used for basic database interaction mature. After the basics are implemented, more effort can be devoted to solving real-world problems with generic interfaces. Two modules that hold great promise in this area are DBIx::Recordset and DBD::Multiplex, both of which try to present simplified interfaces to procedures that existing database servers make complex.

DBIx::Recordset

SQL databases can be very useful for sorting, aggregating, and searching through a large amount of data efficiently, but the SQL interface itself doesn't necessarily provide a robust way of dealing with the resulting data. *Record sets*, which encapsulate a set of responses to a specific class of database query, might provide a better way of interacting with database results than SQL normally provides. For instance, the results of a database search on a site such as Google usually spans a number of Web pages. The traditional way of generating these pages from a SQL query would involve processing the query for each page, displaying only the results needed for the page, and discarding the rest of the results returned from the database. For search queries that return ten or twenty pages, this process can be very inefficient. However, the database server itself usually provides no way of saving the results of a query or partitioning those results into usable chunks.

DBIx::Recordset implements an abstraction layer between a Perl program and the DBI interface to treat a particular search less like a SQL query and more like an abstract record set. It does this for a number of reasons:

- Composing an SQL query based on a large number of input or result fields can be tedious work to program.

- SQL syntax tends to be more strict than most Web applications need, which makes it difficult to change applications without explicit testing.

- The results of an SQL query might need to be returned over a series of requests or in other arbitrary groups based solely on order.

One method that DBIx::Recordset provides specifically for Web applications is `PrevNextForm`, which creates a search results list based on the contents of a data set. As new requests come in for additional records from the same query, `PrevNextForm` finds the next subset of results from the record set and displays it, along with controls for accessing the previous or next set. The current version of this function isn't implemented in a very efficient fashion. However, the basic idea of abstracting the function itself away from the underlying implementation enables the implementation to be optimized over time—using more efficient techniques as they become available—without requiring any changes in the Web applications that use the function.

Eventually, an interface such as DBIx::Recordset could implement a generic form of result caching, which satisfies many uses for record sets with an efficient implementation. Results from common queries could be stored for use as master record sets, which could be parceled out based on the needs of each application request. These sets could be kept in memory, in a cache table created in the same database, or in a separate database specifically for record sets. Each case would require a cache control mechanism that would keep track of data updates and the age of each record set, but such a mechanism could use widely implemented caching techniques. In fact, the module might enable an implementation to be specified for each type of record set, which would provide the greatest flexibility for different performance needs.

DBD::Multiplex

Scaling a Web server architecture sometimes creates a bottleneck in accessing a database back end. The best solution to this would be to create a load-balanced database in the same way Web servers are balanced. Unfortunately, most database servers don't have the capability to handle their own load balancing or synchronization. Those that do require either an expensive addition to the software or complex configuration—with no guarantee that the new configuration will solve the initial performance problem.

A Perl-based solution to this problem is offered by the DBD::Multiplex module, which enables multiple databases to be accessed as a single data source. The module is in early development, but its potential uses make it promising. The idea behind DBD::Multiplex is that each call to the data source would be sent to one or more servers in a list of subordinate data sources. A SELECT statement, for instance, could be handled by a database server chosen randomly from a list to spread the processing load across multiple servers. An INSERT or UPDATE statement, on the other hand, would be sent to all servers in the list to keep them synchronized with each other. Between the two, any type of database could be balanced across servers without requiring its own synchronization or load balancing capability. Additionally, the Multiplex driver could be configured to resend failed statements to another server and warn administrators of the failure. Results from multiple servers could be compared and incorrect results discarded, as is done in a redundant disk array (RAID).

Initially, DBD::Multiplex will provide the capability to interact with symmetrically load-balanced database servers. Each server would have to start as a copy of all the others, both in server type and in the data stored. Eventually, the possibility exists that database servers could be clustered around a single DBD::Multiplex data source. Databases could be split into functional groups of tables that reside on different clusters of balanced servers. Routing between Web applications and the necessary servers would be handled by DBD::Multiplex. For instance, a SELECT statement involving the messages and users table might be routed to a server that holds copies of those tables, while one involving the headlines table would be routed to another cluster. This type of clustering would reduce the size of each database and remove some of the need for synchronization between servers. Combined with application engine clustering, it also could reduce the number of cached database connections overall.

In addition, different types of servers could be clustered into equivalent groups based on a match between the data they carry. For instance, a PostgreSQL server being installed could be listed in parallel with an Oracle server it's replacing. Queries would be sent to both servers, with the result from the Oracle database taking priority. Errors in the configuration of the PostgreSQL server would show up under continuous real-world use, but the Web application user would be shielded from such errors. Eventually the new database could be certified error-free in continuous use, and the older database could be removed from the access list or relegated to a fail-over backup. The progression from one database system to the next would be seamless from the point of view of Web application users.

Summary

Even the most efficient Perl-based Web applications eventually need to scale to meet increased traffic demands. One approach, load balancing, involves duplicating each Web server exactly. Traffic can be routed to load-balanced servers using an external solution to route requests. This can be done before they are processed by the Web server or a Perl solution and after the Web server has received the requests. Another approach, clustering, involves breaking a Web site into functional components that can reside on different machines and then using a more sophisticated load balancer to route requests to the appropriate components. With either approach, it usually becomes necessary to manage server and Web application configurations using a development server and a publishing mechanism. Databases don't always scale well, however, so Perl solutions such as DBIx::Recordset and DBD::Multiplex will become more important as Web applications are required to reduce their impact on the database and potentially use multiple databases in parallel.

21

Perl 6 and the Future

PERL IS A LANGUAGE THAT HAS UNDERGONE MANY changes. (It has grown a great deal.) As Perl grew, the core constructs of each new version were updated to help serve the needs of the latest generation of Perl programmers. Perl 5, for instance, marked a turning point in Perl development by providing a framework for writing standardized extension modules in Perl. Perl 5 also added the capability to access these modules using an object-oriented idiom instead of importing functions. This enabled module programmers to concentrate on writing useful functions without worrying about naming conventions or overlap with other modules. These language changes paved the way for a profusion of Perl modules that customized the language to suit any number of tasks, including the design of Web applications.

Perl 6 provides an opportunity to remake the language again to suit the needs of current and future Perl programmers. Lessons have been learned from the way programmers used and extended Perl 5. There now are more programmers with intimate Perl knowledge than when Perl 5 was being designed. The core language designers, Larry Wall included, have learned a great deal from new languages, such as Java, that didn't exist when Perl 5 was designed. As a result, the change in Perl will be radical to incorporate these new insights; Perl will be rewritten from scratch for Perl 6. Support for new technologies such as Unicode will be built into the language from the ground up instead of tacked on, and special attention will be given to making the internals of Perl more accessible to programmers who want to seamlessly extend the language.

Perl 5 to Perl 6 Translation

One exciting aspect of Perl 6 development is the emphasis on an easy transition between Perl 5 and Perl 6. Many of the programmers working on Perl 6 remember the difficulties that were caused by the switch from Perl 4 style to Perl 5 style. The need to retain backward compatibility with Perl 4 programs made it difficult to add new features to Perl 5. At the same time, the few changes made were enough to break many existing Perl packages. With these lessons in mind, it was decided that backward compatibility with Perl 5 was important, but that it shouldn't impede the progress of Perl 6 toward bigger and better things.

Fortunately, an ingenious solution was found to the problem of updating Perl 5 programs to be compatible with Perl 6 syntax. Instead of trying to implement Perl 5 syntax as a subset of Perl 6, the decision was made to incorporate the automated translation of Perl 5 programs into Perl 6 style (or vice versa, if necessary). In fact, one test of completeness will be the ability to use all CPAN modules with Perl 6 by simply running them through the translator. This amazing idea frees Perl 6 designers to make even radical changes to the structure of the Perl language without worrying about leaving older Perl programs and modules behind. Of course, another principle adopted for Perl 6 design is "Perl should stay Perl," so the changes aren't likely to be so radical that Perl won't be recognizable.

The Perl Compiler

The essence of a Perl 5 to Perl 6 translator comes from the way in which Perl compiles source code into an executable program. When a Perl program is run, the Perl compiler loads the source code of the program and compiles it into bytecode that the Perl runtime can execute. This compiled bytecode normally is discarded after the program exits, unlike the bytecode output of a Java compiler. However, the bytecode itself serves a similar purpose—it's a cross-platform compiled representation of the Perl program that has been parsed, optimized, and prepared for the Perl runtime.

Perl 5.6 offers a suite of compiler backend modules, collected under the B module, that can be used to control the behavior of the Perl compiler. Using the B::Bytecode module through the O interface module, Perl programs can be compiled into the bytecode format without executing them. For instance, a Perl program called `generate_table.pl` could be precompiled into bytecode using the following Perl command line:

```
perl -MO=Bytecode generate_table.pl
```

The `-M` switch tells the Perl executable to load the O interface module with the Bytecode backend module to process the `generate_table.pl` program. Additional options can be specified to include additional modules when compiling or controlling the effects of compilation. The resulting bytecode file is sent to standard output, so it then could be stored for later use, either in memory or on disk. See the "Compiling Stand-Alone Programs" section later in this chapter for examples of how bytecode could be used to improve application performance.

The Perl 6 Decompiler

Unlike the compiled versions of programs in most languages, Perl programs can be decompiled from the bytecode back into Perl source code. In fact, this process can be modified to produce different versions of source code that would produce the same bytecode result. In Perl 5.6, this is accomplished using the B::Deparse backend module, which can produce valid Perl source code of various types from a Perl program. B::Deparse most commonly is used to check for unwanted behaviors in the way Perl interprets the original source code by making it produce an annotated or expanded version of the code after parsing. For Perl 6, though, additional options could be added to cause B::Deparse to emit Perl 6 code from a Perl 5 source, or vice versa. The command-line options for such a conversion might be similar to the following:

```
perl -MO=Deparse,-ogenerate_table.pl6 generate_table.pl5
```

It still remains to be seen how the translation will be implemented, whether as a Perl 5 module for conversion to Perl 6 or as a Perl 6 module with backward-compatibility built in solely for the translation process. Additional features will probably need to be added to deal with formatting—including indentation and idiomatic style—and comments, which are currently stripped out of the source code during optimization. Other options will be implemented specifically to handle the translation of modules, including those modules that have a C library component.

Language-Independent Perl

Another exciting aspect of the Perl 6 compiler is the possibility of compiling code from other languages into Perl binaries. Perl 5 enables this in a limited sense; the XS extension mechanism can be used to incorporate C libraries into Perl modules, and the Java-Perl Lingo (JPL) was developed to incorporate Java programs into a Perl framework. However, both mechanisms are so difficult to use that they are reserved for modules that desperately need them. In addition, neither mechanism provides a framework for other languages, so each new language supported has to be incorporated separately. With Perl 6, the idea is to elevate other languages to first-class citizens in the Perl compiler. A Perl program or module could be written in Perl, but it also could be written in Java, Python, C, or Ruby.

This might seem like a frivolous use of a compiled environment. After all, most languages already have some form of compiler or interpreter, so there should be little need to compile programs in those languages into Perl. However, this assumes that each program is being developed in a vacuum, with no need to run programs from multiple languages in the same shared environment. With Web programming in particular, this couldn't be further from reality. In most Web environments, applications can come from a wide variety of sources, spread both over time and over multiple organizations. You can't assume that all these groups will use the same language or environment, so it's sometimes necessary to collaborate between groups that use incompatible tools. If Perl has the capability to run the original code written by each group, no matter what the language, it has a much greater chance of being the platform chosen to implement a combined solution.

Java to Perl

One language that is bound to be important to Perl developers is Java. Despite the excellent track record of Perl in implementing Web applications, many application designers still are more comfortable learning to program in Java than in Perl. Regardless of their motivations, programmers who prefer Java or who have existing code written in Java might end up on a Web application project developed in a Perl environment. Rather than discard their existing code and experience, it would be good to allow them to program in the Perl environment using the Java code they're used to. Even better would be to allow them to program parts of a program in Java and parts in Perl so that they become used to both languages over time.

In addition, Java does have the advantage of a vigorous corporate following. Many projects coming out of large corporations, such as IBM, are being developed in Java first—or Java only—with the idea that the Java code will serve as a reference implementation for others. Instead of tossing the reference code aside while reimplementing the project entirely in Perl, it would be good to allow these projects to be incorporated as Perl modules in their native form. Even better would be to allow Perl programmers to optimize parts of a Java module in Perl as the project progresses. This could serve to improve the availability and completeness of Perl modules in crucial areas such as Extensible Markup Language (XML) processing and legacy system interaction.

The Inline Module

The beginnings of a standardized approach to incorporating other languages into Perl comes from the Inline module. New to Perl 5.6 and still experimental, the Inline module enables code from other languages to be used directly in a Perl program as though it were native. The module creates a framework similar to the DBI module, in which additional languages can be added as drivers while the API for using them stays constant. A program using the Inline module can specify a language (or languages) to include inline. It then can write and call subroutines from the additional languages as though they were Perl subroutines. Code segments in other languages aren't included in the main Perl block, but they can be included as DATA sections in the same file as the Perl program. Alternately, source code in other languages can be imported from other files into the Perl program using the Inline module and then accessed as though the subroutines were imported Perl subroutines.

A crucial purpose to which this kind of language-neutral implementation can be put is the creation of Perl modules in other languages. Sometimes, Perl isn't able to benefit from work carried out initially in another language. In addition, the Perl modules created as derivative works might be missing some of the features of the original libraries. For instance, Perl support for the XML Document Object Model (DOM) lagged behind other languages, such as C and Java. Perl's XML::DOM module stagnated for nearly a year while similar C libraries added new DOM features and improved performance. If the process of adapting C or Java libraries for use as Perl modules were streamlined, Perl could benefit from work done in any language as soon as it became available.

In Perl 5, the Inline module is implemented by automating the process of creating XS modules, which then are imported into the namespace of the main Perl program. However, early information about the direction of Perl 6 hints that this kind of multi-language support will be built in at the compiler level, so implementing Inline language drivers will become considerably easier in Perl 6. Support for code in C, C++, and Python already is incorporated into the Perl 5.6 version of Inline. Java, Ruby, and other new languages are expected to be added as drivers before Perl 6 is released. Perl 6, in turn, probably will bring about a marked increase in the number of languages supported as well as the number of Inline-based modules created, just as Perl 5 brought about the rapid growth of Perl modules.

Perl 6 Performance Improvements

One area in which Perl 6 is hoped to surpass Perl 5 is performance. Perl performance is usually the subject of fierce debates, with C programmers claiming that Perl programs are too slow overall and Perl programmers claiming that Perl programs are capable of being as fast as C programs. (Perl programmers also add that the development time necessary for a C program generally makes up for any performance loss in a Perl program.) Regardless of the current state of Perl performance, all sides would agree that making Perl faster overall would be a good thing.

As a result, the development of Perl 6 is being carried out with an eye toward improving both the perceived performance and the benchmarked performance of Perl programs. The internals of Perl are undergoing great scrutiny, with an eye toward reducing the memory footprint of the Perl runtime by moving unessential functions from the core into loadable modules. The implementation of the Perl compiler also is being rethought from the standpoint of optimizing even more Perl functions based on the way in which programmers are likely to implement them. In addition, aspects of the Perl language from object-oriented syntax to the behavior of unary operators are being updated to make both development and execution of Perl programs faster.

Compiling Stand-Alone Programs

One area in which the perceived performance of Perl programs can be improved is the time taken for compiling the program and loading the Perl runtime. As mentioned throughout this book, there are many situations in which compiling a Perl program every time it is executed can cause a considerable performance drain. If it were possible to keep Perl programs in precompiled states and use the precompiled versions when available, much of the time spent compiling programs could be saved. This would improve performance not only for Web applications, but also for complex stand-alone applications that currently take seconds or minutes to compile before executing.

As mentioned, Perl programs are compiled to a platform-independent bytecode before being executed by the Perl runtime. To reduce the need for compiling Perl programs at runtime, it would be possible to keep compiled bytecode either in memory or on disk and use the precompiled copy rather than the source copy to run a program. The B::Bytecode module currently provides a way to save bytecode and the B module enables it to be imported into a Perl program at runtime. For Perl 6, both systems could be streamlined and offered as universal Perl options, which would automate the process to some extent. Web environments would benefit from such a system by using compiled bytecode versions of Perl programs instead of subroutine-based execution. Bytecode execution would provide a more pristine environment to Perl programs, which otherwise would have difficulty running in a persistent environment. It would do this while providing most of the benefits of persistence.

Perl to C Compiling

Aside from bytecode, it's also possible to compile Perl programs into a system-specific language such as C. This enables the program to be compiled into a binary executable using a C compiler. Although this won't necessarily result in a program that runs faster than the equivalent Perl program overall, it can dramatically reduce the perceived performance by removing the compile step at runtime. In addition, compiled binaries are sometimes more compact and easier to distribute than the equivalent Perl programs. Compiling C programs would enable developers to control which version of Perl is used by a program, as well as the modules made available to it.

Compiling a Perl program to C code is currently made possible by the B::C module. An additional module, B::CC, compiles Perl programs into optimized C code with more restrictions. Both modules are considered experimental in Perl 5.6. Neither module generates a program that would be familiar to C coders translating a Perl program by hand. Rather, the program is closer to a representation of the process carried out by the Perl compiler and runtime when executing Perl bytecode. However it is implemented, the end result of the compiled code is a program that should work just as the original Perl program would have. Using the current modules, a Perl program named `generate_table.pl` could be compiled into C source code using the following command-line options:

```
perl -MO=CC generate_table.pl > generate_table.c
```

As with the Bytecode and Deparse backend modules, the O interface module is used to invoke the CC backend module. Options can be provided to the CC module to affect the way the C code is optimized as well as how it is likely to be compiled. Other options can be specified to control which Perl modules are included when creating C code.

Historically, compiling a Perl program into C code has been a difficult prospect. The code produced by the C and CC backend module tended to be overly complex because it needed to reimplement much of the processing that would ordinarily happen inside the Perl runtime. The complexity of programs also tends to increase rapidly when resource-intensive modules such as Tk or XML::DOM are incorporated. The compiled code also has a few less-than-optimized side effects due to the Perl 5 implementation of the Perl compiler. For one, a full copy of the Perl runtime library is included in every compiled program. This means that the memory footprint of a compiled Perl program is likely to be as large or larger than the same program run through the Perl runtime. These kinds of problems are at the front of developers' minds as they create Perl 6, so it's likely that solutions will be implemented to enable fast executables to be generated from standard Perl programs.

Larry Wall and Damian Conway

By and large, the design of Perl has come from the mind of one person: Larry Wall. Larry wrote the first versions of Perl, and he has served as the chief language designer and spiritual leader for Perl design for each subsequent version. It's not too much to say that Perl would not be Perl without Larry; his intelligence, wit, and sheer practicality are embedded into the structure of Perl as deeply as the semicolon. (Sorry, Larry.) The Perl community also has benefited from his example. More than any computer technology I've encountered, Perl has a community of recognizable faces—accessible ones, even! Specific names are identified with each Perl project, and the result is an environment that encourages personal responsibility for code and pride in a job well done. Again, without Larry's example, I'm not sure that Perl would have such a genuinely competent community surrounding it.

More recently, another recognizable face has come along with a passion for Perl that rivals even Larry's. Damian Conway is a Perl programmer, lecturer, and author extraordinaire who is widely known for doing the work of a dozen eccentric geniuses. He has written truly amazing Perl modules such as Coy, which creates poetic error messages, and Lingua::Romana::Perligata, which enables Perl programs to be written using the position-independent syntax of Latin. His pursuits aren't frivolous, though. He has a knowledge of Perl to rival Larry himself, and each new module is an exercise in stretching the limits of Perl programming. His creations are so impressive that he's been barred from winning any further Larry Wall awards at the Perl Conference in exchange for having the Best Technical Paper category renamed the Damian Conway award. Every aspect of Perl touched by Damian seems to sparkle afterward, and it's work such as his that renews my faith that Perl development will be extraordinary for years to come.

Summary

The future of Perl looks bright. Perl 6 promises a complete rewrite of the Perl language and Perl internals, with a specific focus on improving the performance and usability of Perl. Radical changes can be made to Perl 6 because of a decision to implement backward compatibility by translating Perl 5 programs into Perl 6 automatically. This kind of translation also provides a promising framework for incorporating code from other languages directly into Perl programs. Support for these languages is being added experimentally by the Inline module, but Perl 6 should provide more seamless integration possibilities. Updates to Perl internals also will be a boon to efforts surrounding compilation of Perl programs as bytecode or executable binaries, both of which will find many uses in the years to come.

IV

Appendix

Alphabet Soup—Glossary and References

IF WEB TECHNOLOGIES HAVE ONE THING IN common, it's a profusion of standards and acronyms. The madness started with the World Wide Web itself, which gave rise to the first acronym, WWW, which actually is more difficult to say than the term it references. The tradition continues with a variety of new Web acronyms such as SVG, XHTML, PNG, SOAP, and WSDL. To clear up some of the jargon, I've created this appendix with a glossary of terms and acronyms associated with Web servers and Web standards. I've also added a glossary devoted to XML because it seems to give rise to more jargon than all other Web technologies combined.

Because most information about the Web can be found on the Web, I've included URLs for each definition, where available. These locations were correct at the time this book was written; an updated list will be available on the Web site for the book at http://www.newriders.com or http://www.globalspin.com/thebook/ if the locations change or new terms are added.

Web Server Glossary

Apache The most widely used Web server software, offered under the GNU General Public License (GPL). http://server.apache.org/

Apache::ASP   A Perl module that enables Perl code to be embedded in HTML in a style similar to that of Active Server Pages (ASP). http://www.apache-asp.org/

component   In HTML::Mason, a component is a basic unit of Web application processing. Components might include HTML, Perl, or a combination of the two. http://www.masonhq.com/

DBI   A Perl module that provides a generic interface to any Structured Query Language (SQL) database. http://www.perldoc.com/cpan/DBI.html

embedded Perl   Perl code added directly to sections of an HTML page. The code is evaluated and results are printed in place.

EmbPerl   An embedded Perl environment. http://perl.apache.org/embperl/

endpoint   The location of a SOAP server application to which SOAP requests are sent.

FastCGI   A protocol that enables arbitrary server applications to access the Web server API. http://www.fastcgi.com/

HTML   The Hypertext Markup Language is the system of tags used to specify formatting and content in Web pages. http://www.w3.org/MarkUp/

HTML::Mason   A component-based embedded Perl environment. http://www.masonhq.com/

iPlanet   A brand of threaded Web server software developed by the Sun-Netscape Alliance. http://www.iplanet.com/

IIS   The Internet Information Server is a Microsoft Web server included with Windows server products. http://www.microsoft.com/

ISAPI   The Internet Server Application Programming Interface enables custom modules to be written for IIS.

mod_perl   A plug-in module for the Apache Web server that enables Apache API modules to be written in persistent Perl. http://perl.apache.org/

Netscape   A brand of threaded Web server software that has been replaced by the iPlanet line of servers. http://www.iplanet.com/

NSAPI   The Netscape Server Application Programming Interface enables custom modules to be written for Netscape or iPlanet servers.

Perl   The Practical Extraction and Reporting Language is a general-purpose programming language modeled after C, awk, and English. `http://www.perl.org/`

PerlEx   An environment for embedded or persistent Perl. `http://www.activestate.com/`

persistent Perl   Any Web server environment that enables Perl programs to reside in memory and process multiple requests.

post-processor   A code segment that is executed by the server environment after any program or static file in a defined class.

pperl   A persistent Perl page format used by the VelociGen environment.

preprocessor   A code segment that is executed by the server environment before any program or static file in a defined class.

PSP   Perl Server Pages are HTML-like files with embedded Perl code and custom server-side processing tags.

request   From a Web server perspective, a single connection from a browser requesting the contents of a URL.

SlashDot   A news Web site targeted at the technical community with special emphasis on open source software projects. `http://www.slashdot.org/`

template   An HTML or other text document used to specify unchanging aspects of Web application output.

URL   A Uniform Resource Locator is used to specify the location of a document or program on the Internet. `http://www.w3.org/Addressing/`

VelociGen   An environment for embedded or persistent Perl. `http://www.velocigen.com/`

VeloMeter   A Web server load testing application that simulates the activity of site visitors. `http://www.velometer.com/`

Web application   An application with an HTML and forms interface made up of programs running on a Web server.

Web service   An application with a SOAP or other XML interface made up of programs running on a Web server.

Zeus   A brand of performance-oriented Web server software. `http://www.zeus.com/`

Standards and Organizations

Apache Project   The Apache Project produces the Apache Web server and other server-side technologies. `http://www.apache.org/`

CGI   The Common Gateway Interface is a protocol for executing arbitrary server-side applications to respond to Web requests.

CPAN   The Comprehensive Perl Archive Network is a distributed repository of Perl code, modules, and documentation. `http://www.cpan.org/`

GPL   The GNU General Public License gives users the right to use, modify, and redistribute program code as long as derivative works also are licensed under the GPL. `http://www.fsf.org/`

HTTP   The Hypertext Transfer Protocol is a standard for retrieving documents from the Web. `http://www.w3.org/Protocols/`

PerlMonks   The PerlMonks site offers articles and discussions about Perl by members of the Perl community. `http://www.perlmonks.org/`

Perl Mongers   The Perl Mongers are a worldwide user group devoted to promoting Perl and bringing Perl programmers together. `http://www.pm.org/`

UDDI   The Universal Discovery, Description, and Integration standard defines a set of methods for automated discovery of businesses and their services. `http://www.uddi.org/`

W3C   The World Wide Web Consortium is a neutral standards organization that focuses on Web-related standards and technologies. `http://www.w3.org/`

XML Bestiary

DTD   A Document Type Definition is one way of representing the structure of an XML language. XML documents can be checked against a DTD to determine their validity.

DOM   The Document Object Model is a method of accessing parts of an XML document by representing it as a tree of objects. Each object has a set of methods used to access or manipulate it.

element   In DOM, an element is a node representing a tag or set of matched tags.

expat   The expat parser is a C program created to parse XML documents into a usable data structure. It is the basis of most Perl XML modules.

node   In DOM, a node is an object representing a location in the parsed XML tree. For instance, an element node would contain the complete contents of a set of matched XML tags, including the name of the tag and its attributes. Nodes might contain other nodes.

Schema   An XML Schema is one way of describing the structure of an XML language. Documents written in a particular language can be checked for validity against the language's XML Schema. `http://www.w3.org/XML/Schema/`

SOAP   The Simple Object Access Protocol offers a standard way to access object methods using XML over Internet protocols. `http:://www.w3.org/TR/SOAP/`

SOAP::Lite   The SOAP::Lite module provides a Perl interface to SOAP clients and servers. `http://www.soaplite.com/`

SVG   The Scalable Vector Graphics format is an XML language that describes the appearance of vector images. `http://www.w3.org/Graphics/SVG/`

tag   In XML, a tag is a string enclosed in angle brackets that labels the text appearing between it and a matched tag. For instance, `<word>taradiddle</word>` is the string `taradiddle` enclosed in `word` tags.

WSDL   The Web Services Description Language is an XML language used to describe the location, protocols, and request format for a Web service.

XHTML The Extensible Hypertext Markup Language is an XML language designed to duplicate the tags used in HTML. A subset of valid XHTML documents are valid HTML, but XHTML also can be extended to provide new features. http://www.w3.org/MarkUp/

XHTML Basic An XML language that includes a subset of XHTML tags tailored to the needs of wireless devices. http://www.w3.org/MarkUp/

XML The Extensible Markup Language is a generic language format specification that is designed to be both machine- and human-readable. XML languages share a common syntax and can be parsed using a common set of tools. http://www.w3.org/XML/

XML-RPC The Extensible Markup Language Remote Procedure Call protocol provides a standard way to invoke object methods on remote servers through standard Internet networking protocols. http://www.xmlrpc.org/

XML::Simple A Perl module that translates XML documents into a Perl data structure made up of hashes and arrays.

XSL The Extensible Style Language enables formatting and transformations to be specified for a given class of XML documents. XSL is commonly used to produce HTML from XML.

XSLT The Extensible Style Language for Transformations is a subset of XSL designed to translate one form of XML into another.

Index

U–V

HOW TO CONTACT US

VISIT OUR WEB SITE

WWW.NEWRIDERS.COM

On our Web site, you'll find information about our other books, authors, tables of contents, and book errata. You will also find information about book registration and how to purchase our books, both domestically and internationally.

EMAIL US

Contact us at: **nrfeedback@newriders.com**

- If you have comments or questions about this book
- To report errors that you have found in this book
- If you have a book proposal to submit or are interested in writing for New Riders
- If you are an expert in a computer topic or technology and are interested in being a technical editor who reviews manuscripts for technical accuracy

Contact us at: **nreducation@newriders.com**

- If you are an instructor from an educational institution who wants to preview New Riders books for classroom use. Email should include your name, title, school, department, address, phone number, office days/hours, text in use, and enrollment, along with your request for desk/examination copies and/or additional information.

Contact us at: **nrmedia@newriders.com**

- If you are a member of the media who is interested in reviewing copies of New Riders books. Send your name, mailing address, and email address, along with the name of the publication or Web site you work for.

BULK PURCHASES/CORPORATE SALES

If you are interested in buying 10 or more copies of a title or want to set up an account for your company to purchase directly from the publisher at a substantial discount, contact us at 800-382-3419 or email your contact information to corpsales@pearsontechgroup.com. A sales representative will contact you with more information.

WRITE TO US

New Riders Publishing
201 W. 103rd St.
Indianapolis, IN 46290-1097

CALL/FAX US

Toll-free (800) 571-5840
If outside U.S. (317) 581-3500
Ask for New Riders
FAX: (317) 581-4663

New Riders

WWW.NEWRIDERS.COM

RELATED NEW RIDERS TITLES

ISBN 157870216X
760 pages
US $50.00

Win32 Perl Programming: The Standard Extensions, Second Edition

Dave Roth

This book is a guide to Perl's most common Win32 extensions, grouped by their functionality. This new edition updates coverage from Perl 5.05 to current Perl version 5.6. It also includes new chapters offering critical, badly-needed information regarding security for Win32 Perl, the topic most highly requested by reviewers.

MySQL and Perl for the Web

Paul DuBois

MySQL and Perl for the Web focuses on Perl scripting combined with the MySQL database because the combination is an important one that has not been adequately documented, even though it is one of the more robust systems available today. This book covers how to put a database on the Web, related performance issues, form processing, searching abilities, security, common e-commerce tasks, and more.

ISBN 0735710546
500 pages
US $44.99

PHP Functions Essential Reference

Zak Graent, et al.

The *PHP Functions Essential Reference* is a simple, clear, and authoritative function reference that clarifies and expands upon PHP's existing documentation. This book will help the reader write effective code that makes full use of the rich variety of functions available in PHP.

ISBN 073570970X
500 pages
US $44.99

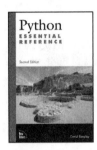

ISBN 0735710910
416 pages
US $34.99

Python Essential Reference, Second Edition

David Beazley

Python Essential Reference, Second Edition, concisely describes the Python programming language and its large library of standard modules—collectively known as the Python programming environment. It is arranged into four major parts. First, a brief tutorial and introduction is presented, then an informal language reference covers lexical conventions, functions, statements, control flow, datatypes, classes, and execution models. The third section covers the Python library, and the final section covers the Python C API that is used to write Python extensions. This book is highly focused and clearly provides the things a reader needs to know to best utilize Python.

ISBN 1578702151
416 pages
US $35.00

Win32 Perl Scripting: The Administrator's Handbook

Dave Roth

"Concise, well-written, pragmatic, and lots of exemplary code. If you need to automate administrative tasks, ignore the O'Reilly Perl-Admin books, this one has a lot more substance and a lot less fluff. Dave Roth has a lot of real-world experience with Perl and Win32. He's solved a lot of difficult problems. More than that, he does a great job of regularly taking the time to document and convey that knowledge on to others. The book is a great distillation of that knowledge."

—An online reviewer

Solutions from experts you know and trust.

www.informit.com

ERATING SYSTEMS

B DEVELOPMENT

OGRAMMING

TWORKING

RTIFICATION

D MORE...

xpert Access.
ree Content.

New Riders has partnered with **InformIT.com** to bring technical information to your desktop. Drawing on New Riders authors and reviewers to provide additional information on topics you're interested in, **InformIT.com** has free, in-depth information you won't find anywhere else.

- **Master the skills you need, when you need them**

- **Call on resources from some of the best minds in the industry**

- **Get answers when you need them, using InformIT's comprehensive library or live experts online**

- **Go above and beyond what you find in New Riders books, extending your knowledge**

As an **InformIT** partner, **New Riders** has shared the wisdom and knowledge of our authors with you online. Visit **InformIT.com** to see what you're missing.

www.informit.com ▪ www.newriders.com

Colophon

Photographer Jes Alford captured the image on the cover of this book, which is a ladder at the entrance of a cliff dwelling. Although the specific location of this particular dwelling is not noted, some of the most well-preserved North American cliff dwellings are located at Mesa Verde National Park near Cortez, Colorado, and Tonto National Park, which is near Roosevelt, Arizona. Studies suggest that these cliff dwellings were used largely among the Anasazi and Salado Native Americans.

Cliff dwellings were built into the sandstone layers of the alcoves in canyon walls, or they were built in natural caves. Several theories exist regarding their purpose. Some believe these dwellings freed Mesa land for cultivation; others believe that they served as protection against enemies because access to cliff dwellings required a ladder, making them easy to defend.

This book was written and edited in Microsoft Word and laid out in QuarkXPress. The fonts used for the body text are Bembo and MCPdigital. It was printed on 50# Husky Offset Smooth paper at VonHoffman Graphics, Inc. in Owensville, Missouri. Prepress consisted of PostScript computer-to-plate technology, filmless process. The cover was printed at Moore Langen Printing in Terre Haute, Indiana, on 12pt, coated on one side.